KT-119-547

CONTEMPORARY WALES

Volume 26

Edited by

**Elin Royles (Aberystwyth University)
Paul Chaney (Cardiff University)**

*Published on behalf
of the University of Wales*

**Cardiff
University of Wales Press
2013**

© University of Wales, 2013

All rights reserved. No part of this book may be reproduced, stored in a retrieval system, or transmitted, in any form or by any means, electronic, mechanical, photocopying, recording or otherwise, without clearance from the University of Wales Press, 10 Columbus Walk, Brigantine Place, Cardiff CF10 4UP.

www.uwp.co.uk

British Library Cataloguing in Publication Data
A catalogue record for this book is available from the British Library.

ISBN 978-0-7083-2683-1
ISSN 0951-4937

Original cover design by Marian Delyth
Cover photograph © Keith Morris/Photo Library Wales
Printed by CPI Antony Rowe, Chippenham, Wiltshire

CONTENTS

FIGURES AND TABLES

FIGURES

TABLES

MAPS

CONTRIBUTORS

Sally Baker is an independent scholar with an interest in Wales and neoliberal welfare reform.

Derek Birrell is Professor of Social Policy and Administration in the School of Criminology, Politics and Social Policy at the University of Ulster.

Brian J. Brown is Professor of Health Communication at De Montfort University, Leicester, but has a longstanding interest in the history of Wales.

Jane Bryan is based in the Welsh Economy Research Unit at Cardiff Business School, Cardiff University.

Nickie Charles is Professor and Director of the Centre for the Study of Women and Gender in the Sociology Department at the University of Warwick.

Einion Dafydd is a PhD Candidate at the Department of International Politics, Aberystwyth University.

Kirrin Davidson works as a researcher for Mark Drakeford AM at the National Assembly for Wales and is an MSc student in the School of Social Sciences at Cardiff University.

Rhys Davies is a senior research fellow in the Wales Institute of Social & Economic Research, Data & Methods (WISERD).

Howard Davis is Professor of Social Theory and Institutions in the School of Social Sciences, Bangor University and Co-Director of the Wales Institute of Social & Economic Research, Data & Methods (WISERD).

Mark Drakeford is a Labour Member of the National Assembly for Wales and remains affiliated to Cardiff University, as Professor of Social Policy and Applied Social Sciences. In March 2013, Mark became the Minister for Health and Social Services in Wales.

Adam B. Evans is a PhD student at the Wales Governance Centre, Cardiff University.

Martina Y. Feilzer is a Senior Lecturer in Criminology and Criminal Justice at Bangor University.

Paul Furlong is Professor of European Studies at Cardiff University and has been involved in WISERD since its inception.

Andrew Henley is Professor of Entrepreneurship and Regional Economic Development at Aberystwyth University and was formerly Director of the LEAD Wales programme at Swansea University.

Karen Jones is a Research Officer on the LEAD Wales programme at Bangor Business School, Bangor University.

Robert Jones is a PhD student at Cardiff Law School. His research is looking into the situation of imprisonment in Wales and the devolution of criminal justice.

Stephanie Jones is currently working as a freelance social researcher and trainer. Her research interests include gender, disability, participatory methodology and social exclusion. She is based in Swansea.

Marie Navarro is a specialist in public law, was editor and Chief Researcher to Wales Legislation Online and now runs YourLegalEyes offering training and consultancy in Cardiff and London.

Heather Norbury was formerly a researcher on the LEAD Wales programme at the School of Business and Economics, Swansea University.

Laura Norris is an early career researcher at the Centre for Advanced Studies at Cardiff University and is embarking on a cross-departmental PhD in innovation and system transition.

Mamata Parhi is a lecturer in Swansea University; her research interests include technological change and economic development, economic growth in space and time, innovation and organizational behaviour in industry.

Alexandra Plows is an independent consultant specializing in regional sustainable development and forms of public engagement. She was previously a Research Fellow at the Wales Institute of Social and Economic Research, Data and Methods (WISERD).

Julie Porter is a Research Associate in the Department of Planning & Geography at Cardiff University and is finishing her PhD research in the School of Social Sciences at Cardiff University on migration motivations and labour market dynamics.

Martin Powell is Professor of Health and Social Policy at the Health Services Management Centre, University of Birmingham.

Gareth Rees is Professor and Director of the Wales Institute of Social & Economic Research, Data & Methods (WISERD).

Neil Roche is based in the Welsh Economy Research Unit at Cardiff Business School, Cardiff University.

Sally Sambrook is Professor of Human Resource Development at Bangor Business School, Bangor University.

Luke Sloan is a lecturer in quantitative methods in the School of Social Sciences at Cardiff University.

Chris Taylor is Professor of Education at Cardiff University and is currently leading the Welsh Government funded evaluation of the Foundation Phase in Wales for the Wales Institute of Social & Economic Research, Data & Methods (WISERD).

Stephen Tierney is Professor of Constitutional Theory in the School of Law, University of Edinburgh and Director of the Edinburgh Centre for Constitutional Law.

Katherine S. Williams is a Senior Lecturer in Criminology and Criminal Justice at Aberystwyth University.

Jo Yates was a key part of the research team working on the evaluation of the North Wales Women's Turnaround Project. She has an MA in Social Research and Social Policy, Bangor University.

1. LEARNING TO LEAD FOR BUSINESS GROWTH – IMPLICATIONS FOR SUPPORTING SMEs IN WALES

*Karen Jones, Andrew Henley, Sally Sambrook
and Heather Norbury*

ABSTRACT

The Welsh private and third sectors are heavily dependent on SMEs. Consequently the performance of SMEs is critical to the performance of the Welsh economy. Substantial public funds, particularly from European Structural Funds, have been allocated to support these since 2000. The majority of programmes thus funded have been led from within the Welsh Government. This paper reports interim evaluation findings from one intervention led by two Welsh higher education institutions (HEIs), namely the LEAD Wales programme. The programme is an extended intervention to support the leadership skills of owner-managers and incorporates a range of learning methods, including formal masterclasses, but emphasizes situated and experiential learning through action learning, coaching and peer-to-peer exchange exercises.

The programme's impact is assessed on the experiences of 325 participants, of whom 217 have completed the programme. The paper concludes that situated learning methods, through which participants are able to draw from shared history and experience over an extended period, are critical to programme success. By contrast, short-term thematic teaching, based around more formal, hierarchical learning, is less likely to yield significant and sustainable economic benefits. The implications of this for business support in Wales are discussed.

INTRODUCTION

There is pervasive interest in entrepreneurship within the small and medium sized enterprise (SME) sector at the highest political level (European Commission,

2008), not least because entrepreneurship is recognized as a major driver of innovation, competitiveness and economic growth; it can unlock personal potential and contribute to social cohesion (European Commission, 2004). Some commentators claim entrepreneurship is 'the engine of economic and social development throughout the World' (Audretsch, 2003, p. 5). The subject of how entrepreneurs learn, and therefore improve leadership and management skills, has recently attracted significant academic and practitioner interest (Cope, 2005; Jones et al., 2010).

Research in Europe indicates that entrepreneurial potential is not being fully exploited (European Commission, 2003). Consequently the needs of SMEs have been placed at the heart of the Lisbon Growth and Jobs Strategy in Europe (European Commission, 2005). Within its framework of actions, special attention is placed on entrepreneurship skills to improve the potential for growth in the SME sector.

Similarly, the Welsh Assembly Government in its document 'One Wales' (2007) sets out its vision for a sustainable society that includes action to stimulate enterprise and business growth to enable SMEs to thrive. Through its document 'Wales: A Vibrant Economy' (Welsh Assembly Government, 2005), and a range of emerging programmes, the Welsh Government commits to support SME development and stimulate business growth. This support is vital to the Welsh economy as SMEs (defined as those with less than 250 employees) account for 60 per cent of all employment in the private sector in Wales (Welsh Government, 2011).

This policy context has informed the strategic direction of European structural funds in Wales, initially through the 2000–6 Objectives 1 and 2 programmes, and particularly, since 2007, through the Convergence and Competitiveness programmes. This paper reports early findings from the LEAD Wales programme, which provides leadership development to owner-managers of SMEs, including some managing directors of social enterprises, in Wales. The programme focuses on leadership capability because research has indicated leadership is a key factor in SME survival and growth (Smith and Peters, 2006). Leadership can create an important source of competitive advantage (Hirst et al., 2004).

The programme is funded through the European Social Fund to support approximately 700 businesses in the West Wales and the Valleys Convergence Region from 2009 to 2015. LEAD Wales is managed and delivered by two Welsh (HEIs), Swansea and Bangor universities, and therefore also supports increased engagement between higher education and the small business and social enterprise sectors. This paper provides an interim assessment of the benefit and impact of the programme based on the experiences of 325 participants between 2010 and 2012, of whom 217 have completed the programme to date.

In a smaller business context, understanding learning and development is key to driving economic development and imperative to the creation of a knowledge economy. Insights into the potential value of extended management and leadership development support may inform future policy and the specific design of particular programmes. The findings complement other recent analyses (Meliou and Kennard, 2012).

The paper is structured in the following way. First, the Welsh context of the intervention is discussed, followed by the programme's history, its underpinning philosophy and design. Next, we discuss research methods. We report interim findings on the personal and professional development of participants, changes in leadership style, business development and growth, followed by a discussion on learning methods. We conclude with implications for policy and research.

THE WELSH CONTEXT

The total business population in Wales is currently estimated at just under 193,000 (Department for Business, Innovation and Skills, 2011a). The number of businesses per 10,000 of the adult population is considerably lower in Wales compared to England (784 compared to 927). Portraying a similar picture to other UK regions 99.9 per cent of businesses in Wales are SMEs, and almost 74 per cent are sole traders. However, businesses in Wales are somewhat smaller than in England, with slightly higher proportions in the small and micro sub-groups (under fifty and under ten employees respectively). As a percentage of the total business population, Wales has a higher proportion of businesses in the agriculture, forestry and fishing sector (7.2 per cent), compared to England (2.2 per cent) (see Figure 1.1). Farming and food is important to the Welsh economy, particularly as this sector has the greatest proportion of SMEs (Welsh Government, 2011). More significantly, businesses in Wales are under-represented in the more innovative professional, scientific and technical activities sector compared to England (7.6 per cent of the total business population compared to 13.9 per cent).

Lower levels of private sector productivity have been recognized as an important factor in explaining lower levels of economic prosperity in Wales. Extensive evidence suggests innovative economies are more productive and

Figure 1.1
Percentage share of enterprises per industry sector, 2011

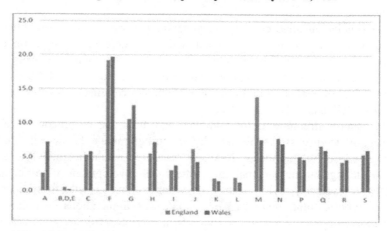

Key to industry sections

A	Agriculture, Forestry & Fishing
B,D,E	Mining/Quarrying; Electricity/Gas/ Air Con Supply; Water Supply; Sewerage/Waste Management/Remediation Activities
C	Manufacturing
F	Construction
G	Wholesale & Retail Trade; Repair of Vehicles/Motorcycles
H	Transportation & Storage
I	Accommodation & Food Service Activities
J	Information & Communication
K	Financial & Insurance Activities
L	Real Estate Activities
M	Professional, Scientific & Technical Activities
N	Administrative & Support Service Activities
P	Education
Q	Human Health & Social Work Activities
R	Arts, Entertainment & Recreation
S	Other Service Activities

Source: Department for Business Innovation and Skills (2011a).

faster growing (Department for Business Innovation and Skills, 2011b, p. 5). Successive economic policy statements from the Welsh Government have recognised this: *A Winning Wales* (Welsh Assembly Government, 2002); *Wales: A Vibrant Economy* (Welsh Assembly Government, 2005); *Economic Renewal: A New Direction* (Welsh Assembly Government, 2010). Additionally, strategic plans for key sectors include, for example: Science for Wales (Welsh

Government, 2012). This identifies barriers and enablers of business development, which include: infrastructure and skills; research and development; financial incentives such as access to funding sources, investment, procurement, and favourable regulatory standards.

Other influences include the nature of capital and technology employed, and innovative capacity, as well as business competitiveness and strategic positioning. This can be deconstructed into elements, capturing both lack of skills and poor occupational mix in the workforce, lack of economic mass, as well as a residual component, which economists usually attribute to lack of management and leadership capacity (Welsh Assembly Government, 2005). Some regions in Wales typify the overwhelming difficulties experienced with the decline of traditional industries. Employers in regions severely affected sometimes question the work-readiness of job applicants (Adamson et al., 2010). As the Leitch review of skills (2006) highlighted, improving business leadership skills is essential to raising the need for skills and for getting the most from employees. It is essential for promoting business innovation and creativity, and for exploiting business networking and supply chain opportunities to overcome the disadvantages of geographical peripherality.

There are therefore many reasons for lower ability or willingness to seek and achieve business innovation and growth in Wales. The leadership programme, upon which this paper is based, is concerned with the 'individual challenges' (Riverin, 2007) of the SME context. This cannot alone provide a solution to deeper causes of lower levels of private sector productivity. However, it is widely recognized that overall employee productivity may be influenced by the quality of management and leadership, and therefore interventions to support organizational management and leadership development may reap positive economic benefits. This has long informed the case for the provision of formal management training and qualifications in both public and private sectors.

It has been noted that there is a plethora of management and leadership provision in Wales (Wales Management Council, 2005), which can be bewildering for the small business owner, who might be uncertain about both his or her own needs, and the quality of provision on offer. Welsh HEIs typically focus on full-time undergraduate and specialist postgraduate provision. MBA programmes typically target recent graduates and part-time versions usually cater for middle managers in public and larger private sector organizations. Gibb (2009) argues that low levels of interest from small businesses arises because delivery is supply-driven by the expertise of the provider and therefore often designed to be appropriate to the needs of large organizations.

Unsurprisingly, levels of satisfaction with the provision of publically funded support for small and medium sized businesses in the UK are low (Carter et al., 2000). Sargent (1996) notes programmes are often regarded as highly academic, with insufficient practical focus for small businesses. Anecdotal evidence from LEAD Wales confirms this to some extent. Other researchers are more positive about the potential benefits of a supply-driven approach (Morrison, 2003; Fuller-Love, 2006). However, others suggest that low levels of interest may reflect weak observed impacts on business performance (Storey, 2004). The issue of how SME demand can be stimulated needs to be considered and problematized. Small businesses need to be able to perceive readily the benefits of programme participation, particularly if that participation is costly in terms of either fees or time committed. Recognizing the idiosyncratic nature of small business life, the Council for Excellence in Management and Leadership proposed:

> The key to solving the problem is to join the entrepreneurs in their world and to tap seamlessly into the activities that they would be undertaking as a normal part of running their businesses (Perren and Grant, 2001, p. 16).

Small business owners are more likely to understand how value is added if interventions are tailored to their needs. Against this background we present the leadership programme upon which the paper is based.

LEADERSHIP PROGRAMME INTERVENTION

LEAD Wales adopts a design developed between 2004 and 2006 by Lancaster University Management School (Wren and Jones, 2006). This design was informed by concerns about the salience of traditional leadership and management development for small business owners, as well as by research concerning the way in which entrepreneurs learn to lead (Kempster and Watts, 2002; Kempster, 2009). The LEAD ('Leading Enterprise and Development') model was delivered to over 1000 SME owners and managers across the north-west of England between 2008 and 2012 with funding support from the former North West Regional Development Agency. In Wales, LEAD is delivered by Swansea University and Bangor University.

Previous research (see for example, Bolden, 2001; Kempster and Watts, 2002; Stewart and Birchall, 2005; Walker et al., 2007; Gold and Thorpe, 2010) has highlighted the following as defining characteristics of leadership in small businesses:

- a sense of isolation experienced by many business owners (Inglis, 1994; Stewart and Birchall, 2005; Peters, 2008), particularly those operating as sole owners;
- a suspicion towards formal taught programmes, such as MBAs, since these are perceived as focused around the needs of middle managers in large organizations (Sargent, 1996; Gibb, 2009);
- a limited confidence to achieve effective delegation of responsibility to employees (Bolden, 2001);
- constraints on strategic thinking imposed by the pressure of day-to-day operational issues (Bolden, 2001; Smith and Peters, 2006).

Thus the ten-month programme is built around an integrated learning model (Figure 1.2), with activities designed to enhance situated learning (learning created from the activity, culture or context) and promote the creation of learning spaces (Peters, 2010). These encompass formal learning, as well as experiential learning and peer-to-peer learning approaches (Smith, 2011). Programme activities include masterclasses, action learning sets for small facilitated group work on business issues, business coaching, peer-to-peer business shadowing and exchange, and learning and reflection sessions. A secure e-forum allows access to programme resources and discussion facilities. Accreditation is provided by an independent UK management education accreditation body.

Figure 1.2
Integrated learning model

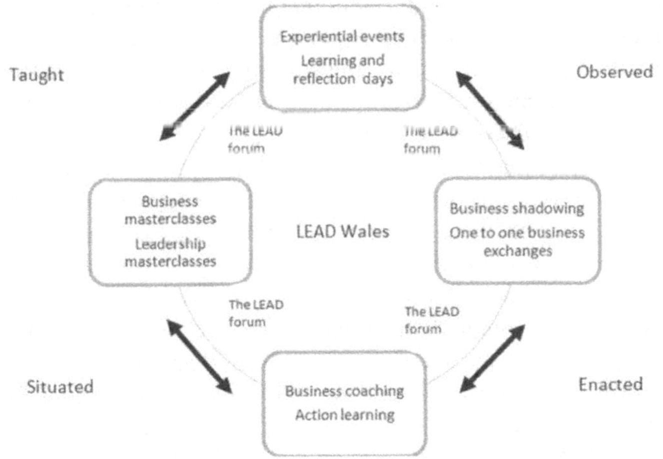

Adapted from Smith (2011, p. 18).

Participants are recruited in groups of between twenty and twenty-eight owner-managers of SMEs and strategic leaders of social enterprises with at least three employees, trading for at least two years, within the West Wales and Valleys Convergence region. The equal opportunities target is set at 40 per cent female participation in the programme. Participants tend to originate from small and micro businesses (average size twelve employees), with a sectoral break-down reflective of the Welsh business population.[1] Recruitment is targeted at businesses with growth aspirations. This is assessed through questions about the history of the business, applicants' growth aspirations and strategy for growth, which may be expressed as expansion, diversification or by increasing staffing, turnover and/or profit. Additionally, applicants must communicate personal development aspirations, motivation to commit time to the programme, a commitment to team-based learning, and an understanding of the need to exercise integrity and confidentiality in group learning activity. The recruitment process[2] typically involves informal one-to-one interviewing to establish suitability. No firm decision on an offer of a LEAD Wales place is made until confirmed and agreed by a recruitment panel.

RESEARCH DESIGN

The project adopts an evaluation strategy, employing a mixed method approach (Bryman and Bell, 2007), comprising questionnaire surveys, focus groups and autobiographical interviews. The different methods were informed by research philosophy and the research questions that we sought to address. Whilst we sought to provide a clear quantitative approach to investigate the impact of the programme we also wanted to explore and describe this in more depth from a qualitative perspective. These approaches are discussed in turn.

Questionnaires, completed by all participants, gather initial and post-programme quantitative data on participants' business (turnover, number of employees). This enables the estimation of impact as evidenced by growth in business turnover (as a percentage) and size of workforce (as increase in number of new jobs created). Questionnaires also measure levels of satisfaction with different learning methods and entrepreneurial and leadership traits. Descriptive statistical analysis and means are reported based on valid responses from 323 participants who completed the initial questionnaire and 201 who completed the final questionnaire.

As it is difficult for individuals to articulate leadership learning (Kempster and Cope, 2010), qualitative data are gathered through focus groups and interviews to elicit tacit knowledge (Kempster and Parry, 2004). Focus groups take place two months after participants complete the programme. This is voluntary, resulting in a self-selected, convenience sample. Seventeen focus groups have been conducted to date. The focus groups are recorded and transcriptions analysed for emerging themes, employing grounded analysis (Easterby-Smith et al., 2008). Seventeen autobiographical narrative interviews (Schütze, 2007; Wengraf, 2001, 2004) have also been undertaken to explore the participants' life stories (Rae and Carswell, 2000) and entrepreneurial journeys.

We acknowledge that these are self-reported data, at this stage taken only over a 10–12 month period with participants who are self-selected and already growth-orientated. However, business performance will be evaluated annually with an online questionnaire to identify any change in participants' business (expansion, change in structure, diversification, creation, closure, etc.); changes in employment; employee productivity; changes in turnover; annual revenue; and where applicable, the nature of continuing activity with cohort members. This commenced in November 2011 and will continue to 2015, when funding ends, to provide a more robust picture of the programme's economic and social impact.

FINDINGS

Profile of programme participants

A diverse network of business owner-managers and social enterprises is represented in the programme (Table 1.1). Initial profile data indicates 36 per cent of participants are female and 64 per cent are male, ranging in age from early twenties to over seventy. The largest group is aged 35–50. Although 39 per cent possess a higher education qualification, participants typically report high levels of technical skill, but limited formal management training. Conversely, 22 per cent have no formal qualifications or only achieved qualifications up to the compulsory school leaving age of sixteen.

The businesses are broadly representative of the sectoral breakdown in Wales, with manufacturing slightly over-represented and construction under-represented (Table 1.2). Participants' prior business experience ranges from a few years up to thirty years, although nearly a third (31 per cent) has been in business for five years or less. On average, annual business turnover at the beginning of the programme was £735k even though over 57 per cent reported a turnover of £500k or below per annum. Employment is similarly skewed as

Table 1.1
Profile of programme participants

Gender	N	%
Male	207	64
Female	118	36
Age		
Over 50 years	81	25
35-50 years	169	52
Under 35 years	73	23
Education		
No qualifications	20	6
GSCEs/O levels (age 16)	52	16
A levels (age 18)	47	15
HND or further education award	77	24
First degree	76	24
Post graduate degree	50	16

the average number of employees at the start of the programme was thirteen although 58 per cent of participants employed ten people or less.

Upon joining the programme, 61 per cent of participants stated they had a specific business challenge or issue in mind (Table 1.3), 85 per cent of the issues concerned business growth. It is encouraging that upon completion nearly 90 per cent said their initial expectations of the programme were either 'mostly' or 'fully' met.

Personal and professional development

Research findings illustrate that leadership development can have a positive impact on, not only the business but, the personal and professional development of the business leader. The most significant impacts appear to be on self-confidence levels and on management of work-life balance. Exit questionnaire data shows 83 per cent either 'strongly agreed' or 'agreed' with statements relating to improvement in personal self-confidence. Qualitative findings strongly support this. Improvements in personal self-confidence typically translate into an increase in confidence in running the organization and in leading staff, as illustrated below:

> I am naturally confident but in the business setting I was constantly doubting myself. Since LEAD Wales, I believe I can do it and people will listen to me and respect me.

Table 1.2
Profile of businesses

Business sector	N	%
Professional services	78	24
Education; art and recreation; other services	67	21
Wholesale and retail trade; transport and storage; accommodation and food services	58	18
Manufacturing	43	13
Information and communication	32	10
Construction	25	8
General	22	7
Years running business		
1–5 years	100	31
6–10 years	81	25
11–20 years	84	26
>20 years	53	17
Turnover £ p.a.		
<500k	179	57
500k up to 1m	78	25
1m up to 2m	29	9
2m up to 3m	13	4
3m or more	15	5
Number of employees		
1–4	86	27
5–10	96	31
11–25	78	25
26–50	33	11
51–100	15	5
>100	6	2

Table 1.3
Business concerns

Business position at baseline	N	%
Seeking to grow faster	96	55
Were not growing	53	30
Losing sales	12	7
Danger of closing the business	8	5
Other	6	3

Prior to joining the programme many participants worked six, sometimes seven days a week, with little time to devote to holidays. Typically they feared the business would suffer in their absence. 'Time-release' for the programme forces participants to reflect on the nature of their commitment to the business and to confront fear of absence. For some this not only resulted in a positive change in their ability to achieve a better work-life balance but also brought wider benefits to the business, since more work could be delegated and employees empowered. Some found time to work from home, as needed, without feeling stressed about being away from the business. Overall, 37 per cent said the programme had a significant impact on reducing stress. This translates to a more positive outlook on life and business. Many described the experience of participating in the programme as 'energizing' and 'life-changing'.

Leadership style

The programme primarily aims to enhance participants' leadership skills, in order to improve business performance. Exit findings show 60 per cent said the programme had a significant impact on the way they provide leadership for their team and organization. The following extract is illustrative of how the programme raised participants' awareness of their leadership style:

> I learned I was in the wrong place as a leader (far too democratic) and pushed to the extreme when upset. I was able to find a better balance. Now we hold more open meetings, telling staff more about company goals and growth. The staff is part of the company not just me running it on my own.

Participants typically describe some uncertainty at the start of the programme concerning the roles of leader and manager. Qualitative findings suggest that gaining greater clarity in this regard helped participants clarify their own role in the organization. In consequence, they were able to switch focus away from managing day-to-day tasks to a leadership role that gives attention to future business growth, strategies and leading their staff to future success:

> Defined the difference between leadership and management. I never thought of them differently. I am looking for opportunities more and delegating more. I also have the right people on the right job.

> I have increased strategies and schedules. I now measure our [resources] to stream-line and watch costs. I have let the staff take more control and let them try their own ways of solving problems or performing tasks.

Table 1.4
Changes leading and managing employees and teams

	N	%
Developing positive working relationships	131	65
Providing leadership for team	121	60
Improved morale	111	55
Mentoring staff	107	53
Effective communication	102	51
Building effective teams	78	39
Managing conflict	72	36
Workforce planning	65	32
Handling disciplinary action	38	19

Wider impact on employees and teams may result (Table 1.4). Most notably participants reported developing positive relationships, over half were mentoring staff, and a similar proportion noted improved morale. Effective communication is a critical factor behind successful leadership in any organizational context. It is therefore promising that around half the participants said the programme had a significant impact on their ability to provide effective communication.

Qualitative findings reveal specific examples of changed communication practices including the establishment of regular staff meetings, where none had previously taken place, and the introduction of more formal appraisal and employee goal setting systems:

> I've briefed everybody what the goals are and I've planned those goals out. I've started the appraisal systems which we have here, put those appraisals in, set those goals, delivered those. Now, I give a review at the end of each month.

Some participants also observed improvements in employee productivity as a result of explaining to their staff the reasons for, and value of, particular tasks and roles, as illustrated here:

> I appreciate the people, if you get them on board with what you're trying to do and your goals, and where you're trying to take the company, they'll often take things further than you actually expected to yourself and actually bring in ideas you didn't expect.

Business development and growth

Baseline findings highlight that many participants experienced strategic confusion regarding, for example, whether to focus on a particular niche or pursue all business opportunities present. The programme is not designed to support or teach formal strategy analysis; however, it does encourage reflective thinking which can increase capacity to appreciate the current positioning of the organization and fit with the business environment. This can lead to a formal strategy process, but depends also on the nature of the business (size, sector, etc.) and style of the leader.

Nevertheless, exit data shows 97 per cent of participants stated that the programme had a significant impact on them and the way they run their business. The most significant business impacts are strategic thinking and associated business growth. Forty-six per cent said the programme contributed significantly to the development of a strategic business plan. In consequence:

- 62 per cent plan to expand the business;
- 38 per cent plan to start a new business;
- 30 per cent will diversify the primary business;
- 17 per cent will develop a partnership or merger with another business;
- 10 per cent plan to franchise their business to others.

Qualitative findings suggest the opportunity to find a 'sounding board' in the form of coaching or participation in an action learning set makes a significant contribution to these outcomes. Typically participants report it's the first time the business feels organized and focused. The following comments provide specific examples:

> I have a five-year strategy so in five years time, the other people will be doing what I am doing and I'll do as much or as little as I'd like. So LEAD sort of made me really think about it. Not just vaguely think about it, which I've done in the past, but actually do something. Put some steps in place, take some actions so it can be achieved and will be achieved. So that's a major thing that I feel I got from LEAD and if for nothing else, it was worth doing it for that.

> The Coaching and Action Learning Sets have provided me with clarity about our future direction and have helped me to formulate robust strategies that will undoubtedly assist in moving my business forwards.

Business growth is reported by the majority of participants, either in terms of increase in staff or turnover or both. Nevertheless, business growth is not guaranteed and for some participants the programme focused attention on rationalisation or turnaround strategies. The analyses of baseline and exit data

(Table 1.5) shows on average businesses reported an increase of just over £101k in annual turnover. While, in absolute terms, this is not large, given the average initial size of participating businesses, it reflects an average increase of 23 per cent.

Additionally, on average there was an increase of 1.76 jobs per business. Some of these jobs are part-time, and assuming that a part-time job is half of a full-time one, this converts to 1.64 full-time equivalent (FTE) jobs created per business.

As a result, participants who have completed the programme have created a net increase of approximately 297 jobs (277 FTE) within the Welsh economy.

Table 1.5
Business growth

Change in Turnover		
By individual		No. participants
Absolute average change in turnover £	£95,013	189
Percentage change in turnover	22.90%	191
By business (averaging across individual participants from the same business)		
Absolute average change in turnover £	£101,053	163
Percentage change in turnover	23.00%	164
Change in Employment		
By individual		Sample size
Absolute average change in employment	1.65	196
Estimated total net change in jobs	323.5	
By business (averaging across individual participants from the same business)		
Absolute average change in employment	1.76	169
Estimated total net change in jobs	297	
Change in Employment (FTEs, part-time employees = 0.5)		
By individual		Sample size
Absolute average change in FTE employment	1.53	196
Estimated total net change in FTE jobs	299.2	
By business (averaging across individual participants from the same business)		
Absolute average change in FTE employment	1.64	169
Estimated total net change in FTE jobs	277	

Some participants report that they achieved business growth by acting on a business opportunity about which they had previously been hesitant. Improvement in business and personal self-confidence is apparent in reported business growth activity, associated with progress through the programme. For example, reflecting a common theme, one participant said: 'The main thing has been the confidence – confidence to go where I hadn't gone before.'

One caveat regarding these outcomes is that participants are recruited because they have growth aspirations for their business. In this respect the data provide a useful indicator of the outcomes that may be achieved through small business support interventions.

Learning approach and SME engagement

Qualitative findings show the positive outcomes reported here centre on the creation of learning networks.[3] This critically depends on participants' willingness to be open and trusting. In this respect the programme is particularly successful. A significant majority of participants frequently report reduced feelings of isolation associated with running a smaller business, as illustrated in this excerpt:

> The biggest thing has been sharing commonalities with other businesses in a way that you can't do at a classic networking type group or event or something. There's something instantly deep about the relationships on the course and I don't really know why . . . so there's real support and empathy between people. It's quite special relationships that we've all got with individual people.

Action learning sets and peer-to-peer shadowing and exchange activities, supported with business coaching, provide an environment where participants are able to freely discuss their hesitations and articulate a successful way forward with business issues. Relationships formed within the programme have also led to business partnerships, joint ventures and continued business support among groups of participants. Preliminary findings from seventy-five participants in the annual survey, which commenced in November 2011, suggest around three-quarters continue to meet socially or through business networking or organized meetings. Twenty per cent engage in action learning set meetings on a self-facilitated basis. Whilst much of this activity is led by participants, there is strong demand for continued involvement and support from the universities and teams delivering the programme. Post LEAD events and masterclasses have enabled opportunities for continued engagement. Some participants provide talks. Additional benefits include enhanced access to enterprises and entrepreneurs for research purposes. Continued involvement is vital to develop relationships with the small business community. Whilst resourcing this activity presents some challenges, it is hoped that these outputs will continue to grow after the project has finished.

DISCUSSION

The LEAD Wales programme employs a range of learning methods intended to enhance the strategic leadership skills of participants. Key benefits include improved personal self-confidence, which helped achieve improved work-life balance through increased delegation and reduced focus on business minutiae. Also, enhanced leadership style, achieved through greater self-awareness and critical reflection, resulted in improved communication skills, both with employees and with other external stakeholders. Economic impact is demonstrated by an average increase in business turnover of £101k per annum and the creation of almost 300 new jobs within Welsh businesses completing the programme. These outcomes are particularly impressive since they have been achieved in challenging economic conditions. Thus, the programme supports the Welsh Government in its objective to promote growth and create jobs and opportunities for people in Wales. Fundamentally, the findings highlight the significant role of HEIs in local, regional and national economies.

We conceptualize the impact of extended development support for entrepreneurial leaders (Figure 1.3) as a flow of knowledge transfer and impact at various levels – individual, organizational, within the business community, and at a wider societal level. For instance, individual development can lead to knowledge transfer and impact on employees or other organizational stakeholders, which may in turn impact on the individual leader's learning and development. 'LEAD graduateness' creates a willingness to engage with, listen to and learn from other businesses who may or may not have been part of the programme. Some of this activity can impact directly on the organization. Through engagement with HEIs, networks can be extended, creating social capital and thus supporting business development (Gordon and Jack, 2010, p. 534). Business and HEI engagement can be nurtured through the creation and development of relationships (Abreu et al., 2008). At a broader societal level, knowledge transfer and impact may occur, for instance, with HEIs, the regional economy, communities and so on (Cox and Taylor, 2006; Gordon et al., 2010).

Figure 1.3
Illustrating the wider impact of extended development
support for entrepreneurial leaders

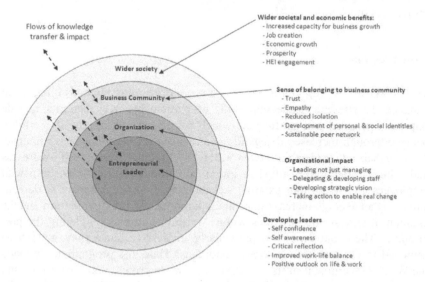

Although there are almost 200,000 small businesses in Wales, the experience of owning and managing these businesses appears, for many, an isolating experience. Breaking this cycle is critical. In this respect, our findings support earlier research (Inglis, 1994; Stewart and Birchall, 2005; Peters, 2008; 2010). Self-confidence may be low and the ability to achieve the best from staff, however loyal they may be, can be hindered by limited leadership skills. Support needs not only to address market failures in the provision of 'hard' financial and infrastructure support, but also the issue of 'soft' management and leadership skills (Gold and Thorpe, 2010). These two aspects are complementary. Businesses will fail to make full advantage of 'hard' support, if they suffer from management and leadership skills gaps. Leadership development for the business owner or social entrepreneur may also be a precondition if management training for employee managers lower in the business is to be effective (Leitch, 2006).

However, a more holistic approach needs to be taken forward in pedagogic design. Too much support is 'supply-driven', that is based on the expertise of available experts rather than seeking to unlock the knowledge within the entrepreneur (Perren and Grant, 2001). Adding support to Meliou and Kennard's recent report from Leadership and Management Wales (2012), we propose that a 'slow-burn' approach, involving support over an extended period of time, can provide opportunity for reflection, and is more likely to be effective over the medium term.

Finally, the success of the LEAD programme in north-west England highlighted the potential for engagement between SMEs and HEIs. Whilst this is important for knowledge transfer and skills development (Johnston et al., 2008), this relationship may and can lead to future benefits for wider stake-holders, for example through increased SME participation in student work placement activity, or greater willingness on the part of entrepreneurs to engage with students to share business experience and 'tell their stories'.

CONCLUSION

As previously noted, one caveat regarding reported outcomes in business growth is that participants are recruited because they have growth aspirations for their business. Therefore business performance is likely to some extent, regardless of participation, to be above average. Nevertheless, the effective design and impact of the LEAD programme in supporting business growth has been acknowledged elsewhere (Smith and Peters, 2006; Gordon et al., 2010). Since it is important to assess the impact of a particular intervention in a different context (Pawson and Tilley, 1997) we have demonstrated early benefits of the programme in Wales. Ongoing contact with participants will allow this to be assessed until, at least, 2015 when the current funding expires.

Small businesses rely on effective leadership to survive and grow, and the currency of any support programme to the needs of business owners is important. Their survival and growth is vital, not only in job creation but also in contributing to regional innovation, competitiveness and growth. In the current economic climate, supporting the development needs of SMEs in Wales is imperative.

NOTES

[1] The LEAD Wales Business Plan sets out indicative recruitment targets by unitary authority (UA) to ensure a good geographical coverage of recruitment across the West Wales and Valleys Convergence Region. These targets have been allocated proportionate to the total small business population in each unitary authority. Recruitment is targeted in the Welsh Government's leading sectors and complies with WEFO

Equal Opportunities Cross-Cutting Theme and University Equal Opportunities policies
to target female, BME, disabled and young people who are owner-managers.

2   Participants are engaged with through networking events; referrals from business
support organizations, banks and past participants; advertising in key locations such
as business support centres and incubator units; through collaboration with business
development managers and relevant services within the universities delivering the
programme; preview events; and workshops at sectoral conferences. Links also exist
in networks such as Chwarae Teg, All Wales Ethnic Minority Association, other
relevant organizations, such as MEWN (Minority Ethnic Women's Network), BEN
(Black Environment Network), Race for Opportunity, SHAW Trust, Social Firms
Wales, Disabled Workers Co-operative and Leonard Cheshire.

3   A complementary perspective here is that the programme serves to create 'communities
of practice' (Lave and Wenger, 1991), through which each group of participants
jointly constructs knowledge and practice about entrepreneurial leadership (Peters,
2008).

REFERENCES

Abreu, M., Grinevich, V., Hughes, A., Kitson, M. and Ternouth, P. (2008). *Universities, Business and Knowledge Exchange*, London: Council for Industry and Higher Education and Centre for Business Research.

Adamson, D., Angove, M., Bromiley, R. and Thomas, B. (2010). *Reaching the Untapped Potential in the Upper Valleys,* Pontypridd: University of Glamorgan.

Audretsch, D. B. (2003). *Entrepreneurship: A Survey of the Literature*, Enterprise Paper No: 14, Belgium: European Commission.

Bolden, R. (2001). *Leadership Development in Small and Medium Sized Enterprises*, University of Exeter: Centre for Leadership Studies.

Bryman, A. and Bell, E. (2007). *Business Research Methods*, Oxford: Oxford University Press.

Carter, S., Ennis, S., Lowe, A., Tagg, S., Tzokas, N., Webb, J. and Andriopoulos, C. (2000). *Barriers to Survival and Growth in UK Small Firms*, London: Federation of Small Businesses, October 2000.

Cope, J. (2005). 'Toward a dynamic learning perspective of entrepreneurship', *Entrepreneurship Theory and Practice*, 29, 4, 373–97.

Cox, S. and Taylor, J. (2006). 'The impact of a business school on regional economic development: a case study', *Local Economy,* 21, 2, 117-35.

Department for Business Innovation and Skills (2011a). *Business Population Estimates for the UK and Regions, http://www.bis.gov.uk/assets/BISCore/statistics/docs/B/Business-Population-Estimates-2011_Statistical-Release.pdf* (accessed 6 December 2012).

Department for Business Innovation and Skills (2011b). *Innovation and Research Strategy for Growth*, London: Her Majesty's Stationery Office.

Easterby-Smith, M., Thorpe, R. and Jackson, P. R. (2008). *Management Research*, London: Sage.

European Commission (2003). *Green Paper 'Entrepreneurship in Europe'*. Brussels: European Commission, 21.01.2003 COM 27 final.

European Commission (2004). *Action Plan: The European Agenda for Entrepreneurship*. Brussels: European Commission, 11.02.2004 COM 70 final.

European Commission (2005). *Implementing the Community Lisbon Programme – Modern SME policy for Growth and Employment*, Brussels: European Commission, 10.11.2005 COM 551 final.

European Commission (2008). *'Think Small First': A 'Small Business Act' for Europe*, Brussels: European Commission, 25.6.2008 COM 394 final.

Fuller-Love, N. (2006). 'Management development in small firms', *International Journal of Management Reviews*, 8, 3, 175–90.

Gibb, A. (2009). 'Meeting the development needs of owner managed small enterprise: a discussion of the centrality of action learning', *Action Learning: Research and Practice*, 6, 3, 209–27.

Gold, J. and Thorpe, R. (2010). 'Leadership and management development in small and medium-sized enterprises: SME worlds', in Gold, J., Thorpe, R. and Mumford, A. (eds) *Gower Handbook of Leadership and Management Development*, Surrey: Gower Publishing Limited.

Gordon, I., Hamilton, E. and Jack, S. (2010). *A Study of the Regional Economic Development Impact of a University Led Entrepreneurship Education Programme for Small Business Owners*, Lancaster: Institute for Entrepreneurship and Enterprise Development, Lancaster University Management School.

Gordon, I. and Jack, S. (2010). 'HEI Engagement with SMEs: developing social capital', *International Journal of Entrepreneurial Behaviour and Research*, 16, 6, 517–39.

Hirst, G., Mann, L., Bain, P., Pirola-Merlo, A. and Richver, A. (2004). 'Learning to lead: the development and testing of a model of leadership learning', *The Leadership Quarterly*, 15, 311–27.

Inglis, S. (1994). *Making the Most of Action Learning*, Hampshire: Gower.

Johnston, L., Hamilton, E. and Zhang, J. (2008). 'Learning through engaging with higher education institutions: a small business perspective', *International Small Business Journal*, 26, 6, 651–60.

Jones, O. A., Macpherson, A. and Thorpe, R. (2010). 'Learning in owner-managed small firms: mediating artefacts and strategic space', *Entrepreneurship & Regional Development*, 22, 7/8, 649–73.

Kempster, S. J. (2009). *How Managers Have Learnt to Lead – Exploring the Development of Leadership Practice*, Basingstoke: Palgrave Macmillan.

Kempster, S. J. and Cope, J. (2010). 'Learning to lead in the entrepreneurial context', *International Journal of Entrepreneurial Behaviour and Research*, 16, 1, 6–35.

Kempster, S. J. and Parry, K. W. (2004). *The Lived Experience as Leadership Development*. Paper presented at the Australian and New Zealand Academy of Management (ANZAM) 18th annual conference. Dunedin, New Zealand. December 2004.

Kempster, S. and Watts, G. (2002). *The Entrepreneur as Leader: an Exploration of Leadership Development amongst Small Business Owner-managers.* Paper presented at the 25th ISBA National Small Firms conference.

Lave, J. and Wenger, E. (1991). *Situated Learning: Legitimate Peripheral Participation,* Cambridge: Cambridge University Press.

Leitch, S. (2006). *Leitch Report of Skills: Prosperity for All in the Global Economy – World Class Skills,* Norwich: HMSO.

Meliou, E. and Kennard, B. (2012). *The Impact of Leadership and Management Development on Organizations,* Cardiff: Leadership and Management Wales.

Morrison, A. (2003). 'SME management and leadership development: market reorientation', *Journal of Management Development,* 22, 9, 796–808.

Pawson, R. and Tilley, N. (1997). *Realistic Evaluation,* London: Sage.

Perren, L. and Grant, J. (2001). *Management and Leadership in UK SMEs,* London: Council for Excellence in Management and Leadership.

Peters, S. (2008). *Building Communities of Practice Across SMEs: The Case of LEAD,* South East Leadership Academy Newsletter, Leadership Academy, Special Edition, Leadership, Innovation and Communities of Practice, Vol. 1, November 2008.

Peters, S. (2010). *Where Does the Learning Take Place? Learning Spaces and the Situated Curriculum within Networked Learning,* Proceedings of the 7th International Conference on Networked Learning.

Rae, D. and Carswell, M. (2000). 'Using a life-story approach in researching entrepreneurial learning: the development of a conceptual model and its implications in the design of learning experiences', *Education and Training,* 42, 4/5, 220–7.

Riverin, N. (2007). *Policies for Developing Entrepreneurship Skills and Culture,* OECD, USAID, LEEDS program: 97–114.

Sargent, A. (1996). 'Training for growth: how can education assist in the development of small businesses', *Industrial and Commercial Training,* 28, 2, 3–9.

Schütze, F. (2007). *Biographical Analysis on the Empirical Base of Autobiographical Narratives. How to Analyse Autobiographical Interviews – Part One.* Germany: Otto-von-Guericke University, Magdeburg.

Smith, S. (2011). *SME Leaders' Learning in Networked Learning: An Actor-network Theory and Communities of Practice Theory Informed Analysis,* University of Lancaster: Unpublished PhD thesis.

Smith, L. and Peters, S. (2006). *Leading by Design: The Case of LEAD.* Full paper for Symposium: Entrepreneurial Leadership Learning, Belfast: British Academy Management.

Stewart, J. A. and Birchall, D. (2005). *Leadership Development for SMEs,* Research Report, London: DTI/CITB.

Storey, D. J. (2004). 'Exploring the link, among small firms, between management training and firm performance: a comparison between the UK and OECD countries', *International Journal of Human Resource Management,* 15, 1, 112–30.

Wales Management Council (2005). *Management Development in Wales: A Survey of Current Practice 2004–5,* Cardiff: Wales Management Council.

Walker, E., Redmond, J., Webster, B., and Le Clus, M. (2007).'Small business owners: too busy to train?' *Journal of Small Business and Enterprise Development*, 14, 2, 294–306.

Welsh Assembly Government (2002). *A Winning Wales*, Cardiff: Welsh Assembly Government.

Welsh Assembly Government (2005). *Wales a Vibrant Economy: The Welsh Assembly Government's Strategic Framework for Economic Development*, Cardiff: Welsh Assembly Government.

Welsh Assembly Government (2007). *One Wales: A Progressive Agenda for the Government of Wales*, Cardiff: Welsh Assembly Government.

Welsh Assembly Government (2010). *Economic Renewal: A New Direction*, Cardiff: Welsh Assembly Government.

Welsh Government (2011). *Business Structure Analysis by Size Band, Wales and UK (NS)* Stats Wales, *http://www.statswales.wales.gov.uk* (accessed 1 August 2012).

Welsh Government (2012). *Science for Wales: Strategic Agenda for Science and Innovation in Wales*, Cardiff: Welsh Government.

Wengraf, T. (2001). *Qualitative Research Interviewing: Biographic Narrative and Semi-structured Method*. London: Sage Publications.

Wengraf, T. (2004). *The Biographic-Narrative Interpretive Method (BNIM) – Short Guide November 2004 Version 22*, London: Middlesex University and University of East London.

Wren, C. and Jones J. (2006). *Ex Post Evaluation of the LEAD Programme*, Lancaster: Lancaster University Management School.

2. INNOVATION IN THE WELSH AUTOMOTIVE INDUSTRY: CHALLENGES AND STRATEGIES

Mamata Parhi

ABSTRACT

Hailed as a budding leader in Europe in terms of auto-component production, Wales's ambition to maintain or improve innovation and a competitive edge in this sector appears to have been seriously thwarted in recent years by developments in the world economy. This paper takes stock of the ongoing structural and organizational 'revolution' in the value-added chain in the automotive industry in Wales and discusses the strengths and weaknesses of the industry from a systemic innovation point of view. This approach draws on basic concepts of evolutionary theory and innovation systems in order to analyse the structure and boundaries of sectors – and identify the factors affecting innovation, competitiveness and the development of public policy.

INTRODUCTION

The automotive industry, sometimes referred to as the 'industry of industries', is synonymous with twentieth-century industrial development and is intertwined with the twin aspects of mass production and mass consumption. In recent years the battle for markets and customers has reached an all time high leading to far-reaching structural and regional re-organization along the supply-chain of the automotive industry. Prominent in the industrial revolution, Wales continues to be a major part of the manufacturing landscape in the UK in general – and the automotive industry in particular. The automotive industry in Wales faces both market and production site competition not only from elsewhere in the European Union, but also the newly industrializing countries such as India and

China. The current crisis has further exposed the limitations of the existing business model of many companies, whilst the need for scale efficiency has led to over-investment in production capacity (Bailey et al., 2008). Key questions that emerge from this scenario are: what happens in – and to – an oligopolistically structured industry when its underlying foundation is being shaken by the emergence of new competitors in the global market? And, do Wales-based automotive suppliers have a chance of survival in the long run?

Any attempt to understand the dynamics of modern industrial growth and competitiveness requires us to study the evolution of the core of the process, especially the speed at which micro agents are becoming interdependent. Adopting this strategy, the objective here is: 1. To understand the present state of the Welsh automotive industry, and its evolution over past decades and; 2. to examine whether and how this sector can become adept in adjusting to contemporary competitive conditions. The main strands of the analysis will focus on the boundaries and depths of the automotive sector, drawing out its strengths, weaknesses and limitations, so as to provide an incisive and theoretically informed assessment of the industry.

Building on recent theoretical and empirical research into innovation systems (Lundvall, 1992; Nelson, 1993) the current paper sets out to assess the expected connection between innovation and firm performance in the automotive industry in Wales. It has become almost a cliché to argue that the innovation by firms can only be fully understood by examining them in relation to the system in which they are embedded. This is because the innovation process involves the transformation of an idea into a marketable product or process and requires an adaptive network of institutions that encompass a variety of informal and formal rules and procedures; an *innovation ecosystem*, that shapes how corporate entities create knowledge and collaborate successfully to bring new products and services to market.

Innovation processes, like any process, evolve over time and are influenced by many factors during the course of their evolution. Because of the complex nature of the process requiring several complementary dimensions of technology, knowledge, skills, as well as the uncertainty about outcomes vis-à-vis the costs incurred, firms almost never innovate in isolation. Rather they interact with each other and with other organizations to gain, develop or exchange knowledge, information and other resources. In fact, a firm's activities (including technological activities) are likely to involve other firms or organizations operating in the same system. Thus the behaviour of a firm is as much affected (constrained or furthered) by other firms and institutions as, in turn, it influences them, thereby underpinning a two way process of interaction.[1] Following from this simple notion, innovation is therefore widely perceived to result from a coalescence of inputs and ideas from a multitude of sources within and outside firms. These sources could be other firms (e.g. suppliers, customers and competitors) and institutions (e.g. universities, research institutes, financial institutions, government regulators) make a significant contribution to the firms' innovative activities. Indeed, the very essence of the systems of innovation approach is its emphasis on the importance of innovating firms working together with other firms and with a range of other organizations. Here, the firm is seen as working within a context composed of a broader scientific and technological community, influenced by relationships with suppliers, customers, regulators and research and training organizations. Building on this perspective, this paper analyses the structure and boundaries of the automotive industry in Wales and identifies the factors affecting innovation and competitiveness of the industry.

Accordingly, the remainder of the paper is organized as follows. First, the evolutionary characteristics of the Welsh automotive industry are discussed and recent trends analyzed. Subsequently, the systems of innovation approach is used to describe the model for innovation and growth in the Welsh automotive sector. The strengths and weaknesses of the sector's innovation system are then elaborated using a version of systems of innovation. The final section discusses prospects, strategies, and outline policy implications for overcoming the challenges faced by the Welsh automotive sector.

WHITHER THE WALES AUTOMOTIVE INDUSTRY IN WALES?

The significance of the automotive industry in Wales

Having been the seedbed of the industrial revolution, Wales continues to be a major part of the manufacturing landscape of the UK. Over the last two centuries, it has been transformed from a predominantly agricultural country to an industrial, and now a post-industrial economy. Significant restructuring in recent years has reduced the number of people working in manufacturing, yet it still accounts for a large proportion (27 per cent) of the nation's Gross Value Added (GVA) (a share greater than the UK average, ONS, 2010). In absolute terms, approximately 1.18 million people constitute the Welsh workforce, of which 161,500 are engaged in manufacturing (StatsWales, 2009).[2] In 2009, total Gross Value Added (GVA) in Wales was £44.5 billion, 74.3 per cent of the UK average. Table 2.1 presents a description of key structural characteristics of the Welsh economy and, in particular, the manufacturing sector.

Table 2.1
Structural characteristics of Wales and UK

		Wales	United Kingdom
A.	**Land Area and Population**		
	Land area (1000*km^2)	20.78	1,728
	Population (x million, 2007)	3	60.9
	Population density (per km^2, 2007)	142	246
B.	**Labour Market and Per Capita Income**		
	Working age employment rate (%, 2010)	67.1	70.6
	Unemployment rate (%, 2010)	8.1	7.9
	GDP per capita income (£, 2008)	15,237	20,520
C.	**GVA, Manufacturing Share, Employment**		
	Agriculture (% of GVA, 2007)	0.5	0.8
	Industry (% of GVA, 2007)	27.1	21.4
	Services (% of GVA, 2007)	72.4	77.8
	GVA in manufacturing (£ million at basic prices, 2007)	7,841	154,881
	GVA in auto industry (SIC 2007 Division: 29) (£ million, 2008)	*	38,886
	Total Employment Costs (£ million, 2008)	479	5,699
D.	**Expenditure on R&D (2008, in £ million)**		
	Businesses	244	15,631
	Government	45	2,290
	Higher education institutions	254	6,519
	Total	543	24,440
E.	**Allocation of EU Structural Funds (Objective 1, 2 and 3; £ million at 2004 prices)**		
	2000	219	1500
	2001	214	1751
	2002	209	1631
	2003	203	1608
	2004	200	1585
	2005	211	1575
	2006	209	1526

* = Not available

Sources: National Statistics, *http://www.statistics.gov.uk*

Wales currently has one of the lowest workforce employment rates, and a relatively low per-capita income (see Table 2.1). This has led to regional policies focused on promoting inward investment in high-tech sectors, strengthening the skills base and encouraging innovation and enterprise (Cooke et al., 1995; Cooke, 2004). Inward investment has been most significant. In this regard, an intensive regional support regime has contributed to a shift in the industrial sector from a traditional concentration in metals manufacturing and processing towards electronics and white goods production (Cooke et al., 1995; Cooke, 2004). Although the effectiveness of this strategy has been questioned (e.g. Fuller and Phelps, 2006), it is clear that over recent years inward investment has been a major factor in reshaping the Welsh manufacturing sector. Manufacturing inward investment to the region has been concentrated in two main sectors: electronic and electrical engineering, and automotive components (although there have also been large-scale investments in other sectors (e.g. aeronautical engineering) (Cooke et al., 1995; Cooke, 2004)).

The automotive sector in Wales, which is the mainstay of its manufacturing sector, is what has remained (or rather was resurrected) during the lengthy period of restructuring that the region has experienced over recent decades. This included several waves of plant closures, relocations (to lower-cost locations) and downsizing. While the successive Welsh Governments have encouraged and mapped out a stimulus plan to re-vitalize the growth of the automotive sector, the recent global meltdown and the growing number of low-cost destinations are creating additional challenges to securing faster growth. It is therefore necessary to examine the evolutionary trend of the industry and examine the extent to which these factors contributed, at least partially, to the recent trend of laggardly growth.[3]

WALES'S AUTOMOTIVE INDUSTRY: IMPERFECT PAST AND VOLATILE PRESENT

(i) Early years (1780 until mid-1980s)
Wales's centrality in the industrial development of the UK recently came into prominence once again, due to the heavy foreign investment and leadership in cutting-edge technology in manufacturing. But from the 1780s until the mid-1980s, the country's share in overall (manufacturing) income in the UK was limited to heavy industrial inputs, especially steel and coal (while agricultural supply predominated in overall income generation). In the twentieth century Wales experienced a lengthy period of restructuring from the early post-war years until the effective ending of major coal production following the defeat of the miners in the 1984–85 strike. Since 1985 Wales has once again taken a significant role in manufacturing production in the UK and led the race among other regions in terms of attracting foreign direct investment.

The lengthy restructuring of the Welsh economy during the post-war years stood it in good stead. During this time government policy encouraged the relocation of engineering and other manufacturing firms to south and north Wales. This encouraged the establishment of companies, such as Ford, Ferodo, GEC, Hoover, Hotpoint, Borg-Warner, etc., many of which underlined the importance of American investment in a UK economy. But between 1945 and 1975, there was no obvious pattern to the incoming foreign investments except for the fact that they were classical branch-plants. The scenario changed, however, after the establishment of the Welsh Development Agency (WDA) in 1976, which for the first time took a leading role in promoting strategic economic development. Although an economic plan was absent until 1992, the WDA nevertheless tacitly developed and followed a sectoral strategy to intensify the level of investment, both domestic and foreign, in automotive and electronic engineering. Given that the period of intense job loss in the heavy industries was in the 1980s, the strategy of promoting investment paid off well during the period (Cooke et al., 1995; Cooke, 2004).

(ii) Recent developments (1985 to date)

Between 1983 and 1993 Wales consistently attracted between 15 per cent and 20 per cent of UK inward investment (Cooke, 1995). Much of this investment in engineering industries came from Japanese, American and European (especially German) firms. Ford opened its new high range engine plant at Bridgend in 1978 and this was followed by investments by several companies (e.g. Calsonic, Valeo, Robert Bosch, Trico, Gillet, etc.). In 1992, Toyota began production of 200,000 engines a year to supply to their assembly plant in Derby (to export back to Japan). With the Ford engine plant producing 500,000 Zeta engines as well as Jaguar's new AJ26 V8 engine, Wales became one of the key centres of high quality, high-skilled automotive engine components production in Europe. These indigenously developed supplier companies started to build a customer base that included all the UK and major European automotive manufacturers.

By early 2000, there were over 250 automotive companies in Wales (around 40 of the top 100 global leaders) woven into a diverse established supply-chain.[4] In addition, the sector manufactured a high proportion of the engines made by both Ford and Toyota in Europe. The experience in engine manufacture placed Wales in a leading position in the production of drive-train technology globally. Companies like TRW, Visteon, Meritor and Magna have been competing with global leaders since 1995 and have a customer base that spans the whole of the UK and major European manufacturers in the sector (Rhys, 2002). These firms have much deeper supply-chain links with UK-based, domestic and foreign-owned assemblers such as Rover, Ford, Toyota,

Honda, GM and Peugeot, and more recently with Tata (who acquired Land Rover and Jaguar). Welsh suppliers have over sixty direct supply contracts with these firms and some 130 indirect supply contracts (i.e., through another firm in the supply chain). However, it has also been noted (e.g., Rhys, 2002), that, in Wales, per capita gross value added is about 7 per cent less than the UK average and capital expenditure is lower by 20 per cent. Thus, although it is increasingly capital-intensive, the industry currently lags in productivity.

The Welsh manufacturing sector in general, and the automotive supply-chain in particular, have declined significantly in the more recent years. In contrast to the growth trajectory between 1991 and 1998, most of the large and medium-sized firms have reduced their workforce.[5] Official statistics at UK level show large firms (>250 employees) accounted for approximately two-thirds of manufacturing job losses between 1998 and 2001. This trend in Wales was no different to the rest of the UK (Office of National Statistics, 2003). However, Wales slipped from fourth to sixth in the regional manufacturing employment share in approximately one year. Wales was now closer to the profile of the 'post-industrial' regions like the South East and South West of England in its modest share of manufacturing employment; in contrast to manufacturing regions such as the English Midlands where the trajectory was positive up to 1998 (Cooke, 2002). The speed of this change, and the manner in which inward investment firms and the linked remnants of the Welsh steel heritage contracted, impacted heavily on the innovation potential of the region and its engineering industries including the automotive sector.

CURRENT ECONOMIC AND STRUCTURAL TRENDS IN THE INDUSTRY

Regional and industrial policy guiding Wales's automotive industry

The regional institutions in Wales (such as Welsh Government) and their policies have clearly had a big impact on the automotive industry. At the European level, the industry is affected by three major types of policy: the macroeconomics of free trade inside and outside the EU; common standards (regulation) on emissions (EURO-IV, EURO-V late 2009 and EURO-VI, 2014) and safety (EURO NCAP tests) which are compulsory in all member states; and the re-cycling and the End-of-Life Vehicle (ELV) Directive which came into force at the beginning of 2007.

At UK national level, policies have been, for the most part, non-interventionist and have concentrated on improving the business environment (Bailey and

Driffield, 2007). For example, labour laws have remained 'flexible' in order to attract and retain inward investment. Thus, while indigenous companies have declined, through new overseas investments (either though FDI or acquisition) foreign-owned transnational firms have maintained 'an automotive industry in the UK' (as opposed to a UK automotive industry). However, the non-interventionist approach has been shelved for the present with the Automotive Assistance Package[6] and the promise of support to Vauxhall (Opel) and the introduction of a scrappage scheme in common with other EU member states. In manufacturing national policy has shifted away from sector-specific support to general support for all manufacturing sectors (i.e. from vertical to horizontal industrial policy measures) (MacNeill and Bailey, 2009).

Against this backdrop research funding has, however, remained largely sector-based (although there is support for research in horizontal or 'platform' technologies). Much of the automotive-specific effort has been directed through the Foresight Vehicle Programme which has sought to fund collaboration amongst companies and research organizations in order to address forecasts for 'future vehicle capabilities'. Reduction of life cycle emissions (LCE) has been a major UK national policy imperative. One example is the CENEX[7] initiative to promote UK market development and competitiveness in low carbon and fuel cell technologies for transport applications. Much of this has been prompted by recognition of the environmental challenge.

At the regional level, policy is implemented by the Welsh Government through its Department of Economy and Transport. The Welsh Government's strategy is aligned with the national UK strategy to support low carbon vehicles and intelligent traffic systems. Since its inception in its various programmes, WG has developed an action and implementation plan to map the actions for the development and delivery of businesses across Wales. The Entrepreneurship Action Plan (2000) was a Welsh Development Agency milestone and the subsequent government policy documents viz., *WAVE: (Wales: A Vibrant Economy)* (WAG, 2005) and more recently the *Economic Renewal Plan* (WG, 2010), promote manufacturing productivity as a key objective. In addition, policy has supported technology development through funding local universities and building technological capability by promoting centres of excellence in the region to facilitate synergies between private and public sector.

Automotive demography: Key characteristics
In this section, we provide an overview of the existing aggregate indicators to provide a picture of the current growth of this industry and its position in the UK automotive sector. Given the paucity of consistent data for indicators for

the Welsh automotive industry (such as R&D, entry-exit characteristics and innovation structure – product or process innovation) we present only the broad sectoral trends in the industry, comparing it with the UK trend, wherever possible.

The automotive sector is vital for Wales's economy accounting for over one-fifth of its manufacturing turnover and it is critical in bringing FDI into the region. Automotive manufacturing is one of the largest sectors in Wales, generating over £3 billion annually. The 250 companies in the automotive sector employ over 20,000 people.[8] Wales is home to a few big vehicle manufacturers (Ford, Toyota) and a number of world class supplier firms. The sector manufactures a high proportion of the engines made by both Ford and Toyota in Europe. Major global companies such as Toyota, TRB, TRW and more recently SPX Contech have their manufacturing footprint in Wales. There have been some recent investments (e.g. by Connaught, Takao Europe Manufacturing Limited and Stevens Vehicles) in Wales. The Wales automotive industry also possesses some technology-intensive and innovative electro-mechanical components and system manufacturers (e.g. Mollertech, Schaeffler, TRW, Tata).[9] These are additional to firms like Ford and Toyota which produce core technology products such as engines.

Wales therefore has several mechanisms for stimulating innovation and rapid company incubation as well as an extensive network of business support with a high degree of regional penetration. The automotive sector is supported by several Centres of Excellence in research and innovation in power electronics, electric motors, energy storage systems and combustion expertise. For instance: the University of Glamorgan's Fuel Cell Technology Centre (developing vehicles of the future utilizing hybrids of fuel cells, batteries, ultra capacitors and advanced internal combustion engines in various configurations); Swansea University's electronic systems design group (worked with Toyota to further develop hybrid vehicle technology); and Cardiff University's Centre of Research in Energy, Waste and the Environment (working with Ricardo to research GDI engine fuel injection).

Yet, in spite of having some well-established centres of excellence, the industry has been mainly composed of relatively low value, low technology generic and bulky non-mechanical component manufacturers.[10] This resonates with the status of manufacturing in the region. Generally, the manufacturing sector in Wales is set against the background of low levels of new firm creation (Keeble and Walker, 1994), combined with factors likely to hinder enterprise growth including low levels of capital availability, high levels of external control. The current skill structure also continues to show a poor occupational mix – low-skilled occupations are over-represented whilst professional, scientific and technical workers are under-represented (IMI, 2009).

The IMI (2009) report notes that skilled trade occupations, including technical skills, are relatively important and also says that the industry shows the volume of managers and customer service and sales staff is high compared to other occupations. Thus the industry is still characterized by low-skilled workers. This partly corroborates the conclusion that there is a legacy problem inherited from the heavy industries. However, the recent recession does not appear to have affected the occupational mix.

CONSEQUENCES OF THE STRUCTURAL AND ECONOMIC TRENDS IN WALES'S AUTOMOTIVE INDUSTRY

The automotive sector is beset with low levels of new firm creation in the region, together with the presence of other weakening factors (*inter alia*, a poorly diversified industry and occupational structure, low levels of capital availability and high levels of external control). In general, the firms have more ability to adapt and redesign products than to really push the technology frontier. Instances of technological upgrading are conspicuously few in number except for the pockets of excellence such as the European Technical Centre of Calsonic Llanelli Radiators. This could be linked to the branch-plant syndrome and low R&D profits of inward investment. This has been confirmed by studies which show that the initial operations of the multinational firms were merely assembling rather than generating technological capability in the region (Munday, 2000). Several micro-level studies have shown that many of the firms have low decision-making discretion with respect to investment in plant and equipment as well as sales and marketing of products, though they have considerable decision making power over the output levels and work force expansion or contraction (Munday, 2000).

Thus, even though several years have passed since devolution, the state of innovation in Wales has remained largely hierarchical and dependent on public policy.[11] The manufacturing sector in general and the automotive industry in particular is no exception. In fact, the industry has been significantly shaped by the strategic goals of the public sector agencies (such as the Welsh Assembly Government which absorbed the erstwhile WDA). Though some of the goals and objectives of the regional government are also shared by industry, the innovation system in Wales has a structure resembling a pyramid, with a large proportion of innovation under-achievers dominating the manufacturing activity at the bottom, while the top comes to a point with a very small number of 'star' players. The automotive sector in particular has been mostly FDI-led, so multinationals have a key role in the sector's competitiveness. Unfortunately, there is not much evidence to prove that these foreign firms are contributing to the innovation in the industry. On the contrary there is increasing evidence that although many of these foreign firms are global leaders in their own right, the activities they are undertaking in Wales are mostly assembly operations rather than developing innovative products or processes. The situation has worsened lately due to the relocation of some of the large automotive OEMs as well as the more recent financial crisis. This has resulted in a lack of 'critical mass'.

All these factors may be symptomatic of a weakening '*system of innovation*' in the sector. In fact, since the 'emerging' system of innovation was focussed around the engineering sectors and these sectors were particularly hard hit (when the large firms contracted) it started to have a cascade effect on the automotive supply chain. With the withdrawal of some large players or thinning of their businesses in Wales, the sector started losing the 'regional interlocutors' who were the kingpins of its strength and performance. This also led to the breakdown of the embryonic relationships between universities, government and business which were just starting to take off, thus resulting in a hollowing out of the automotive manufacturing base in Wales.[12] In order to tease out the systemic dimensions of the problem, we now look at the strengths and weaknesses of the automotive industry in Wales using a systems-of-innovation approach.

WALES'S AUTOMOTIVE INNOVATION PERFORMANCE THROUGH AN 'INNOVATION SYSTEM' LENS

The innovation system in the automotive industry: motivating innovation trends

'Systems' approach to innovation is founded on one of the most persistent themes in modern innovation studies, namely the idea that innovation by firms cannot be understood purely in terms of independent decision-making at the level of the firm. Rather, as noted, innovation involves complex interactions between a firm and its environment. On one level the environment consists of interactions between firms especially between a firm and its network of customers and suppliers. Here the argument is that inter-firm linkages often involve sustained relationships which shape learning and technology creation rather than being arm's-length market relationships. On a second level the environment involves broader factors shaping the behaviour of firms: the social (and perhaps cultural) context; the institutional and organizational framework; infrastructures; and so on.

This notion of innovation as a systemic process, based on a series of networked interactions and institutional learning, stems from the writings of authors such as Lundvall (1992), Nelson (1993) and Nelson and Rosenberg (1993). Innovation systems can be characterized at national (Lundvall, 1992) level and regional level (Cooke, 1992), and even sectoral level (Carlsson and Stankiewicz, 1995; Breschi and Malerba, 1997).[13] Subsequent writings have defined the concept more closely (see Cooke, 1998). The theoretical roots of this systemic notion lie in 'interactive learning theories' and 'evolutionary theories' (Edquist, 1997). According to this perspective of innovation, inter-action among firms and specificities concerning the patterns of interaction constitute the breeding ground for the creation, application and diffusion of knowledge. The interactions, often sustained rather than arms-length, lead to synergetic creation of knowledge and learning which is so crucial for innovation. Indeed, the very essence of the systems-of-innovation approach is its emphasis on the importance of innovating firms working together with other firms and with a range of other organizations. Here, the firm is seen as working within a context composed of a broader scientific and technological community, influenced by relationships with suppliers, customers, regulators and research and training organizations. This is the systemic perspective.

Figure 2.1 is a graphical illustration of innovation dynamics from a systemic viewpoint. One can observe that every firm operates in an environment which is partly given by the economic and physical infrastructure of the industry – and influenced by government policies. The major actors which influence the firm are: the other firms in its value chain (customers/suppliers), the government, educational institutions, research bodies and industry associations. The environ-ment of the firm can be thought of as both an immediate or primary environ-ment and a secondary one. The major actors which influence the firm in its primary environment can be characterised as organizations having day-to-day interactions through the value chain.[14] The firm – together with these other actors – can be said to form a local system of innovation. Also, one can note that the macro environment is given by the existing physical, socio-economic and tech-nological infrastructure available in the region or country. Moreover, there could also be feedbacks from other systems of innovations.[15]

Innovation systems related to the automotive industry can be divided between those closely connected to company headquarters where innovation is developed, and those in 'branch plant' countries or regions that are primarily users, rather than producers of knowledge and therefore innovation followers

Figure 2.1
A framework for Wales' automotive industry

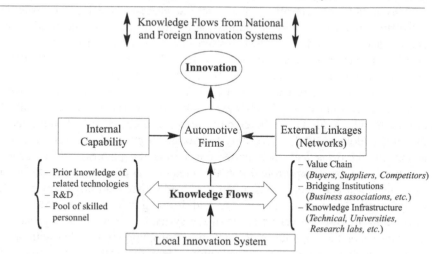

Source: Adapted from Parhi (2006).

(MacNeill and Bailey, 2009). In the latter case, the innovation system is geared to incremental process improvement with networks aimed at cost reduction. New, radical change is controlled by gatekeepers outside the region or the country in question. Relationships between the players tend to be old fashioned and adversarial and based on asymmetries of power and knowledge (Taylor, 1995). Innovation systems tend to be reactive and reflect a production system being for the most part closed, proprietary and dominated by a small number of large transnational companies. In contrast, more proactive innovation systems are characterized by high levels of trust and reciprocity like the well-documented case of Japanese firms. Thus, Cooke (1998) distinguishes three types of innovation system: 'dirigiste', where external control is exerted by industries or governance organizations; those that are 'networked' amongst different levels of governance and funding sources; and those that function from the 'bottom up' or 'grassroots' level. Given the nature of divisions in the automotive sector described above, we may expect to see the differences between innovation systems reinforced with the more radical developments taking place in those areas where the major firms have their headquarters and only incremental developments occurring in the follower regions.

As the industry changes to deal with the political and economic constraints of the 'post fiscal crisis' period, there is a challenge for policy to be geared to the transition. In subsequent work Cooke (2005) distinguishes between what he terms the 'industrial paradigm' of policy based upon sectors (or clusters), closed innovation, closed sources and disciplinary science and a new 'knowledge-based paradigm' of networks, open sources and inter-disciplinary science. Policy in the former circumstances has tended to be geared towards support for efficiency savings through business support mechanisms such as subsidized management consultancy or training. Such policy measures have often followed the expressed 'needs' of the major OEMs and suppliers in their quest to reduce costs. These companies have been adept at playing countries, regions and plants against each other within their own 'internal bidding' procedures (Bailey and Cowling, 2006).

Characterizing Wales's automotive innovation system
In the following, we provide a detailed mapping out of the system of innovation in the automotive sector in Wales identifying the principal elements in the system. A system consists of: (i) institutions (ii) actors, relationships and networks, and (iii) knowledge, technological domain and boundaries. Figure 2.2 maps out the system of innovation in the automotive industry in Wales. Broadly, one can identify four essential elements to the system: policy and strategic direction, human resource development or the supply of technical skills, technology generating sectors and the manufacturing sector.

The elements of the automotive industry in Wales as identified in Figure 2.2 and the discussion of the key characteristics of the state of Wales's automotive industry (see above) show several weaknesses in the system of innovation. In spite of being a favoured candidate of policy makers in Wales, the automotive industry in recent years has not prevented the withdrawal of large firms from the region and a consequent lack of 'critical mass'. As might be expected for a region with a significant level of overseas ownership in the automotive sector, strategic decision-making is quite limited as far as the industry in Wales is concerned. As noted, most of the decision-making is carried out elsewhere, generally limited to the headquarters of these companies. Thus, high level technical knowledge inputs to the larger businesses come from outside the region. Even those companies most embedded in the region, such as the top tier suppliers like TRW, have transferred much of their advanced R&D work to Germany in order to be closer to major OEMs and the 'centre of gravity' of automotive technologies. It is therefore clear that the region has missed a generation of investment in many modern technologies. As a result, local

Figure 2.2
Systemic elements of Wales' automotive industry

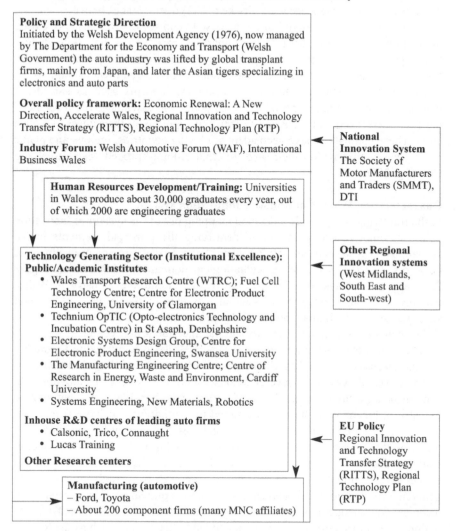

knowledge networks are mostly concerned with manufacturing and with incremental innovation. The innovation system therefore fits Cooke's (1998) dirigiste model dominated by outside interests combined with little in the way of unique or 'sticky' knowledge within the region (Malmberg and Maskell, 1997).

However, for the knowledge-intensive business and niche sector (such as power train technology), the knowledge balance is rather different. Here Wales is clearly a producer of knowledge since the companies are either knowledge-producers *per se* or are able to control their own knowledge flows by virtue of local ownership. Amongst these niche and specialist companies, one significant group is the 'Niche Vehicle Network'. For instance, Narrow Car Company, Abercynon is developing the Naro car series which is a range of 'free leaning' vehicles that improves mobility and addresses the key issues of efficiency and emissions. Similarly, the Connaught Motor company, Llanelli produces petrol/ electric hybrid sports cars through innovative engineering, including the world's first performance hybrid sports coupé, while Stevens Vehicles Cwmbran have designed and developed a small electric zero emissions vehicle and have set up in Wales to manufacture and develop the range. In like manner, Calsonic Kansei leads an international line-up covering power train, steering and braking systems, interior trim and seating, and power electronics. Most of these examples are in high-technology parts production. The participants are developing particular technologies but are too small to be able to market these in whole vehicles for general sale. Inevitably these will be prototyped and sold or licensed to major companies which are mostly outside the region or which will be controlled at least by companies outside the region. Hence, there is a need for more flexible, responsive governance in order to push these private sector firms to build a sustainable innovation system in the sector.

CONCLUSION AND POLICY IMPLICATIONS

In this paper we have investigated how the innovation systems approach can be used to understand the changing dynamics of Wales's automotive industry as witnessed over recent years. Innovation systems approaches tend to be founded on two strong hypotheses. The first is that innovation is a pervasive phenomenon; central rather than marginal to the operations of firms. The second is that interactions between firms, and between firms and other knowledge-producing agencies, are central to innovation performance. Having said this, it is clear that public policies have a central role in the evolution of systems, both in development of underlying knowledge bases, and in provision of the physical and knowledge infrastructures on which the systems rest and progress.

The automotive sector is an important sector not only from a private perspective; it is also important viewed from a public sector and societal perspective. Hence policy makers in regions like Wales – where the automotive

industry has a strong presence, have an interest in strengthening the surviv-
ability of the automotive sector. The traditional base of low-to-medium technology
manufacturing in Wales has seen the development of an innovation system
dominated by external influences. The positive impetus induced by the public
sector in the 1980s did create a positive growth effect in the manufacturing
sector although the trends started to reverse by the end of the century due to the
rapid structural changes in the industry. The 'take-off' phase of the manufacturing sector in general – and the automotive sector in particular – was therefore
only transitory in nature. Whether Wales can remain a long-term location for
automotive production depends substantially on whether the OEMs can hold
their sway as the central core of the automotive clusters in this economic
region. If the OEMs were to successively thin out their Wales plants and in the
end shut them down completely, this would then automatically force suppliers
to migrate. As long as the OEMs remain in Wales with essential real world
functions in production and development so will a considerable part of the
supply industry.

It is true that the global landscape of automotive manufacturing has been
transformed in a way which is less than favourable to the old and mature
industrial regions like Wales. But the industry is also driven by incremental
innovations giving a comparative advantage to a mature industry and the firms
within it. So the strength of the industry lies in promoting innovation and
strengthening it qualitatively by concentrating on the high value-added segments.
Wales has a clear advantage in the niche sectors such as power train technology.
The players in this sector have a real potential to upset the balance that has
weakened the automotive base. However, given that the knowledge-base of
these companies is outside the 'traditional' areas, they need to be allied to the
traditional knowledge of the major companies and linked to their networks in
order to create the required impact in the market.

The acceleration in Wales's manufacturing economic performance was
triggered by an attitudinal shift of the government towards a pro-business
approach. But, until very recently, regional policy towards the automotive
sector was motivated by the prevalent top-down lean manufacturing paradigm
and the short-term needs of a small number of large companies (Bailey et al.,
2008). However, public policy needs to adapt to the changing regional circumstances of the industry and the demise of volume car production. A key
policy direction arising from the systems approaches is to identify and perhaps
support nodal points in the creation and distribution systems in the automotive
industry, keeping in mind that these are likely to be changing over time. Since
knowledge systems are complex in practice, and usually managed by quite

separate institutions (as demonstrated in Figure 2.2), there is a need for policy co-ordination and for adequate information systems to ensure that such co-ordination is possible.

The new vision of knowledge production (as being a multi-faceted, cumulative and collective process) implies that a policy oriented towards solving only appropriation problems at the detriment of co-ordination problems would be misleading. Instead of focussing only on appropriation issues (such as incentives to invest in R&D, etc.), the policies should be geared to ensure co-ordination between knowledge producers and knowledge users and to facilitate the circulation of knowledge. Innovation process takes place in an environment of incomplete information and this may put a constraint on the cooperation of firms. Thus there is a need to implement public policies aiming at co-ordination among individual firms who are part of the innovation process.

NOTES

[1] The institutions, as used here can be laws, social rules, cultural norms, and technical standards, etc.

[2] See *http://www.statswales.wales.gov.uk/TableViewer/document.aspx?ReportId=10579# peopleworkemployment* (accessed 15 January 2013).

[3] Munday (2000) raised concerns about the stability of foreign companies producing standardized products at the mature phases of life cycles.

[4] By 2009, the total number of automotive companies in Wales was reported to be over 200 companies including 40 international companies (Welsh Automotive Forum, 2009).

[5] The cascade effect is said to have been started by Corus, the Anglo-Dutch joint venture that absorbed British Steel which cut a significant employment (Cooke, 2002).

[6] The Automotive Assistance Programme (AAP) is a support package that offers a total of £2.3bn of loan guarantees or loans to the UK automotive sector, which were available for draw down over a two-year period ending December 2010. The final maturity dates of such loans and guarantees can extend beyond 2010. The scheme was designed primarily to use Government guarantees to unlock up to £1.3bn loans from the European Investment Bank (EIB) and a further £1bn in loans from other lenders. The Automotive Assistance Programme was announced on 27 January 2009 and received state aid approval from the European Commission on 27 February 2009.

[7] CENEX which was established with support from the Department for Business, Enterprise and Regulatory Reform (BERR), seeks to stimulate market transformation and networking amongst providers and end users including the Low Carbon Vehicle Procurement Programme and the Low Carbon and Fuel Cell Technology Knowledge Transfer Network.

8   As reported by Welsh Automotive Forum by 2009 the total number of automotive companies in Wales have been reported to be over 200 companies which includes 40 international companies (Welsh Automotive Forum, 2009).
9   Electro-mechanical includes brake, steering, ignition and engine management systems, etc.
10 Generic components include fasteners and stampings, and bulky non-mechanical components include glass, forgings, castings, seats, etc.
11 Although the current policies are not WDA-animated as they were in the 1990s, heavy public intervention still persists.
12 The closing down or thinning of businesses also meant suspension of research grants to universities and/or closing down of the regional R&D laboratories (e.g., Corus shut down its 200-person materials research laboratory in 2001) leading to the dying out of the connecting links between the main pillars of the innovation ecosystem (businesses, government and universities).
13 Systemic notions are commonly found in the literature. Some of the important concepts include industrial networks (Hakansson, 1989); production complexes (Scott and Storper, 1992), value chains (Porter, 1990), industry clusters (Porter, 1990), industrial systems (Saxenian, 1994), innovation systems (Lundvall, 1992; Nelson, 1993), etc.
14 Others, while still important for innovation, may be hard to quantify in practice.
15 Trade or knowledge exchanges across regions/countries may be understood to contribute to these dynamics.

REFERENCES

Bailey, D., and Cowling, K. (2006). 'Industrial policy and vulnerable capitalism', *Institute for Economic Development Policy Discussion Paper Series,* Birmingham: University of Birmingham.
Bailey, D. and Driffield, N. (2007). 'Industrial policy, FDI and employment: still 'missing a strategy', *Journal of Industry, Competition and Trade*, 7, 2, 189–211.
Bailey, D., Kobayashi, S. and MacNeill, S. (2008). ' "Rover and Out" Globalisation: The West Midlands auto cluster and the end of MG-Rover', *Policy Studies*, 29, 3, 267–80.
BERR, (2009). *An independent report on the future of the automotive industry in the UK New Automotive Innovation and Growth Team* (NAIGT), *http://www.bis.gov.uk/files/file51139.pdf* (accessed 29 January 2013).
Breschi, S. and Malerba, F. (1997). 'Sectoral systems of innovation: technological regimes, Schumpeterian dynamics and spatial boundaries', in C. Edquist (ed.), *Systems of Innovation*, London: F. Pinter.
Carlsson, B. and Stankiewicz, R. (1995). 'On the nature, function and composition of technological systems', in B. Carlsson (ed.), *Technological Systems and Economic Performance: The Case of Factory Automation*, Dordrecht: Kluwer Academic Publishers.

Cooke, P. (1992). 'Regional innovation systems: competitive regulation in the new Europe', *Geoform*, 33, 365–82.

Cooke P. (1995). 'Innovative regional clusters: the automotive and electronics industries in Wales', *Regional Industrial Research Reports*, Cardiff: CASS.

Cooke P. (1998). 'Regional innovation systems: introduction', in H.-J. Braczyk, P. Cooke and M. Heidenreich (eds), *Regional Innovation Systems: The Role of Governances in a Globalized World*, London: UCL Press.

Cooke, P. (2002). 'Industrial innovation and learning systems: sector strategies for value chain linkage in less favoured regional economies', *Regional Industrial Research Reports*, Cardiff: CASS.

Cooke, P. (2004). 'The regional innovation system in Wales', in H.-J. Braczyk, P. Cooke and M. Heidenreich (eds), *Regional Innovation Systems: The Role of Governances in a Globalized World*, London: Routledge.

Cooke, P. (2005). 'Regionally asymmetric knowledge capabilities and open innovation: exploring 'Globalisation 2' – a new model of industry organization', *Research Policy*, 34, 8, 1128–49.

Cooke, P., Morgan, K. and Price, A. (1995). 'Regulating regional economies: Wales and Baden-Wurttemberg in transition', in M. Rhodes (ed.), *The Regions and the New Europe: Patterns in Core and Periphery Development*, Manchester: Manchester University Press.

Edquist, C. (ed.) (1997). *Systems of Innovation*, London: F. Pinter.

Fuller, C. and Phelps, N. A. (2006). 'Multinational enterprises, repeat investment and the role of aftercare services in Wales and Ireland', *Regional Studies*, 38, 7, 783–801.

IMI (2009). 'Skills priorities for the automotive retail sector – Wales', Final Report, IMI Research Department, London: The Institute of the Motor Academy.

Hakansson, H. (1989). *Corporate Technological Behaviour – Co-operation and Networks*, London: Routledge.

Keeble, D. and Walker, S. (1994). 'New firms, small firms and dead firms: spatial patterns and determinants in the United Kingdom', *Regional Studies*, 28, 411–27.

King, J. (2008). *The King Review of Low Carbon Cars*. London: HM Treasury.

Lundvall, B-A. (ed.) (1992). *National Systems of Innovation: Towards a Theory of Innovation and Interactive Learning*, London: Pinter.

MacNeill, S. and Bailey, D. (2009). 'Changing policies for the automotive industry in the UK West Midlands: an open innovation model', *Applied Research Working Paper Series*, Coventry: Coventry University.

Malmberg, A. and Maskell, P. (1997). 'Towards an explanation of regional specialisation and industry agglomeration. Europe', *Planning Studies*, 5, 1, 25–43.

Munday. M. (2000). 'Foreign direct investment in Wales: lifeline of leash?', in J. Bryan and C. Jones (eds), *Wales in the 21st Century: An Economic Future*, Basingstoke: MacMillan Business.

Nelson, R. (ed.) (1993). *National Innovation Systems: A Comparative Study*, Oxford: Oxford University Press.

Nelson, R. and Rosenberg N. (1993). 'Technical innovation and national systems', in Nelson, R. (ed.), *National Systems of Innovation: A Comparative Study*, Oxford: Oxford University Press.

Office of National Statistics (2003). *Small Business Statistics*, London: ONS.
Office of National Statistics (2010). *Small Business Statistics*, London: ONS.
Parhi, M. (2006). *Dynamics of New Technology Diffusion: A Study of the Indian Automotive Industry*, Maastricht: University Press Maastricht.
Porter, M. (1990). *The Competitive Advantage of Nations*, New York: Free Press.
Rhys, G. (2002). *The Automotive Sector in Wales: Still Alive and Well*, Report to Third Auto Conference, London, November (*http://www.autoconference.co.uk*)
Saxenian, A. (1994). *Regional Advantage: Culture and Competition in Silicon Valley and Route 128*, Cambridge MA: Harvard University Press.
Scott, A. J. and Storper, M. (1992). 'Regional development reconsidered', in H. Erneste and V. Meier (eds), *Regional Development and Contemporary Industrial Response: Extending Flexible Specialisation*, London: Belhaven.
Taylor, M. (1995). 'The business enterprise, power and patterns of geographical industrialisation', in S. Conti, E. J. Malecki and P. Oinas (eds), *The Industrial Enterprise and its Environment: Spatial Perspectives*, Aldershot: Ashgate.
Welsh Assembly Government (2005). *Wales, A Vibrant Economy, the Welsh Assembly Government's Strategic Framework for Economic Development*, Cardiff: WAG.
Welsh Automotive Forum (2009). *Welsh Automotive Forum: Directory of Membership Companies 2009*, http://www.welshautomotiveforum.co.uk/WAF-Members-Directory.pdf (accessed 15 January 2013).
Welsh Government (2010). *Economic Renewal: A New Direction*, Cardiff: Welsh Government.
Womack, J., Jones, D. and Roos, D. (1990). *The Machine that Changed the World*, New York: Rawson Associates.

3. CHALLENGES FOR RENEWABLE ENERGY DEVELOPMENT IN WALES

Julie Porter and Laura Norris

ABSTRACT

Over the past decade, renewable energy development has received increased attention in response to challenges posed by climate change, peak oil and, more recently, the global recession. Due to this multitude of factors, 'green jobs' focusing on renewable energy development have been identified by policy-makers as a way of transitioning economic systems in the post-recession society. Using qualitative research gathered during the KIMERAA project, from 2010–2011, this paper will discuss the regional conditions needed for this sustainable transition. The south west Wales region is the case study location due to its prominent non-renewable energy industry of liquefied natural gas, and its emerging marine energy industry, particularly wave and tidal energy. In this context, the impact of this transition in renewable energy policy will also feature, evaluating limitations it may pose in the case of Wales. This policy will be contrasted with other renewable energy development policies found within the UK.

INTRODUCTION

Historically, the region of south west Wales (SWW) has utilised its position on the edge of the Atlantic Ocean to its advantage, evolving from a fishing outpost to a major non-renewable energy hub. In regards to fishing, SWW is a commercial and recreational fishing destination, which is still economically significant to the region today. Recently, commercial fishing output in this area was rated fifth in the UK (Visit Wales, 2011). The recreational fishing sector still exists and is considered a valuable part of the commercial tourism industry in the region. In addition, commercial tourism brings in an estimated £350m per year to the region (Visit Wales, 2009). In regards to non-renewable energy development, the Milford Haven Port Authority (MHPA) is considered the 'energy capital of the UK' as it is the third largest port in the UK and the largest port in Wales (MHPA, 2011). It is home to a large oil refinery in Pembrokeshire (see Figure 3.1) as well as two Liquefied Natural Gas (LNG) terminals which are linked across the UK. Considering both the LNG and oil refineries, the MHPA provides 25 per cent of the UK's energy needs (2011).

Figure 3.1
UK oil refineries and output (2010)

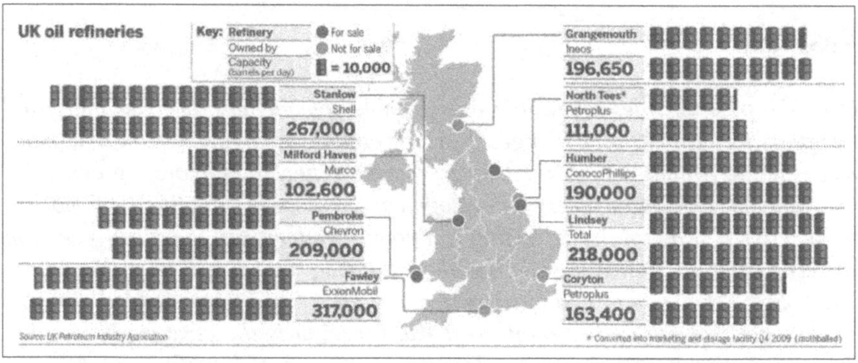

The port provides a major non-renewable energy industrial presence in the region with the traditional supply chains, grid connections and university connections that would be essential for a small renewable energy sector to form. Beyond the services and supply chain that the existing non-renewable energy industry provides, there are also the desirable conditions present in the region and the UK Government interest to be a world-leader in renewable energy production (Carrington, 2012). The former is the attractive point to firms but the latter may be the catalyst for sector growth and success. The 'desirable conditions' are the peak flow found in Ramsey Sound which is the Northern part of SWW. Please see Map 3.1 for further details.

The light areas in Map 3.1 indicate a peak tidal flow of more than 2m/s. The dashed arrow points to the Pembrokeshire area of SWW where the MHPA, LNG terminals and oil refineries are located. The solid arrow points to the location of the Ramsey Sound tidal flow. At this location the water flows between the Welsh coast and Ramsey Island providing optimal peak tidal flows for tidal energy testing. At the time of writing, the marine energy firms in

Map 3.1
Peak tidal flows in the UK

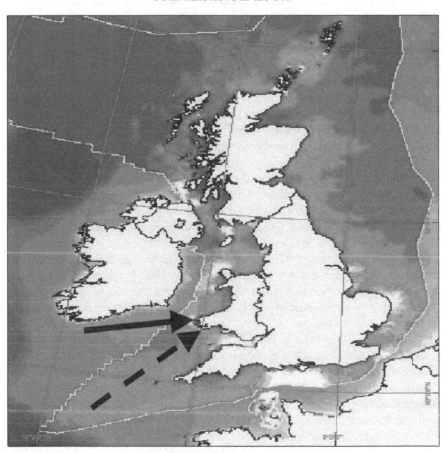

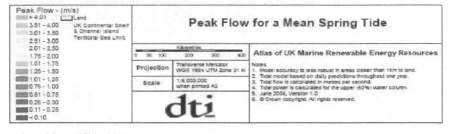

Adapted from Willis, 2010.

the region are at the testing phase of their technology. In transitioning from testing to energy production in the region, several non-technical variables need to be addressed, namely: the support for the technology, the revenue that could be generated (particularly if venture capital is involved) and the potential to develop off-shore space. It is important to note that unlike many other development sites, there is a developed grid connection. There are also firms in the region developing wave energy technology. The vast majority of these firms are engaged in collaborative projects with larger non-renewable energy firms based in the region. These regional actors can network through the Marine Energy Pembrokeshire forum which following its formation, is increasingly supported by the Welsh Government (WG).

When discussing marine energy in Wales, it is important to remember that renewable energy is not a devolved power and that unlike the other countries within the UK, Wales is considered one region without a regional development agency (RDA). This was not always the case as the Welsh Development Agency (WDA) previously oversaw these activities; however, it has been closed since 2006. Nonetheless, the WG oversees policy for the region as well as taking on the role that a traditional RDA would provide including, but not limited to: encouraging entrepreneurship, promoting innovation, providing funding and developing plans for economic growth. Throughout the course of this article, 'the region' will be referenced which, in this case, will solely refer to the south west Wales (SWW) region.

The article will continue as follows. The next section will present a theoretical discussion of path dependent economic development and the triple helix.[1] This will be followed by a brief overview of the methodology set forth by the KIMERAA partnership. The data from this project is the basis for this article. Building on the literature review, the next section will use the information gathered through the semi-structured interviews to discuss the triple helix in SWW highlighting the level of knowledge transfer within the regional knowledge network. This will be followed by a brief review of obstacles, particularly in the form of government policy, to growth in the sector in the region. Finally, concluding remarks will reflect on what needs to happen in the future to sustain this sector and promote intra- and inter-network collaboration.

PATH DEPENDENCE THEORY AND TRANSITION MANAGEMENT

A large body of work addresses the tendency of systems to become 'locked-in' and path dependent (David, 2010; Martin, 2009; Martin and Sunley, 2006).

This path dependence occurs as a result of the way in which system actors utilize behavioural patterns that are based on previous, successful courses of action. However, these successful behaviours will eventually provide diminishing returns, rendering the understanding of how a system can transition, or adapt, significant. Walker (2002) commented that path dependency with an evolutionary 'twist' is the most exciting concept in modern economic geography. Boschma and Frenken (2006) agree that path dependence, focusing on historical continuity, lock-in and new path creation, is fundamental in evolutionary economic geography.

A key attribute of evolutionary economic geography is the ability of the economy to self-transform from within or adapt. This adaptation is needed in evolutionary terms because without it, path lock-in is far from evolutionary; rather, with the absence of adaptation, it is equilibrium-based (Boschma and Martin, 2010). Ideally, history would dictate the path that a system is on and it would be locked-into that path until (or if) there was a significant event/force that could force the existing path to adapt or to create a new path. If discussing resilience theory in the evolutionary economic geography context, this force would be considered a type of shock. According to David (2010), an external force, or a shock, would be what is needed to 'de-lock' the economy from that particular path. This 'force' could be in the form of competition, industrial communities of practice, innovation, an economic crisis or other events. For example, the economy of Pittsburgh was locked-in to the path created by the steel industry until the external 'slow-burn' shock of deindustrialization forced the economy to de-lock from the path. While we acknowledge that paths can adapt in a multitude of ways, such as new path creation, branching, etc., in discussing transition management, the focus will be on the conditions for path adaptation as a result of the de-locking of the path.

This understanding of path de-locking through external forces has led to the proliferation of theories that address the transition of systems and how they can be de-locked by various actors. This is particularly significant under the guises of green development as transition management is a model for governance developed to deal with persistent problems that require systemic change: 'Persistent problems are complex, uncertain, difficult to manage, hard to grasp and operate at different scale levels' (Kemp et al., 2007, p. 319; Rotmans, 2005). So why is it important to think about how and why a system may undergo a transition?

Transitions defy control but can be influenced (Palmer and Dunford, 2002). They cannot be created at will by people or by central government, any less than large technical systems can be created by system builders. Assessing the evidence on this issue Joerges (1988, p. 26) finds that:

studies of LTS [Large Technical Systems] show that they never develop according to the designs and projections of dominant actors: LTS evolve behind the back of the system builders, as it were. It has been shown, too . . . that typically none of the agencies contained in LTS manage to form a somewhat complete picture of their workings.

This poor understanding of technical systems could call into question why it is useful to engage in transition management, namely because of the issues surrounding system innovation. These barriers have to do with uncertainty, the need for change at various levels and vested interests. As a result of this, we are locked into trajectories driven by short-term benefits instead of longer-term optimality (Kemp and Soete, 1992). Because public policy is highly fragmented and oriented towards short-term goals, transitions require the coordination of various policy fields: Science and Technology (S&T) policy, economic policy, innovation policy, environmental policy, transport policy and agriculture policy. One such theory that seeks to understand the interplay between regional actors is the Triple Helix theory. As S&T became increasingly important to regional developments (Braczyk et al., 1998), Etzkowitz and Leydesdorff (2000) advanced this concept that seeks to highlight the role that university, industry and government have in shaping the path of innovations (Leydesdorff and Etzkowitz, 1996, 1998). See Figure 3.2.

The underlying model was analytically different from the national systems of innovation approach (Lundvall, 1988, 1992) which considers the firm to have the leading role in innovation. The triple helix also differed from the 'Triangle' model of Sábato (1975), in which the state is privileged with this role (Sábato and Mackenzie, 1982) in leading innovation. In that case, the focus lay in the network overlay of communications and expectations that reshape the institutional arrangements among universities, industries and governmental agencies.

There are three considered models of the triple helix, that feature historical elements such as a strong Keynesian role of the state or highly prescribed relations between the three spheres. However, the model that is of most relevance is that of the Triple Helix III which generates a knowledge infrastructure in terms of overlapping institutional spheres, with each taking the role of the other and with hybrid organizations emerging at the interfaces.

Increasingly it could be considered that most countries and regions model activities on the Triple Helix III. The desire to attain an environment that supports innovation is high, and as such has been referenced as the exit-strategy from the current recession, outlined in many policy documents, one of which is the Europe 20:20 Strategy (European Commission, 2012). This innovative

Figure 3.2
Triple Helix III

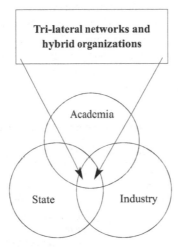

Source: Leydesdorff and Etzkowitz (1996).

environment could consist of university spin-off firms, tri-lateral initiatives for knowledge-based economic development, and strategic alliances among firms large and small, operating in different areas, and with different levels of technology, government laboratories and academic research groups (Etzkowitz and Leydesdorff, 2000, p. 112). It is rare for these arrangements to be controlled by the government, but they are often encouraged using fiscal and policy measures.

As a result, the sources of innovation in a Triple Helix configuration are no longer synchronized a priori. They do not have a pre-given order, but can be thought of as a puzzle for regional actors to solve. This network of relations generates a reflexive subdynamics of intentions, strategies and projects that adds surplus value by reorganizing and harmonizing continuously the underlying infrastructure (Etzkowitz, Leydesdorff, 2000, p. 112).

METHODOLOGY

As part of the wider KIMERAA project, an extensive secondary source analysis for the region was conducted focusing on a sector that had significant growth potential, such as the marine energy sector in Pembrokeshire. The innovation actors in the region – government, university, small and medium sized enterprise (SME), and large industry – were identified and the semi-structured interviews built on this analysis by allowing open engagement. The semi-structured interviews with the key actors in the marine energy cluster were recorded either in person or over-the-phone. Over the course of the data collection period, from 2010–11, ten interviews were completed predominantly with SMEs and university actors as demonstrated in Table 3.1. The data has been used to construct the KIMERAA research report (2011).

Table 3.1
Interview results for south west Wales region

Wales Interview Overview		
Type of Interview	*Number of Interviews Completed*	*Main Findings*
Government	3	– expensive technology to fund – no response to policy question as at UK level – issue between development of marine energy in a sustainable manner due to other sectors in operation in region (fishing, tourism, etc.)
University	2	– some collaboration with SMEs for conservation – although nascent stage sector, competitors are collaborating
SME	3	– need more funding options – need change of policy
Large Industry	2	– need result of assessment to decide future involvement – need change of policy to be lucrative investment – industry at nascent stage in region

Adapted from KIMERAA Report, 2011.

DISCUSSION OF SWW FINDINGS

In SWW, the region is economically in a state of equilibrium due to the prominent non-renewable energy industry as well as the coastal tourism industry. Historically, it is highly path dependent on its coastal position with a significant non-renewable energy sector, which was discussed in the Introduction. The renewable energy firms that focus on marine energy are taking advantage of the existing structure created by the non-renewable energy industry, namely through utilising the supply chain, grid connections and human capital. Theoretically, the external force that caused the de-locking of the path – global climate change, peak oil, global recession – encouraged path branching as a form of adaptation instead of new path creation. This branching from non-renewable energy production to renewable energy development is supported through the triple-helix of regional universities as well as the national government in Wales. Due to the user-driven innovation, which at this stage of R&D is relatively low, the innovations will provide a relatively incremental change. The next radical innovation for the marine energy market may not come from SWW; but, smaller innovations that assist the industry may be produced. While understanding the level of path adaptation, what conditions in the region beyond the supply chain allow this to occur?

Thus far, the existing regional industries, namely the non-renewable energy industry due to its economic significance, support the system transition along with the regional universities and the WG. The meeting of these three 'triple helix' entities, as well as the marine energy-based firms is most noticeable with the knowledge network Marine Energy Pembrokeshire (MEP). Prior to the development of the marine energy sector in SWW, there were no specific knowledge networks that focused on the non-renewable energy system in the region. The main facilitator of knowledge transfer for marine-related activities within the region, at the current time, is the Marine Energy Pembrokeshire (MEP) knowledge network (2011) that was the result of the Spatial Plan in Wales. The membership of MEP is a combination of universities, SMEs and large industry. Some of the members are solely focusing on renewable energy R&D, namely the SMEs, while other members are remnants of the original path, namely the larger non-renewable energy firms, who are increasingly interested in the renewable energy R&D. Through the KIMERAA research findings, the significance of the MEP to facilitate knowledge transfer and collaboration amongst the actors has been identified:

> Even though they are potentially conflicting or competing organisations [in MEP], some of the barriers we are looking at are mutual problems so there are definitely discussions on how the individual companies can work together to overcome these barriers . . . and for making people aware of research and a general sort of partnership even though in the future they are competing. (MEP Facilitator)

> . . . [in SWW] we have developers who are trying to put technology in the water and they realise that although some of them are going to be competitors they are better off sharing their best practice. We had Jane Davidson the minister come down to

co-chair one of the meetings and she left saying that it was quite refreshing to see competitive, early stage companies around the table, which is even worse because at that stage they can be quite guarded, just being quite friendly. They are a quite tight knit community so they are solving problems, sharing potential solutions. (Marine Energy Task Group, Swansea University)

. . . (The MEP is) very good for networking as other developers are in the room at the same time as well as consultants and individuals oriented toward the supply chain as well so it is good to get everyone in one room, swap stories, and see how they can advance especially with the procedures of developing the area . . . it has aided us to know who is in the industry. (Tidal Energy Ltd.)

In addition to firm-to-firm knowledge transfer, there is also knowledge being transferred between university and SMEs, as the technology developers and researchers have a co-dependent relationship. For example, the technology developers need to understand how their equipment, particularly for tidal energy, will impact the ocean floor environment while the researchers can pro-vide modelling for varying scenarios. Researchers are interested in partaking in this modelling as they can see the real-life results during the developer testing phases in SWW.

While knowledge transfer amongst these triple helix organizations are important for transition, a change of societal consciousness is also needed. In relation to climate change, a change of societal consciousness is needed to see substantial breakthroughs in renewable energy innovation or even the use and acceptance of incremental innovations. To a certain extent, this 'change of consciousness' has already occurred in SWW making it a fertile area to accept and produce sustainable technology. Socially, the conservation aspect is already integrated into SWW, which is most notable amongst the firms that comprise the coastal tourism industry who position sustainable tourism as a core responsibility to maintain the coastline. However, economically, with the prominence of the non-renewable energy industry in the region, the renewable energy significance is not as advanced as other regions in Denmark or Sweden for example (Cooke et al., 2011). At the current time, this sustainable mindset for economic growth is mostly demonstrated by the substantial technology development by SMEs in the region, particularly in biomass and solar panels as well the number of successful ecotourism firms that use these local, sustainable suppliers for energy (e.g. Bluestone National Park Resort in Pembrokeshire, West Wales).

This section has demonstrated that the region is ready to accept renewable energy alternatives; however, the technology is at a nascent stage. In light of the low level of long-term, financial support from the WG as highlighted through the case study interviews, the nascent stage of renewable energy development in the region is impressive. If, as in other regions of the UK such as Scotland, the marine energy firms were provided with more competitive long-term financial support, mainly through the Renewable Obligation Certificate (ROC) return, the industry could be a viable source of economic growth in the region. It is important to highlight at this juncture, that outside of the ROCs, the Welsh Government could play an important role in this triple helix through developing alternative funding mechanisms.

OBSTACLES TO OVERCOME

The main obstacle cited by the regional actors that needs to be overcome in order to develop this network further in SWW is the renewable energy policy regarding the ROCs. The ROCs offer renewable energy generators an extra payment on top of the income they receive from electricity sales and the sale of climate change levy exemption certificates (Scottish Government, 2011). As mentioned in the Introduction, there is a delicate balance of power between the national governments and the UK Government in Great Britain, where renewable energy policy is devolved in Scotland but not in Wales. Scotland currently provides a higher return on investment to both wave (5 ROCs/MWh) and tidal (3 ROCs/MWh) energy producers than anywhere else in the UK (Scottish Government, 2011). For comparison, Wales (and England) provide 2 ROCs/MWh for both tidal and wave energy producers.

> At the moment, if you're a developer that produces electricity you get paid £0.70/kWh for it, on top of that payment you get a ROC which gives you more money and the way that's raised is all big businesses have to show that part of their electricity comes from renewable sources so they buy these ROCs so those are traded on the open market at about £0.45/kWh, a considerable amount of money. If you're a wave developer or a tidal stream developer in the UK for every kWh you get 2 ROCs until you see that if you go to Scotland and you're a tidal stream developer you get 3ROCs or 5 if you're a wave developer. So if you've just taken money off an investor who is desperate to get some money off of you and you say I'm going to go to Wales and get 2 ROCs he says you're going to Scotland. We're lobbying government on that because it's not a level playing field. (Marine Energy Task Group, Swansea University)

> The other factor is that in Scotland the support mechanism that is in place in offering 3–5 ROCs with the effect of concentrating activity in and around Scottish waters. Scotland's devolved administration has a role in setting that figure while the Welsh

Assembly Government does not have that same role and cannot set that support mechanism that is comparable to Scotland. (E.On)

While the WG, as well as the UK Government, has provided employment incentives focusing on 'green jobs' for the short-term unemployed as well as the long-term unemployed, this uneven political playing field within the UK supports uneven development of the renewable energy sector (Cowell et al., 2013; see Welsh Assembly Government policy document, *Capturing the Potential: A Green Jobs Strategy for Wales* (2009) and *New Industries, New Jobs* (HM Government, 2009)). In SWW, the entrepreneurs who could potentially be major employers are being overlooked in government policy which will not support the regional economic development in the future. In addition, as many of the firms based in SWW are at the nascent stage and currently focus on conducting research and testing, there are no mechanisms in place that would discourage them from completing this phase in SWW and moving their base to Scotland to capitalize on the ROCs return once they have an actual product.

CONCLUSION

The main message of this analysis of the marine energy industry in SWW is that there is a shift in regional economic development, supported by the triple helix organizations in the region that could support the region with employment opportunities, knowledge transfer and collaborative funding through renewable energy development. Through theoretical discussions and case comparisons, it has been demonstrated that both tidal and wave energy have successfully branched from the non-renewable energy path in SWW. While this has occurred over time, and is largely reliant on the framework of the non-renewable energy industry in the region, there is potential for future growth and economic development. This potential is based on a combination of factors; however, the knowledge networks and level of knowledge transfer occurring within the region are invaluable assets.

In support of this development, the MEP has successfully gathered actors from the non-renewable energy industry with the marine energy sector to facilitate successful knowledge transfer and a few collaborative ideas. To further support this development, the WG needs to address the main obstacles to further industry involvement, such as the ROC policy. This policy is a serious issue for the sustainability of this regional marine energy industry. Through MEP, cluster emergence is possible at this stage; however, for continued growth of the sector in terms of firms, as well as growth of the sector beyond R&D, the ROC policy must be changed or circumvented with other policy measures. This will involve a major shift in policy between England and Wales and would require funding for the increased energy returns. Outside of competition between Scotland and the rest of the UK in regards to renewable energy policy, future research will focus on this interplay between the government, the firm and the knowledge network in future projects.

ACKNOWLEDGEMENTS

This article was stimulated by research funded under the KIMERAA: Knowledge Transfer to Improve the Marine Economy in Regions from the Atlantic Area project, co-financed by the European Cooperation Programme 2007–2013 Atlantic Area. The sponsors are thanked for their support and responsibility for this article lies entirely with the authors.

NOTES

[1] The authors acknowledge that this work has been further developed into the quadruple helix, which includes civil society (Arbo & Benneworth, 2007). However, in the context of wave and tidal energy, civil society does not play as significant a role as would be the case in, for example, wind energy development.

REFERENCES

Arbo, P. and Benneworth P. (2007). 'Understanding the regional contribution of higher education institutions: a literature review', *OECD Education Working Papers*, No. 9, Paris: OECD Publishing.

BBC (2011). 'DeltaStream tidal power Pembrokeshire trial approved', *BBC News Wales,* 11 April 2011, *http://www.bbc.co.uk/news/uk-wales-12929493* (accessed 18 October 2011).

Bluestone (2010). *Energy & Biodiversity, http://www.bluestonewales.com/content/about_us/ environment.aspx.* (accessed 19 October 2011).

Boschma, R. and Frenken, K. (2006). 'Why is economic geography not an evolutionary science?', *Journal of Economic Geography*, 6, 273–302.

Boschma, R. and Martin, R. (2010). 'The aims and scope of evolutionary economic geography', in R. Boschma and R. Martin (eds), *The Handbook of Evolutionary Economic Geography,* Cheltenham: Edward Elgar.

Braczyk, H. J., Cooke, P. and Heidenreich, M. (eds) (1998). *Regional Innovation Systems*, London: University College London Press.

Carrington, D. (2012). 'David Cameron: this is the greenest government ever', *Guardian*, 26 April 2012, *http://www.guardian.co.uk/environment/2012/apr/26/david-cameron-greenest-government-ever* (accessed 21 January 2013).

Cooke, P., Asheim, B., Boschma, R., Martin, R., Schwartz, D. and Toedtling, F. (2011). *Handbook of Regional Innovation and Growth*, Cheltenham: Edward Elgar.

Cowell, R., Ellis, G., Sherry-Brennan, F., Strachan, P. A. and Toke, D. (2013). 'Promoting renewable energy in the UK: what difference has devolution made?', *Cardiff University*, 23 January 2013, *http://www.cardiff.ac.uk/cplan/research/delivering-renewable-energy/dissemination-and-user-engagement* (accessed 25 January 2013).

David, P. (2010). 'Path dependence in economic processes: implications for policy analysis in dynamical systems contexts', in K. Dopfer (ed), *The Evolutionary Foundations of Economics*, Cambridge: Cambridge University Press.

Etzkowitz, H. and Leydesdorff, L. (2000). 'The dynamics of innovation: from National Systems and "Mode 2" to a Triple Helix of university-industry-government relations', *Research Policy, 29*, 109–23.

European Commission (2012). *Europe 20:20 Strategy, http://ec.europa.eu/europe2020/index_en.htm* (accessed 21 January 2013).

HM Government (2009). *New Industry, New Jobs*, Department for Business, Innovation and Skills, *http://www.bis.gov.uk/files/file51023.pdf* (accessed 31 January 2013).

Joerges, B. (1988). 'Large technical systems: concepts and issues', in R. Mayntz and T. R. Hughes (eds), *The Development of Large Technical Systems*, pp. 9–36, Frankfurt am Main: Campus.

Kemp, R., Rotmans, J. and Loorbach, D. (2007). 'Assessing the Dutch Energy transition policy: how does it deal with dilemmas of managing transitions?', *Journal of Environmental Policy and Planning*, 9, 3, 315–31.

Kemp, R. and Soete, L. (1992). 'The greening of technological progress: an evolutionary perspective', *Futures*, 24, 5, 437–45.

KIMERAA Report (2011). *Maritime Clusters: Institutions and Innovation Actors in the Atlantic Area, http://www.cria.pt/cria/admin/app/CRIA/uploads/KIMERAA/maritime_clusters.pdf* (accessed 18 October 2011).

Leydesdorff, L. and Etzkowitz, H. (1996). 'Emergence of a Triple Helix of university–industry–government relations', *Science and Public Policy, 23*, 279–86.

Leydesdorff, L. and Etzkowitz, H. (1998). 'The Triple Helix as a model for innovation studies', *Science and Public Policy, 25*, 195–203.

Lundvall, B.-Å. (1988). 'Innovation as an interactive process: from user–producer interaction to the national system of innovation', in G. Dosi, C. Freeman, R. Nelson, G. Silverberg and L. Soete (eds), *Technical Change and Economic Theory*, London: Pinter.

Lundvall, B.-Å. (ed.) (1992). *National Systems of Innovation*, London: Pinter.

Martin, R. (2009). *Rethinking Regional Path Dependence: Beyond Lock-In to Evolution.* Papers in Evolutionary Economic Geography # 09.10, *http://econ.geo.uu.nl/peeg/peeg0910.pdf* (accessed 24 January 2013).

Martin, R. and Sunley, P. (2006). 'Path dependence and regional economic evolution', *Journal of Economic Geography*, 7, 573–602.

Milford Haven Port Authority (2011). *About Us, www.mhpc.co.uk.* (accessed 16 June 2011).

Palmer, I. and Dunford, R. (2002). 'Out with the old and in with the new? The relationship between traditional and new organizational practices', *International Journal of Organizational Analysis,* 10, 209–25.

Rotmans, J. (2005). 'Societal innovation: between dream and reality lies complexity', *Shortened Inaugural Speech*, Rotterdam School of Management, ERIM, Erasmus University Rotterdam.

Sábato, J. (1975). *El pensamiento latino americano en la problemática ciencia–technología–desarrollo-dependencia*, Buenos Aires: Paido's.

Sábato, J. and Mackenzie, M. (1982). *La Producción de Technología. Autónoma o Transnacional*, Mexico City: Nueva Imagen.

Scottish Government (2011). *Marine Energy Road Map, http://www.scotland.gov.uk/ Publications/2009/08/14094700/3* (accessed 16 June 2011).

Tidal Energy Ltd. (2011). *The Delta Stream Solution, http://www.tidalenergyltd.com/ ?page_id=640* (accessed 18 October 2011).

UK Department of Business, Innovation & Skills (2009). *New Industries New Jobs, Policy Document, http://www.bis.gov.uk/policies/new-industry-new-jobs* (accessed 25 January 2013).

University of Exeter (2009). *Beyond Nimbyism Case Study: Wave Dragon Wave Energy Project, Pembrokeshire, South Wales, http://geography.exeter.ac.uk/beyond_nimbyism/ deliverables/reports_WaveDragon_Final.pdf* (accessed on 28 October 2011).

Visit Wales (2009). *Coastal Tourism Strategy, http://wales.gov.uk/docs/drah/publications/ Tourism/090612coastaleng.pdf* (accessed 17 June 2011).

Visit Wales (2011). *Impact of Commercial Fishing in Wales, http://wales.gov.uk/topics/ environmentcountryside/foodandfisheries/fisheries/commercialfishing/;jsessionid=F8 BC03D14C5971F262570D606D1672CB?lang=en* (accessed 25 January 2013).

Welsh Assembly Government (2008). *Green Jobs in Wales, Policy document, http:// wales.gov.uk/consultations/businessandeconomy/greenjobs/?lang=en* (accessed 17 June 2011).

Welsh Assembly Government (2009). *Capturing the Potential: A Green Jobs Strategy for Wales, http://wales.gov.uk/docs/det/publications/090709capturingthepotentialagreenjobs strategyforwalesen.pdf* (accessed 31 January 2013).

Walker, R. (2002). 'The geography of production', in E. Sheppard and T. Barnes (eds), *A Companion to Economic Geography*, Oxford: Blackwell.

Williamson, D. (2011). 'Inward investment programmes deliver "next to nothing" for Wales', *Western Mail,* 15 June 2011, *http://www.walesonline.co.uk/news/wales-news/ 2011/06/15/inward-investment-programmes-deliver-next-to-nothing-for-wales-91466- 28880086/#.Tfg_-U950GU;twitter* (accessed 16 June 2011).

Willis, M. (2010). *Ocean Energy in Wales – Ambitions and Opportunities, Presentation, http://welshcomposites.co.uk/downloads/OceanEnergyWales.pdf* (accessed 17 June 2011).

Interviews
Interview, Eon, 2010. Personal communication.
Interview, Low Carbon Research Institute (Architecture Department, Cardiff University), 2010. Personal communication.
Interview, Marine Energy Pembrokeshire, 2010. Personal communication.
Interview, Marine Energy Task Group, Swansea University, 2010. Personal communication.
Interview, Milford Haven Port Authority, 2010. Personal communication.
Interview, Tidal Energy Ltd., 2010. Personal communication.

4. LOCAL STRATEGIES IN WELSH ECONOMIC DEVELOPMENT POLICY

Paul Furlong

ABSTRACT

This article considers the main characteristics of the decision-making strategies of public sector senior managers operating in the economic development sector in Wales, with particular reference to their relationship with the Welsh Government, to their perceptions of their objectives within their localities, and their understandings of their roles as professionals. The article identifies four distinct patterns in decision-making strategies: isolated, dependent, communitarian and entrepreneurial. These vary by understandings of locality, by perceptions of conflict or agreement over professional skills and knowledge, and by levels of disagreement over political interests, objectives and resources. In conclusion, some of the policy implications are considered, in particular the importance of a better and more detailed understanding of variations in local implementation of policy.

INTRODUCTION

This article concerns how senior managers in local government and para-state agencies in Wales interpret, apply and seek to implement the policies of the Welsh Government with regard to economic development and community regeneration. The article is based on an analysis of a sub-set of interviews undertaken by the Wales Institute of Social and Economic Research Data and Methods (WISERD) in late 2009 and early 2010. WISERD is a consortium of five Welsh universities (Aberystwyth, Bangor, Cardiff, Glamorgan and Swansea) established in 2009 and funded initially by the Economic and Social Research Council (UK) and the Higher Education Funding Council for Wales.

As part of its mission to promote social science research in Wales, WISERD undertook a large scale research project on locality in Welsh public policy, comprising 122 interviews of senior managers in the public sector in selected authorities and agencies across Wales. This article is based on an analysis of twenty interviews of managers in the economic development sector and related areas. I begin by explaining briefly some of the origins, the scope and the limitations inherent in the use of this dataset. I then refer to the issue of how we understand the role of the state in economic development both in Wales and more broadly in the UK and elsewhere, before moving on to the interview material itself. I use this material to show how strategies adopted by these managers follow some distinctive patterns that shed light on their role as important actors in the local implementation of Welsh economic development policy, and in particular how this varies across Wales in ways that significantly affect implementation and delivery.

There are several important aspects of the dataset to note. First, the full set of 122 interviews covers senior managers working in a wide range of policy sectors, including health, education, environment, social services and transport as well as economic development. The scope of the wider project, as indicated above, was to investigate how senior managers in Wales identify and operation-alize notions of locality, broadly understood, in public policy-making. As part of this, the semi-structured interviews asked, among others, a series of questions that relate directly to the issues I discuss below on which my analysis is structured, namely the relationship of their perceptions of professional knowledge to their perceptions of how conflict and agreement structures their decision-making. The subset used here covers those involved in economic development either within local authorities or in agencies and public sector consortia. These are selected because the material available in these interviews relates directly to my primary concern, which is how public policy in economic development is made in Wales. I discuss below why I consider this issue important and how the framework is relevant to it.

This relates directly to the second aspect, which is the key issue of locality. As indicated above, this was one of the central organizing concepts for the project as a whole. This is an important factor in my analysis, but the extent to which this can be fully exploited in a relatively small subset is limited. The reason for this is not difficult to explain, but none the less critical, and it is one that has implications for qualitative research in the social sciences in the Welsh context. Within a small country with a relatively small population of senior managers, generally regarded as characterized by close interpersonal contact both among themselves and with the central authorities in Cardiff, exhaustive use of all the material available in a sub-set of twenty would risk infringing the respondents' need for anonymity. Locality is important, but it is not the most important factor. My interest is explicitly and primarily in how the range of factors impact on the politics of the policy process, by which I mean in this case how perceptions of power interact with understandings of professional knowledge and expertise. Applying this dichotomy, I identify four distinct ideal-types within the sub-set. These ideal-types are associated strongly with respondents interviewed in specific regions within Wales: hence the relevance and sensitivity of the locality factor.

To retain the commitment to anonymity on which the project was based, I do not exploit the relevance of locality fully here. The relevant political, economic, cultural and historical factors that may help explain the formation of the distinct strategies adopted are rich in local detail. In the Welsh context, this of itself precludes the full use of the material available in this anonymized dataset. It may be worth considering in future the implications of this constraint for qualitative research in the social sciences in small close-knit populations such as those in the public sector in Wales. This would be less of a problem if the entire dataset was used, but a preliminary analysis of this has demonstrated, not surprisingly, that material that covers economic development in the remainder of the interviews is sparse and not obviously relevant. My contention is that the use of the sub-set is justified by the clarity and focus of the material from respondents whose main role is in this area, and by its relevance to the issue at hand. There may be ways around this constraint, and at the least my analysis can contribute to the development of innovative methods that do so, as well as to the substantive issue of policy-making in economic development.

A brief word is also needed on the broader context. The policy relevance of studies of economic development in Wales derives from two related factors. First, whether under Labour or Conservative-led coalition administrations in London, devolution in Wales has shared a common discourse of economic modernization, with different tonalities for each. Under Labour, the emphasis was on a top-down regionalism in which the Welsh Assembly Government was sometimes seen by its critics as mirroring the central monitoring of detailed targets set for local agencies by managerial elites (for the Labour policy, see Blair, 2000; more generally, Geyer, 2012). Under the Conservatives, following the UK White Paper of February 2011, the tone shifted to a 'new localism' based on 'more freedom, more choice and more local control' (Cameron, 2011). Whatever the response of the Welsh Government may be considered to have been, the important issue is that devolution has been consistently expected to produce an economic and social dividend. In that sense, as Jones et al. argue, devolution has profound implications for the nature and practice of economic governance. It provides political space for adjusting and altering trajectories of economic governance. In turn, the 'success' of economic governance has consequences for further rounds of devolution, set within the limits of constitutional change. (2005, p. 398)

Under both Labour and Conservative-led governments in London, it is supposed to do this by stimulating improved decision-making at local levels. The role of senior managers in economic development is therefore of central relevance in delivering policy advances in a sector where the previous record is poor and the political salience is high (see for example, Welsh Assembly Government, 2002; for the academic debate, Christopoulos, 2006; Hoppe, 2010; Kim, 2010; Roberts and King, 1991).

As devolution in Wales embeds itself and develops its own identity, it becomes possible to reach reasonable assessments of its impact and its prospects. Whether we have the theoretical understanding for this, let alone the empirical grounding, may be disputed. The academic debate so far has struggled to come to a consensus about how to characterize the state formations, structures and processes that are now emerging. What is clear however is that there is a tension between on the one hand the levels of public support for devolution in Wales, undoubtedly in the majority and increasing (Scully, 2011; Wyn Jones and Scully, 2004), and on the other hand, an inability on the part of politicians and civil servants, still less of academics, to identify and articulate just what devolution has achieved in the period since 1999.

The evidence appears to be that devolution has not been associated with any improvement in Wales's relative economic performance so far. In fact Wales has fallen further behind its comparators in the UK (Davies, 2011). Of course, we do not know if the position would have been even worse without devolution; counter-factual evidence is not available. However, whatever the causality, we do know about worsening of the relativities, because since devolution in 1999, there has been a significant increase in the scope, quality and richness of data relating to important indicators of economic and social activity in Wales. With regard to quantifiable outcomes, it is safe to say that notwithstanding acknowledged gaps and limitations in the data, for example with regard to differentiation at a sufficient level of analysis within Wales, much more is now known about major aspects of social and economic development. We therefore know that some policies are not working, and others are not working as well as expected, but we do not necessarily know why, and quantitative research is not always able to reveal the answers.

This applies especially to the field of economic regeneration. The improvement in collection and use of quantifiable data relating to economic and social conditions, which is still in progress, has not been matched by a similar improvement in our detailed understanding of how economic development policies are framed and implemented at levels other than that of government initiatives and outputs. Yet this is a key aspect of the transformation of governance that is a constant feature of government rhetoric over many years, whatever the political colour. Underlying this are important and unresolved debates about the role, capacities and functions of the state in protecting society against external conditions deriving from uncontrolled processes of global markets, or better in promoting the capacity of society to respond and adapt in its own way to pressures of economic globalization.

In the aftermath of the devolution settlement, arguments were not slow to emerge to the effect that it is not clear whether the new localism is preferable to a strong central state, notionally able to regulate capital markets and, at the margins, direct other forms of flows of economic resources into desirable sectors (Walker, 2002). In a more optimistic discussion about the scope of regional development policy, Hudson (2007, p. 1158) argues that, though there are

> limits that are an unavoidable consequence of capitalist social relations, . . . this does not mean there are no possibilities for political choices within these parameters. So in contrast, and instead of deterministic inevitability, the emphasis should be placed firmly upon political choice and the political possibilities offered by recognition of multiple paths and developmental trajectories and modalities of power.

This emphasis on political choice, in the arguments of Hudson and others (Anderson, 1992; Keating and Loughlin, 2004), is explicitly based on a willingness to recognize a heterogeneity of interests and values within a generic shared regional identity, and the need to uncover whose interests prevail within regions and how.

This analysis is intended as a contribution to the debate about 'whose interests . . . and how'. It therefore does not seek to characterize 'the state' as an actor in itself, whether polycentric or united around a common purpose, consciousness and organization. The focus rather is on state agency and on actors whose roles are determined by a wide range of factors, among which the choices of the central government are only one among a complex set of factors determining the range of options available, albeit one of the most important.

The primary concern is in identifying the strategies of senior managers as they seek to carry out their roles. The focus is on empirical description and analysis of this neglected and significant factor, the evaluation of which may help us to understand better the diverse ways in which public policy in economic development in Wales is delivered outside the confines of the Welsh Government, and to a certain extent to explain some of its failures and successes. Notwithstanding frequent perceptions of heavy-handed central control imposing uniformity of practice, found also here, the interview data demonstrates that in implementing government policy in this area, senior managers in local government and in public sector agencies adopt strategies that differ widely from one another; to differing extents, these appear to them to have a significant role in determining how government policy actually works in their locality, even where, as many do, they bemoan the extent of central direction of policy. The role of local government and other local stakeholders is especially relevant in some areas since the introduction of Communities First in 2004, of which more later, since this is explicitly a selective and 'bottom-up' approach to community regeneration.

Underlying the analysis, readers may be able to perceive the influence of a perhaps familiar theoretical framework. An accessible and recent version of this may be found in Hoppe (Hoppe, 2010; for a critique of this general approach, see Rose, 1993). The conceptual and theoretical underpinnings are developed in more detail in extended versions of the conference papers on which this article is based (Furlong, 2011), but the typology developed here should be understood as 'thick description' derived from the interview data, not as an attempt to apply a prior framework to a set of cases. The interview data is analyzed primarily in terms of what it tells us about public policy as it is actually implemented. The two main axes used to differentiate the responses relate to, on the one hand, the perceptions of local economic development managers about the certainty or uncertainty of the professional knowledge they and others bring to bear on the issues, and on the other hand, their perceptions about the extent of conflict or agreement over values and aims of public policy relative to the issues.

In brief, this analysis describes the responses in terms of perceptions about knowledge and perceptions about power. This dichotomy is sometimes seen as representing the conflict of professional expertise and political interest, and that is one of the ways it is used here. In turn, in the Welsh context, this relationship opens up another dimension, that of local-central relations, in which professional expertise may to a greater or lesser extent be identified by local managers as their preserve, because of the perceived importance of a deep understanding of local, often very local, economic and social conditions. Policy emanating from the central authorities is then readily categorized, by some in these interviews, as mainly determined by politics rather than by expertise.

Because of their relationship with these two key frames, knowledge-power and locality-centre, this analysis reveals other factors, such as understandings of locality, historical legacy, political culture and political identity, but given the space available, it does no more than allude to these as variables appropriate for further more detailed research. For the purposes of presentation, the decision-making strategies associated with the complex relationships of knowledge and power in the policy process are often reduced to a four-cell schema in a simple box-cell matrix. The version given in Table 4.1 is derived originally from a classic study of political economy by Dahl and Lindblom (Dahl and Lindblom, 1953), and much adapted and modified since.

Table 4.1
Decision-making strategies in the public policy process – basic categories

Power axis / Knowledge axis	*Close to certainty*	*Far from certainty*
Far from agreement	A. Complex/political	B. Anarchic/creative
Close to agreement	C. Rational-calculative	D. Incremental

I now go on to consider the interview material in more detail. In the real world of policy-making, strategies do not conform to these abstract reference points. Rather, what we find is clusters of responses grouped around types of behaviour that can be mapped onto the matrix at a range of points. This does not mean that examples of these cannot be found in other areas, only that these are the predominant types in specific localities. In order to preserve anonymity as far as possible, the localities of the interviewees are referred to only as North East Wales (NEW), North West Wales (NWW), Mid and West Wales (MWW) and South Wales Valleys (SWV). Clear differences of strategy between the interviewees emerge, that relate to specific aspects of these localities, especially to political culture and socio-economic legacy. The specific analysis of these aspects is developed only as far as the obligation to preserve anonymity allows. Names of people and places are concealed.

PERCEPTIONS OF POLICY: ISSUES OF KNOWLEDGE AND POWER

If we look first at how the respondents characterize the general relationship between their own locality and central government in Cardiff, the differences between the strategies are striking. One set of responses, localized strongly in the five interviews from MWW, is typified by this comment,

> I think that we as an area have to look to our own innovation initiative. The evidence is certainly for the last ten, well frankly if I am brutally honest, it is probably since the Welsh Assembly Government came into being we are not perceived to be a priority.

This is the most negative of the different approaches, in this regard. In these responses, there is a strong sense of distance from the centre, of conflict with it and of the importance of asserting professional expertise: I refer to this type as the isolated professional. Of the others, the communitarian type (mainly in the four respondents in NWW) tends to talk at some length about 'partnership, rather than having to answer up', for example arguing that 'we have to collaborate across the board before any money can be targeted'. Perhaps mixing aspiration with interpretation, one manager in this area characterizes the relationship with the Assembly Government (as it was at the time of the interview) in much more positive terms than those of the isolated professional: 'I wouldn't say we are servants to the Assembly – I would say we are partners because we have the same purpose' (NWW). The other two approaches are more pragmatic in their understanding, and less inclined to see scope for independent action outside the constraints of the Welsh Government. This can play out in different ways, however. The dependent professional seems to regard the objectives set by Cardiff as leaving little local discretion. One manager in the SWV area gives a clear indication of perceptions of their own role in this regard:

> *Interviewer*: '. . . those key decisions that affect what goes here in terms of your role, who makes those?'

> *Respondent*: 'I suppose it's Welsh Assembly, because we're dependent on the investments, . . . so it's funding, and they've got the purse strings. Strategy, I've some local sort of dimension there with local politicians, but again we've got to fit in with national strategy.'

This is scarcely surprising, as government funding for economic development and community in the Valleys is a major source of revenue and has been for several decades. Even so, it is not a banal point to make that for this manager, and for others in the same area, this is referred to mainly as a constraint. Another manager in the Valleys, asked about a specific large economic development programme, FS4B, describes it as 'very centralized and controlled

. . . very anonymous, and it basically marginalizes local authorities'. It should be noted here however that this is not specifically a reference to economic development managers alone, but to the local authority in general, and might even include politicians. This is a characteristic we will see later in other contexts, that one of the roles of the dependent Economic Development Officer (EDO), in this typology, is seen as that of promoting the interests of the local authority against threats from other local stakeholders and the overweening power of central government.

Rather clearer and more positive about how to make the most out of the constraints is the entrepreneur. The term 'policy entrepreneur' is used by Kingdon and others to refer to actors who are usually either elected politicians or top level administrators and who adopt opportunistic strategies to promote policy innovation through legislation or administrative regulation (Kingdon, 1995; Mintrom, 1997). That is not the sense here. I am using the term 'entrepreneur' with specific reference to sub-national authorities who have little scope for normative policy innovation, and whose role is to interpret and implement statutory norms approved elsewhere, and who do this so as to maximize short-term objectives.

Unlike the isolated professional, this type of manager makes a professional assessment that solutions lie outside the region; this necessitates an opportunistic approach to alliances wherever appropriate, granted the economic, social and locational constraints and strengths. Political influence and professional expertise are seen as different resources for achieving a flexible set of goals. This strategic approach is explicit and reflective:

> You know changes in the world and in the economic trends, as we've seen in the last eighteen months, have had more impact on the economy in [our area] than we've had in eighteen years . . . so what we've done is we've adopted the Welsh Assembly Government's economic strategy and we've looked at the economic forum strategy and what we've tried to do is align ourselves to add value to that . . . adding value in a positive way to the direction of travel of the Welsh Assembly Government and [North Wales] economic forum to make sure that our area is playing its part, which is a different approach. (NEW)

There is a strong sense in this interview that the EDO is comfortable with having adopted a strategy that starts from a recognition of local limitation. The perception is that local bids for strategic independence are unlikely to succeed:

> We've banned the idea of creating our own economic development strategies even though we're a very big department because I've found at times that many authorities

who have tried to invent strategies to change the world in their own little patch have failed dismally, because you can't change GDP, you can't change unemployment, and you can't change economic activity rates in the global sense . . . it comes about from more national strategic changes.

There is a stark contrast between this respondent and the one first quoted, who talked in terms of a locally determined strategy that put them in conflict with central government. In summary, from the interview data, as the above analysis indicates, I have identified four different types of response, which I categorize respectively as isolated, dependent, communitarian and entrepreneurial. The first two are broadly characterized by complex and politicized strategies, in which the strategies are determined strongly by perceptions of political disagreement and professional certainty; in terms of the cell matrix in Table 4.1, these are two variants of the complex/political strategy (A); the last two reflect much more incremental understandings, with relatively balanced approaches to the relationship of political objectives and professional expertise, predominantly in cell C. There is a strong area identification of the types of responses as follows:

> Isolated strategy – Mid and West Wales (MWW)
> Dependent strategy – South Wales Valleys (SWV)
> Communitarian strategy – North West Wales (NWW)
> Entrepreneurial strategy – North East Wales (NEW)

If we then consider what these responses tell us about how managers think of their own professional understandings and their own role, there is a range from the objective expert certainty of the dependent and isolated professionals to the more guarded professional uncertainty of the communitarian and the entrepreneur; however, this masks some complex interactions with senses of local knowledge and of the political aspects of the role.

The clearest sense that the expertise of the economic development manager provides a uniquely qualified vantage point comes from the isolated professional:

You always have to be cautious about the degree of parochialism that you bring to the table. And the only way really to deal with on one hand, that subjective parochialism and on the other hand the political experiences and remoteness from our area, is to have good quality business intelligence and objective knowledge and understanding. . . . And one of the things that we are seeking to do at the moment is to say to Welsh Assembly Government we are happy to share with you, information that we gather. (MWW)

Here, though politics is what the centre practises, the manager resists implicitly the notion that localism is the source of professional understanding. On the contrary, it can be associated with 'subjective parochialism'; the political centre and the parochial limited vision are both contrasted neatly with 'objective knowledge and understanding' that the manager alone can 'bring to the table'.

The dependent professional (SWV) also has a stable view of their role that brings them into conflict with central authority. We saw that in some of its activities the Welsh Government is regarded in this area (though not only there) as anonymous and controlling, so this conflict is hardly surprising and probably not new. Reforms such as the Communities First programme (CF) introduced new forms of policy-making that required a more fundamental re-assessment of the role of the EDO. EDOs in this area exhibited a perhaps surprising degree of unanimity in their willingness to criticize CF; one of them, who stated categorically about CF 'let's be honest, it's beyond hope', contrasted the demands imposed on them by CF's highly localistic and deliberative procedures with what they saw as the proper role of the EDO:

> The way we've always done this now is, a funding stream comes up . . . and it's specific. And you go to the book, and the book will tell you what it's for . . . and what you can spend it on. So if your problem matches any of those things that you can spend it on, and you write an application . . . then that's what you can get. And that, that's the way professionals have always worked. (SWV)

In this 'traditional' view of the role of the EDO, the boundaries between the political centre and the professional in the locality are stable and are seen by the EDO as respecting their autonomy and expertise. CF upset these boundaries, and by their own accounts here proved very problematic for them, notwithstanding that their area was the major beneficiary of this highly selective programme. As a result, according to the same respondent, though Communities First was 'a revolutionary way of looking at community regeneration', it was fundamentally flawed in execution, in that

> it was kicked off without any process in place . . . wasn't linked to anything out there . . . local authorities didn't know anything about it . . . so what it created was an awful lot of frustrated and battered community based staff. And, activists within communities.

We saw that with the isolated professional, there was a clear distinction between the local professional certainties and the political decisions made in Cardiff. In this case, with the dependent professional, the level of conflict with the politicians in Cardiff appears much more limited, and the issue of professional expertise interacting with political decision-making is overlaid by a direct criticism of the competence of the Assembly Government in general. The respondent who made the comments about the anonymity and control of the Assembly Government also treated this as an issue of expertise and competence, as well as one of centre-locality relations, arguing that 'the public sector shouldn't be giving direct support to business, because it doesn't understand it . . .'. This may appear rather inconsistent, but it becomes clear that the interviewee is criticizing not the principle of subsidy but the way in which public support is distributed, especially (as it is perceived) through central micro-management or excessively communitarian approaches. It also becomes clear in this interview that the argument about the competence of the civil servants in Cardiff masks concerns about the role of local authorities and their apparently generalised complaints in the Valleys, at least in this sample, that the new roles and processes marginalize them.

> RES: Empowering communities, now that's on the spectrum of, of revolution . . . in a social context, you can't have state sponsored revolution, and in effect that's what the bit of the Assembly, that's what they were peddling . . . My personal view again, it should have gone through local government . . . and been used as a lever to force change.
>
> INT: What, from the people?
>
> RES: From the service providers. It's just hard isn't it, to crack . . . Irrespective of what the needs of the community might be, to get the statutory, or statutory based public service to then be responsive to delivering services to address those needs, doesn't happen.

The dependence on WAG therefore is by no means unconditional nor is it seen as inevitable, and if communities are to be 'empowered', the EDO would like to be in control of that so as to get leverage over what are seen as the main local obstacles, the service providers.

Where the locality is identified more positively, it produces more nuanced views of how the manager can use local understanding to their advantage. These involve different perspectives on the role of the development manager, but reflecting a more politicized approach. The entrepreneur, as we have seen, sees the scope for the deployment of independent certainties in their role as extremely limited. There is no vision here of 'objective understanding'. On the contrary, the uncertainties are both political (which can be local as well as central) and professional.

The biggest problem I've got, is [elected] members over there saying 'prove it . . . and if you don't prove it we'll take money off you' . . . They are very difficult to persuade and I don't know whether they are being negative about it deliberately or what, but it's still a big challenge for us, so . . . anybody who can effectively show us a mechanism on measuring impact and saying how successful or otherwise they've been . . . People might think that they're getting there but in truth nobody seems to get a grasp . . . And so it's really difficult to prove impact . . . And yet that's what we're being required to do, to maintain investment. I suppose the other way of doing it is turn the tap off and see what happens and if it goes pear shaped then we can say 'I told you so'. But that's a bit drastic. (NEW)

The role of the economic development manager in this case, where alignment of means and goals is seen as highly uncertain, is one of making the most of local resources. The entrepreneur-manager shows limited confidence in knowledge about means relative to outcomes, and adopts an explicit focus on local and national deliberation around opportunistic goals. So when asked to reflect on their own power and resources, the response of one such manager, perhaps deliberately, was very restrictive:

My decision making and that of the council in determining the economic fortunes of the county is limited to be perfectly honest, so we just have to be very good at what we do. And be very good at what's within our control. (NEW)

This is an approach that explicitly recognizes how the role of the EDO has to change. The communitarian acknowledges this also but has a different understanding of the new role. In this case, the partnership perspective we saw with reference to relations with the Welsh Assembly Government extends strongly, at least in aspiration, to local communities, and this is seen as crucial for effective policy.

There is an opportunity for people to influence through collaboration and being part of a partnership. I would say, by now, it is part of normal practice that the community is part of projects in the first place. (NWW)

There is no sense that the EDO is a privileged bearer of knowledge. On the contrary, in contrast both to the isolated professional and to the entrepreneur, the local interests and opinions have supplanted the professional certainties and provide a form of resistance to the uncertain world beyond the community's boundaries. As a result:

Communities will have to take the lead and this comes down to training and skills . . . We must change from being a service to giving tools to the communities to do things themselves. (NWW)

Coherently with this, this EDO has a much more positive view of Communities First, and seems much more at ease with the new roles it entails in how local authorities work, though they have a specific understanding of CF which appears tailored to their own perceived needs and approaches. CF is welcomed explicitly because it allows local, meaning small-scale, development, which may work because local understanding can weigh appropriately:

INT: Are there any local projects or policies like Communities First or other schemes that have had a positive effect on your work?

RES: Yes, I think there are plans, but I don't think they are acknowledged enough, and they are small plans. The reason for this, I think, is that the plans that are successful are small plans or projects and very often it is these that don't get enough praise. It's been said that we have to have strategic plans or projects, and we have to have large projects that touch a lot of people. This is hard because it is the large plans and projects that touch the most people and very often those are the ones that break down . . . There are pockets of small projects and we are trying to promote them locally. There are also examples where it just doesn't work, and I think that the projects that don't work are those where nobody understands and knows the community and its people. (NWW)

This is acknowledged as a role with its own challenges, with a strong potential for disagreement between local communities, as 'whichever community people are in, there is a feeling that it isn't being seen'. Therefore, encouraging local mobilization may entail significant lost opportunities, including also where local disagreement within the community itself apparently blocks development:

There are recent examples where, if you take [*locality*], at policy level, it has been acknowledged that there is a need here; at policy level it has been acknowledged that we are prioritizing and targeting, have managed to successfully get money; but can't achieve local agreement on these plans. There was so much disagreement at local level, which is an example of where there was money available to develop, but it was impossible to achieve agreement.

In general, EDOs with these responses, characterized in this typology as communitarian, have adopted a distinctive strategy that subsumes narrow professional skills into a broader and much more political view of their role that requires them to mediate between conflicting interests at different levels within their community and with external forces including the final arbiter and resource holder, the central authority in Cardiff.

CONCLUSION

The argument in this article can be summarized directly. First, I have started with the premise, not a hazardous one, that decision-making strategies in economic development in the public sector in Wales, broadly defined, and the policy process in Wales more generally, are determined by professional managers in the sector as well as by elected representatives, and perhaps in some cases more by managers than by elected representatives (Boyne and Walker, 2004; Hudson, 2007; Andrews et al., 2011). Second, I have sought to provide evidence from a reliable large scale primary source, the WISERD stakeholder interviews, that these decision-making strategies are strongly differentiated across regions of Wales. I have hypothesized on the basis of the evidence that this differentiation has its origins in a range of factors including political culture, but more significantly and perhaps more contentiously, also including the perceptions, professional resources and priorities of the managers themselves. Third, the effectiveness of public policy in Wales is conditioned strongly by these differences; specifically, I mean by this that both the forms and the quality of public policy, especially in its implementation, are deter- mined by the strategies adopted by professional public sector managers, to an extent not previously recognized. The Communities First programme in part sought to respond to concerns about excessive centralization in Wales by seeking to stimulate a stronger local role in the choice of funding targets and implementation. The analysis, as others have done (Melbeck, 1998), shows how decision-making strategies adopted by managers at the local level result in significantly different interpretations of how the programme can be applied, and in different assessments of its effectiveness.

Finally, the broader political context cannot be ignored. Devolution has been justified by political actors with arguments about decision-making that is expected to be more efficient, more effective and more equitable, because it is more 'local'. The process of modernization in the public sector in England and Wales has been framed by the Coalition Government in London in terms of localism, meaning both more local control and more professional discretion (Cameron, 2011). This analysis reveals how difficult it is to combine these two, if local control means responsiveness to local political interests, and how the synthesis between them may vary even across areas of Wales that might conventionally be regarded as sharing problems and opportunities. The analysis also reveals how central government is not regarded as a neutral actor in this process, even when it is apparently committed to developing bottom-up community based interventions (Walker, 2002). In particular, the perceptions of the professionals in all four areas were strongly coloured by their previous experience of how the Welsh Office and then WAG had sought to direct the strategies of twenty-two unitary local authorities, and several interviewees compared WAG unfavourably to the Welsh Development Agency, merged into WAG in 2004.

A further issue is the extent to which these reforms represent a real departure for Welsh public administration, or rather should be seen as continuing within a devolved context the process of partial and unsatisfactory solutions to the dissatisfaction of central government with the responses of local authorities and local representatives of national policy sectors (Imrie and Raco, 1999). Of all of the initiatives referred to in the interviews, it is (once again) Communities First that seems to represent the most striking element of discontinuity. This is especially noticeable in the Welsh context, where there are strong perceptions within the group of interviewees about the longevity of the 'top-down control culture' that some of them identify as distinctively Welsh, and about the extent to which Communities First breaks with this, again in a distinctively Welsh manner.

More broadly, devolution is expected to produce a social and economic dividend, the fruits of this new localism (Rodriguez-Pose, 2005). As discussed above, notwithstanding the lack of evidence in favour of the economic dividend, political support for devolution in Wales is clearly in the majority and appears to be increasing (Scully 2011; Wyn Jones and Scully, 2004; Wyn Jones and Scully, 2010). This disjuncture between support and outcomes should focus attention on identifying sub-national effects, and relating these to the how and the why of political choice as it occurs in the implementation of economic development policy beyond the twin sites of Cathays Park and the Bay in Cardiff. This article has attempted to shed some initial light on these issues, and in the process has revealed a rich and significant range of differences across Wales. To many readers, it may not appear novel or original to suggest that localism thrives in Welsh political culture. If this article has any contribution to make to that particular debate, it may be that we need to know more about how that localism in its various forms relates to differences in decision-making and differences in performance at sub-national level.

ACKNOWLEDGEMENTS

I am grateful to the editor and to the anonymous reviewers for their helpful comments.

NOTE

[1] Further details of the WISERD stakeholder interviews, including information about access to them, can be found at *http://www.wiserd.ac.uk/research/localities/work programme/stakeholder-interviews/*

REFERENCES

Anderson, J. J. (1992). *The Territorial Imperative: Pluralism, Corporatism and the Economic Crisis*, Cambridge: Cambridge University Press.

Andrews, R., Boyne, G. A., Law, J. and Walker, R. M. (2011). 'Strategy implementation and public service performance', *Administration & Society*, 43, 643–71.

Blair, T. (2000). *Britishness and the Government's Agenda of Constitutional Reform*, London: The Labour Party.

Boyne, G. A. and Walker, R. M. (2004). 'Strategy content and public service organizations', *Journal of Public Administration Research and Theory*, 14, 231–52.

Cameron, D. (2011). 'How we will release the grip of state control', *The Daily Telegraph*, 20 February 2011.

Christopolous, D. C. (2006). 'Governance capacity and regionalist dynamics', *Regional & Federal Studies*, 16, 363–83.

Dahl, R. and Lindblom, C. (1953). *Politics, Economics and Welfare: Planning and Politico Economic Systems Resolved into Basic Social Processes*, New York: Harper and Row.

Davies, R. (2011). *An Anatomy of Income Inequality in Wales: A Report Prepared on Behalf of the Wales Equality and Human Rights Commission*, Cardiff: Wales Institute of Social and Economic Research, Data and Methods.

Furlong, P. (2011). 'Uncertainty and control in Welsh economic development: an analysis of WISERD stakeholder interviews'. WISERD Conference, 'Devolution, Place and Change', Bangor University.

Geyer, R. (2012). 'Can complexity move UK policy beyond "evidence-based policy making" and the "audit culture"? Applying a "complexity cascade" to education and health policy', *Political Studies*, 60, 20–43.

Keating, M. and Loughlin, J. (eds) (2004). *The Political Economy of Regionalism*, Abingdon: Routledge.

Hoppe, R. (2010). *The Governance of Problems: Puzzling, Powering and Participation*, Bristol: Policy Press.

Hudson, R. (2007). 'Regions and regional uneven development forever? Some reflective comments upon theory and practice', *Regional Studies*, 41, 1149–60.

Imrie, R. and Raco, M. (1999). 'How new is the new local governance? Lessons from the United Kingdom', *Transactions of the Institute of British Geographers*, 24, 45–63.

Jones, M., Goodwin, M. and Jones, R. (2005). 'State modernization, devolution and economic governance', *Regional Studies*, 39, 4, 397–403.

Kim, Y. (2010). 'Stimulating entrepreneurial practices in the public sector', *Administration & Society*, 42, 780–814.

Kingdon, J. (1995). *Agendas, Alternatives and Public Policies*, New York: Addison Wesley Longman Ltd.

Melbeck, C. (1998). 'Comparing local policy networks', *Journal of Theoretical Politics*, 10, 531–52.

Mintrom, M. (1997). 'Policy entrepreneurs and the diffusion of innovation', *American Journal of Political Science*, 41, 738–70.

Roberts, N. C. and King, P. J. (1991). 'Policy entrepreneurs: their activity structure and function in the policy process', *Journal of Public Administration Research and Theory*, 1, 147–75.

Rodriguez-Pose, A. (2005). 'On the "economic dividend" of devolution', *Regional Studies*, 39, 405–20.

Rose, N. (1993). 'Government, authority and expertise in advanced liberalism', *Economy and Society*, 22, 283–98.

Scully, R. (2011). 'What will Wales powers referendum result mean?', *http://www.bbc.co.uk/news/uk-wales-12587227* (accessed 18 October 2011).

Walker, D. (2002). *In Praise of Centralism: A Critique of the New Localism*, London: Catalyst.

Welsh Assembly Government (2002). *A Winning Wales: The National Economic Development Strategy of the Welsh Assembly Government*. Cardiff: Welsh Assembly Government.

Wyn Jones, R. and Scully, R. (2004). *Devolution in Wales: What Does the Public Think?* Swindon: Economic and Social Research Council.

Wyn Jones, R. and Scully, R. (2010). 'Territorial politics in post-devolution Britain', in R. Heffernan, P. Cowley and C. Hay (eds), *Developments in British Politics*, 9. Basingstoke: Palgrave Macmillan.

5. LOCALISM, COMMUNITIES AND WOMEN'S CRIMINAL JUSTICE: A WELSH PERSPECTIVE

Martina Y. Feilzer and Katherine S. Williams,
with Alex Plows and Jo Yates

ABSTRACT

This paper explores what community provision for women offenders can tell us about the implementation of the recommendations included in the Corston Report (– a review of women with vulnerabilities in the criminal justice system) and the promise of the Big Society for Welsh communities. The authors do this by reflecting on research carried out to evaluate the Women's Turnaround Service (WTS) delivered in north Wales. Specifically, we explore two key aspects which have emerged from recent political rhetoric in relation to criminal justice practices, namely the role of communities in providing the space and capacity for offering services to women offenders to aid their reintegration into local communities; and the role of the new localism in allowing locally responsive services to develop and be sustained. The paper suggests that the failure to integrate women's services effectively in local communities is a result of inherent contradictions between the proclaimed processes of the new localism and the practices of centralized governance of criminal justice services.

INTRODUCTION

This paper explores what community provision for women offenders can tell us about the implementation of the recommendations included in the Corston Report (a review of women with vulnerabilities in the criminal justice system) (Corston, 2007), and the promise of the Big Society for Welsh communities. It suggests that the failure to integrate women services effectively in local communities is a result of inherent contradictions between the proclaimed processes of the new localism and the practices of centralized governance of criminal justice services.

The reflections in this paper are based on the evaluation of the Women's Turnaround Service (WTS) delivered in north Wales which provides holistic one-to-one support for women in the criminal justice system or those at risk of offending. The evaluation was funded by NOMS Cymru (the then National Offender Management Service's regional office for Wales) and covered the period of April 2010 to April 2011. The main research methods used were focus groups with clients and WTS case workers; interviews with clients, WTS staff, and workers at referral agencies; a number of case studies of specific clients drawn from the service's case management system and from focus groups and follow-up interviews; and the analysis of quantitative data on project clients using the case management system.

Women's Turnaround Services were set up in response to increasing concern about the rise in the female prison population and the particular problems faced by female offenders. The Corston report (Corston, 2007) heralded locally responsive, intense community provision as an appropriate and effective response to female offending and this approach resonated strongly with government policy in 2009 – in its prioritization of dealing with the causes of crime and the moving of decision-making and delivery back into local communities (Faulkner, 2003). It also resonated with governmental rhetoric post-2010, notably, emphasizing the importance of the community in the concepts of the Big Society[1] and the new localism (Halpern, 2010).

Researchers of local community services are left with a dilemma: decide to conduct community studies which highlight how a community supports 'successful' service provision with the danger of producing research which is merely of local interest and which neglects wider questions of power and governance (Crow, 2000, p. 176); or develop broader arguments in relation to 'what works' in the provision of criminal justice services neglecting the specifics and providing generalized statements about the value of programmes which can be close to meaningless without the context in which these programmes and services have arisen and are delivered. This paper treads a third way: it uses the specifics gleaned from research on WTS in north Wales to highlight wider debates in relation to the promises of the new localism and the realities of the lived localism on the ground. It first sets out how communities are used as units of increasing relevance in criminal justice; then explores how communities were expected to provide a supportive backdrop for women offenders in the Corston Report; and finally reflects on the challenges of local community provision of criminal justice services for female offenders post 2010 as well as the wider implications for the notion of the Big Society in Wales.

COMMUNITIES, CRIMINAL JUSTICE AND WALES

For many years communities have played a significant role in governmental rhetoric in relation to criminal justice policy. The rhetoric has included consideration of whether communities are: worthy of protection; justifiably vengeful towards offenders; capable of forgiveness and of reintegrating those who have wronged them; or merely tools for rehabilitation of offenders (Spalek, 2008, pp. 83–104; Hughes and Gilling, 2004). Communities are at the heart of concepts such as social capital, resilience and local governance. Under the current Coalition Government in Westminster, communities have been given special status as the units that can take over the provision of social services from a retreating public sector (Cabinet Office, 2010). Governmental emphasis on the 'new localism' appears to transfer responsibility (if not power) from central government to local government as well as more vaguely to 'communities' themselves. Bringing decision-making closer to 'the people' (Sagar and Croxall, 2012, p. 1) is regarded as a cornerstone of government policy. However, the question of how close is tricky. Government use of 'community' is not clearly defined but careful reading of rhetoric and policy suggest that local authorities are central to the agenda (Cabinet Office, 2010; Jordan, 2010; Sagar and Croxall, 2012, p. 3).

In the criminal justice arena this new localism has found expression partly in the introduction of locally elected Police and Crime Commissioners (PCCs), seen as being at the heart of the Big Society's policing plans (Morgan, 2012, p. 473). The first elections took place in November 2012 but suffered from very low electoral turnout (below 20 per cent across Wales), raising significant questions over their political mandate. The 'new' localism is anything but new, in the 1980s the Conservative government recognized the limitations of formal state responses to crime and in the 1990s the New Labour Government placed significant emphasis on involving local communities in the delivery of services (Faulkner, 2003). The creation of Crime and Disorder Reduction Partnerships in England and Community Safety Partnerships in Wales in the 1998 Crime and Disorder Act resulted in the devolution of community safety powers to a local level which includes, for example, the power to impose fixed penalty notices (Sagar and Croxall, 2012, p. 4). In their latest incarnation communities and the new localism come together in the UK Coalition Government's ambition to build a Big Society.[2] The policies supporting the building of the Big Society are in a 3-page document which suggests that the Government wants '. . . to give citizens, communities and local government the power and information they need to come together, solve the problems they face and build the Britain they want' (Cabinet Office, 2010, p. 7). The context, broader meaning and intentions are elucidated by Halpern (2010, pp. 64–6) as rewarding individuals and communities for positive contributions, so supporting social capital and therefore communities.

So what are these communities at the heart of the Big Society and other concepts? Work in rural studies suggests they are geographically based 'units of belonging', or 'locally meaningful social relationships' (Charles and Davies, 2005, p. 673), yet the concept of communities has been expanded by some to relate to any symbolically constructed relationships which lead to shared meanings and the development of group identities (Kennedy and Roudometof, 2004, p. 6). In this sense, communities do not need to be locality based, they can be imagined, transcend national boundaries and be bound only by 'shared cultural meanings and identities' (Kennedy and Roudometof, 2004, p. 4). It must be acknowledged that the concept of community is contested and there are significant ongoing debates (not relevant to the present discussion) about the influence of globalization and the changes to the core institutions and structural set-ups in Britain for our understanding of communities (Spalek, 2008, pp. 83–6; Charles and Davies, 2005; Kennedy and Roudometof, 2004). There are also distinctly negative interpretations of community which allude to the effect of specific community interests as triggering conflict between different communities, and warn of the dangers of self-interested and inward looking communities (Faulkner, 2003, p. 291).

Government rhetoric does not engage with such discussions about the meaning and structure of community or any changes those may be undergoing and use the word community 'rather unproblematically', as a 'catch-all phrase' (Spalek, 2008, p. 84), and predominantly carrying a positive connotation of cohesion, inclusion and supportive structures which 'trumpet the virtues of "community"' embracing a positive spin on social capital (Crow, 2000, p. 185). Therefore new localism sees communities primarily as units of local governance in which to find active citizens (a willing and free workforce) to implement decentralized services often through third sector organizations (TSOs)[3] to everyone's mutual advantage (Sagar and Croxall, 2012, p. 3).

In Wales, the term communities is seen to have a particular meaning and resonance, partly due to the large sways of rural areas in the country, their link to national movements, and role as a base for Welsh patriotism (Charles and Davies, 2005, p. 673). Cooper and Innes (2009) note a more complex and nuanced linking with community, taking account of inequalities. Charles and Davies (2005) claim that Wales maintains traditional, locality-based communities and has been resilient to some extent to the perceived erosion of communities based on geographically-placed social relations in contemporary societies. Welsh studies of local communities highlight the role of women in traditional communities built on networks of extended families and kinship, as well as in contemporary communities where women often facilitate and sustain the community and local organizations (Charles and Davies, 2005). In a criminal justice context, many focus on the importance of Welsh communities and Welsh exceptionalism in the form of a more progressive and communitarian approach to offenders and crime (see Drakeford, 2010 on youth justice in Wales or Edwards and Hughes, 2008 and Edwards and Hughes, 2009 on community safety in Wales); this notion will be further explored below.

COMMUNITIES IN CORSTON

The Corston Report (Corston, 2007), reviewing the treatment of women with particular vulnerabilities in the criminal justice system, was published in 2007. It was commissioned following growing concern about the rise in custodial sentences imposed on women which was increasing at a faster rate than that of men (Social Exclusion Unit, 2002; Gelsthorpe and Morris, 2002; Deakin and Spencer, 2003; Hedderman, 2004) and an awareness of the detrimental effects of prison sentences on women, their families and their communities (Gelsthorpe et al., 2007). As a result, the Corston Report called for a radical overhaul of the way in which women were treated by the criminal justice system with an emphasis of keeping women out of prison and providing supportive structures in women's own communities. Clearly this links in with women being the lynchpin of social capital (Charles and Davies, 2005). Similar to government rhetoric, Corston (2007) operated on an uncritical understanding of community as a cohesive, inclusive and friendly space (Corcoran, 2011, p. 35); a notion which may not be consistent with the experiences of many of the women involved with the criminal justice system. However, unlike government, Corston's understanding of 'community' is not rooted in local authorities but arises out of practical and 'real' supportive networks and cohesive units.

Corston saw women's community centres as the backbone of such supportive structures, designed to facilitate women's easy access to a full range of statutory and voluntary agencies ('one-stop shops'), as well as allowing these agencies access to vulnerable women who are often 'hard to reach'; these are frequently termed Women's Turnaround projects. It should be noted that since 2004, the UK Government had committed to developing a new approach to women's offending (The Women's Offending Reduction Programme) and, in 2005, the New Labour Government committed £9 million to a demonstration project consisting of women's centres with the intention of preventing offending by women (see Gelsthorpe et al., 2007; Heddermann et al., 2008; and Jolliffe et al., 2011).[4] In a similar vein, Corston (2007) argued that preventing female offending could be achieved by an holistic approach: supporting women as individuals, mothers and members of communities to improve their lives, deal with their problems and build more positive futures within their communities which was best achieved through local community centres, bringing support to women.

In Wales, the lack of a women's prison heightened the perceived need to offer community services in order to avoid sending women to prisons in England which are, in many cases, significant distances from their homes, communities and families and have no Welsh language provision. Wales had been left out of the original tranche of government funding so there was an urgent need for alternatives to custody, for effective community provision. Thus, it may be no accident that Wales 'volunteered' to provide 'Corston-style' community provision for female offenders, recognizing that women in Wales are seen to be at the heart of community structures (Corston, 2007, p. 10; Charles and Davies, 2005): so Women's Turnaround projects were born in Wales.

CRIMINAL JUSTICE SERVICES IN THE COMMUNITY – THE CHANGING INVOLVEMENT OF THE THIRD SECTOR

The criminal justice sector has undergone significant changes over the past two decades. Some of these seem to support government rhetoric in relation to localism and community focus, for example, the introduction of local community safety partnerships. These were formed following the Crime and Disorder Act (1998) and were designed to build a local 'voice'. Community Safety Partnerships gained responsibility for reducing offending with the Policing and Crime Act (2009) which was hoped to improve local partnerships and ownership of local crime problems (House of Commons Justice Committee, 2011, p. 2). Under the Police Reform and Social Responsibility Act (2011) many of these responsibilities will be moved to the newly elected PCCs, leaving local community safety partnerships weakened and in considerable uncertainty over their future shape and influence. The partnerships ensure local education, health, youth justice and other policy areas are respected, they are answerable to local councils, the Welsh Government and Westminster whereas PCCs are single individuals answerable locally in elections once every four years and nationally through the Crime and Police Panels to Westminster.[5] Arguably, PCCs reduce rather than strengthen local accountability. Other changes clearly do not sit easily with community involvement and local accountability, for example, the rather quietly implemented consolidation of probation areas into larger geographical probation trusts – the Wales Probation Trust covering the whole of Wales was established in April 2010 – and the restructuring of the National Offender Management Service (NOMS) with the abolition of the regional offices.

In the area of third sector (TS) service provision, there have also been numerous changes. The renewed state reliance since the 1980s, and particularly during the era of New Labour Governments, on welfare provision through private and TS services has led to a growth in organizations offering penal services and the number of partnerships between TS and public sector (Faulkner, 2003, p. 294; Gelsthorpe, 2011, p. 128) and, arguably, to changes in the nature and ethos of those organizations (ACEVO, 2003; Gibbs 1996; Haney 2010; Gelsthorpe, 2011, p. 136; Corcoran, 2011, p. 34; Maguire, 2012, p. 485) with attendant legal problems (Morris, 2012). In the last decade, the commissioning of TS services supporting the criminal justice system has changed towards more competitive and short-term funding coming from a wider range of service commissioners (local or national government, European Union funds, charities such as the Big Lottery, etc. (Meek, Gojkovic, and Mills, 2010, p. 9; Feilzer et al., 2012)). The effect on TSOs is not altogether clear at this stage although there is some indication that small local organizations are struggling to compete for funding with bigger national charities (Wright, 2008, p. 30; Corcoran, 2011; Maguire, 2012), private firms and public sector agencies (some of which now compete for funding e.g. probation). Some suggest that the TS is suffering from 'organizational cloning', i.e. of the TS becoming more like the public sector (Corcoran, 2011, p. 34; ESRC 2011–12); and from 'goal distortion' (Neilson, 2009, p. 406) through the creation of consortia between TSOs and both the private sector and public sector agencies. Examples of this are: crime reduction charity Nacro's (unsuccessful) bid jointly with global private security firm G4S and others to run two prisons in 2008; youth charity Catch 22's alliance with international service company SERCO, and health and social care charity provider Turning Point; and two of the newly formed probation trusts, the Wales and the Staffordshire and West Midlands Probation Trusts, are also setting up partnerships with the private sector in order to deliver the first payment by results pilots[6] involving public sector organizations (Ministry of Justice, 2012).

The increasing dependency on government financing of a larger proportion of charities operating in the criminal justice sector raises much wider questions about the TS's independence, its welfare role, and its function as a promoter of social progress and brakes on the expansion of the crime control industry (Vennard and Hedderman, 2009, p. 38; Corcoran, 2011, p. 32; Maguire, 2012, p. 485). In effect, many TSOs are becoming part of the crime control industry. Additionally, the central role of the budget holder/commissioner and the need to centrally regulate a plethora of local partnerships raise concerns over the reality of the proclaimed transfer of power from central government to local areas (Vennard and Hedderman, 2009, p. 230; Corcoran, 2011, p. 39). For example, since the dissolution of the NOMS regional offices including NOMS Cymru, all commissioning comes directly from London and the Ministry of Justice, which is keeping tight control over all payment by results commissioning and contracted services.

Throughout England and Wales these local pressures are evident and were clearly at work in the project we evaluated (Feilzer et al., 2012). Managers of smaller voluntary sector organizations are spending large amounts of their time trying to secure further funding either on their own, by building consortia with other voluntary organizations to bid for larger national contracts, or as sub-contractors to larger private or TSOs. As subcontractors, smaller organizations have almost no control over their contracts or any input into the policy which underpins the main contracts as set by central commissioners which may be set by a national rather than local agenda. Additionally, being at the 'beck and call' of different commissioners expecting different outcomes and operating from very different perspectives inevitably puts a strain on the coherence of an organization's purpose (Billis and Harris, 1992, p. 215; Neilson, 2009; ESRC, 2011–12; Feilzer et al., 2012) and their autonomy (Seddon, 2007). Being awarded large (if short-term) contracts from central commissioners may require delivery of national rather than locally relevant services or coercive as well as welfare elements (Gibbs, 1996 and Haney, 2010) – and allows organizations to grow to levels they may not have the capacity to sustain in the long term. As a result, the need to secure funding for a growing organization puts enormous strain on the organization and constrains a manager's ability to perform other duties (Neilson, 2009; Corcoran, 2011; ESRC, 2011–12). It thus blinkers organizations' ambitions to develop more localized initiatives or the meeting of local needs (Maguire, 2012). In Wales, where partnership working has slowly grown out of local Community Safety Partnerships (Edwards and Hughes, 2009, pp. 78–9), this more competitive environment is likely to undermine some of the existing trust and information sharing as organizations may perceive this to weaken their chances of winning contracts (the right information can be a powerful tool in bidding for contracts so sharing of information may be less likely).

Finally, in the criminal justice sector a critical question is an organization's ability to take on the responsibilities of dealing with vulnerable women at risk of causing harm to others and/or themselves. Although the Women's Turnaround projects do not deliver services with a probation purpose, they do provide services to female offenders and ex-offenders, many of whom are serving community sentences or have been released from prison. It is not altogether clear how commissioners vet services for their ability both to provide support to vulnerable women whilst also considering public protection and the protection of their workers. Of course, only a small minority of women offenders pose a risk to others but in the main those at risk are children (see for example, Gelsthorpe et al., 2007, p. 7) and therefore the need for support and recognition of potential risk is of great importance. The assumption seems to be that the TS will somehow be equipped to work with vulnerable and sometimes dangerous people without the need for any of the qualifications or organizational procedures or safeguards required for public sector workers in similar positions, for example, social workers or probation officers. Generally, the TS is not trained to deliver such specialist, potentially coercive work (Neilson, 2009).

PROVIDING SERVICES FOR FEMALE OFFENDERS IN WELSH COMMUNITIES

In Wales, the first community provision for female offenders was launched in Cardiff in November 2007; the Women's Turnaround project was delivered by the Women's Safety Unit of Safer Wales – a charity providing support to victims of abuse – for south Wales and later on for parts of West and mid-Wales. The project started out as a 6-month demonstrator project, but Safer Wales successfully gained follow-on funding until April 2011. The provision of support and welfare services to female offenders through community centre provision was expanded to north Wales in 2009. The North Wales Women's

Centre (NWWC) is based in Rhyl in north Wales and was initially established in 1999 as a limited company (Interactive Rhyl Ltd) providing information and communication technology (ICT) services to the local business community. In 2009, the Welsh Assembly Government provided funding for the organization to purchase their current premises to deliver a range of services for women suffering from domestic violence. In common with most women's centres until 2009, the North Wales Women's Centre was only ever envisaged as a general support service for the women of north Wales. In the wake of the Corston Report, the Ministry of Justice made funds available for the provision of community services to female offenders and rather than investing in a completely separate infrastructure they chose to tap into services which were already being provided for women and so they called on women's centres to apply for this funding. This strategy also achieved a second aim which was to integrate offenders with non-offenders so as to normalize female offenders' experiences and provide an environment in which they are most likely to respond to support and intervention programmes (Fawcett Society, 2004, 2005 and 2009; Corston, 2007).

In May 2009, in a similar process, and with help and support from the south Wales Project, the NWWC applied (to NOMS Cymru) and were awarded funding for a demonstrator Women's Turnaround project in north Wales to support women in the criminal justice system or at risk of offending. The new service ran alongside the NWWC's ongoing provision of services to women who had more general needs. The Women's Turnaround Service provides support for women involved in the criminal justice service or those at a clear risk of becoming so involved; and provides a safe, non-judgemental environment in which women can make progress towards reducing their risk of offending behaviour, and improving their life chances and lived reality. Importantly, unlike a statutory service it does not compel women to attend; and it is not tied to a community sentence or supervision requirements. The WTS in Wales relies on referrals from other agencies, mainly probation, as well as drop-ins or self-referrals, and all women attend on a voluntary basis.

One of the key lessons learnt in both Turnaround projects in Wales was the need to respond to women in their own geographical communities (which can be quite small). Expecting women to attend a central point is insufficient; service provision needs to come to the women, through outreach or satellite offices close to the women's communities. Rhyl and Caernarfon are less than forty miles apart yet required very different localized services and in rural areas the provision of outreach services is essential. In part, this is a reflection of the extent to which some women are excluded from mainstream society (i.e. they cannot travel; having no personal transport and no money for public transport) nor do they have access to the childcare (or adult care) needed to be away from home for long periods, or they are suffering from the stigma of being recognized as an offender (Holloway and Brookman, 2010; Feilzer et al., 2012).

There is no question that both Welsh Women's Turnaround projects responded to real need for community provision for vulnerable women, including female offenders. In their initial two-year period (November 2007–October 2009) the south Wales Turnaround project received 400 referrals, whilst the north Wales project received nearly 140 referrals over a ten-month period (April 2010–January 2011). Both projects achieved those figures despite difficult circumstances relating to short-term funding; budgetary pressures; shortages of human resources; and other general implementation problems, such as limited publicity of services; negotiation of targets with commissioners; clarification of purpose, target group and referral processes, etc. (for the full evaluation of the south Wales WTP, see Holloway and Brookman, 2010; for the north Wales WTS, see Feilzer et al., 2012). The levels of need uncovered in Wales clearly support the continuation of the service.

In April 2011, after a competitive tendering process, another provider, Platform 51 (based outside Wales) took over the Women's Turnaround projects covering the whole of Wales. It was run in conjunction with the NewDay project – an employment project for offenders and ex-offenders funded by the European Social Fund across Wales which aims to reduce offending and re-offending by providing training and qualification for offenders in order to address existing barriers into employment (Wales Probation Trust, 2012, see also Convergence Priority 2, 2007). This focus on one UK Government and EU initiative, namely getting women into employment, seems counter to the Corston principles of delivering women-led services and highlights the dangers of central commissioning and its tendency to impose uni-dimensional objectives onto local provision. Platform 51 subcontracts another organization, the Kim projects to deliver the WTS in north Wales.[7] The new Wales-wide contract came with reduced funding and therefore a reduction in case workers with major implications for the lesson of providing services to women 'where they are' rather than from a central point. This may reduce 'real' local provision and make services and case workers less accessible. The decision to roll out the service Wales-wide through one provider seems to be counterintuitive given the UK Government's emphasis on locally responsive community services, even if services are more locally subcontracted (e.g. Kim project in north Wales, (Maguire, 2012)). As Corston notes, local provision is often better able to meet local community and individual needs through alternative roots, more effectively achieving both the social capital and employment objectives (Feilzer et al., 2012).

In Wales, there are a number of complicating factors in relation to service delivery. The nature of some parts of Wales as rural with a significant geographical spread and pockets of demographic diversity complicates notions of community and localism as well as raising significant questions for effective service delivery. The diversity of the landscape of service provision and differing funding streams effectively targeting and competing for similar populations (e.g. health and criminal justice services targeting drug users) combined with the geography of Wales and general problems of accessing central services highlights the need to design locally appropriate outreach community provision. It is no surprise that successful interventions are more likely where agencies work well together in true partnership rather than in 'mandated partnerships' (Squirrell, 2007, p. 63) or 'contractual partnerships' and in an era of a more diverse landscape of service provision and increasing competition this is both vitally important and more difficult to achieve.

WELSH COMMUNITIES' RELIANCE ON LOCAL SERVICES

Community studies in many parts of Britain, and worldwide, claim that 'traditional' communities built on geographical area and on strong personal ties, and the social capital that is supposed to derive from such ties, are disappearing or weakening (Charles and Davies, 2005). Social capital is interpreted as the 'ability of actors to secure benefits by virtue of membership in social networks or other social structures' (Portes, 1998, p. 6). As mentioned above, Wales is often seen as the exception to this wider trend (Drakeford, 2010, p. 142). Community can be described as being made up of two elements, informal ties through an individual's embeddedness in networks of kinship, neighbourhood, or friendship and formal ties through locally based organizations (Charles and Davies, 2005, p. 686). Communities have also been defined as being held together by a 'sense of common identity and mutual obligation and respect', bringing with them positive connotations of social responsibility, support and local initiative (Faulkner, 2003, p. 191).

In more demographically stable areas such as large areas of mid and north Wales, and in areas where the incoming population has settled permanently and/or brings with it some of the informal ties and may be willing to adopt the existing format of community ties such as in parts of south Wales, the 'traditional' community based on kinship and location is still strong (Charles and Davies,

2005, p. 687). In these communities, women have been found to be crucially important in retaining community ties and partnership working or supportive structures both formal and informal are essential to the well-being of such areas (Charles and Davies, 2005; Cooper and Innes, 2009). Whilst the utility and limitations of the concept of social capital might be debated it is clear that civil society and voluntary or more informal supportive structures can connect people and consolidate stronger and more effective communities (Foley and Edwards, 1997). Women are key to this and to the effective inclusion of families into communities. Thus, underpinning the ideals of community provision for women in the criminal justice system is that women, in particular, should be able to draw on, and benefit from, the social capital still existing in the community. The assumption being that women offenders are members of the community and therefore will be able to draw on support, or if they have been excluded should be reintegrated in the community. There is, of course, the danger of underestimating the extent to which some women are excluded from local communities and how much difference a women centre provision can make to those levels of exclusion. Additionally, although more deprived communities often have strong cohesion the most deprived areas have been found to have lower levels of social capital or community cohesion (Cooper and Innes, 2009; Morgan, 2012, p. 469) and a disproportionate number of female offenders live in those communities.

In terms of governance, the devolution of some of the statutory powers relating to community safety, such as substance misuse, and children's services to the Welsh Government and a 'dragonising' of this area of policy through an emphasis of social integration (Edwards and Hughes, 2009, pp. 78–9), clearly hints at a distinctive Welsh way of delivering local services. As a 'newborn democratic country' (Stephens, 2004, p. 133), local structures and services in Wales are still developing and trying to find their place. This is more difficult in non-devolved areas of governance, such as criminal justice, which are so closely tied to devolved areas of policy such as health and welfare.

Effective information sharing and growing a knowledge base of local services and people is of particular importance in the criminal justice arena in Wales. In this context, we observed the running of an alliance set up in recognition of the need to address offending by women in a multi-agency, holistic approach. The terms of reference for the Women of Wales Alliance (WOW) specify its intentions to reduce the number of women entering the criminal justice system, reduce the number of women receiving custodial sentences, and act to inform and influence policy makers (WOW, 2012). The WOW group facilitated inter-agency links in north Wales, met every six weeks and was made up of representatives of a number of statutory and TSOs, including probation, the North Wales Women's Centre, Nacro, Arch Initiatives, and others. Meetings were used to share information about all the services available to women in Wales; to avoid duplication of efforts; to set up contacts and links between services; and to provide mutual support. The WOW group agreed terms of reference and produced strategic objectives with action points and delivery time frames.[8]

The value of structured inter-agency communication at a local level cannot be over-estimated; the WOW group was instrumental in helping the NWWC to set up links with HMP Styal and with the police and courts. The NWWC drew on group members' experiences and knowledge of a range of factors including prison system, policies and practices and it used contacts provided by other members of the group. WOW developed into a space in which organizations were able to build up links, develop better working relationships and therefore practice more effective information sharing and support of each other and the women who rely on their services. The alliance was able to provide training and strengthened discussions and negotiations with locally powerful organizations, such as North Wales Police and Local Health Boards. The ability of local services to be jointly proactive about the priorities of local service delivery rather than being responsive to changing goalposts from national government (Hughes and Gilling, 2004, p. 135) is an important element of establishing a sustainable 'community' response to the challenges of offending behaviour and the reintegration of previously excluded populations. Such a set-up can also provide some stability against changes in service provision as witnessed in the Women's Turnaround projects by integrating new service providers in the alliance and ensuring that developments and relationships established in the service are not lost. However, it will be severely limited in scope and power if the organizations involved can only be passive participants lacking control over service delivery, such as being subcontractors of services. Furthermore, in an environment where organizations compete for contracts/subcontracts the willingness to share information may decline so reducing the effectiveness of community groups in delivering local services.

In addition to local alliances which aim to bring agencies together to facilitate real and practical support and enable information exchange, some organizations have formed bodies which represent their activities or particular client group. Women's Breakout (formerly Women's Centre Forum) formed in 2008 and acts as the 'representative body for a national network of women-centred services' (Women's Breakout, 2012). As an 'organization' its aims are strategic and it is set up to serve as a contact point and lobbyist for policy makers rather than as a structure to enable effective working partnerships at a local level. Such organizations hint at an increasing fragmentation of the TS into distinct interest groups actively vying for policy attention and priority status. There are similar organizations working on behalf of groups working with young people (e.g. Transition to Adulthood Alliance), the homeless (e.g. Homeless Link), etc. Whilst these are important in getting issues onto a policy agenda their focus is not on local social integration or community provision.

CONCLUSION

The Westminster Government has very enthusiastically espoused a localism agenda and claimed to support local solutions for local communities which require local partnerships to achieve responsive services fully embedded in local communities. Delivery of these policies relies on the third sector. However, other policies, such as payment by results, the introduction of PCCs and some other changes to the criminal justice arena, undermine the agenda, distort and control the third sector drawing them into delivery of national priorities. For example, local services, particularly in the third sector, are dependent on increasingly short-term and stringently regulated funding, distorting their goals, expecting ambitious results in short timescales, introducing competition among local services and demoting many local providers to subcontractors tied to contractual requirements rather than local needs. In Wales, this is particularly problematic as it interferes with the Welsh Government's even stronger commitment to local delivery and their growing understanding of the problems of, and solutions to, effective service delivery in rural areas.

Nevertheless, there is no denying that the right combination of individual determination, creative energy and financial and human resources can produce good and effective local criminal justice services which make a difference to people's lives. However, this is not as a result of recent emphases on community and localism by politicians and policy makers but rather despite governance and social structures which work *against* sustainable local structures. Such local set-ups can be fragile, often dependent on individuals, and are easily disrupted by commissioning processes. Some local structures have proved more resilient in Wales, where organizations and partnerships seem to have got used to reinventing themselves under different guises to fit the latest policy fad. In Wales, the already strong civil society/community ties may allow 'genuine' local responses to continue to offer effective solutions but this situation is under mounting pressure.

On a more macro-level, it is often difficult to see through the numerous small local TSOs which are centrally controlled and understand what is available at a local level, how these services fit into the general structure of criminal justice service provision and how they are held to account. Additionally, it seems that recent changes in the sector and the 'take-over' of TSOs through public funding has resulted in the elimination of a strong coherent voice favouring penal reform and restraint in the use of criminal justice for everyone caught up in the criminal justice system, not for particular subgroups. Instead, there appears to be an increasing array of different UK-wide interest groups vying for special status, such as groups representing women, or young people, or those with mental health problems, and different treatment for their clientele, many of which pay only lip-service to differing local needs.

On reflection, new localism undermines the social and community integration that the Welsh Government aims to deliver (see, for example, Welsh Assembly Government's Community Cohesion Strategy, 2009; Welsh Government, Child Poverty Strategy, 2011; and Children First, Offenders Second and, the ongoing Communities First Programme) and interferes with delivery of services to local communities by providers who understand and respond to the needs of those communities. Less central policy control would help deliver the localism the Westminster Government claim to support. In Wales, at least, interventionist and heavy-handed delivery of localism policies from Westminster look poised to destroy what they claim to desire.

One way forward in resolving this conflict between rhetoric and practice may be to reduce central (Westminster) policy control, encourage devolution – both to the Welsh Government and local areas – and receive commitment to longer-term funding and a comprehensive service transfer enabling local areas to set up sustainable and reliable services responding to local needs. There are of course dangers to a wholesale adoption of the new localism and local service provision and these should not be neglected. Relying on local TSOs and networks may result in less well qualified staff and less well equipped services working with vulnerable and, at times, 'risky' offenders. Locally responsive service provision will lead to justice by geography and some individual and community needs will not be served: it also raises issues around equality and social justice.

NOTES

[1] A rhetorical notion espousing normative values of the community and volunteering and the claim that localism is more responsive compared to state provision (Levitas, 2011, p. 330).

[2] The concept and origin of the Big Society is contested but there is considerable support for the notion that it is a continuation of the 'Third Way' and the communitarian ideals of the New Labour era; for a discussion of the Big Society, see Jordan, 2010.

[3] We use the term third sector to encompass not-for-profit charitable organizations regardless of whether they rely primarily on paid or voluntary staff. Third sector may be a more accurate term as the majority of not-for-profit charitable organizations rely on paid staff as well as voluntary service provision.

[4] The Women's Offending Reduction Programme was launched in 2004 and five Together Women centres in the North West of England opened in December 2006, see Gelsthorpe et al., 2007; Heddermann et al., 2008; and Jolliffe et al., 2011. Note: Scotland was leading on the development of women's centre provision by opening the 218 Centre in Glasgow in 2003, see Loucks et al., 2006.

[5] See Home Office, Police and crime panel scrutiny of the precept, *http://www.home office.gov.uk/publications/police/pcc/scrutiny-of-precept-guidance?view=Standard& pubID=1089872* (accessed 22 December 2012).

[6] A new approach in which providers of rehabilitation services will only be paid if they deliver certain contractually agreed results, such as a reduction in re-offending, i.e. the government will pay only for 'what works'.

[7] It is very difficult to find information about the new Turnaround service provision.

[8] However, even such partnerships are fragile. In January 2012 we were included in an e-mail circular aiming to 're-launch' WOW which suggested that the alliance is struggling to survive the general reduction of resources across the sector as well as the multitude of changes to services and organizations. As of December 2012, the WOW meetings have not been re-launched successfully.

REFERENCES

Association of Chief Executives of Voluntary Organizations (ACEVO) (2003). *Replacing the State: The Case for Third Sector Public Service Delivery*, London: ACEVO.

Billis, D. and Harris, M. (1992). 'Taking the strain of change. Local voluntary agencies enter the post-Thatcher period', *Non-Profit and Voluntary Sector Quarterly*, 21, 3, 211–25.

Cabinet Office (2010). *Building the Big Society*, London: Cabinet Office, *http://www. cabinetoffice.gov.uk/news/building-big-society* (accessed 10 July 2012).

Charles, N. and Davies, C. A. (2005). 'Studying the particular, illuminating the general: community studies and community in Wales', *Sociological Review*, 53, 4, 672–90.

Convergence Priority 2, T1 and ESF Regional Competitiveness Priority 1 ESF Convergence P2 T1&2, ESF Regional Competitiveness P1 (2007). *Increasing Employment and Tackling Economic Inactivity Strategic Framework 2007–2013*.

Cooper, H. and Innes, M. (2009). *The Causes and Consequences of Community Cohesion in Wales: A Secondary Analysis,* Cardiff: UPSI, Cardiff University.

Corcoran, M. (2011). 'Dilemmas of institutionalisation in the penal voluntary sector', *Critical Social Policy*, 31, 1, 30–52.

Corston, J. (2007). *A report by Baroness Jean Corston of a Review of Women with Particular Vulnerabilities in the Criminal Justice System (Corston Report)*, London: Home Office, *http://www.justice.gov.uk/publications/docs/corston-report-march-2007.pdf* (accessed 22 December 2012).

Crow, G. (2000). 'Developing sociological arguments through community studies', *International Journal of Research Methodology*, 3, 3, 173–87.

Deakin, J. and Spencer, J. (2003). 'Women behind bars: explanations and implications', *Howard Journal for Penal Reform,* 42, 2, 123–36.

Drakeford, M. (2010). 'Devolution and youth justice in Wales', *Criminology and Criminal Justice*, 10, 2, 137–54.

Edwards, A. and Hughes, G. (2008). 'Resilient Fabians? Anti-social behaviour and community safety work in Wales', in P. Squires (ed.), *Asbo Nation: The Criminalisation of Nuisance,* Bristol: Policy Press.

Edwards, A. and Hughes, G. (2009). 'The preventative turn and the promotion of safer communities in England and Wales: political inventiveness and governmental instabilities', in A. Crawford (ed.), *Crime Prevention Policies in Comparative Perspective*, Cullompton: Willan.

ESRC (2011–12). *The Third Sector Role in Criminal Justice,* ESRC Research Seminar Series, organized by Corcoran, M., Hucklesby A., and Mills, A. Keele University and Leeds University. *http://www.law.leeds.ac.uk/research/projects/the-third-sector-in-criminal-justice.php* and *http://www.law.leeds.ac.uk/assets/files/research/ccjs/towards/hucklesby.pdf* (accessed 21 December 2012).

Faulkner, D. (2003). 'Taking citizenship seriously: social capital and criminal justice in a changing world', *Criminal Justice*, 3, 287–315.

Fawcett Society (2004). *Women and the Criminal Justice System: A Report of the Commission on Women and the Criminal Justice System,* London: Fawcett Group.

Fawcett Society (2005). *One Year On: A Report of the Commission on Women and the Criminal Justice System,* London: Fawcett Group.

Fawcett Society (2009). *Engendering Justice – from Policy to Practice: Final Report of the Commission on Women and the Criminal Justice System,* London: Fawcett Group.

Feilzer, M. Y., Plows, A., Williams, K. S. and Yates, J. (2012). *An Evaluation of the Women's Turnaround Service in North Wales.* Final Report to NOMS Cymru, *http://www.wiserd.ac.uk/wp-content/uploads/2010/03/WISERD_RRS_008.pdf* (accessed 21 December 2012).

Foley, M. W. and Edwards, B. (1997). 'Escape from politics?', *American Behavioral Scientist,* 40, 5, 550–61.

Gelsthorpe, L. and Morris, A. (2002). 'Women's imprisonment in England and Wales: a penal paradox', *Criminal Justice*, 2, 3, 277–301.

Gelsthorpe, L., Sharpe, G. and Roberts, J. (2007). *Provision for Women Offenders in the Community*, London: Fawcett Group.

Gelsthorpe, L. (2011). 'Working with women offenders in the community: a view from England and Wales', in R. Sheehan, G. McIvor, and C. Trotter (eds), *Working with Women Offenders in the Community*, Abingdon: Willan.

Gibbs, A. (1996). 'Probation service users as volunteers in partnership projects', *Probation Journal*, 43, 142–6.

Halpern, D. (2010). *The Hidden Wealth of Nations,* Cambridge: Polity.

Haney, L. (2010). *Offending Women: Power, Punishment and the Regulation of Desire,* Berkeley: University of California Press.

Hedderman, C. (2004). 'Why are more women being sentenced to custody?', in G. McIvor (ed.), *Women Who Offend,* London: Jessica Kingsley.

Hedderman, C., Palmer, E. and Hollin, C. (2008). *Implementing Services for Women Offenders and Those 'At Risk' of Offending: Action Research with Together Women,* Ministry of Justice Research Series, 12/08.

Holloway, K. and Brookman, F. (2010). *An Evaluation of the Women's Turnaround Project. Final Report for NOMS Cymru,* Cardiff: Glamorgan University.

Home Office (2012). *Home Office Police and Crime Commissioners Update Bulletin Wales Version – July 2012,* London: Home Office, *http://www.homeoffice.gov.uk/publications/police/police-crime-comms-bulletin/* (accessed 21 December 2012).

House of Commons (2011). *The Role of the Probation Service.* House of Commons Justice Committee, Eighth Report of the Session, 2010–2012. Vol. 1. London: The Stationery Office.

Hughes, G. and Gilling, D. (2004). '"Mission impossible"?: the habitus of the community safety manager and the new expertise in the local partnership governance of crime and safety', *Criminology and Criminal Justice*, 4, 2, 129–49.

Jolliffe, D., Hedderman, C., Palmer, E. and Hollin, C. (2011). 'Re-offending analysis of women offenders referred to Together Women (TW) and the scope to divert from custody', Ministry of Justice Research Series 11/11, London: Ministry of Justice.

Jordan, B. (2010). *Why the Third Way Failed. Economics, Morality and the Origins of the 'Big Society'*, Bristol: The Policy Press.

Kennedy, P. and Roudometof, V. (2004). 'Transnationalism in a global age', in P. Kennedy and V. Roudometof (eds), *Communities across Borders,* London: Routledge.

Levitas, R. (2011). 'The just's umbrella: austerity and the Big Society in coalition policy and beyond', *Critical Social Policy*, 81, 320–41.

Loucks, N., Malloch, M., McIvor, G. and Gelsthorpe, L. (2006). *Evaluation of the 218 Centre*, Edinburgh: The Scottish Executive.

Maguire, M. (2012). 'Response 1: Big Society, the voluntary sector, and the marketization of criminal justice', *Criminology and Criminal Justice*, 12, 5, 483–94.

Meek, R., Gojkovic, D., and Mills, A. (2010). *The Role of the Third Sector in Work with Offenders: the Perceptions of Criminal Justice and Third Sector Stakeholders*, Southampton: Third Sector Research Centre.

Ministry of Justice (2012). *Payment by Results, http://www.justice.gov.uk/offenders/ payment-by-results/community-pilots* (accessed 1 November 2012).

Morgan, R. (2012). 'Crime and justice in the "Big Society"', *Criminology and Criminal Justice*, 12, 5, 463–81.

Morris, D. (2012). 'Charities and the Big Society: a doomed coalition?', *Legal Studies*, 32, 1, 132–53.

Neilson, A. (2009). 'A crisis of identity: Nacro's bid to run a prison and what it means for the voluntary sector', *Howard Journal of Criminology and Criminal Justice*, 48, 4, 401–10.

Portes, A. (1998). 'Social capital: its origins and applications in modern sociology', *Annual Review of Sociology*, 24, 1–24.

Sagar, T. and Croxall, J. (2012). 'New localism: implications for the governance of street sex work in England and Wales', *Social Policy & Society*, 11, 4, 483–94.

Seddon, N. (2007). *Who Cares? How State Funding and Political Activism Change Charity*, London: Civitas.

Social Exclusion Unit (2002). *Reducing Re-Offending by Ex-Prisoners*, London: Office of the Deputy Prime Minister, Social Exclusion Unit.

Spalek, B. (2008). *Communities, Identities and Crime*, Bristol: The Policy Press.

Squirrell, G. (2007). 'Seeking desistance in the community: drug users' experience of the criminal justice system', *Therapeutic Communities*, 28, 1, 59–73.

Stephens, A. C. (2004). 'Democratizing local government in Wales', *Contemporary Wales*, 16, 1, 133–49.

Vennard, J. and Hedderman, C. (2009). 'Helping offenders into employment: how far is voluntary sector expertise valued in a contracting-out environment?', *Criminology & Criminal Justice*, 9, 2, 225–45.

Wales Probation Trust (2012). *Newday, http://www.walesprobationtrust.gov.uk/english/ local-communities-and-partners/newday/* (accessed 12 December 2012).

Welsh Assembly Government (2009). *Cohesion Strategy*, Cardiff: Welsh Assembly Government.

Welsh Government (2011). *Child Poverty Strategy*, Cardiff: Welsh Government.

Women's Breakout (2012). *http://www.womensbreakout.org.uk/* (accessed 29 January 2013).

WOW, Women of Wales Alliance (2012). *Terms of Reference*. Hard copy only. Copy available from authors on request.

Wright, A. (2008). *Public Services and the Third Sector: Rhetoric and Reality*, House of Commons Public Administration Select Committee, Eleventh Report of the Session 2007–8, London: TSO.

6. A WELSH CRIMINOLOGICAL IMAGINARY: THE STATE OF CRIMINOLOGY IN WALES

Robert Jones

ABSTRACT

The following paper intends to lay down the foundations for a Welsh school of criminological thinking. Assessing the nature of criminological research and teaching in Wales within the context of devolution and debates concerning the transfer of further powers to the Welsh Government, the paper intends to examine why criminologists have failed to address the context of criminal justice in Wales. In doing so, the paper will draw critical attention to changes that have taken place within higher education as well as the mutually reinforcing role that particular criminological traditions have played in suppressing debates around the Welsh context. As a response, attention is paid to the importance of developing a Welsh Criminological Imaginary to ensure that future scholars and criminological thinkers in Wales, born into the post-devolution era, are able to develop and articulate responses to crime and justice to help move Wales beyond approaches currently taken in Westminster.

INTRODUCTION

In a speech given to the Law Society in 2007 the then Counsel General for Wales, Carwyn Jones AM, raised concerns over the sustainability and suitability of a single *legal* jurisdiction for both England and Wales. Also drawing attention to the potential for a devolved system of *criminal justice* Mr Jones's words echoed sentiments which had been clearly outlined within the Welsh Labour and Plaid Cymru coalition government's *One Wales* strategy. An approach that demonstrated the coalition government's outward commitment to:

. . . consider the evidence for the devolution of the criminal justice system. This is within the context of devolution of funding and moves towards the establishment of a single administration of justice in Wales. A full debate with the legal community on the creation of a separate criminal justice system for Wales is inevitable if the National Assembly gains greater powers. (Welsh Assembly Government, 2007, p. 29)

Despite the National Assembly gaining such powers following the outcome of the 2011 devolution referendum, debates around a devolved criminal justice system[1] have merely emerged as a consequence or by-product of arguments currently being made around the establishment of a separate legal jurisdiction in Wales. In addressing what academics have described as the emergence of a unique approach to law making in Wales (Navarro, 2012; Rees, 2012), legal scholars have disproportionately carried the baton in terms of researching and successfully framing Wales and the Welsh context as a meaningful unit of study. Even when attention has been paid to the potential to devolve criminal justice powers to Wales, such calls have emerged from those working in the field of law (e.g. Jones, 2008).

However, despite the commitment shown by legal scholars to at least address the Welsh context in law, in criminological terms the study of Welsh criminal justice remains under-researched and excluded from higher education teaching programmes. Whilst this paper acknowledges that a significant amount of criminology, both research and teaching, is actually being carried out in Wales, it aims to draw critically upon the fact that very little is actually being done *on* Wales. Importantly, the paper's consideration of the Welsh context can be understood in relation to two different components:

(i) The study of Welsh criminal justice issues at the level of those working within or alongside criminal justice services in Wales, and those who find themselves subject to the criminal justice process (e.g. police, courts, prison).

(ii) The study of Welsh criminal justice at the level of governance within the era of devolution and increasing concerns with Welsh governance (e.g. policy making, constitutional affairs).

Whilst the later part of the paper intends to lay down the foundations for an approach to the study of crime and justice which is more befitting to post-devolution Wales, the paper firstly aims to discuss the reasons why the Welsh context of criminal justice remains an underdeveloped narrative. Central to this will be the processes that have managed to reproduce and maintain the hegemony of what will be referred to throughout as an Anglocentric criminology.

MARKET LIBERALISM AND THE ANGLOCENTRIC UNIVERSITY

Propelled by the 'ascendance' of a set of neoliberal principles heralded by the Conservative government of Margaret Thatcher (Walters, 2007, p. 17), higher educational institutions from the 1980s onwards have found themselves increasingly exposed to the kinds of processes previously associated with institutions and organizations in operation in the private sector. No longer reliant upon centralized government for the majority of its funding, the state's desire to roll away from its former responsibilities has ignited a need for universities to begin searching for ways to generate income (Walters, 2007). Overrun by the language of managerialism, phrases such as efficiency, management, effectiveness and even profit have begun to dominate talk within the corridors of even some of the most 'prestigious' academic institutions.

In the face of extraordinary changes to the way in which universities in Wales and throughout the UK are being funded, universities themselves have become increasingly susceptible to the processes of an academic capitalism in which every sphere of their activity has become subject to market forces (Rhoades and Slaughter, 2004b). In Wales, notwithstanding the fact that higher education falls under the responsibilities of the Welsh Government, universities appear unable to resist the forces of a neoliberal-led academic capitalism. Examples of such activities can be traced throughout almost every aspect of the university; take for example the student survey[2] or the generic evaluation form that confronts students upon completion of every module of study. The business-like mantra that the 'customer is always right' which has been propelled by a 'customer revolution' within higher education is having significant effects upon the conditions in which universities and academics are expected to perform.

Within the higher education sector in Wales, universities are currently experiencing the effects of such transformations first hand. Propelled by cuts to the higher education budget which were announced by the Welsh Government in 2010, universities in Wales have faced a considerable reduction in their overall budget from £420 million in 2010/2011 to £382 million in 2011/2012 (Learned Society of Wales, 2012). For some, including Professor Richard Davies from the Learned Society of Wales, such cuts which amount to an overall 5 per cent budget reduction, are confining Welsh universities to the 'slow lane' of higher education (Learned Society of Wales, 2012). Told to 'adapt or die' by Education and Skills Minister Leighton Andrews AM in a keynote speech to the Institute of Welsh Affairs in 2010, plans are already in place for a rapid overhaul of higher education in Wales (Andrews, 2010). This includes an announcement made by the Higher Education Funding Council for

Wales (HEFCW) to cut the number of universities in Wales from eleven to six by merging the University of Wales Institute Cardiff (UWIC), University of Wales, Newport and the University of Glamorgan as the University of South Wales.

Ultimately, as the values of market liberalism begin to permeate and transform the landscape of higher education in Wales and beyond, such developments are having a significant effect upon the performance of the academy. Exposing universities to unprecedented new pressures, critical attention must be paid to the ways in which, against a backdrop of increasing financial insecurity, the values underpinning academic capitalism have become 'prioritized over the core educational activities of the academy' (Rhoades and Slaughter, 2004a, p. 38). As outlined by Walters (2007, p. 18):

> Ministers and senior university management, as a necessary transformation within changing economic landscapes, have presented the new business-like culture of universities. As a result, individual disciplines within universities are expected to be profit-making or alternatively face disestablishment. For many scholars, knowledge must coexist with, or be subservient to, market demand.

Significant here are the effects that an income-led approach to higher education has had, and continues to have, upon criminological departments in Wales. In particular, against a backdrop of financial insecurity and increasing cuts to the higher education budget, critical attention must be drawn to the effects that the neoliberal university has had upon efforts to frame Wales as a worthwhile topic of study within criminological research.

Research Assessment
In face of the increasingly difficult funding situation facing higher education institutions, one of the ways in which UK universities and individual depart-ments seek to increase their income is through external research grants, the amount of which is dependent upon what standard each university department is perceived to be performing at in terms of its research. The way in which this standard has previously been assessed is through the Research Assessment Exercise (RAE). For universities in Wales, the RAE is conducted by the Higher Education Funding Council for Wales (HEFCW). Under the system of scoring subject departments and the research they produce the rewards of working in a well-performing department can be great:

> Blessings flow in terms of respect and esteem . . . big money flows into our institutions in the wake of high scores, directly in terms of money from the Funding

Council and indirectly in the wake of the fact that students increasingly wish to study in departments that have a good reputation for research work. (Wyn Jones, 2004, p. 13)

However, whilst academics in universities across the UK vie to compete with each other for the highest score and the rewards that inevitably follow, to fully appreciate the effects that the research assessment is having upon the trajectory of criminological research in Wales it is necessary to consider the assessment criteria that it employs. The last assessment conducted in the UK was in 2008. It scrutinised sixty-seven subject panels or Units of Assessment (UOA) and each department was graded from a score of one to four. Central to the RAE's judgment on 'quality' research lies in its ability to be recognized on an international level. Awarding a lowest possible score[3] of one to departments whose research is only 'recognised nationally in terms of originality, significance and structure', the RAE provides the greatest rewards (a score of four) to departments whose research might be considered 'world-leading' or internationally renowned for its 'originality, significance and rigour' (RAE, 2008, p. 8).

In consequence such an approach punishes those whose research is only deemed relevant at a national level. It is important here to point out that the RAE's employment of the term 'national' refers to all constituent parts of the UK. This therefore raises the question; under such a criterion what does the research assessment make of research which has been conducted exclusively on the situation of crime and justice in Wales (let alone the other constituent parts of the UK)? Encouraging and rewarding criminologists working in Wales for research that attracts international recognition, the research assessment can be held, albeit partly, responsible for the promotion and reproduction of a narrative that encourages criminologists to overlook matters relating to Wales and reinforce the view that matters of crime and justice remain one that extends well beyond the borders of Wales. Reproducing the processes in which universities have become subject to the forces of neo-liberal governance, according to Broadhead and Howard (1998), the research assessment has exposed universities to an extended form of disciplinary power which seeks to regulate academics and researchers in accordance with a set of institutional aims. In the case of criminology in Wales, this disciplinary power manages to naturalize and reproduce an Anglocentric outlook that currently dominates discussions of crime and justice in Wales.

In its existing form, the research assessment has played a major role in supressing the issues that affect Wales from criminological research. Whilst the RAE will be replaced in 2014 with a new form of assessment, its predecessor, the Research Excellence Framework,[4] looks set to employ its very own fixation with 'world leading' and 'international' research (REF, 2011). However, whilst the circumstances that surround external research funding undoubtedly play a significant role in helping to discourage the study of matters relating to Wales, the reluctance shown by universities in Wales may also be understood within the context of another important and equally competitive means of income generation.

Recruitment

Besides research funding which is made available to universities by funding councils such as the HEFCW, Economic and Social Research Council (ESRC), Home Office, Welsh Government and European Commission, a major source of income for higher educational institutions is through student recruitment. Whilst attention here will not be paid to the controversies surrounding the cost of university tuition or the differences that exist between different parts of the United Kingdom, of utmost concern are the effects that market forces are having upon the 'criminological curriculum' in Wales.

Table 6.1
Place of domicile: UK students who applied to study at university in 2011-12

By UK country	2011	2012
England	426,208	384,170
Northern Ireland	19,130	18,292
Scotland	39,761	39,169
Wales	21,289	20,876
Total	**506,388**	**462,507**

Source: *http://www.ucas.com/about_us/media_enquiries/media_releases/2012/20120130* (accessed 3 February 2012).

According to information obtained from Universities and Colleges Admissions Service (UCAS) (see Table 6.1) 84.2 per cent of all UK students who applied to university in 2011 and 83.1 per cent in 2012 are domiciled in England. Put another way, four out of five students applying to university in Wales are from across the border. In contrast, in 2011 students from Wales represented just 4.2 per cent of the overall total, and 4.5 per cent in 2012. It is at this juncture that Welsh universities' increasing commitment to 'international' research agendas can begin to be understood amongst the wider forces governing university departments. In an attempt to 'sell' their research departments and criminological programmes to the largest section of the 'market', Welsh univer sities have come to engage in the kinds of processes that seek to prioritize income generation over student education. It is a situation allied to that described by Rhoades and Slaughter (2004b, p. 286):

> In marketing, the needs and interests of the enterprise take precedence over the needs of the customer. The aim of marketing activities is to persuade the consumer to buy (to increase revenues) rather than to inform the consumer in some neutral sense so that they can make the best choice. In the case of higher education institutions, a marketing campaign may have multiple aims to do with the characteristics an institution wants in its freshman class.

In Wales, the characteristic referred to by Rhoades and Slaughter (2004b) is that the marketing activities of its universities target students from England. In seeking to attract the largest amount of students possible, as demonstrated by data obtained from UCAS, English students represent the largest 'market share' in terms of university applicants. For fear of deterring prospective students from England, Welsh universities have entered into an almost irreversible process of Anglicization. Ensuring minimal reference to the study of Wales or Welsh criminal justice, criminological departments in Wales have come to represent an almost 'Wales free zone'. Nowhere is this point made clearer than in the teaching programmes made available throughout universities across Wales.

There are eleven universities in Wales. Criminology is a taught discipline at undergraduate level in seven of these institutions whilst criminological pro- grammes are offered at the postgraduate level within four. With the inclusion of joint honours programmes, there are a total of twenty-one criminology-related degree programmes being delivered throughout Welsh universities. To date, not one programme offers a module that specifically aims to consider or discuss the Welsh context of crime, justice or punishment. Whilst this fact is not at all surprising given the significant lack of research that has been conducted into issues surrounding Wales, it does however epitomize the Anglicized trajectory of criminological departments currently operating in Welsh universities.

When it comes to addressing the developments or effects that devolution has had on life in Wales, criminological departments have much to learn from other areas of academia. For example, in Cardiff Law School the undergraduate LLB Law programme offers students the chance to undertake a module on 'Welsh Devolution' whilst its postgraduate LLM in Governance and Devolution offers students the chance to undertake modules in 'Constitutionalism and

Governance' and 'The Law of Devolution in Wales'. In Bangor University, LLM Law students can study modules in the 'Law of Devolution in Wales and Europe', 'Welsh Public Law' and 'Bilingualism in Wales and Other European Countries'. In Swansea University, students on the undergraduate LLB Law can take a module in the 'Legal History of Wales' whilst staff at the university are currently working on a new module in Welsh, *Cymru'r Gyfraith,*[5] which aims to look at the development of Welsh legal identity, including the role of the National Assembly as a legislature. Similarly in Scotland, Sterling University offers a module on 'Scottish Society' as part of their undergraduate BA Crime and Society programme which aims to run alongside the other modules it delivers (Sterling University, 2012).

Whilst the issues of research funding, student recruitment and teaching mutually reinforce one another in helping to normalize and reproduce a hegemonized view of criminology that fails to see Wales as a valuable unit of study, equally important is the extent to which the discipline of criminology itself has contributed to the suppression of the Welsh context. Central to this point is the supremacy that *realist criminology* has assumed within an era in which universities have been forced to concern themselves with a capacity to generate income.

AR WERTH:[6] CRIMINOLOGY IN WALES

Developed in the 1980s as a response to the 'punitiveness and exclusionary' policies of the newly elected Margaret Thatcher government, realist criminology also emerged in response to what it described as the 'utopianism' and idealism contained within the Marxist criminology of the radical new Left (Young, 2006, p. 234). Dismayed with the way in which the new Left had sought to provide, what is felt was, an overindulgent fixation with the role of the state, realist criminology aimed to provide an alternative approach which strayed beyond the theoretical underpinnings of Marxism towards the generation of a research agenda and development of a statistical analyses on crime, its causes and its consequences. At the time of its emergence, key realist thinkers including Ian Taylor were increasingly influenced by the Labour Party and their own efforts to oppose the rise of the popular New Right. In particular, Taylor's (1981) *Law and Order: Arguments for Socialism* was influenced heavily by Tony Benn's writings upon the values of social democracy (Sim et al., 1987). However, whilst new realist thinkers immediately 'nailed their colours to the mast of the Labour Party' (Sim et al., 1987, p. 51), the values espoused by new realist criminologists were soon to play a central role in the party's rise to power. On October 4 1994, in his first address to the Labour Party conference as the party's leader, Tony Blair outlined New Labour's vision to tackle crime. Inspired by realist concerns towards aetiology, the plight of victims (Young, 1986) and debates around the 'seriousness' of crime, the Labour Party's outward commitment to be *tough on crime and its causes* owed a lot to the advocacy of realist criminology. However, upon reaching power in 1997, the relationship between New Labour and realist criminology was about to take a marked shift as the criminology of New Labour became the criminology of the state. Whilst realist criminology before 1997 played a significant role in the formation of New Labour's law and order agenda, of utmost concern for the purposes of this paper are the ways in which realist criminologists, in the age of 'money led research' (Walters, 2007, p. 24), have neatly positioned themselves to service the vehicle of the state's criminology. Crucially however, are the hegemonizing effects that a state-led criminology has had upon criminology in Wales.

Realism pays: servicing the vehicle of state criminology

Key to the dominance of Left realist criminology is 'profitability' and the way in which criminological departments have been able to make themselves attractive to government-funded research. Whilst realism's concern with aetiology, victims and the 'seriousness of crime' has played a key role in informing the nature of state responses (Young, 2006), it was realist criminology's increasing concern with the promotion of a research agenda and statistical explorations of crime (and its causes) that was instrumental in the government's outward desire to approach the problem of crime through an 'evidence based' framework. According to the *Modernising of Government* white paper (Cabinet Office, 1999), the creation of policies based on research findings was central to New Labour's 'revised' approach to government:

> Policy decisions should be based on sound evidence. The raw ingredient of evidence is information. Good quality policy making depends on high quality information, derived from a variety of sources – expert knowledge; existing domestic and inter-national research; existing statistics; stakeholder consultation; evaluation of previous policies. (Cabinet Office, 1999, p. 31)

In the wake of an increasing reliance upon the role of 'experts' within the 'what works' era, realist criminologists have vied to make themselves as attractive as possible to funders following an explosion in state-funded research. One of the ways in which realist thinkers have achieved this is through an unwitting political alliance to the state's crime control directives (Cohen, 1988). Accepting, utilizing and employing the language and terms of reference used by the state to discuss crime and justice, realist thinkers have become complicit with the trajectory of a state criminology plagued with the values of an actuarial and managerial agenda (Feeley and Simon, 1994; Clarke and Newman, 1992). In an effort to remain as attractive as possible to government contracted research, terms such as 'community safety', 'risk', 'social control', 'security', 'partnerships', 'networks' and 'offender management' have uncritically entered into the hegemonic discourse of criminological research and teaching within higher education institutions.

Understood as both a result of an enhanced level of government commitment to criminological research and the continuing pressures imposed by the neo-liberal university, the 'commercialization' and 'commodification' of criminological research has had a significant effect upon the character of critical scholarship (Walters, 2007, p. 25). As criminological perspectives become 'embedded' not only with the state's definition of crime control but also the forces of market liberalism (for fear of a reaction from potential funders), a reluctance to provide any meaningful critique has led to what might be foreseen as the dilution of 'critical scholarship' and a significant reduction in the 'value' of criminological research (Walters, 2007, p. 25). As such, a paradox emerges in which increasing levels of concern with 'evidence' and 'expertise' has led to a decline in the real autonomy of academic expertise this includes attempts in Wales to even envisage, yet alone develop, an approach to the study of crime and justice which considers the Welsh context.

Left realism in Wales
Left realism holds a tight grasp over criminology in Wales. Amongst the universities and individual schools that offer criminology programmes, the state's language on crime control has infiltrated departmental research themes and independent academic-led research projects. In addition, the language central to the state's crime control apparatus may also be traced within the criminological programmes that are taught in Wales. This includes a module offered in Swansea University on 'Crime Prevention and Community Safety'; 'Crime Control and Prevention' in Aberystwyth; 'Regulating Society' in Bangor; 'Penology: Punishment, Prisons and Offender Management' in Glamorgan; and a 'Crime Control, Regulation and Policing' module in Cardiff.

By adopting the state's language on crime control issues, realist criminologists (or the individual departments that espouse it) have made themselves particularly appealing to funders. To illustrate, attention should be drawn to Cardiff University's School of Social Science 'Crime, Security and Justice' research theme and more specifically the aims of the theme itself.

> Researchers in the Crime, Security and Justice Theme have a significant *international* reputation for the application of innovative and rigorous research designs to substantive *'real world'* problems. Their research has advanced theory and knowledge across key areas of sociological interest, including: policing and social control, the governance of community safety and security; and offending and identities. (Cardiff University, 2012)

Whilst the interest areas central to the theme can be traced back to the actuarial and managerial criminology of the state, important reference is also made to the significance of an *international* reputation and the centre's increasing concern with *real world* problems. Interestingly however, since 2001 researchers involved in the theme have been in receipt of over £5 million in research grants from funding agencies which have included the Home Office, the Economic and Social Research Council and the European Commission. Such significant investment is illustrative of the attractiveness that realist criminologies pose to potential funders which include the Westminster Government.

Further to the award of research grants, universities in Wales have also taken advantage of the 'generous funding' (Scraton, 2002, p. 33) made available by the Home Office to undertake evaluation research into state measures of crime prevention. Under both 'what works' and 'evidence based' agendas, criminologists in Wales have embraced the prospect of developing evaluative research agendas. For example, in Bangor University academics have worked to develop The Centre for Applied Research and Evaluation Sciences (CARES), whilst in Glamorgan University a section on their website titled 'Research and Consultancy' boasts a list of evaluation projects that have been undertaken by academics working within the University's Centre for Criminology. Whilst the existence of such efforts are symptomatic of a criminology embedded with the state (Walters, 2007), this state-funded reliance upon the 'expert knowledges' of evaluation research has much wider consequences.

Within the context of Wales, this continual state-funded reliance upon the role of 'expert knowledges' has had a significant effect upon the ability of academics to help frame issues that relate to the Welsh context. Through such a fixation with the role of 'expert knowledges', according to the work of Žižek (2001, p. 3), the politicality of some of the fundamental questions facing academics in Wales are being 'violently displaced' by a form of post-politics which lays emphasis upon:

. . . the need to leave behind old ideological divisions and to confront new issues, armed with the necessary expert knowledge and free deliberation that takes into account concrete people's needs and demands. (Žižek, 2001, p. 3)

Within the context of criminological research, this manifests itself on two levels. First, this kind of displacement has removed critical attention away from the punitiveness and authoritarianism contained within the state's attempts to respond to the 'problem' of crime and justice (Pratt et al., 2005). Second, it has managed to displace meaningful politicization over the definition and situation of justice in Wales. As such, issues relating to the socio-political context in Wales, including changes to the devolution dispensation, are displaced and therefore excluded from debates around criminal justice. This, in coexistence with the forces propelling university researchers to try and maximize the amount of income brought in via external research grants, manages to secure the legitimacy of an Anglocentric imaginary that constructs England and developments in Westminster as its template and Wales as a subject not quite 'real' enough to warrant such attention.

Within the context of a 'survival of the fittest' culture that has swept through higher education institutions since the political and economic transformation to market liberalism, realist approaches to the study of crime have neatly positioned themselves as the front runner for funded research. However, they have done so at a cost. In Wales, the supremacy of realist teaching and research has played a significant role in hegemonizing an approach to the study of criminal justice that has left a body of Welsh criminology well and truly malnourished. In particular, the 'commercialization' of criminological research has served to undermine the authenticity of 'critical' scholarship (Walters, 2007, p. 25). For fear of putting off potential funders with the use of language deemed anarchistic or potentially controversial, the income-generation principles underpinning research in Wales are managing to ensure that 'the menial and the mundane prevails over the creative and the critical' (Walters, 2007, p. 20).

Whilst legal scholars lead the way in learning more about the Welsh context, for criminologists in Wales, what is required is an approach to the study of crime and justice that strives to move beyond the hegemonized narrative of Anglocentric criminology, an approach that not only descends from the criminological positions espoused by the state, but one that continues to encourage concern amongst criminologists in Wales with developments in Westminster. Therefore, in an effort to promote what Scraton (2001, p. 2) calls 'knowledges of resistance', the final passage of this paper intends to outline the preconditions for the development of a new form of criminological intellectualism which ambitiously seeks to re-appropriate analyses of crime and justice in the post-devolution era.

DYCHMYGU:[7] A WELSH CRIMINOLOGICAL IMAGINARY

At the very beginning of Alana Barton et al.'s (2007) *Expanding the Criminological Imagination*, the authors ask a series of important and hypothetical questions. Encouraging readers from the outset to consider the nature of contemporary responses to crime and criminal justice, they are instantly asked to consider how current developments will be reflected upon in years to come:

> Future generations of social scientists will look back critically at this period and ask why liberal democracies continued to expand their apparatuses of criminal justice when, at the same time, officially measured and defined rates of 'crime' had been in steady decline. They will question why the UK government's response had been to create more and more criminal offences (over 1,000 since 1997 at the last count), expand the range of 'interventions' in the lives of the young, fill the prisons to bursting point and build a new generation of prisons for profit. They will question how and why some of the fundamental principles of due process, such as the right to trial by jury and *habeas corpus*, were being eroded. They will question why police costs were spiralling out of control and why more police officers and new legions of community safety officers were being recruited when they had little impact on reducing reported crime rates or even on reducing the fear of crime. (Barton et al., 2007, p. 1)

Whilst the questions raised within *Expanding the Criminological Imagination* will be applicable to criminologists throughout different parts of the United Kingdom, in Wales against the backdrop of fifteen years of devolved government, six years since the amended Government of Wales Act 2006, two years since powers of criminal justice were devolved to the Northern Ireland Government and a year on from the 2011 referendum that granted Wales primary law making powers, a whole range of additional questions may be raised. For example, why despite the efforts that have been made by academics in other areas of academia (Jones, 2008; Navarro, 2008) was an agenda *for* Welsh criminal justice not developed? Why despite an outward commitment by the Welsh Government to discover more about the potential to devolve powers of criminal justice did criminologists in Wales not do more to support their efforts? And why, despite suggestions of a more progressive approach to *youth justice* in Wales when contrasted to those being conjured up in Westminster

(Drakeford, 2010), did criminologists fail to challenge the Anglicized view that surrounds *criminal justice* in Wales? Against the backdrop of these failures, and in addition to those outlined by Barton and colleagues (2007), the following intends to lay the foundations for the development of a progressive counter-hegemonic criminological imaginary, an imaginary reliant upon an 'organic' form of intellectualism; an organic criminology *of* Wales (Gramsci, 1971, p. 6).

A Welsh criminological imaginary

At present, a Welsh criminological imaginary has yet to be envisaged – let alone realized. For such an imaginary to emerge in Wales it must assume hegemony amongst the criminological departments that operate within its universities. Central to the development of a Welsh criminological imaginary are a number of factors which present themselves as preconditions to the hegemonization of a Welsh criminological perspective. What these preconditions must do is to ensure that a progressive Welsh criminological imaginary is able to move beyond the logics that simply legitimize and reinforce the dominance of Anglocentric criminology, a logic institutionalized within the very funding systems that universities in Wales have become both subject to and reliant upon in the age of neoliberalism.

One of the ways in which criminologists in Wales might achieve this is through changes to the Research Assessment itself. At present, an Anglocentric criminology is institutionalized within the very funding systems that universities in Wales have become subject to within the market-led era of higher education. With an approach that rewards research for its 'international' or 'world lead-ing' status, radical changes to the way in which criminological research is assessed in Wales would undoubtedly help nurture the development of a Welsh criminological position. As illustrated by Wyn Jones (2004, p. 19);

> So if we accept that there is not enough research on Wales emanating from our universities we must ensure that the Research Assessment, or an alternative funding system, encourages it. There is no mystery here. Indeed, I would be very surprised if the funding wasted on trying to force shotgun weddings between higher education institutions were not enough in itself, it itself could in some way be connected to the research assessment, to give research on Wales a great boost.

Nevertheless, whilst recognition of the Welsh context is vital to attempts to move beyond an institutionalized fixation with 'international' and 'world leading' research; this must not blur the wider and future aims of a Welsh criminological perspective. For instance, the development of an approach to the study of crime and justice in Wales does not propose that all academics and researchers in Wales immediately turn their attention to the situation of criminal justice in Wales. Nor does it suggest that matters which exclusively relate to Wales are the only issues of any notable value. Rather, the Welsh criminological imaginary is about the creation of a space in which *greater* attention not *complete* attention can be given to the Welsh context. Contrary to any notion of an all-encompassing perspective, Welsh criminology should endeavour to research and explore responses to crime and punishment which are themselves 'world leading' and can be recognized 'internationally' by comparative criminologists. In the same way that Portugal has been acclaimed for its efforts to provide a resistant culture to drug control in an era of criminalization (Greenwald, 2009), Finland for a move away from repressive practice (Lappi-Seppälä, 2001) and other Scandinavian countries for an 'exceptional' approach to penal policy characterized by low levels of imprisonment (Pratt, 2008), Wales has an opportunity develop its very own unique resistances against the rising tide of a universalizing punitive turn (Coleman and Sim, 2005). Such a resistant approach can build upon the advances made in the area of *youth justice* in Wales which has attracted widespread praise for its ability to resist the punitive forces that have swept across *youth justice* policy in England (Drakeford, 2010; Haines, 2009; Morgan, 2009).

However, whilst changes to the research assessment would undoubtedly help the Welsh criminological imaginary to emerge, the role and significance of institutional leadership within university departments must not be overlooked. For example, why despite being exposed to the same funding structures and forms of research assessment have law departments and legal scholars been able to devote more attention to the issues affecting Wales? And why, despite the same pressures to recruit as many students as possible in the income-led era, have law schools been able to include matters relating to Wales into their teaching programmes? In as much as changes to the research assessment will play a fundamental role in any attempts to increase levels of research and teaching on Wales, criminology departments in Wales also require a stronger sense of leadership that will place added value to the study of Wales in an attempt to challenge the hegemony of a Westminster-led criminology.

A criminology of Wales

Whilst some may argue that efforts to research crime and justice are already being made in Wales, critical attention must be drawn to the tokenistic nature of attempts currently being made to study criminology in Wales. In particular, what is most alarming is the amount of research that is being done *in* Wales when compared to the amount of work being done *on* Wales. As outlined by Richard Wyn Jones (2004, p. 2) in his review of the failures of higher education in Wales in 2004:

> If one looks at the research produced by Wales's universities, one is struck by how little work is done on Wales within our educational institutions. As a result, our knowledge of many aspects of the life of contemporary Wales is pitifully inadequate. This in turn constrains the task of creating policies which could deal successfully with the complex economic, social and cultural problems of our country.

To illustrate, take the Welsh Centre for Crime and Social Justice (WCCSJ). Formally launched at the end of 2010, according to the centre's website the WCCSJ (2012) aims to provide 'high quality, theoretically informed, policy-relevant research on crime and social justice in Wales and beyond'. Drawing together criminologists from eight universities across Wales as well as criminal justice practitioners, what is particularly problematic is the Centre's outward concern with research that is being done *in* Wales as opposed to research that is actually being conducted *on* or *for* Wales. In doing so, some of the major questions that relate to the Welsh context continue to be neglected. Alternatively, within the context of any attempt to hegemonize a Welsh criminological imaginary the WCCSJ should seek to create a platform for criminological research into Wales as opposed to what research is being churned out by academics and researchers who are simply employed or funded by Welsh universities.

Silk and beyond
In October 2011, the then Secretary of State for Wales Cheryl Gillan MP announced that an independent commission led by former Clerk to the National Assembly for Wales, Paul Silk, would be conducted in two parts. Whilst the first addressed issues of taxation and financial accountability, the second part of the commission according to a report published shortly after Ms Gillan's announcement in 2011, aims:

> To review the powers of the National Assembly for Wales in the light of experience and to recommend modifications to the present constitutional arrangements that would enable the United Kingdom Parliament and the National Assembly for Wales to better serve the people of Wales. (House of Commons, 2012, pp. 10–11)

At present the outcomes of this review are unknown. However, even if we allow ourselves very briefly to consider the report's potential findings this poses a number of hypothetical problems for criminologists working in Wales. For example, what if the Silk Commission recommends that powers of criminal justice be extended to the Welsh Government? At present, universities and criminologists in Wales are not prepared for such an eventuality. Ironically, despite the dominance of criminological approaches in Wales which centre themselves upon the realities of crime and its control, criminologists in Wales must wake up to the *realities* of the situation that twenty-first-century Wales now finds itself in.

In waking up to such a 'reality', greater attention must be afforded to the development of a criminological perspective that *better serves the people of Wales*. Whilst this must include efforts to try and match the steps taken by law departments to offer programmes through the medium of the Welsh language,[8] criminology programmes must try to ensure that matters of Welsh criminal justice are included within teaching frameworks. Whilst many will fear the effects this might have upon the large majority of students applying to universities from England, criminologists in Wales must look to use the Welsh criminological imaginary to *attract* as opposed to *deter prospective* students. By developing a potentially innovative and 'world leading' approach to the study of crime and justice those who choose to study in Wales will be afforded an opportunity to work amongst and contribute towards such a progressive and different approach, a school of thought which is better placed to resist the constraining forces of a Westminster-led criminology and to take advantage of the autonomous space brought about by changes to the devolution settlement in Wales (Wyn Jones and Scully, 2012). In doing so, criminologists in Wales will be ideally placed to help inform debates around devolution and criminal justice and may even help to influence the nature and trajectory of policy responses if such matters are ever devolved to the National Assembly. As outlined within a Welsh Affairs Committee review into the situation of imprisonment in Wales in 2006, in an era in which Wales, relatively speaking, finds itself with unprecedented levels of political and legislative autonomy it:

> now has an opportunity to develop its own distinctive approach to criminal justice which better reflect the needs of Wales and which could serve as a model for developments elsewhere in the UK. (House of Commons, 2007a, p. 4)

These sentiments, alongside the view that Wales now has the chance to bring 'initiative and flair into non-custodial sentences' (House of Commons, 2007b,

Ev 133), must find themselves at the very heart of any attempt to develop a progressive approach to criminology that not only exists in Wales, but organically belongs to Wales. In true Gramscian terms, it surrounds the development of an 'organic' form of intellectualism fully capable of subverting the nullifying forces of a hegemonized Anglocentric criminology that has for so long remained completely unchallenged.

SUMMARY

Have you ever read any criminology texts? They are staggering. And I say this out of astonishment, not aggressiveness, because I fail to comprehend how the discourse of criminology has been able to go on at this level. One has the impression that it is of such utility, is needed so urgently and rendered so vital for the working of the system, that is does not even need to seek a theoretical justification for itself, or even simply a coherent framework. (Foucault, 1980, p. 47)

Since the birth of the 'what works' agenda, criminologists have sought to provide themselves a theoretical justification under the working title of 'evidence based policy' and an outward commitment to research and explore 'what works' best. If Foucault's reflection is something that criminologists in general have found difficult to respond to, for criminologists in Wales this sense of justification is even more problematic. With very little known about the Welsh context, criminology in its current setup is failing the people of Wales, whether that is victims of crime in Wales, practitioners working in the justice system, the voluntary sector or those who find themselves swept up by an ever widening net of criminal justice interventionism (Cohen, 1985). In Wales, criminologists must seek to do more and to take advantage of a receptive climate of change swept in under a tide of devolution and greater powers afforded to the Welsh Government. This includes efforts currently being made in higher education. In Cardiff University, the Wales Governance Centre (WGC) aims to facilitate and encourage research into the issues surrounding governance and constitutional affairs in Wales. At present, the WGC has four key areas of research *Public Policy; Political Economy, Politics and Government* and *The Law of Wales*. In view of some of the arguments which have been put forward in this paper, as Welsh criminology and the study of crime and criminal justice in Wales begins to be taken more seriously, it may be conceivable to suggest that the WGC may wish to add a fifth element to its research activity.

Finally, whilst criminologists in Wales may look to the efforts made by law departments and legal scholars as a marker in their attempts to develop a Welsh criminological perspective, it must be noted that whilst current debates in Wales are dominated by talk of legal jurisdiction, legal scholars themselves may soon come to look towards and reflect upon the ideas emerging from Welsh criminology. As outlined by the Counsel General for Wales, Theodore Huckle QC, in 2012 gave a speech to the Society for Legal Scholars at Cardiff Law School, questions relating to criminal justice in Wales are likely to impinge heavily upon future discussions around devolution.

> If, for whatever reason, the Welsh Government cannot at present move forward with proposals for taking on Policing and Justice responsibilities, the case for a separate legal jurisdiction may be considerably weakened. It would be of limited or even dubious worth pursuing a separate legal jurisdiction 'in principle' if Welsh Ministers and the Assembly did not also obtain a reasonably full set of powers in relation to Justice; crucial aspects of the supposedly separate jurisdiction would still be the responsibility of the Ministry of Justice. (Huckle, 2012)

As debates relating to the devolution of criminal justice in Wales look set to take centre stage as the Welsh Government prepares to submit its evidence to Part II of the Silk Commission in the spring of 2013, it should be of considerable concern to any criminologist reading this that criminology in Wales, in its current format, has very little contribution to make to such debates. Given some of the arguments made throughout this paper and the words contained within the Counsel General's address, never has there been a more crucial time to kick-start Welsh criminology.

NOTES

[1] This refers to the adult system; this is not to be confused with discussions relating to Youth Justice in Wales.

[2] *http://www.thestudentsurvey.com/*

[3] Research can be considered unclassifiable. This is research which cannot be considered relevant even at a national level.

[4] *http://www.ref.ac.uk/*

[5] Welsh, translation 'Legal Wales'.

[6] Welsh, translation 'For Sale'.

[7] Welsh, translation 'To imagine'.

[8] Currently the only criminology programme in Wales that offers modules in Welsh is the BSCEC Criminology at Aberystwyth. Modules are only available at Level 4.

However, the undergraduate Law programme at Aberystwyth offers students the chance to take modules in Welsh throughout the full three years of their degree. In addition, Law departments in Cardiff University and Bangor University both offer modules through the medium of Welsh.

REFERENCES

Andrews, L. (2010). *Opportunities for a Confederal University for South West Wales*, Keynote address at the Institute of Welsh Affairs Conference, Trinity Saint David, 3 December 2010, *http://www.leightonandrews.com/#!speeches/ceea* (accessed 3 February 2013).

Barton, A., Corteen, K., Scott, D. and Whyte, D. (2007). *Expanding the Criminological Imagination: Critical Readings in Criminology*, Cullompton: Willan.

Broadhead, L. and Howard, S. (1998). 'The art of punishing: the research assessment exercise and the ritualisation of power in higher education', *Education Policy Analysis*, 8, 1–14.

Cabinet Office (1999). *Modernising Government White Paper, Presented to Parliament by the Prime Minister and the Minister for the Cabinet Office by Command of Her Majesty*, March 1999, London: Cabinet Office.

Cardiff University (2012). *Crime, Security and Justice Research Theme*, Cardiff School of Social Sciences, *http://www.cardiff.ac.uk/socsi/research/researchthemes/crimes ecurityjustice/index.html* (accessed 6 March 2012).

Clarke, J. and Newman, J. (1992). *The Managerial State: Power, Politics and Ideology in the Remaking of Social Welfare*, London: Sage.

Cohen, S. (1985). *Visions of Social Control*, Cambridge: Polity Press.

Cohen, S (1988). *Against Criminology*, New Brunswick: Transaction Books.

Coleman, R. and Sim, J. (2005). 'Contemporary statecraft and the "punitive obsession": a critique of the new penology', in J. Pratt, D. Brown, M. Brown, S. Hallsworth and W. Morrison (eds), The *New Punitiveness: Trends Theories, Perspectives*, London: Routledge.

Drakeford, M. (2010). 'Devolution and youth justice in Wales', *Criminology and Criminal Justice*, 10, 137-54.

Feeley, M. and Simon, J. (1994). 'Actuarial justice: the emerging new criminal law', in D. Nelken (ed.), *The Futures of Criminology*, London: Sage Publications.

Foucault, M. (1980). *Power/Knowledge: Selected Interviews and Other Writings, 1972–1977*, Brighton: Harvester.

Gramsci, A. (1971). *Selections from the Prison Notebooks*, London: Lawrence and Wishart.

Greenwald, G. (2009). *Drug Decriminalization in Portugal: Lessons for Creating Fair and Successful Drug Policies*, Washington DC: Cato Institute.

Haines, K. (2009). 'The dragonisation of youth justice', in W. Taylor, R. Earle and R. Hester (eds), *Youth Justice Handbook: Theory, Policy and Practice*, Cullompton: Willan.

House of Commons (2007a). *Welsh Prisoners in the Prison Estate*, Welsh Affairs Committee Third Report of Session 2006–07, London: The Stationery Office Limited.

House of Commons (2007b). 'Memorandum submitted by The Prison Governors Association', Evidence given to the Welsh Affairs Select Committee, Ev 133 (P. Tidball), *Welsh Prisoners in the Prison Estate*, Welsh Affairs Select Committee Third Report of Session 2006–07, London: The Stationery Office Limited.

House of Commons (2012). *Devolution in Wales: The Silk Commission*, House of Commons, 9th March 2012.

Huckle, T. (2012). *Wales, a Jurisdiction?*, Speech given to the Society of Legal Scholars, Cardiff Law School, 15 November 2012.

Jones, J. (2008). 'The next stage of devolution: a (d)evolving criminal justice system for Wales', *Crimes and Misdemeanours*, 2, 1, 1–39.

Lappi-Seppälä, T. (2001). 'Sentencing and punishment in Finland: the decline of the repressive ideal', in M. Tonry and R. Frase (eds), *Sentencing and Sanctions in Western Countries*, Oxford: Oxford University Press.

Learned Society of Wales (2012). *The Funding Gap*, Cardiff: The Learned Society of Wales.

Morgan, R. (2009). 'Report to the Welsh Assembly Government on the question of Devolution of Youth Justice Responsibilities', 14 December 2009.

Navarro, M. (2008). 'The coming of law making powers to the National Assembly', in D. Balsom (ed.), *The Wales Year Book 2008*, Aberystwyth: HTV.

Navarro, M. (2012). 'A substantial body of different Welsh law: a consideration of Welsh subordinate legislation', *Statute Law Review*, 33, 2, 163–91.

Pratt, J. (2008). 'Scandinavian exceptionalism in an era of penal excess: Part I: The nature and roots of Scandinavian exceptionalism', *British Journal of Criminology*, 48, 2, 119–37.

Pratt, J., Brown, D., Brown, M., Hallsworth, S. and Morrison, W. (2005). *The New Punitiveness: Trends, Theories, Perspectives*, London: Routledge.

Rees, O. (2012). 'Devolution and family law in Wales: a potential for doing things differently?', *Statute Law Review*, 33, 2, 192–206.

Research Assessment Exercise (2008). *Research Assessment Exercise 2008: The Outcome*, December 2008, *http://www.rae.ac.uk/pubs/2008/01/* (accessed 16 December 2012).

Research Excellence Framework (2011). *Assessment Framework and Guidance on Submissions*, July 2011. *http://www.ref.ac.uk/pubs/2011-02/* (accessed 16 December 2012).

Rhoades, G. and Slaughter, S. (2004a). 'Academic capitalism and the new economy: challenges and choices', *American Academic*, 1, 1, 37–60.

Rhoades, G. and Slaughter, S. (2004b). *Academic Capitalism and the New Economy: Markets, State, and Higher Education*, Maryland: The Johns Hopkins University Press.

Scraton, P. (2001). 'A response to Lynch and Schwendingers', *The Critical Criminologist: Newsletter of the ASC's Division on Critical Criminology*, 11.

Scraton, P. (2002). 'Defining "power" and challenging "knowledge": critical analysis as resistance in the UK'. in K. Carrington and R. Hogg (eds), *Critical Criminology: Issues, Debates, Challenges*, Cullumpton: Willan.

Sim, J., Scraton, P. and Gordon, P. (1987). 'Introduction: crime, the state and critical analysis', in P. Scraton (ed.), *Law, Order and the Authoritarian State*, Milton Keynes: Open University Press.

Taylor, I. (1981). *Law and Order: Arguments for Socialism*, London: Macmillan.

University of Sterling (2012). *Criminology, http://www.stir.ac.uk/undergraduate-study/course-information/courses-a-to-z/school-of-applied-social-science/criminology/* (accessed 5 February 2012).

Walters, R. (2007). 'Critical criminology and the intensification of the authoritarian state' in Barton et al. (eds.) *Expanding the Criminological Imagination: Critical Readings in Criminology*, Cullompton: Willan, pp. 15–37.

Welsh Assembly Government (2007). *One Wales: A Progressive Agenda for the Government of Wales*, Cardiff: Welsh Assembly Government.

WCCSJ (2012). *About WCCSJ,* Canolfan Troseddeg a Cyfiawnder Chymdeithasol Cymru, Welsh Centre for Crime and Social Justice, *http://wccsj.ac.uk/about-wccsj.html* (accessed 5 February 2012).

Wyn Jones, R. (2004). *The Failure of the Universities of Wales*, National Eisteddfod Lecture, Newport 2004, Cardiff: Institute of Welsh Affairs.

Wyn Jones, R. and Scully, R. (2012). *Wales Says Yes: Welsh Devolution and the 2011 Referendum*, Cardiff: University of Wales Press.

Young, J. (1986). 'The failure of criminology: the need for a radical realism', in J. Young and R. Matthews (eds), *Confronting Crime*, London: Sage.

Young, J. (2006). 'Left realism', in E. McLaughlin and J. Muncie (eds), *The Sage Dictionary of Criminology*, London: Sage.

Žižek, S. (2001). *On Belief*, London: Routledge.

7. HOMICIDE, SCANDAL AND MAKING MENTAL HEALTH POLICY IN WALES

Mark Drakeford and Kirrin Davidson

ABSTRACT

The paper considers the development of mental health policy in Wales in the period immediately before and after devolution. In particular, it traces the impact of scandal following homicides by people suffering from mental ill health on policy production. While scandal has continued to be an endemic condition of this policy field through the period under consideration, the paper argues that its impact has been much diminished in the period after the inauguration of the National Assembly for Wales. It concludes by offering some explanations for this finding.

INTRODUCTION

Late in October 2012 the Welsh Government published its new Mental Health Strategy, *Together for Mental Health,* together with a Delivery Plan for the following three years (Welsh Government, 2012a). The document represented the culmination of more than a decade of policy-making in this field, in the post devolution period. A leading third sector mental health charity set out its verdict in this way: 'the Strategy is welcome and it can now be said that Wales has both a good quality legislative framework for mental health and a good quality policy for moving mental health services forward' (Hafal, 2012). This paper compares and contrasts the state of public policy in relation to mental health in the period immediately before and since the creation of the National Assembly in 1999. In particular it focuses on the impact of homicides by people suffering from a mental illness, and the public reaction to such scandals, on the policy making process. It is not the purpose here to consider whether the incidence of such homicides is rising or falling in Wales. The numbers involved are simply too small to make such a determination (University of Manchester, 2012, p. 100). Rather, the paper concentrates on an exploration of the relationship between the generation of scandal and public policy making, concluding that while scandal has proved an endemic context for mental health services, both before and after the creation of the National Assembly, its impact on policy-making has been very different in the two eras.

Methods
Of approximately forty homicides committed in Wales by people with a mental health problem (Hendy, 2010) during the first three Assembly terms (May 1999–April 2011), only nine were the subject of inquiry by the Healthcare Inspectorate Wales (HIW).[1] Because these HIW reports bring together the most comprehensive accounts of such events, and represent a concerted attempt to generate what Brown (2004, p. 95) terms 'authoritative sense-making', this paper focuses exclusively upon these instances of homicide. A thematic analysis of each report was undertaken, involving a close reading of each text, annotation of common themes and examination of the explanatory framework within which reports have been produced (see Butler and Drakeford, 2005, p. 222ff for an extended account of the methodological issues involved in 'anatomising scandal'). As far as scandal generation is concerned, the investigation reported here utilized online newspaper archives, searching particular terms and themes found in a sample of broadsheet, middle-range and tabloid accounts of homicides involving people with a mental health condition in Wales. Not all nine of the HIW reports attracted national media attention. This paper concentrates on those which did. These articles were then subjected to a comparative discourse analysis in order to identify those elements which were productive of scandal.

HOMICIDE, SCANDAL AND POLICY SHIFTS

Wales has long experience of the connection between scandal and policy-making in mental health. The Ely Hospital Inquiry of 1969 was a landmark event which provided a unique fresh impetus to the closure of long-stay Victorian asylums (Korman and Glennerster, 1990). Yet, even as this resettlement policy was at its height, below the surface there were already signs that the programme was coming under increasing strain as the social fabric frayed under the retrenchment of the 1980s (Goodwin, 1989). In 1984, for example, social worker Isabel Schwarz was killed at her place of work, Bexley Hospital, by former patient Sharon Campbell (DHSS, 1988). It took two years of determined campaigning by Isabel's father, GP Victor Schwarz, to secure an inquiry into the events which led to that tragedy (see Butler and Drakeford, 2005, p. 141ff, for an extended account of this case). A rash of further scandals in the 1990s changed both the public mood and the policy direction (Muijen, 1995; Tidmarsh, 1997). Rose (1997, p. 30) for example, traces the way in which a 'new narrative' emerged from mental health scandals during the mid 1990s, bringing together problems in community care and violent crime in a 'relationship of causality' and a culture of allocating blame and responsibility.

The scandalizing process began in earnest with the 1992 case of Christopher Clunis. It captured and cemented a set of public anxieties that, as the influential *Spectator* (1994) magazine put it, care in the community had been transposed into 'carnage in the community'. Mr Clunis, a discharged mental health patient, had murdered a complete stranger, Jonathan Zito, on the platform of a London underground station, plunging a knife into his head. A sustained – but brief – campaign by Jonathan Zito's wife, a Welsh social work student, led to the creation of a full blown public inquiry. The Ritchie Report (1994) into these events and the care and treatment which Mr Clunis had received laid bare a system fragmented beyond the point of coherence and incapable of delivering a sense of safety, either to patients or the community at large. It was clear, the Report said, that the system had 'served Christopher Clunis very badly'.

In itself, the Clunis case has been widely regarded as a pivotal moment in mental health policy making. Maden (2007, p. 1) went so far as to describe it as 'the most important event in the history of modern British mental health services'. Yet, the Clunis case was both preceded and succeeded by similar events in the mental health field, as successive scandals fed a growing public mood of disillusionment. Against that background, and under intense pressure to demonstrate that 'action' was being taken by government, the Department of Health published *Guidance on the Discharge of Mentally Disordered People and their Continuing Care in the Community* (1994, p. 11) which made it clear that, 'In cases of homicide, it will always be necessary to hold an inquiry which is independent of the providers involved'.

Each new inquiry now became fodder for a narrative linking mental health with policy collapse. Their texts, ruthlessly deploying hindsight in order to create coherence from 'a jigsaw puzzle in random order' (Ritchie, 1994, p. 1), came to 'function hegemonically to impose a particular version of reality on its readers' (Brown, 2004, p. 107). Almost any new piece of information was capable of being reported within a framework which emphasized danger and policy collapse. A BBC Panorama programme in the autumn of 1997 produced a crop of headlines, in which the *Times* (1997) reported that 'Mental Patients "Have Killed 104"', and the *Independent* (1997) informed its readers that 'Mental patients commit a murder every two weeks'. When the *Times* used the phrase 'knife-crazy mental patient' (1993) to describe Christopher Clunis it was, Payne (1999, p. 192) argues, 'all the more powerful by contrast with other, more restrained articles in the same paper'.

Wales was not immune from this scandal explosion. In 1996, just at the cusp of the New Labour and devolution eras, Andrew Cole murdered Fiona Ovis and William Crompton in circumstances which combined the by-now well-established components of mental health scandal with a new set of tabloid ingredients of its own. Andrew Cole was a patient at Bronllys Hospital in Brecon when he met Fiona Ovis, a local doctor's daughter, herself suffering from mental ill-health. He became obsessed with her, but that obsession turned to violence when she formed a new relationship with 18-year-old William Crompton. Thirty hours after being discharged from Bronllys, he tracked the couple to a bungalow in Llandrindod Wells where he killed them both. Mass circulation newspaper headlines tell their own story. The *Sun* (1996) led with: 'Lovers' bloodbath – Doc's daughter and secret toyboy knifed to death in their love nest'. The *Daily Mirror* (1997), explicitly linking the case with that of Christopher Clunis, reported the outcome of the subsequent court hearing under the headline 'Stab frenzy lover jailed'. The national attention which these events and their aftermath attracted continued for over a decade.

Porter (1996, p. 403) suggests that the cumulative effect of this explosion of scandal was to turn community care into 'an object of rampant public suspicion'. 'Community care has failed', concluded the in-coming Health Secretary, Frank Dobson (Department of Health, 1998). 'It has left many vulnerable patients to try to cope on their own. Others have been left to become a danger to themselves and a nuisance to others . . . A small but significant minority have become a danger to the public as well as themselves.' The New Labour administration ordered an immediate halt to the programme of mental hospital closure (Department of Health, 1997) and quickly set out a new policy direction, in which 'assertive outreach' and compulsory treatment in the community were now to be pursued. Boardman (2005, p. 33), echoing other analysts, describes the new policy mix as contributing 'to the return to the asylums along with the virtual asylums of hostels and homes for the mentally ill'. As noted further below, mental health policy in England, under New Labour, was very largely shaped through a lens of social authoritarianism, in which the dangers posed by a small minority of patients, amplified through the medium of scandal, dominated policy-making for all. Whilst the risk to the general public was in reality very low (Fawcett and Karban, 2005, pp. 36–7), the 'unique horror' of psychotic homicide meant that 'low is not always the same as insignificant' (Maden, 2007, p. 43).

MENTAL HEALTH POLICY AND SCANDAL IN THE POST DEVOLUTION ERA

The National Assembly for Wales thus came into being just as the impact of scandal on policy making in mental health was at its most intense. Yet, despite the strength of these repeated conclusions and reactions, devolution meant that from the outset, and in a number of key ways, mental health policy was an early candidate for policy differentiation. By July 1999, just eight weeks after the first Assembly elections, Jane Hutt, as Health and Social Services Minister, had set up two advisory groups 'made up of members from all interest groups to draw up all Wales strategies for both adult and child and adolescent mental health services' (Hutt, 1999). The work of these groups led to early strategy documents, including *Adult Mental Health Services for Wales*, published in September 2001. It made it clear that

> the National Assembly has made mental health one of its three health priorities. This in itself is highly significant given the Cinderella status from which mental health has suffered over many years. (National Assembly for Wales, 2001, p. 1)

In sharp contradistinction to the slow down (and, in some instances, reversal) of the policy of closing mental health hospitals in England, the *Partnership Agreement*, which brought into being the first post devolution coalition between Labour and the Liberal Democrats, contained an explicit commitment to accelerate the closure of Wales' remaining long-stay hospitals (National Assembly for Wales, 2000, p. 9). In the period which followed, two distinct policy projects were at play in Wales. On the one hand, a sustained effort can be detected to *normalize* mental health services and to introduce a far greater involvement of service users and carers alongside those who provide mental health services, including planning and commissioning (e.g. WAG, 2004, 2009a; Thomas et al., 2010, p. 526). The 2001 All Wales Mental Health Strategy set out an ambition to 'provide the best possible care for those with mental health problems', based on four underpinning principles – equity, empowerment, effectiveness and efficiency (National Assembly for Wales, 2001, p. 5). It promised a National Service Framework for mental health services in Wales. Such a document had been produced for England in 1999, the year in which the Assembly came into being. The Welsh equivalent appeared in 2002. Implementation was generally considered to be slow (Hafal, 2006). An updated version was published in 2005, this time accompanied by an Action Plan to set standards, drive up quality and reduce unacceptable variation in services in different parts of Wales.

While policy making within Wales was characterized by a set of clear principles, inconsistently matched by service development on the ground, the same period was also characterized by both overt and covert opposition to successive attempts, at Westminster, to reform mental health legislation in the direction of further compulsory treatment of the mentally ill in the community. In 2002, the *Western Mail* reported 'a special meeting of the Assembly's health committee', at which the Royal College of Psychiatrists, Royal College of Nursing, the Law Society and a series of mental health voluntary groups combined to condemn Westminster's Mental Health Bill as at odds with, and in contradiction of, Welsh policies. In a rare show of interest in Welsh politics, the *Times* (2004) reported then-First Minister Rhodri Morgan as predicting the demise of the latest attempt at reform, when he told reporters that, '[w]e do not expect the draft, pre-legislative Bill to come forward this side of a general election'. When the election was over, however, the bill reappeared, to further protests in Wales against its over-emphasis on 'protecting the public from a small minority of dangerous mentally-ill people' (*South Wales Echo*, 2005). By contrast, in England, the 'over-riding influence on 21st century mental health policy, due to the public, media and political outcry over "madness and murder" in the late 20th century, is control' (Morrall, 2005, p. 37).

SCANDAL STILL

Does all this mean that Welsh policy making, post devolution, has been able to proceed free of the occurrence of scandal? The evidence is quite to the contrary. In the 40 homicides committed in Wales by people with a mental health problem (Hendy, 2010) during the first three Assembly terms (May 1999–April 2011), all the raw material for scandal is to be discovered, as the brief selection below demonstrates.

Stranger danger
The Christopher Clunis case drew much of its potency from the random nature of the killing. His victim, Jonathan Zito, was wholly unknown to him, and it was entirely a matter of chance that had brought him to the same underground station platform. Just after midday on 19 October 2005, Ms A[2] stabbed a female shopper at a Cardiff city centre store. The event was captured on CCTV where Ms A is seen first to approach another woman, before attacking her victim. 'I picked her out' (HIW, 2008, 1.3) she told police but, in another central debate of mental health homicides, both the Court which dealt with the case and the Inquiry report which followed concluded that 'the homicide was not predictable' (HIW, 2008, 2.1). A number of further recurrent themes occur in this case: Ms A was 'hard to help' (HIW, 2008, 1.14), discharging herself from hospital despite being 'urged' not to do so. Nor was her condition easy to treat. During the two years leading up to October 2005 she had been diagnosed as suffering from 'borderline personality disorder' with 'no mental health intervention' (HIW, 2008, 1.28). Moreover, in another echo of the Clunis case, Ms A's treatment had been made more difficult because of her own peripatetic life-style, including not only movement within Wales, but across the border between Wales and England. In the process she had not only lost contact with mental health services, but had become progressively more alienated from her own family. The sense of randomness which permeates the act of homicide in this case plays powerfully to an ungovernable sense of danger. The generation of scandal often depends on evoking a vicarious identification with the possibility that this could be an experience met directly in the reader's own life. As we envisage shoppers going about their everyday business, the message is power-fully communicated that, as far as the victim is concerned – *it could be you.*

The case of Ms A made headlines in all the major national and local papers in the days following the homicide. Here was a killing which took place in the middle of the day in a shop on a busy city centre street, 'just 200 yards from the Millennium Stadium' (*Times*, 2005). The *Express* (2005) concluded that 'the attack underlines the horror of life in violent Britain today'.

Family matters
On 16 May 2009, Mr G violently attacked his 84-year-old mother Mrs H, with a knife, at her Pembrokeshire home (HIW, 2011). Mrs H died as a direct result of the wounds she received, and her son was arrested on the same day. Press coverage and the Inquiry report focused on the many years during which Mrs H had been her son's main carer. Following a 'perfectly normal' upbringing and early life, in which he had attended university and obtained a degree in

engineering, Mr G fell ill at the age of 24. Thereafter his condition fluctuated considerably, with long periods of controlled ill-health, interspersed with more serious episodes which required hospitalization and which had involved concerns for his mother's safety. The Inquiry report provides an unusually vivid account of events which led up to Mrs H's death, detailing the exact timings of incidents preceding the homicide, with various 'missed opportunities', where if the authorities involved had acted differently, Mrs H's death may have been avoided.

Unlike most homicides of this sort in the post devolution period, that of Mrs H attracted some media coverage beyond Wales. It did so partly because of the way in which the events contained so many archetypal ingredients of scandal-making. As in Greek tragedy, the qualities of dramatic tension and tragic inevitability (because the reader knows the final outcome) are balanced by an equally powerful sense that the final outcome could have been different if only individuals or organizations *acted otherwise*. Moreover, homicides within the home also evoke powerful feelings of violation, in which violent events are made all the more disturbing for having happened in a place of safety. Describing Mrs H as 'gentle and much-loved', her family pointed to the contrast from which horror was created: 'Her death was violent and cruel, after a life of love and caring' (*Carmarthen Journal*, 2009).

By now, however, even events with a powerful set of scandalizing ingredients were not, in themselves, sufficient to attract media attention. In this case, the novelty was provided because, at a time when a ban on smoking in public places was a matter of current debate, coverage focused on the fact that the immediately precipitating case of the killing had been a quarrel in which Mrs H had forbidden her son to smoke within the family home. The *Daily Mirror* (2009) account, for example, was headlined 'Son killed mum after smoke ban'. Beyond that, attention focused on a more established theme – that the tragedy had been the result of NHS failure. Mrs H's family issued a statement in which they said that:

> The health service relied upon 84-year-old Mrs H to support G. In turn, we relied on the health service to hospitalise him when needed. The tragedy happened when the safety net of hospitalisation was not activated. (*Daily Post*, 2009)

This was the theme taken up in reporting away from West Wales where the homicide took place. 'Family of mum stabbed by son criticises his supervision' reported the *Birmingham Post* (2009). 'Family of mentally ill killer slams NHS', said the *Daily Post*, in North Wales on the same day.

Good and evil

Scandals which succeed in reaching a national audience, and in making a lasting impact, are those which reach towards an unambiguous division of the world into good and evil. One mental health scandal of this sort stands out in the post devolution period: it involved the death of Father Paul Bennett, in March 2007, on the doorstep of his own vicarage in Trecynon, in the Cynon Valley. Father Paul's assailant was Mr D and the subsequent HIW Inquiry Report (HIW, 2009) traces a developing period of mental ill-health from 2004 onwards. By 2006 Mr D 'was engrossed with religion, the Bible and the belief that he was God' (HIW, 2009, 1.23). His mother had moved to a flat located near the church in Trecynon, and overlooking the vicarage where, in July 2006 Mr D slit his own throat using a Stanley knife (HIW, 2009, 1.24). After his admission to hospital, an arrangement was made for him to be seen by the Mental Health Crisis Team but, 'fearing that he would be sectioned' (HIW, 2009, 1.23), Mr D left the hospital before he could be seen. Police were informed and, within a few hours, he was discovered at his mother's address, 'calm, compliant and very quiet' (HIW, 2009, 1.48). It was to prove the only occasion on which Mr D might have come into formal contact with mental health services. The HIW Inquiry concluded that, 'in retrospect it is clear that between 2006 and 2007, Mr D was at a serious risk of committing harm to the general public, to Father Paul, in particular and to himself . . . but at no point had Mr D been seen by any psychiatric service that could have identified the disorder and initiated treatment' (HIW, 2009, 2.5).

Of all the mental health-related homicides reported in Wales after 1999, the Father Paul case attracted the greatest degree of attention, across the media spectrum. From the *Sun* (2007a) – 'Bible Nut Killer' – to the *Guardian* – 'Man charged with vicar's murder' (2007) – every national newspaper in the United Kingdom carried extensive accounts of what had taken place. The contrast between good and evil was a prominent theme of all reports – a man who 'spent his whole life putting the feelings of others ahead of his own' (*Sun*, 2007b) counterpoised with an attacker 'obsessed with Satanism' (*Daily Mail*, 2007a) – as was the sense of violation in a place of sanctity – 'Priest Stabbed to Death in Front of Family at Vicarage' (*Times*, 2007). The distress and difficulty for Father Paul's family continued to attract media attention well beyond the immediate events themselves, and the homicide became swept up in attempts, in some parts of the newspaper world in particular, to forge a narrative of 'broken Britain'. 'Another day, another wave of knife crime', said the *Daily Mail* (2007b), ever anxious to feed public anxiety over knife crime amongst young men, a fear which it had played a prominent role in creating, and which peaked in the first half of 2008 (Squires, 2009, pp. 127–8). Quite certainly, the Father Paul case and the other instances reported here captured headlines far outside Wales.

DID SCANDAL MATTER IN THE POST DEVOLUTION PERIOD?

The previous section has demonstrated that, since 1999, Wales has not seen any significant diminution in scandals associated with homicides by individuals suffering from mental ill-health. Did this have an impact on policy-making, consistent with the impact produced by similar events in the years leading up to devolution? The answer appears to be that it did not. The focus on mental health services at the National Assembly did not diminish in the second half of its first decade. A very lively debate surrounded the call for a separate Mental Health Trust for Wales (Williams, 2008), during the structural reforms of the *One Wales* administration after 2007, before the then-Health Minister Edwina Hart concluded that 'normalization' would be better served by including responsibility for such services within the remit of the seven newly integrated LHBs which came into being on 1 October 2009.

Following the 2006 Government of Wales Act the Assembly was able, in certain circumstances, to draw power down from Westminster to make primary legislation in Wales. The first ever use of such powers by a backbencher focused on mental health, with the Mental Health (Wales) Measure making its way to the statute book in 2010. Its four main parts aimed to: ensure that more mental health services were available within primary care; provide all patients in secondary services with a Care and Treatment Plan; enable all adults discharged from secondary services to refer themselves back to those services; and support every in-patient to have help from an independent mental health advocate if wanted (Welsh Government, 2012b). Passed into law with strong all-party support and considerable assistance from the Welsh Government, the Measure showed no signs of being influenced by scandal to shift policy in a more authoritarian direction. Indeed, the Chief Medical Office of the period, Dr Tony Jewell, regularly emphasised the rarity of mental-health linked homicides. In response to the findings of the review into the Father Paul homicide of 2007, for example, he said 'I would like to assure people that those living with mental health conditions remain more likely to be the victims of harm, than the perpetrators' (WAG, 2009b).

Together for Mental Health, the most recent mental health strategy referred to in the opening section of this paper, aims to address issues relating to the assessment of mental health and the treatment of mental disorders, as well as providing additional support to service users through independent specialist mental health advocacy. The primary objective of the strategy, according to the Welsh Government, is to 'improve attitudes towards mental health, reducing stigma and discrimination' (Welsh Government, 2012c).

CONCLUSION

How can the relative lack of impact of scandal on policy in Wales best be explained? To begin with, it is important to be aware of the dynamics of scandal itself (see Butler and Drakeford, 2005 for a fuller account of these processes). Scandals operate to a media beat, in which a gathering tide results in a fierce beating on the shore of policy-making, before public interest begins to recede. Simple repetition of events previously found, in themselves, to be scandalous now quickly loses impact. The rash of hospital inquiries which followed Ely met exactly this fate. Media reporting leads to scandal-inflation, in which events have to be outrageous or disturbing in order to merit attention; and even then with diminishing force on both public opinion and policy-making. By the time devolution came into being, the scandal tsunami of the mid-1990s had already passed its peak. While scandal remained a regular feature of the mental health landscape in Wales in the decade which followed, its ability to exercise an impact on policy-making was in decline.

It is also the case, we would argue, that the basic conditions for generating scandal in the mental health field had diminished in Wales in the period just before and after devolution. In this context, some important distinctions can be made between circumstances in Wales and England. Following Cairney (2008), for example, it can be suggested that mental health policy in the post 1997 period was driven by two scandal-fuelled policy problems in England, of which only one existed in Wales. English policy makers, and their counterparts in Wales, faced the problem of effective care in the community and the impact of scandals (such as that involving Christopher Clunis) where patients became dangerous following a lapse in treatment compliance. In England, however, they also had to deal with new media attention focused upon a group of patients for whom no effective treatment – within hospital or beyond it – appeared to be available. The 1996 case of Michael Stone, involving the death of Lin Russell and her six-year-old daughter Megan, threw into sharp relief the 1983 Mental Health Act's 'treatability' test, which meant that only patients whose conditions were considered treatable could be detained. Cases of 'personality disorder', such as that of Michael Stone, were deemed untreatable, and so beyond the scope of the Act. Addressing this issue meant that, in England, mental health had become associated with crime and public safety, rather than the previously dominant paradigm of strengthening the rights of patients of mental health services. This strand ran far less powerfully in Welsh debates, chiefly as a result of the absence of Home Office responsibilities in the Welsh devolution settlement. In England, in the post-Michael Stone period, 'the Home Office became a major player in the development of new mental health legislation' (Cairney, 2007). In Wales, the clear separation of 'health' and 'justice' made it easier for Welsh interest to concentrate on issues of care and treatment. Put simply, the scope for scandal was narrower in Wales, as a result.

Within this small space, though, a number of characteristics existed, in the particular circumstances of Wales in the first decade of the present century, which also helped create a context which was inimical to the generation of scandal. Some have argued, for example, that a 'honeymoon period' (Cairney, 2007, p. 14) existed in the earliest days of devolution in which the space for scandal generation was diminished. Others have suggested (see, for example, Greer, 2004; 2005) that policy conditions in Wales have narrowed the possibilities for scandal, by drawing potential opponents in the health field into the policy-making process. The small number of key individuals involved in any policy area, their geographical proximity and their access to ministers and key civil servants all combine to diminish the dissenting voices through which claims to scandal can be generated. If Wales has a different set of policy conditions, then it has also been argued (see Cairney, 2008) that devolution brought with it a new policy *style* which applied in the field of mental health, and placed further limits on the scope for scandal. Quite certainly, the National Assembly was established with a set of claims to a 'new politics' (McAllister, 2000) in which inclusivity and widened participation were to be the hallmark of the emerging institution. The first Government of Wales Act, in 1998, constituted the Assembly as a 'corporate body', in which the demarcation between 'government' and 'parliament' was deliberately blurred. Formal consultation with local government, the voluntary sector and wider economic interests were formalised in three statutory 'partnership councils' (see Chaney, 2003). The closeness of key actors and organizations, in the post-devolution period, may thus have squeezed down the space in which scandal could have taken root.

The result has been that, in Wales, the emphasis since 1999 has been on providing mental health services which meet the needs of the vast majority of users, rather than designed around exceptional, but high profile cases. In that sense, the basic policy disposition since devolution has been different. To an extent this can be explained by the wider set of principles which have guided social and health policy making over this period (see Chaney and Drakeford, 2004; Sullivan, 2004; Drakeford, 2012). However, it is also a position buttressed and promoted by a strong third sector which has, from the start, operated on a partnership basis with the Welsh Government, with 'close consultation between civil servants and voluntary groups such as MIND' (Cairney, 2008, p. 363). As discussed earlier in this paper, mental health received very early attention in the life of the first Assembly. Health Minister, Jane Hutt, in providing a Foreword to *Adult Mental Health Services for Wales* (National Assembly for Wales, 2001) highlighted this theme:

> The process of consultation was as open and inclusive as we could make it and provoked the most wide-ranging debate ever in Wales on mental health. This has ensured a balanced approach, with the contribution of the voluntary sector, users and carers fully recognised alongside the work of the NHS and local government.

Ultimately, it is this sense of cross-party and cross-sector unity which has been effective in influencing mental health policy and service provision in Wales. Together it has, so far, succeeded in providing a bulwark against the onslaught of scandal which, in other eras and in other places, has proved to be so hard to resist.

NOTES

[1] Inquiry reports by Health Inspectorate Wales (HIW) adopt a convention of referring to those caught up in homicides by a single initial of the alphabet, usually unrelated to the names of those involved. The effort to secure anonymity or confidentiality is very largely compromised by newspaper reporting of all these cases where actual names, addresses and much other material is readily accessible through the use of internet search engines. Nevertheless, in this paper, we adhere to the HIW formalities, in line with material cited.

[2] Healthcare Inspectorate Wales was established on 1 April 2004, under the Health and Social Care (Community Health and Standards) Act 2003. The National Assembly for Wales, with the assent of this Act, gained 'powers to inspect and undertake investigations into the provision of NHS funded care either by or for Welsh NHS organisations' (HIW, 2005, p. 4). As of January 2007, independent external reviews became the task of Healthcare Inspectorate Wales (HIW, 2011, p. 1).

REFERENCES

Birmingham Post (2009). 'Family of mum stabbed by son criticises his supervision', October 6.

Boardman, J. (2005). 'New services for old – an overview of mental health policy', in Sainsbury Centre for Mental Health *Beyond the Water Towers*, London: Sainsbury Centre for Mental Health.

Brown, A. D. (2004). 'Authoritative sensemaking in a public inquiry report' *Organization Studies*, 25, 1, 95–112.

Butler, I. and Drakeford, M. (2005). *Scandal, Social Policy and Social Welfare*, Bristol: Policy Press.

Cairney, P. (2007). 'Policy styles, devolution and mental health in Britain: beyond the headlines', PAC Conference, Belfast, September.

Cairney, P. (2008). 'Has devolution changed the 'British policy style'?', *British Politics*, 3, 350–72.

Carmarthen Journal (2009). 'Mentally ill son killed mum', October 7.

Chaney, P. (2003). 'Social capital and the participation of marginalized groups in government: a study of the statutory partnership between the third sector and devolved government in Wales', *Public Policy and Administration*, 17, 4, 22–39.

Chaney, P. and Drakeford, M. (2004). 'The primacy of ideology: social policy and the first term of the National Assembly for Wales', in N. Ellison, L. Bauld and M. Powell (eds), *Social Policy Review 16*, Bristol: Policy Press.

Daily Mail (2007a). 'Cannabis maniac hacked vicar to death in graveyard', October 17.

Daily Mail (2007b). 'Another day, another wave of knife crimes', March 19.

Daily Mirror (1997). 'Stab frenzy lover jailed', 22 January.

Daily Mirror (2009). 'Son killed mum after smoke ban', October 6.

Daily Post (2009). 'Family of mentally ill killer slams NHS', October 6.

Department of Health (1994). *Guidance on the Discharge of Mentally Disordered People and their Continuing Care in the Community*, HSE (94) 27. London: Department of Health.

Department of Health (1997). 'Plans for psychiatric hospital closures to be vetted by new group', *Press Release*, 97/222.

Department of Health (1998). 'Frank Dobson outlines the third way for mental health', *Press Release*, 29 July.

Department of Health and Social Security (1988). *Report of the Committee of Inquiry into the Care and After Care of Sharon Campbell*, London: HMSO.

Drakeford, M. (2012). 'Wales in the age of austerity', *Critical Social Policy*, 32, 3, 454–66.

Express (2005). 'Pensioner stabbed to death at checkout', October 20.

Fawcett, B. and Karban, K. (2005). *Contemporary Mental Health: Theory, Policy and Practice*, New York: Routledge.

Goodwin, S. (1989). 'Community care for the mentally ill in England and Wales: myths, assumptions and reality', *Journal of Social Policy*, 18, 1, 27–52.

Greer, S. L. (2004). *Territorial Politics and Health Policy*, Manchester: Manchester University Press.

Greer, S. L. (2005). 'The territorial bases of health policymaking in the UK after devolution', *Regional and Federal Studies*, 15, 4, 501–18.

Guardian (2007). 'Man charged with vicar's murder', March 16.

Hafal (2006). *The Mental Health National Service Framework, http://www.mentalhealth wales.net/mhw/framework_wales.php* (accessed 21 December 2012).

Hafal (2012). *What's in Wales' New Mental Health Strategy?, http://www.hafal.org/hafal/news.php?id=298* (accessed 30 October 2012).

Healthcare Inspectorate Wales (2005). *Annual Report 2004–05: Supporting improvement through Inspection and Review, http://www.hiw.org.uk/Documents/477/Healthcare%20 Inspectorate%20Wales%20Annual%20Report%202004-05.pdf* (accessed 17 October 2012).

Healthcare Inspectorate Wales (2008). *Report of a Review in Respect of Ms A and the Provision of Mental Health Services, Following a Homicide Committed in October 2005*, Caerphilly: Healthcare Inspectorate Wales.

Healthcare Inspectorate Wales (2009). *Report of a Review in Respect of Mr D and the Provision of Mental Health Services, Following the Homicide of Father Paul Committed in March 2007and the Ambulance Response and Care Provided to Father Paul's Family and Local Community*, Caerphilly: Healthcare Inspectorate Wales.

Healthcare Inspectorate Wales (2011). *Report of a Review in Respect of Mr G and the Provision of Mental Health Services, Following a Homicide Committed in May 2009*, Caerphilly: Healthcare Inspectorate Wales.

Hendy, J. (2010). 'The victims in Wales' *Hundred Families Website, http://hundred families.org/TheVictims/wales.htm* (accessed 17 October 2012).

Hutt, J. (1999). 'Answers to questions not reached in plenary' *National Assembly for Wales Record of Proceedings*, 14 July, *http://www.assemblywales.org/bus-home/bus-first-assembly/bus-chamber-first-assembly/bus-chamber-first-assembly-rop.htm?act= dis&id=9056&ds=//1999* (accessed 31 October 2012).

Independent (1997). 'Mental patients commit a murder every two weeks', October 13.

Korman, N. and Glennerster, H. (1990). *Hospital Closure: A Political and Economic Study*, Milton Keynes: Open University Press.

Maden, A. (2007). *Treating Violence: A Guide to Risk Management in Mental Health*, Oxford: Oxford University Press.

McAllister, L. (2000). 'The new politics in Wales: rhetoric or reality?', *Parliamentary Affairs*, 53, 3, 591–604.

Morrall, P. (2005). 'Mental health policy in England: chaos and control!', *NI Ethics Forum 2005*, 2, 26–37, *http://www.qub.ac.uk/methics/MorrallP.pdf* (accessed 20 December 2012).

Muijen, M. (1995). 'Scare in the community: Britain in moral panic', *Community Care*, 7–13, September.

National Assembly for Wales (2000). *Putting Wales First: A Partnership for the People of Wales,* Cardiff: National Assembly for Wales.

National Assembly for Wales (2001). *Adult Mental Health Services for Wales: Equity, Empowerment, Effectiveness, Efficiency. A Strategy Document* (online), available at: *http://www.wales.nhs.uk/publications/adult-health-e.pdf* (accessed 25 October 2012).

Payne, S. (1999). 'Dangerous and different: reconstructions of madness in the 1990s and the role of mental health policy', in S. Watson, L. Doyle (eds.), *Engendering Social Policy*, Buckingham: Open University Press.

Porter, R. (1996). 'Two cheers for psychiatry! The social history of mental disorder in twentieth-century Britain', in H. Freeman and G. E. Berrios (eds), *150 Years of British Psychiatry, Volume II: The Aftermath*, London: Athlone.

Ritchie, J. (1994). *Report of the Inquiry into the Care and Treatment of Christopher Clunis*. London: HMSO.

Rose, D. (1997). 'Trial by television', *Community Care*, 4–10 December, 30–1.

South Wales Argus (2007) .'Mentally ill man detained indefinitely', December 21.

South Wales Echo (2005). 'Draft Bill criticised', April 8.

Sullivan, M. (2004). 'Wales, devolution and health policy: policy experimentation and differentiation to improve health', *Contemporary Wales, 17*, 44–65.

Spectator (1994). 'Carnage in the community', 7 May.

Squires, P. (2009). 'The knife "epidemic" and British politics', *British Politics*, 4, 1, 127-57.

Sun (1996). 'Lovers' bloodbath – Doc's daughter and secret toyboy knifed to death in their love nest', May 3.

Sun (2007a). 'Bible nut killer', March 16.

Sun (2007b). 'Defiance of Rev "killer"', March 17.

Thomas, P., Wilson, C. and Jones, P. (2010). 'Strengthening the voice of mental health service users and carers in Wales: a focus group study to inform future policy', *International Journal of Consumer Studies*, 34, 525–31.

Tidmarsh, D. (1997). 'Psychiatric risk, safety cultures and homicide inquiries', *Journal of Forensic Psychiatry*, 8, 1, 138–51.

Times (1993). 'Wife seeks enquiry into killer's release', June 29.

Times (1997). 'Mental patients "have killed 104"', October 13.

Times (2004). 'Mental health bill to disappear', June 15.

Times (2005). 'Shopper stabbed to death at checkout', October 20.

Times (2007). 'Priest stabbed to death in front of family at vicarage', March 15.

University of Manchester (2012). 'The national confidential inquiry into suicide and homicide by people with mental illness', *http://www.medicine.manchester.ac.uk/cmhr/centreforsuicideprevention/nci/reports/annual_report_2012.pdf* (accessed 1 October 2012).

Welsh Assembly Government (2004). *Stronger in Partnership. Involving Service Users and Carers in the Design, Planning, Delivery and Evaluation of Mental Health Services in Wales. Policy Implementation Guidance*, Cardiff: WAG.

Welsh Assembly Government (2009a). *Citizens First Wales: Improving Public Service Delivery. Findings from the 2006 Living in Wales Survey into Citizens' Views of Public Services Part 1: Social Services for Carers, http://new.wales.gov.uk/dpsp/research/people/liwresults06/social.pdf?lang=en* (accessed 11 October 2012).

Welsh Assembly Government (2009b). *Welsh Assembly Government Responds to Independent Review of Father Paul Bennett Homicide, http://new.wales.gov.uk/newsroom/healthandsocialcare/2009/091127homicide/?lang=en* (accessed 11 October 2012).

Welsh Government (2012a). *Together for Mental Health, http://wales.gov.uk/docs/dhss/ publications/121022deliveryen.pdf* (accessed 15 October 2012).

Welsh Government (2012b). *Mental Health (Wales) Measure, http://wales.gov.uk/topics/ health/nhswales/healthservice/mentalhealthservices/measure/?lang=en* (accessed 11 October 2012).

Welsh Government (2012c). *Press Notice: Together for Mental Health, http://wales.gov. uk/newsroom/healthandsocialcare/2012/121022mhs/?lang=en* (accessed 25 October 2012).

Western Mail (2002). 'Assembly joins protests over mental health bill', September 12.

Williams, C. (2008). 'Welsh government considers case for single mental health body', *Community Care*, June 6.

8. CREATING AN INCLUSIVE HIGHER EDUCATION SYSTEM? PROGRESSION AND OUTCOMES OF STUDENTS FROM LOW PARTICIPATION NEIGHBOURHOODS AT A WELSH UNIVERSITY

Chris Taylor, Gareth Rees, Luke Sloan and Rhys Davies

ABSTRACT

Widening participation has been one of the most significant and widely debated features of the UK Higher Education policy landscape in the past few years. The dominant approach to this in both England and Wales has been to try and recruit 'new' undergraduate students from areas that have traditionally had low levels of participation. Although there has been research that has examined the access and participation of non-traditional students to university, there has been very little attention given to the progress and outcomes of such students once they are in university. Drawing upon several years of students' data in one Welsh university, this paper explores the association between coming from a 'low participation neighbourhood' and a range of undergraduate outcomes, including withdrawal and degree classifications. Once other factors, such as prior attainment and social class, have been taken into account, we find no significant 'effect' on the progress of students who come from such areas. However, in undertaking this analysis, we also highlight the ecological fallacy of using 'low participation neighbourhoods' in widening participation policies and practices. This is important in assessing whether area-based approaches are a credible way of genuinely widening participation. But we also suggest that this may mitigate any association between non-traditional university students and their university progress and outcomes that we are able to identify.

INTRODUCTION

The role of higher education (HE) in Welsh society has been substantially defined in terms of ensuring that access is open to individuals from as wide a range of social backgrounds as possible. Certainly, the emergence of a modern HE system in Wales during the nineteenth and early twentieth centuries was associated popularly with notions of the essentially democratic and inclusive character of the institutions that were created. And, in reality, participation in the colleges of the University of Wales and the other HE institutions up until the middle of the twentieth century was *somewhat* more favourable towards women and those from lower middle-class and working-class backgrounds than was the case in other parts of the UK (Rees and Istance, 1997).

Of course, the dramatic expansion of HE in Wales – and across the UK – during the second half of the twentieth century and especially during its last decades has transformed the nature of the sector. Not only have the numbers of students in HE increased very significantly, but also this 'massification' of the universities has been associated with the major growth in rates of participation by women, as well as members of ethnic minorities and older-age adults, albeit on a lesser scale. However, changes in patterns of participation by individuals from less advantaged social backgrounds have been less dramatic. Simply expressed, the growing numbers of HE participants from working-class backgrounds have been more than matched by the increase in participation of those from middle-class backgrounds; with the result that the latter have pretty much maintained their advantage in access to HE. This is true of Wales, as well as the other countries of the UK, even if the extent of these inequalities is somewhat reduced here (Rees and Taylor, 2006; Tight, 2012).

Not surprisingly, therefore, strategies aimed at raising the levels of HE participation amongst individuals from less advantaged social backgrounds have remained at the core of HE policy in Wales, especially in a wider UK context of increasing student fees to pay for enlarged university provision. Moreover, parliamentary devolution since 1999 has created opportunities for the pursuit of strategies aimed at – what has come to be termed – 'widening participation' that are distinctive to Wales. Hence, for example, in terms that clearly echo those nineteenth-century, popular notions of a democratic and inclusive Welsh HE system, the Welsh Government – alone amongst the UK administrations – is currently committed to paying the extra costs to students arising from the abolition of the fees cap (allowing universities to charge fees of up to £9,000 per annum) (Gallacher and Raffe, 2012).

Perhaps less well known are the policies that have aimed *directly* to increase levels of participation in HE amongst individuals from less advantaged social backgrounds. Hence, the Higher Education Funding Council for Wales (HEFCW) has used its funding of the universities to raise levels of participation (by 10 per cent between 2008–9 and 2012–13) from the most disadvantaged areas of Wales. These most disadvantaged areas are defined by the Communities First (CF) designation, which is intended to encompass the neighbourhoods in Wales that experience the worst social and economic conditions, as reflected, for example, in scores on the Welsh Index of Multiple Deprivation. HEFCW operate a premium payment to universities for students recruited from CF areas, and students from CF areas are a key part of the *Reaching Wider* initiative in Wales (HEFCW, 2010). In addition, these strategies have, in the past, targeted students whose disadvantage is indicated not only by their financial circumstances, but also critical social characteristics, such as disability, ethnic background and being brought up in care, although this has now been superseded by an exclusive focus on the Communities First areas (HEFCW, 2010).

As with the Welsh Government's policy on student fees, this approach to raising levels of participation amongst those from less advantaged social backgrounds is distinctive. For example, in England, the areas receiving priority are defined in terms of their having historically low rates of participation in HE. Hence, the Higher Education Funding Council for England (HEFCE) uses a classification of local areas in terms of levels of participation in HE, known as POLAR, Participation of Local Areas (HEFCE, 2007). What this indicates, therefore, is that strategy in England is aimed at assisting universities in the recruitment of 'first generation' students in order to 'widen' HE participation. In Wales, on the other hand, the strategy has been to encourage participation from areas of socio-economic disadvantage. Of course, there is inevitably substantial overlap between these two approaches. However, as we shall see later, in practice, they can refer to very different neighbourhoods, and hence the kinds of 'new' students they seek to attract.

It is instructive, however, that despite their differences, both Wales and England have adopted *area-based* strategies to widening participation in identifying, in slightly different ways, what we might term low participation neighbourhoods (LPNs). Area-based approaches in education policy are not uncommon in attempting to address educational inequalities. However, doubts about the appropriateness and analytical underpinnings of such approaches have been expressed repeatedly (Gewirtz et al., 2005; Batey and Brown, 2007; Rees et al., 2007). Indeed, specific concerns about this approach in the HE sector have been raised too. The critical issue here has been the extent to which designating *areas* for special treatment is effective in identifying the *individuals* who need support in order to enter HE. As a result, most research has tended to focus on recruitment and participation (Blicharski, 2000; Osborne and Shuttleworth, 2004; Harrison and Hatt, 2009).

However, there has been considerably less attention paid to how well students from less advantaged backgrounds do once they are at university. Having gained entry, how do they cope with the undoubted demands and pressures of university life? Some studies have suggested that individuals from less advantaged backgrounds find it difficult to adjust to what they experience as the alien cultural milieu of the university. Other research, however, reports that students from such backgrounds perform disproportionately well, as their greater levels of commitment to their studies provide the basis for especially strong outcomes (Hatt et al., 2003; Harrison et al., 2007; and Crozier et al., 2008).

In what follows, we try to contribute to this debate. We do so on the basis of an analysis of a quantitative data-set relating to a relatively large number of students, albeit at only one Welsh university. Most previous studies of student progression and outcomes have depended on qualitative data, providing a rich picture of how HE is experienced by different groups of students. Our focus here is on identifying *patterns* in the relationships between residence in a neighbourhood prioritized for widening participation and progress and out-comes at university; and a large-scale data-set is necessary to achieve this. Of course, both types of study are a necessary part of constructing a rounded overall analysis and thereby providing a robust basis for the development of policy.

Accordingly, in this paper, we aim to provide a systematic analysis of the progression and outcomes of undergraduate students from LPNs attending one Welsh university. Unlike most other studies of university outcomes, we are interested in a range of measures of progress throughout the – typically – three years of an undergraduate course. Moreover, it is important to consider the wide range of factors that can potentially exert an influence on students' progress and outcomes. From previous studies, a number of key influences have been identified as determinants of progression and outcomes in HE. These include prior educational attainment, gender, age and ethnicity (for example, Hoskins et al., 1997). More recently, the relationship between the type of school students previously attended and their university outcomes has also been identified (for example, Smith and Naylor, 2005; Hoare and Johnston, 2010). Therefore, the analysis presented here provides a more sophisticated and hence more robust examination of the progress and outcomes of students from LPN, by considering the *relative* influence of many of these other key determinants, as well as the specific influence of what kind of neighbourhood students come from. We adopt the appropriate statistical methods to enable us to estimate the significance of these diverse factors.

METHODOLOGICAL APPROACH

Data
The main data source for this analysis is a set of undergraduate student records from one Welsh university for six years of entry (2005/06 to 2010/11). This includes administrative information about the students whilst at the university, linked to information from their original UCAS applications. Table 8.1 provides a summary of the number of years of data available for each cohort of entrants. So, for example, for students who enrolled in 2010/11, we do not have any outcome measures, as they had yet to complete their first year in university at the time that the research was completed. However, this cohort of under-graduate entrants is included in some of the descriptive analyses we present later. Conversely, Table 8.1 also illustrates that the data include three years of entrants (2005/6 to 2007/8) where we have information relating to their progress in their first, second and final years of their degree course.

Table 8.1
The student records

Year of Intake 2005/06	2006/07	2007/08	2008/09	2009/10	2010/11
YEAR 1	YEAR 1	YEAR 1	YEAR 1	YEAR 1	
YEAR 2	YEAR 2	YEAR 2	YEAR 2		
YEAR 3	YEAR 3	YEAR 3			

The data are very complex, and sourcing the variables used in the analysis is certainly not straightforward. Whilst there will always be some discrepancies in such educational data, we nevertheless expect that the analyses and modelling we have undertaken are robust enough, and are based on a sufficiently large number of records and students, to produce significant and valid findings.

Sample
The University admits approximately 7,000 undergraduate students per year (approximately 4,500 full-time students), of whom about a third are domiciled

in Wales. The analysis here includes all UK-domiciled undergraduate students who entered the University between 2005/06 and 2010/11, a total of 39,672 students. The University can be considered to be a 'selecting' university, in that applications far exceed the number of places available. It offers a wide range of degree subjects across the arts, humanities, social sciences, physical sciences and human sciences, including subjects allied to medicine.

Progression and outcomes: the dependent variables

In order to examine the progression and outcomes of students, we designed the analysis to utilize a broad suite of measures, ranging from a student's first year at the university right through to their graduation. Each measure reflects a different aspect of a student's performance whilst at university. For the purposes of this paper, we present findings based on six progress and outcome measures. These are summarized in Table 8.2, alongside an indication of the respective sample of data we can draw upon for each measure.

In our main statistical analyses and modelling, it is these outcomes that we are trying to understand in terms of the influence exerted on them by a range of student characteristics and other factors. We use these measures as the *dependent variables* and examine the impact of other factors, *the covariates*, on each of these measures separately.

Table 8.2
Measures of undergraduate progress and outcomes

Measure	Dependent Variable	Data
Student re-sat Year 1*	Year 1 Resit(s)	5 cohorts of students (2005–06 to 2009–10)
Student repeated Year 1*	Repeat Year 1	5 cohorts of students (2005 06 to 2009 10)
Student withdrew (any year of study)*	Withdrawn	5 cohorts of students (2005–06 to 2009–10)
Above University-wide median for average marks	Above Median Year 1 Average Marks	5 cohorts of students (2005–06 to 2009–10)
Above University-wide median for average combined marks at Year 2 and Year 3	Above Median Combined Year 2 and 3 Average Marks	3 cohorts of students (2005–06 to 2007–08)
Student achieved a First Class or Upper Second Degree	First or Upper Second Degree Classification	3 cohorts of students (2005–06 to 2007–08)

* These are 'flag' variables that simply identify whether a student had at least one occurrence of this characteristic. We do not identify the number of occurrences for these characteristics.

Low Participation Neighbourhoods (LPNs)
As has been outlined, our principal interest in this analysis is in the effect that living in an LPN has on a student's performance at university. The study university admits most of its undergraduate students from Wales and England. Therefore, there are two categories of LPNs that are relevant to this university's admissions. The first category of LPNs is Communities First (CF) areas. Communities First areas were initially designated as the 100 most deprived electoral divisions in Wales, according to the Welsh Index of Multiple Deprivation. This definition has subsequently been widened to include a more diffuse categorisation of social and economic disadvantage. Students from CF areas are those whose home postcode is located within these electoral divisions. The second category of LPNs is termed POLAR2 areas. These are based on the participation rates of young people (that is, under 21-years-old on starting their studies) from 2000 to 2004, and are those that fell within the lowest 20 per cent of wards ranked on their rates of young people's participation in HE across Great Britain (HEFCE, 2005).[1]

Owing to the similar focus, but different methodology of these categorizations, some LPNs can be identified as being both a CF area and a POLAR2 area (3.1 per cent of all students in the data); whilst some LPNs are categorized as either CF or POLAR2 (2.3 per cent and 4.7 per cent of all students respectively). Figure 8.1 illustrates the number and proportion of UK-domiciled students in the analysis that are from each of the following sets of LPNs: Communities First areas only; POLAR2 areas only; Communities First *and* POLAR2 areas.[2]

Figure 8.1
Distribution of sample students from Low Participation Neighbourhoods (LPNs)

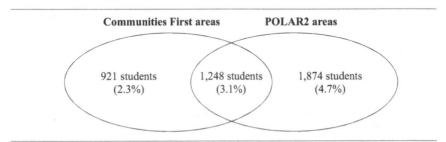

In total, 4,043 students were from LPNs (10.2 per cent of UK-domiciled students), 2,969 of whom were domiciled in Wales (Table 8.3). Of the 1,874 students from POLAR2-only areas, 800 were from Wales, making a total of 2,048 Wales-domiciled students from POLAR2 classified neighbourhoods.

Students domiciled in Wales were more than three times as likely to come from LPNs than UK students domiciled outside Wales (16.6 per cent compared to 4.9 per cent), reflecting the importance (and distinction) of CF neighbourhoods in this measure. However, Wales-domiciled students were still more than twice as likely to come from POLAR2 neighbourhoods (11.5 per cent of Wales-domiciled students compared to 4.9 per cent of other UK-domiciled students).

Table 8.3
Students from Low Participation Neighbourhoods (LPNs) by country of domicile

Domicile	CF only	POLAR2 only	CF and POLAR2	Total LPN Number	% (by domicile)	% (by total LPN)
Wales	921	800	1,248	2,969	16.6	73.4
Rest of UK	0	1,074	0	1,074	4.9	26.6
TOTAL UK	921	1,874	1,248	4,043	10.2	100

Prior attainment of students

The prior educational attainment of students is probably the most important factor in determining any of the outcome measures identified above (for example, Gorard, 2008). It is, therefore, essential that any examination of the differential outcomes of particular groups of students must take into account their prior attainment.

Traditional analyses of the progress and outcomes of students in universities use A Level UCAS tariff points as the main measure of prior attainment, with A* grade attracting 140 points and E grade 40 points. This allows comparisons to be made based on the number of A Levels undertaken or the points score of the highest three A Levels. A major consequence of this approach is that students with other qualifications ('non-standard qualifications') are often removed from the analysis (see, for example, Hoare and Johnston, 2010). However, because the present analysis is primarily interested in the participation of students who are from traditionally low participating neighbourhoods, it is important that students with 'non-standard qualifications' are included. Therefore, our preferred measure of prior attainment here is a student's total UCAS tariff score, using the UCAS standard tariff scores for all qualifications.

The main limitation of this is that we are unable to control for the number of qualifications that a student has. Students with more qualifications will generally have higher total UCAS points scores, despite perhaps not having the equivalent grades to students with fewer qualifications. It is also argued that some qualifications appear to have an 'inflated' UCAS tariff (for example, the Welsh

Baccalaureate Advanced Core Qualification (Taylor et al., 2011)). Nevertheless, there does not appear to be any way of controlling for these issues without removing students with 'non-standard qualifications', counter to the focus of our analysis here.

Other student characteristics

Alongside a measure of prior attainment, we are also interested to see what influence other student characteristics have on their progress and outcomes. The additional covariates we include in the analysis are:

- Year of entry – six years of entry 2005/06 to 2010/11
- Age at entry – continuous variable in years
- Gender – male or female
- Ethnicity – aggregated to White, non-White and not known
- Type of school last attended – comprehensive; college; grammar; independent; or not known
- Socio-economic classification – seven classification types, aggregated to: middle class – higher managerial and professional occupations, lower managerial and professional occupations, and intermediate occupations; and working class – small employers and own account workers, lower supervisory and technical occupations, semi-routine occupations, routine occupations; and not known (which can include unemployed or never worked)
- Disability – aggregated to known disability or no known disability
- Domicile – Wales, England and the rest of the UK.

STUDENTS FROM LOW PARTICIPATION NEIGHBOURHOODS: KEY CHARACTERISTICS

A useful starting point for our analysis is to provide a descriptive account of the undergraduate student characteristics of those from LPNs, noting where appropriate the differences between those from CF and those from POLAR2 neighbourhoods.

The first thing to note is that the proportion of UK-domiciled students from LPNs has been declining slightly over the last six years in this particular university (Figure 8.2) and this appears to be largely due to the falling proportion of students from Communities First areas. Interestingly, female students are slightly more likely to come from LPNs (11 per cent of females compared with 9 per cent of male students) irrespective of the category of LPN they come from (although there are more female students than male ones in the University as a whole).

Figure 8.2
Percentage of UK-domiciled students from LPNs by year of entry

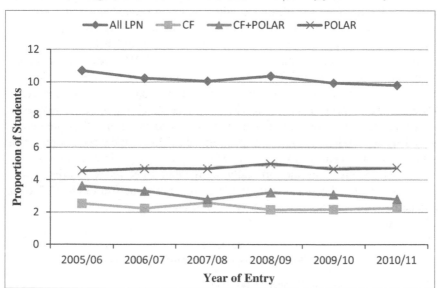

It comes as no surprise that students from LPNs were far more likely to come from working-class households than middle-class households (14.5 per cent compared to 6.8 per cent – see Table 8.4). However, it *is* perhaps surprising that 38.4 per cent of students from all LPNs were from middle-class households, 24.3 per cent from working-class households and 37.2 per cent from households with no known social class (see Harrison and Hatt (2009) for a

Table 8.4
Social class background of students from LPNs

Low Participation	Percentage of Students by Social Class (%)		
Neighbourhood	Working Class	Middle Class	Unknown Social Class
CF only	3.5	1.6	3.2
CF and POLAR2	4	1.7	5.8
POLAR2	7	3.5	5.9
All LPN	14.5	6.8	15
% of LPN	*24.3*	*38.4*	*37.2*
Total number	*6,805*	*22,803*	*10,064*

discussion of the 'unknowns'). Although low participation is not exclusively a concern of working-class families, this does suggest that the *average* scores for LPNs are hiding some significant variations within the neighbourhood. Certainly, we should not assume that every individual from an LPN is disadvantaged in terms of entry to HE; and this applies to both categories of LPN.

In a similar vein, the majority of students from LPNs previously attended comprehensive schools (47.7 per cent) or colleges (42.5 per cent) (Table 8.5). Students from colleges were the most likely to be from LPNs (14.0 per cent), followed by students from comprehensive schools (8.8 per cent). However, interestingly, a small but significant number of students from LPNs previously attended independent schools (6.0 per cent of all LPN students) and grammar schools (3.8 per cent of all LPN students); again perhaps indicating a greater social heterogeneity in the officially designated LPN areas. Students who previously attended colleges were twice as likely to come from POLAR2 areas compared with students from other types of schools.

Table 8.5
Type of last school attended by students from LPNs

| LPN | Students by Social Class (%) | | | |
	Comprehensive	College	Independent	Grammar
CF only	2.7	2.6	0.3	0
CF and POLAR2	2.5	4.2	0.4	0
POLAR2	3.7	7.3	2.7	4.1
All LPN	8.8	14	3.5	4.1
% of LPN	47.7	42.7	6	3.8
Total number	*16,663*	*9,333*	*5,326*	*2,865*

More predictably, given the size and geographical distribution of ethnic minorities in Wales, the vast majority of students from LPNs were White (85.9 per cent of LPN students). However, Non-White students were more likely to come from LPNs (14.1 per cent compared to 9.8 per cent of White students and 11.7 per cent of students with ethnicity unknown). This difference in ethnic background was greater for students from POLAR2 areas (particularly outside Wales) than it was for students from CF areas. There was very little difference in the likelihood that students from LPNs had a disability or not (10.5 per cent of students with a disability were from a LPN compared to 10.2 per cent of students without a disability).

Welsh-speaking students were slightly more likely to come from an LPN than non-Welsh speakers (12.2 per cent compared to 10.2 per cent). However, Welsh speakers were more than twice as likely as non-Welsh speakers to come from a CF-only area (5.4 per cent compared to 2.3 per cent). But non-Welsh speakers were more likely to come from a POLAR2-only area (4.7 per cent compared to 3.1 per cent), much of which is due to students from outside Wales.

In terms of the key factor of previous educational attainment, Figure 8.3 shows that students from LPNs had, on average, only slightly lower UCAS tariff points than students from non-LPN areas. For example, students from CF-only areas had, on average, a UCAS tariff of 359 points, compared to an average UCAS tariff of 367 points for students from non-LPN areas. However, this difference of eight UCAS tariff points in this comparison is the equivalent of less than half a grade in one A Level and may therefore be regarded as relatively insignificant. There was very little difference between the UCAS tariff scores of students from CF and POLAR2 areas. Figure 8.3 does suggest, however, that students from areas that are classified as CF *and* POLAR2 had, on average, the lowest levels of prior attainment (as measured here) – a difference of 24 tariff points compared with students from non-LPN areas. This is a difference of at least one whole grade in an A Level. Nevertheless, Figure 8.3 also illustrates the wide variation in UCAS tariff scores within each category of students, as measured by one standard deviation either side of the average.

Figure 8.3
Average total UCAS tariff by Low Participation Neighbourhood
(with +/- 1.0 standard deviation)

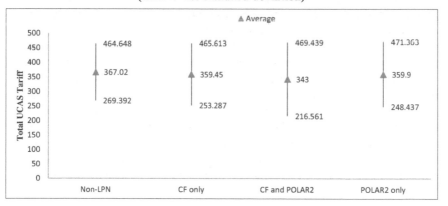

We do not have data on the subjects which make up these levels of prior educational attainment. However, it is perhaps instructive that more UK-domiciled students from LPNs studied non-STEM subjects (39.9 per cent compared to 23.6 per cent studying STEM subjects) (Table 8.6). However, students studying STEM and Professional Medical subjects were slightly more likely to come from LPNs (9.3 per cent and 14.6 per cent respectively, compared to 8.4 per cent of students studying non-STEM subjects). This trend is similar for students from CF areas and POLAR2 areas.

Table 8.6
Subject centre of students from LPNs

LPN	Students by Subject (%)		
	Non-STEM[a]	STEM[a]	Professional Medical
CF only	1.9	2.2	3.3
CF and POLAR2	2.2	2.3	5.8
POLAR2	4.3	4.8	5.5
All LPN	8.4	9.3	14.6
Non-LPN	91.6	90.7	85.4
Total number of LPN	19,279	10,232	10,069

a – Science, Technology, Engineering and Mathematics (STEM).

This descriptive account of students from LPNs raises some interesting issues. Firstly, the evidence on students' social-class backgrounds and the type of school or college that they previously attended suggests that there is much greater social heterogeneity in LPNs than might be imagined. Clearly, not all *individuals* from LPNs come from significantly disadvantaged backgrounds, whatever the average level of social disadvantage in their *neighbourhoods*. This poses important questions in regard to the use of geographical areas as the basis for widening participation strategies. Secondly, it is instructive that levels of prior educational attainment (at least as measured here) appear to be broadly equivalent between students from LPNs and those from other sorts of area. Given that it is well established that overall levels of educational attainment in LPNs are substantially lower than in other areas, this indicates that whatever widening of participation that is taking place at the study university, those students are able to achieve relatively high levels of education attainment, in spite of their coming from LPNs.

PROGRESSION AND OUTCOMES: AN INITIAL ANALYSIS

We can extend our descriptive analysis of students from LPNs to consider their progress whilst at university and the outcomes they achieve in their degrees. Hence, Table 8.7 indicates that students from LPNs generally appear to progress slightly less well at this university and are less likely to secure favourable degree results than other UK-domiciled students. For example, whilst 71.9 per cent of non-LPN students achieved either a First Class or Upper Second Class degree, only 62.1 per cent of students from LPNs were awarded these degree results. Similarly, 51.8 per cent of non-LPN students achieved an average Year 1 mark above the university median compared with only 42.8 per cent of students from LPNs. However, the contrast between non-LPN and LPN students is less pronounced in the likelihood of a student repeating Year 1 (2.2 per cent and 2.9 per cent respectively) and in whether they had withdrawn (5.1 per cent and 6.3 per cent respectively). Indeed, there are almost no differences as to whether they had at least one resit in Year 1 or not.

Table 8.7
Progress and outcomes of students from Low Participation Neighbourhoods

Outcome	CF only	CF and POLAR2	POLAR2 only	All LPN	Non-LPN	Total number
Resit (2) Year 1	13	10.9	11.9	11.7	11.8	4,637
Repeat year 1	2.8	2.9	2.9	2.9	2.2	116
Withdrawn	5.8	6.7	6.2	6.3	5.1	2,068
High Year 1 average[a]	40.6	35.4	48.3	42.8	51.9	11,074
High Year 2/3 combined average[a]	40.8	28.1	48.2	40.6	51.8	4,904
Good degree[b]	55.1	55.3	70	62.1	71.9	8,097

a – above University median.
b – First or Upper Second degree classification.

There are, however, some variations between the different types of LPN. Generally, students from POLAR2-only areas achieved better outcomes at the study university than students from CF-only areas (less likely to have resit(s) in Year 1, more likely to achieve above the university-median average marks, and more likely be awarded a First or Upper Second Class degree). But there was very little difference between students from CF-only and POLAR2-only areas in terms of whether they had withdrawn or had to repeat their first year. Perhaps most interestingly, it was also the case that students from areas that were classified as CF *and* POLAR2 areas, reflecting the most disadvantaged areas (socio-economically and with the lowest rates of participation in HE), were the most likely to be amongst the lowest achieving students in the University.

These patterns of student progression and the outcomes they achieve are, in very broad terms, consistent with previous studies which have emphasised the difficulties that students from disadvantaged – or working-class more widely – backgrounds experience in coping with the demands of university-level work and of the cultural environment more generally (especially at a 'selecting' university of the kind studied here) (for example, Marris, 1964; Crozier et al., 2008). However, it is important to note that our descriptive analyses do not provide a very detailed account of the nature of the relationships between LPN and university progress and outcomes. Hence, it is unclear whether the performance of students from LPNs is simply associated with where students come from or to other characteristics that the students share. For example, it may be that LPN students have other characteristics in common, such as their level of their prior attainment, the type of school they attended, or their gender or ethnic background, which could account for their progression and outcomes. Only by statistically modelling the influence of a range of factors can this be investigated.

MODELLING THE PROGRESS AND OUTCOMES OF STUDENTS FROM LOW PARTICIPATION NEIGHBOURHOODS

In order to explore the relationships between the progress and outcomes of undergraduate students and a *range* of factors, we developed a series of models, one for each progress and outcome measure (see Table 8.2 above), using binary logistic regression. This statistical technique enables us to estimate the contribution that various student characteristics and prior educational attainment make in determining the probability of different progression and outcome measures occurring. In particular, we are able to examine whether students from LPNs were more or less likely (or the same) than students with the same characteristics, but who did not come from Low Participation Neighbourhoods, to 'succeed' at the study university.

Binary logistic regression is used to identify variables or characteristics among the student samples that appear to be *important* in predicting the progression and outcome measures listed above (Table 8.2). In similar fashion to Hoare and Johnston (2010), Table 8.8 presents the odds ratios from the models generated. All the models consider the importance of the same variables and

Table 8.8

Separate logistic regression analyses (odds ratios) of six university outcome measures (using total UCAS tariff points)

		DV: Year 1 Resist(s) [n=31,883]	DV: Repeat Year 1 [n=31,883]	DV: Withdrawn [n=31,883]	DV: Year 1 Marks [n=19,822]	DV: Years 2 and 3 Combined Marks [n=8,618]	DV: Good Degree Classification [n=9,987]
Year of entry	2006/07	0.86**	1.95**	0.87	0.91*	1.11	1.09
	2007/08	0.77**	1.87**	0.91	0.93	0.95	1.19**
	2008/09	0.87**	2.03**	0.81*	0.78**	0.26**	1.27**
	2009/10	0.92	2.33**	0.71**	1.06	0.41**	1.17
	2010/11	0	0	0.41**	1.11	0.11*	
Age	Age on entry	0.89**	0.88**	0.95**	1.08**	1.03	1.12**
Gender	Male	1.73**	2.49**	0.94	0.75**	0.86**	0.63**
Ethnicity	Non-White	1.88**	1.69**	0.73**	0.73**	0.74**	0.53**
	Ethnicity not known	1.2	1.01	1.04	1.11	0.94	1.05
Disability	No known disability	0.83**	0.71**	1.05	1.15*	1.1	1.11
School type	Grammar	1.22**	1.23	1.04	0.89**	1.12	0.95
	Independent	1.33**	1.19	1.03	0.61**	0.73**	0.69**
	College	1.06	1.19	1.05	0.85**	1.03	0.92
	Unknown type	0.83	1.39	1.12	0.91	0.88	1.17
Social class	Working class	1	0.95	1.26**	0.91*	1	0.91
	Not known	1.08	1.07	1.23**	0.89**	0.99	0.99
Welsh language	Welsh speaker	1	1.05	1.15	0.94	0.89	0.83*
	Language unknown	0.31**	2.97**	5.98**	0.14**	0.37	1.16
Domicile	UK (not Wales/England)	1.94**	2.07**	1.51*	0.58**	0.63*	0.61*
	Wales	1.60**	1.98**	1.58**	0.52**	0.57**	0.51**
LPN	CF and POLAR	1.09	1.06	1.15	0.93	0.75	1.15
	POLAR2 only	1.13	1.33	1.25	1.02	1.01	1.02
	CF only	1.13	0.75	0.89	1.06	1.02	0.81
Prior attainment	Total UCAS Points	1.00**	1.00**	1.00**	1.01**	1.01**	1.01**
	Constant	2.7	0.28	0.19	0.05	0.19	0.08

Reference groups: 2005/6 year of entry; Comprehensive Schools; Middle class; White students, non-Welsh speakers, females, domiciled in England, from non-LPN; $* p < .05$. $** p < .01$.

characteristics, and use the same measure of prior attainment, total UCAS points. An odds ratio greater than 1.0 indicates that students with a particular characteristic (for example, working-class background, Welsh-speaking and so forth) performed better than the corresponding reference category (middle-class background, non-Welsh-speaking, etc.). Where the odds ratios are less than 1.0, this indicates that the students in a given category performed less well compared with the corresponding reference category. The odds ratios can also be interpreted as a percentage. For example, Table 8.8 gives an odds ratio of 1.12 for age on entry in relation to getting a good degree result (First or Upper Second). This means that a student who entered one year older than another student is 12 per cent more likely to get a good degree result, all other things being equal. Similarly, Table 8.8 gives an odds ratio of 0.63 for male students in relation to getting a good degree result. Since this odds ratio is less than 1.0, this means that male students are 37 per cent less likely to get a good degree result than female students, all other things being equal.

There is considerable debate whether statistical significance should be reported in studies such as this, as the analysis is based on data for a *population* of *all* students at this university (in the relevant years), rather than on a systematic *sample* of students. In this context, we argue that there are a number of reasons why it is nevertheless helpful to report statistical significance (see also Plewis and Fielding, 2003). The first is that we are concerned with what Plewis and Fielding (2003) refer to as the 'hierarchical structure of effects' or, in other words, the *relative* importance of one variable compared with another in predicting the progression and outcome measures. This allows us to judge the *relative* importance of coming from an LPN on, for instance, degree outcomes, compared with the other variables in the models. Secondly, we are not really interested in the effect of students coming from LPN areas in this single university alone; we are also interested in drawing wider inferences beyond the study university to what we might refer to as the 'super-population' from which our university is chosen. A similar argument could also be made in relation to the other year-cohorts of students at this university that are not included in our analysis. And third, we also wish to acknowledge that, despite drawing upon a large number of students in the analysis, the number with given characteristics may be quite small. This is particularly the case for the number of students from an LPN who had completed their degree during the period from which the data is drawn. Where these numbers of students are small, we want an indicator to help us judge, as far as we can, that these results (the odds ratios) are robust and reliable, in much the same way as would have done if we were using a systematic sample of the population.

Table 8.9
Summary of covariate results, other than LPN (positive relationships (+)
or negative relationships (-))

Dependent variables	Significant covariates						
	Prior attainment	Male	Non-white	Independent schools	Age	Rest of UK[a]	Wales-domiciled
Year 1 resit(s)	-*	+*	+*	+*	-*	+*	+*
Repeat Year 1	-*	+*	+*	+	-*	+*	+*
Withdrawn	-*	+	-*	+	-*	+*	+*
Above median Year 1 average marks	+*	-*	-*	-*	+*	-*	-*
Above median combined Year 2 and 3 average marks	+*	-*	-*	-*	+	-*	-*
First or Upper Second Degree classification	+*	-*	-*	-*	+*	-*	-*

a Not domiciled in England or Wales.
* Statistically significant results ($p<0.05$).

Table 8.9 provides a summary of the models detailed in Table 8.8. For simplicity, this table only identifies those variables that are statistically significant in predicting the various progression and outcome measures (we use $p<0.05$ as an indicator of significance). It also shows the direction of the relationships between the covariates and the outcome measures; whether they are positive or negative. For example, if your prior attainment is relatively high, you are more likely to achieve a First or Upper Second degree (positive relationship); but if you are male, you are less likely to achieve this class of degree (negative relationship). Table 8.10 provides a similar summary for students from LPNs.

Throughout the analyses, clearly the most important predictor of any of the outcomes is prior educational attainment. Hence, Table 8.9 shows that higher levels of prior attainment are likely to reduce the probability that a student will have Year 1 resit(s), to have to repeat Year 1 and to withdraw from university. Such students are also associated with higher levels of marks (Years 1 and 2/3 combined), and are significantly more likely to get a First or Upper Second class degree. There is a sense, therefore, that by the time students reach the point of entry to HE, they are already on an 'educational pathway' from their previous schooling. Even though all individuals entering university (especially a 'selecting' one) will have achieved a relatively high level of educational

Table 8.10
Summary of LPN results (positive relationships (+) or negative relationships (-))

Dependent variables	Low Participation Neighbourhood covariates		
	CF only	CF and POLAR2	POLAR2 only
Year 1 resit(s)	+	+	+
Repeat Year 1	-	+	+
Withdrawn	-	+	+
Above median Year 1 average marks	+	-	+
Above median combined Year 2 and 3 average marks	+	-	+
First or Upper Second Degree classification	-	+	+

a Not domiciled in England or Wales.
* Statistically significant results (p<0.05).

attainment, variations in this attainment are closely associated with subsequent student performance at university.

Other factors that are often associated with these outcome and progress measures include gender, ethnicity, the type of school previously attended and age. Here, our findings are consistent with other equivalent studies of university performance (for example, Hoare and Johnston, 2010). Accordingly, Table 8.9 shows that, all other factors being held constant: male students are less likely to do well than female students; non-white students tend to do less well than their white counterparts (although non-white students are less likely to withdraw); students from independent schools tend to do less well than students from comprehensive schools; and older students tend to do better than their younger counterparts. Importantly, we find there is little or no consistent relationship between social class and these outcomes, once these other characteristics (for example, prior attainment) are taken into consideration. This is not to suggest, of course, that social class has no influence on student performance; but rather that this influence is exercised indirectly through factors such as, for example, previous educational attainment.

Throughout the analyses, the year of entry also appears to be significant in influencing the outcomes. However, there are no clear or distinct patterns or trends to these 'effects', perhaps reflecting the changeable and turbulent influence of different cohorts of students. However, this also demonstrates the importance of analysing student progress and outcomes using several cohorts of students rather than taking a snap-shot using just one year of entry.

Interestingly, we do find that students domiciled in England (the reference group in these models) are far more likely to progress well and achieve favourable outcomes than students domiciled in other parts of the UK, including Wales. This relationship is consistent for all progression and outcome measures considered here. It is not clear, however, why this should be the case. One possible explanation is that there are systematic relationships between the UCAS tariff that students achieve and their country of domicile. For example, if students from Wales and Scotland tend to have higher UCAS tariff scores due to different qualifications in these countries, they may appear to 'underachieve' at university; that is, the statistical models may not actually be comparing students with equivalent levels of attainment prior to entry.

Most importantly for this analysis, we are now in a position to address the question raised earlier as to the direct influence (or otherwise) of residence in an LPN on student performance whilst at university. As Table 8.10 shows, coming from an LPN does *not* appear in the list of influential factors in relation to the suite of progression and outcome measures used in this study; and this is true however the LPN is defined. Hence, coming from an LPN *in itself* makes no significant difference to the likelihood of a student doing well or not at this university. Crucially, once other characteristics – and prior educational attainment, in particular – are taken into consideration, the 'effect' of being resident in an LPN is seen to be negligible; there are no significant differences between the performance of students from LPNs compared with those from other types of area, once we take account of all other factors. To the extent that living in an LPN influences university progression and outcomes, this influence is achieved through other factors (such as previous educational attainment, in particular). Clearly, this is a conclusion that poses important theoretical questions which can only be explored through further research.

CONCLUSIONS

As we noted at the outset, strategies for widening access to university have come to play a very prominent part in HE policy in all the countries of the UK, including Wales. Indeed, HEFCW is currently (at the time of writing) in the process of revising its approach to widening participation. Whilst limited in its empirical scope (to only one Welsh university), we believe that a number of important implications for the debate about widening access to HE follow from our analysis.

Firstly, we have shown that coming from an LPN does not necessarily mean that students are from socio-economically disadvantaged households nor are they necessarily non-traditional or first-generation entrants into HE. It may be argued, of course, that this is no more than an applied illustration of the 'ecological fallacy' (Robinson, 1950). However, it remains the case that area-based approaches remain the corner-stone of widening participation strategies.

As is generally agreed, the underlying priority for widening participation is to encourage more students from working-class backgrounds to become non-traditional or first-generation entrants to HE (for example, DfES, 2003; Green-bank, 2006; HEFCE, 2007; Harrison and Hatt, 2009). However, we have observed that the social-class background of students from designated LPNs, both in terms of CF areas and POLAR2 areas, is frequently quite heterogeneous. This suggests that an area-based approach may not be entirely appropriate to achieve the underpinning aims of widening participation strategy. Indeed, the logic here is that using an individual's household background (or even the school attended) would provide a better basis for identifying those students who should qualify for 'preferential' treatment within widening participation initiatives. Further-more, the limitation of using an area-based approach in identifying possible 'targets' for widening access in HE may also mask important and negative rela-tionships between student outcomes and social and educational advantage that still need identifying and addressing through further research.

Secondly, the most important finding relating to the aims of this analysis is that there does not appear to be a significant relationship between university outcomes and whether a student comes from a Communities First and/or POLAR2 neighbourhood, when controlling for a wide range of other key influ-ences (for example, differences in prior attainment, gender, ethnicity, type of school attended, etc). What this indicates, therefore, is that someone from an LPN is just as likely to have a 'successful' university career as anyone else, all other things being equal.

Clearly, there is a sense in which this provides a strong endorsement of the effectiveness of the overall project of widening access to university. Students from LPNs are able to thrive in HE in terms that are broadly equivalent to their peers whose homes are in other sorts of area. However, it is important to note in this context that all the groups of students analysed in this study had attained relatively high levels of educational attainment (compared with the wider population as a whole) in order to gain entry to our 'selecting' case-study university. In this sense, therefore, the form of widening participation strategy was somewhat limited, in confining entry to these highly qualified individuals (although we do not have direct evidence as to whether the offers made to individual students took account of their social circumstances).

It is also clear that the 'all other things being equal' proviso is crucial too. This is because average levels of educational attainment in LPNs are lower than those in other types of area. What this suggests, therefore, is that those individuals from LPNs who succeeded in attaining the requisite levels of educational attainment were, in some senses, 'exceptional'; they achieved higher levels of attainment than would be expected, given the areas in which they live.

This suggests, in turn, that there are limits to how far policy for HE can affect the distribution of educational opportunities. As others have pointed out, it would be more effective to focus resources on the earlier phases of educational development, to attempt to bring about a fairer distribution of opportunities to achieve the levels of attainment that appear to be necessary to be 'successful' in HE (Gorard, 2008). This is not, of course, to absolve the universities from any responsibility in this area. Rather, it is to indicate where the Welsh Government's priorities would be best directed, if the kind of democratic and inclusive system of higher education that was envisaged in nineteenth-century Wales is to be achieved in the twenty-first century.

NOTES

[1] In October 2012 HEFCE published POLAR3, showing participation rates updated to cover the period 2005–6 to 2010–11. These were not available for the analysis reported here.

[2] Given these figures are based on one university in Wales, where a significant proportion of the students are Wales-domiciled, it should be noted that the ratio of CF students to POLAR2 students is not representative of LPN students in the HE sector as a whole.

REFERENCES

Batey, P. and Brown, P. (2007). 'The spatial targeting of urban policy initiatives: a geodemographic assessment tool', *Environment and Planning A*, 39, 2274–793.

Blicharski, J. (2000). 'Tracking students' progression: learning their lessons', *Widening Participation and Lifelong Learning*, 2, 3, 32–7.

Crozier, G., Reay, D., Clayton, J., Colliander, L. and Grinstead, J. (2008). 'Different strokes for different folks: diverse students in diverse institutions – experiences of higher education', *Research Papers in Education*, 23, 2, 167–77.

DfES (2003). *The Future of Higher Education*, Norwich: HMSO.

Gallacher, J. and Raffe, D. (2012). 'Higher education policy in post-devolution UK: more convergence than divergence?', *Journal of Education Policy*, 27, 4, 467–90.

Gerwirtz, S., Dickson, M., Power, S., Halpin, D. and Whitty, G. (2005).'The deployment of social capital theory in educational policy and provision: the case of Education Action Zones in England', *British Educational Research Journal*, 31, 6, 651–73.

Gorard, S. (2008).'Who is missing from higher education?', *Cambridge Journal of Education*, 38, 3, 421–37.

Greenbank, P. (2006). 'The evolution of government policy on Higher Education', *Higher Education Quarterly*, 60, 2, 141–66.

Harrison, N., Baxter, A. and Hatt, S. (2007). 'From opportunity to OFFA: discretionary bursaries and their impact', *Journal of Access Policy and Practice*, 5, 1, 3–21.

Harrison, N. and Hatt, S. (2009). 'Knowing the "unknowns": investigating the students whose social class is not known at entry to higher education', *Journal of Further and Higher Education*, 33, 4, 347–57.

Hatt, S., Baxter, A. and Harrison, N. (2003). 'The new widening participation students: moral imperative of academic risk', *Journal of Access Policy and Practice*, 1, 1, 16–31.

HEFCE (2005). *Young Participation in Higher Education*, Bristol: HEFCE.

HEFCE (2007). *Higher Education Outreach: Targeting Disadvantaged Learners, Report 2001/12*, Bristol: HEFCE.

HEFCW (2010). *HEFCW Strategic Approach and Plan for Widening Access to Higher Education*, Cardiff: HEFCW.

Hoare, A. and Johnston, R. (2010). 'Widening participation through admissions policy – a British case study of school and university performance', *Studies in Higher Education*, 36, 1, 21–41.

Hoskins, S. L., Newstead, S. E. and Dennis, I. (1997). 'Degree performance as a function of age, gender, prior qualifications and discipline studied', *Assessment & Evaluation in Higher Education*, 22, 3, 317–28.

Osborne, R. D. and Shuttleworth, I. (2004). 'Widening access to higher education in the UK: Querying the geographic approach', *Higher Education Management and Policy*, 16, 1, 101–18.

Marris, P. (1964). *The Experience of Higher Education*, London: Routledge.

Plewis, I. and Fielding, A. (2003). 'What is multi-level modelling for? A critical response to Gorard (2003)', *British Journal of Educational Studies*, 51, 4, 408–19.

Rees, G. and Istance, D. (1997). 'Higher education in Wales: the (re-)emergence of a national system?', *Higher Education Quarterly*, 51, 1, 49–67.

Rees, G. and Taylor, C. (2006). 'Devolution and the restructuring of participation in higher education in Wales', *Higher Education Quarterly*, 60, 4, 370–91.

Rees, G., Power, S. and Taylor, C. (2007). 'The governance of educational inequalities: the limits of area-based initiatives', *Journal of Comparative Policy Analysis: Research and Practice*, 9, 3, 261–74.

Robinson, W. S. (1950). 'Ecological correlations and the behavior of individuals', *American Sociological Review*, 15, 3, 351–7.

Smith, J. and Naylor, R. (2005). 'Schooling effects on subsequent university perform-ance for the UK university population', *Economics of Education Review*, 24, 549–62.

Taylor, C., Rees, G., Davies, R. and Wilkins, C. (2011). *Welsh Baccalaureate Quali-fication: Progression and Outcomes of Students at Cardiff University*, Cardiff: Cardiff University.

Tight, M. (2012). 'Widening participation: a post-war scorecard', *British Journal of Educational Studies*, 60, 3, 211–26.

9. CAUTIOUS AND CREATIVE: UNDERSTANDING THE WELSH GOVERNMENT'S EU INTEREST REPRESENTATION STRATEGY

Einion Dafydd

ABSTRACT

This study examines the strategy employed by the Welsh Government (WG) to promote its policy interests within EU policy-making processes between 1999 and 2012. It argues that working with the UK Government in the formulation and promotion of UK-EU policy forms the centrepiece of the strategy, but that the WG also explores other channels through the work of its representatives in Brussels. The WG has continued to make a conscious effort to refrain from acting in ways which might jeopardize its relationship with Whitehall despite changes in the level of party political congruence, displaying caution both in its engagement with the UK Government and in its interest-promotion activity in Brussels. The main factor explaining the continuity of the WG's approach is Welsh Labour's perception that it stands to gain little from publicizing conflicts with the UK Government on issues related to the EU. This research suggests that while incongruence increases the potential for intergovernmental tension, this tension will not necessarily manifest itself in the context of EU policy. The WG's strategy is also characterized by creativity. It explores various channels to promote its interests, working informally with actors such as the European Commission, MEPs, regional networks and other European regions.

INTRODUCTION

The rise of sub-state EU interest representation activity over the last three decades is a significant development as it appears to challenge established accounts of international relations which stress that the international domain is the realm of states (Waltz, 1979; Putnam, 1988; Moravcsik, 1993; 1998). Existing studies identify substantial variation in the extent and manner in which sub-state entities[1] (SSEs) attempt to promote their interests at the EU level (Criekemans, 2010; Marks et al., 2002; Moore, 2007; 2008). This variation is explained by their constitutional status, the level of resources available, and the degree of party political congruence between the state and sub-state governments (Hooghe and Marks, 1996; Marks et al., 1996; Mamadouh, 2001; Tatham, 2010). This study provides an account of the strategies pursued by the Welsh Government (WG) in its attempts to promote its policy interests within EU policy-making processes between 1999 and 2012. It also provides an explanation of these strategic decisions.

Unlike some SSEs (Marks et al., 2002; Blatter et al., 2008, p. 468), the WG attempts to influence EU policy debates (WG, 2012, p. 5). Powers to conduct international affairs have not been devolved. However, the Concordat on the Co-ordination of EU Issues (Cabinet Office, 2010), an agreement between the UK Government and the devolved administrations, gives the WG the right to engage in a range of activities relating to the formulation and promotion of UK–EU policy, and to mobilize externally by interacting with foreign actors. While not as extensive as that of certain other SSEs such as the larger German *Länder* and Spanish *Comunidades Autónoma*, the WG level of engagement in European affairs is substantial. It has established an office (which in the year 2009–10 had a budget of over £700,000)[2] in the centre of Brussels' EU district, and the External and European Affairs Division in Cardiff. Yet relatively little is known regarding the activity that the WG undertakes in pursuit of its EU goals, and no attempts have been made thus far to analyse this activity in terms of an overall strategy rather than as individual forms of mobilization.

Only a limited number of studies have previously been conducted on aspects of Welsh engagement with foreign actors. In a recent work, Royles examines the 'extensive' international activity of the WG 'beyond the EU' (2010, pp. 142–3), with the research focusing on the fields of trade and international development. Stressing the WG's dependency on UK Government permission to mobilize in this way, she argues that the main motives for such activities include economic interests and 'nation-building' (Royles, 2010, pp. 160–1). The majority of works deal with Welsh activity in the context of EU governance; evaluating Welsh experiences of managing EU Structural Funding (Boland, 2005; Morgan, 2003; Williams, 2003) and analysing engagement by Welsh actors in EU policy-making processes. Jones charts the progress made by the Welsh Office and the Welsh Development Agency to develop a 'complex network of consultative relationships between Wales and the EU' in the 1970s and 1980s (2003, p. 121), and argues that the goal was primarily to gain access to EU Structural Funding. More recent studies have focused on the organizational structure of the offices of Welsh actors in Brussels (Haf, 2003; Lewis, 1998; Moore, 2006, 2007).

Bulmer et al. (2002) and Palmer (2008) outline the role that the WG and the National Assembly for Wales (NAfW) play in UK-EU policy-making. Efforts to formulate and to promote Welsh policy preferences are led by the WG, while the NAfW is unable to scrutinize the WG's work satisfactorily as it is not privy to the confidential information that the WG receives from Whitehall (Palmer, 2008, p. 126; Bulmer et al., 2002, p. 62). The extent to which the WG engages in EU policy-making varies between departments, with this variance attributed to the informal nature of relations between Cardiff and Whitehall (Palmer, 2008, p. 164) and the differing levels of expertise between WG departments (Carter, 2002, unpag. [9]). Rawlings also offers a valuable overview of the relationship between Wales and Europe (2003, pp. 425–57), and provides exemplary analysis of the WG's role in implementing EU law. However, the fieldwork for the three studies discussed above was conducted during the Assembly's first term; intergovernmental working practices have developed considerably since this period, as has the capacity of the WG to engage with EU affairs. Further, one of the main factors posited to influence the strategy of SSEs is the degree of party political congruence between the state and sub-state governments (Tatham, 2010), and it is only recently that scholars have been able to analyse how successive WGs have adapted to changes in the level of governmental congruence (see Wyn Jones and Royles, 2012). Cole and Palmer (2011) make an important contribution by evaluating the bilateral and multi-lateral relationships that the WG has established with EU regions, in an account that is partly based on analysis of recent interview data. However, aspects such as the cooperation between the WG and Welsh MEPs remain understudied. While Loughlin (1997) argues that before devolution Welsh interests were more actively promoted by MEPs than through the formal channels available via the Welsh Office and the UK Permanent Representation to the EU (UKRep), it is currently unknown whether the role of Welsh MEPs has changed since 1999. The general weaknesses of the literature are ameliorated in part by Tatham (2008), who explores how the UK's devolved administrations explore six channels of EU interest representation. However, while the fieldwork included interviews with officials from the WG, it is unclear which findings directly relate to Wales since much of the discussion is based on examples drawn from Scottish and English experiences.

METHODOLOGY

Taking an empirical focus, this study identifies how the WG pursues its EU interests, and explains why it pursues its interests in this manner. To this end it examines the activities that the WG undertakes, paying close attention to the mechanisms and channels that it explores, the manner in which it explores these channels, and the way it relates to and interacts with other actors, such as the UK Government and EU institutions. This article does not propose to evaluate the effectiveness of the WG's strategy. As this study examines the behavioural decisions made by a governmental actor, that actor's perception of the opportunity structure that it faces plays a central role in the analysis. The views and attitudes of the WG's officials and Ministers therefore lie at the heart of the study, with care taken to triangulate their accounts extensively with accounts provided by officials of other governmental organizations.

The findings are based on analysis of primary material such as statistical data gathered under the Freedom of Information Act, and analysis of twenty-three semi-structured interviews conducted in Brussels and in various locations in Wales between April 2010 and June 2012. Interviewees included two former WG Ministers (one of whom was in office at the time of the interview), EU-specialist WG civil servants, Welsh MEPs, European Commission officials and officials from the Brussels representation offices of several state and sub-state actors.

The study draws on Tatham's typology of interaction styles between SSEs and state governments. He finds that SSEs either cooperate with the state government, mobilize independently of it, employ a combination of both, or act in a way that conflicts with the interests of the state government (Tatham, 2010, pp. 30, 60). He identifies six main channels of interest representation that SSEs explore in their efforts to influence EU policy processes: 'the Committee of the Regions, the Council of Ministers, the Commission, the European Parliament, regional Brussels offices and European networks and association' (Tatham, 2008, p. 493). This typology facilitates comparison of the WG's strategy with those of other SSEs. In a large-*n* study, Tatham finds that SSEs tend to co-operate with the state government, while some act independently of the state level, and fewer still mobilize in ways that lead to open conflict with the state governments (2010, p. 80). Moreover, he finds that devolution levels increase 'the frequency of cooperation', that party political incongruence 'decreases cooperation and increases non-interaction', and that 'preference intensity configurations' – the discrepancy in the level of importance attached to an issue by the state and sub-state levels – has a significant effect on the way SSEs mobilize (2010, p. 4).

ENGAGEMENT IN UK-EU POLICY-MAKING

The starting point for understanding the WG's EU interest-representation strategy is that it signed the Concordat on the Co-ordination of EU Issues (Cabinet Office, 2010) with the UK Government in October 1999 of its own volition, that it has consented to minor revisions being made to the Concordat in subsequent years, and that it has refrained from exercising its right to terminate the non-legally biding agreement. The Concordat specifies that devolved Ministers and officials are to be 'fully involved' in discussions relating to UK-EU policy-making 'on all issues . . . which fall within the responsibility of the devolved administrations' (Cabinet Office, 2010, B4.3). Much the same as in the first years of devolution this agreement is operationalized in the form of loosely institutionalized working practices, mainly based on informal com-munication between WG officials and their counterparts in the Whitehall department which takes the lead on policy-formulation (Carter, 2002, unpag. [7; 9]; Cabinet Office, 2010, B4.4). This communication, usually via e-mail and telephone,[3] represents the primary method used by the WG to promote its interests in the UK-EU policy debate. Where the WG has a clear interest, interaction with the UK Government takes place from the earliest point in the EU policy-making cycle, when it is established that the Commission is considering drawing up a policy proposal.[4] WG officials emphasize the need to engage in these discussions at an early stage, as they believe that their views are more likely to be taken into account during official-level discussions. Once a policy is presented to the political level for final discussions, greater effort is required to make any substantial revisions as most policy details have already been resolved.[5] Consultations between the WG and central government continue throughout the policy cycle, until the UK Government takes part in the EU Council discussions. The WG views its ability to work with the UK Government as it defines UK-EU policy as representing its best opportunity for influencing EU policy. Once UK-EU policy has been formulated the devolved administrations must adhere to it, limiting the scope for promoting distinctive Welsh interests.

According to Welsh officials, the quality of personal relationships between WG officials and their Whitehall counterparts greatly influences the effective-ness of the WG's input into UK-EU policy-making processes.[6] There is evidence of substantial variation in the extent and quality of WG-Whitehall contacts. Where there is a long tradition of interaction between officials in Whitehall and Wales, as in the case of agriculture, contacts between officials are far better developed than in other cases, such as the environment. As this

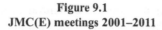

Figure 9.1
JMC(E) meetings 2001–2011

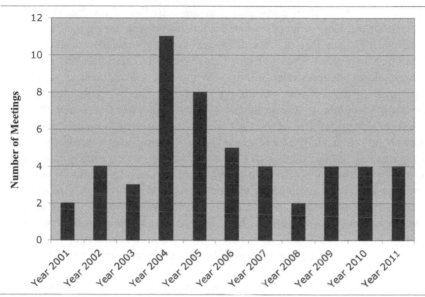

■ JMC(E) meetings.
Source: Cabinet Office FOI 316 158; personal correspondence with Cabinet Office official.

example shows, variation can exist within as well as between departments. The varying degree to which Whitehall departments disseminate information also affects the extent to which Welsh officials are able to engage in consultations[7] (see also Keating, 2005, p. 125). The WG consequently sources additional information through its representatives in Brussels.[8] This information is relayed to officials based in Wales who seek to understand and define Welsh interests.[9]

The WG appears to value participation in meetings of the Joint Ministerial Committee (Europe) (JMC(E)), which are attended by Ministers from the devolved administrations, the Secretary of State for the devolved territories and relevant UK Ministers (Cabinet Office, 2010, A3.12).[10] Meetings take place regularly (see Figure 9.1), usually to discuss issues relating to the UK's negotiating position prior to European Councils.[11] The significance of these meetings for the WG is that they provide a setting for direct face-to-face communication with senior UK Government figures. WG Ministers play a full role in discussions, although officials attempt to resolve any issues through discussions with Whitehall civil servants beforehand.[12] The prestige of the JMC(E) has declined since the early years of devolution when it was chaired by the Prime Minister, Tony Blair.[13] However, it is clear that the devolved administrations believe that they derive some benefit from participating in the activities of the JMC(E). While meetings of the JMC in its other formats fell into disuse during the early years of devolution[14] the JMC(E) has continued to meet regularly in spite of the difficulties involved in arranging meetings (House of Commons, 2010).

Maintaining a good relationship with the UK Government is of central importance to the WG, as substantive input into UK-EU policy-formulation essentially depends on the goodwill of Whitehall officials. While they are obliged to consult Welsh views, they are free to 'proceed to ignore' them,[15] an outcome far more likely where there is lack of sympathy towards the Welsh administration. WG officials strive to avoid conflict, and are ready to sacrifice short-term victories for long-term access to policy-making forums. Where it is clear that the WG's preferences will not be adopted as the UK's negotiating position, its officials turn their attention towards other objectives as early as possible in order to maximize the effectiveness of their broader lobbying strategy.[16] For WG officials, developing good working relationships with their Whitehall counterparts is seen as essential for maximizing influence on UK-EU policy-formulation processes.[17]

A similar approach is seen at the ministerial level. While discussing the diverging preferences of the WG and the UK Government over the use of GM seeds, former WG Rural Affairs Minister Elin Jones (Plaid Cymru) displayed acceptance of the fact that where the interests of administrations diverge, the UK Government has the authority to decide ultimately. In spite of her political affiliation she demonstrated no bitterness or frustration when discussing the issue, noting that 'we have had to agree to disagree'[18] as the fundamental nature of the disagreement left no room for compromise.[19] While a full UK-wide discussion took place, the WG sought a peaceful conclusion, preferring this to open conflict with London.

That the WG prioritizes the maintenance of good relations with the UK Government is further underlined by the methods that it refrains from employing. It has refrained from leaking confidential information and from publicizing conflicts with the UK Government on EU-related issues. At first sight, it appears surprising that the tension predicted by earlier studies (Palmer, 2008, pp. 33–7; Bulmer et al., 2002, p. 166) has failed to materialize in the context of EU policy, especially given that party political incongruence results in less cooperation (Tatham, 2010), and that Cardiff–London relations have experienced partial (2007–10) and full (2010–12) party political incongruence. Several factors explain the continuity in the WG's approach.

SSEs face serious difficulties in influencing EU policy debates, especially when acting without the support of their Member State. A devolved administration therefore requires a very clear incentive to risk sacrificing good relations with the government of its Member State. Party political congruence minimized such incentives between 1999 and 2007. The potential for political damage limited the appeal of public disagreements to successive Labour-led WG administrations, while party structures enabled politicians to resolve differences in private. The context of governmental congruence was conducive to the process of developing intergovernmental trust in the early years of devolution, and the emphasis on the relationship with the UK Government may have been weaker had this trust not developed.

One context in which a devolved administration may perceive that it has an incentive to publicly disagree with the UK Government is within nationalist debates, because of the rich symbolic significance that EU-related activity offers. This held little appeal for the former First Minister, Rhodri Morgan, or to the current First Minister, Carwyn Jones (Shipton, 2009, 2012). Plaid Cymru similarly chose not to seek conflict with the UK Government on EU issues during its time in government. Wyn Jones and Royles (2012, p. 262) are 'unable to unearth any evidence to suggest that partial incongruence following the formation of the Labour–Plaid Cymru WAG in 2007 had any impact whatsoever on relations with London'. They explain this by alluding to the fact that the WG coalition was led by Labour, that the differences between Labour and Plaid Cymru were minor, and that Plaid Cymru 'had no interest in provoking conflict with London' since its main priority was to demonstrate 'its ability to govern' (Wyn Jones and Royles, 2012, p. 262).

There has been a fundamental shift in the way the WG relates to its counterpart in London since the Conservative-Liberal Democrat coalition government was formed in 2010, as the WG has started to regularly criticize the UK Government in public (Wyn Jones and Royles, 2012, pp. 263–4). However, such pronouncements have largely been reserved for policies unrelated to the EU, with most attacks focusing on the way Wales is financed and on the UK's broader fiscal policy. Carwyn Jones' criticism of the way the Prime Minister, David Cameron, handled negotiations at the European Council summit in December 2011 (Shipton, 2011) serves as a rare exception. Even in this instance the First Minister treaded carefully, acknowledging that he agreed with the UK Government's policy, and emphasizing that he had 'a great respect for the UK's representatives in Brussels' (Euractiv.com, 2012). Further, while Jones has also noted his opposition to the idea of holding a referendum on the UK's membership of the EU, he refrained from criticizing the UK Government on the issue during the period 1999–2012 (Jones, 2012). The focus on non-EU issues is not surprising given that policies relating to public spending attain far higher saliency than EU policy and are therefore seen as politically more important. The lack of a discernable change in the WG's approach to EU affairs since 2010 demonstrates that while governmental incongruence increases the likelihood of intergovernmental tension, any conflict that develops will not necessarily emerge in the context of EU policy.

The WG's approach at the official level is similarly characterized by continuity. While there is evidence to suggest that the processes through which the UK Government consults with the devolved administrations have become more formalized during the period of party incongruence (McEwen et al., 2012), WG officials maintain that little has changed in the way they work with and relate to their counterparts in Whitehall departments in the context of EU policy.[20] Devolved officials may feel that many Whitehall civil servants could display a greater willingness to work with the devolved administrations, however they do not view any lack of cooperation in EU policy areas as resulting from governmental incongruence (cf. Wyn Jones and Royles, 2012, pp. 264–5).

REPRESENTING 'UK' INTERESTS IN BRUSSELS

The Concordat makes provisions for the devolved administrations to engage extensively in processes relating to the promotion of UK interests. Privileges include the right to forge a special relationship with UKRep, and to send Ministers and officials to Council meetings with the permission of the lead UK Minister (Cabinet Office, 2010, B4.12–14). WG Ministers and officials are required to 'support and advance the single UK negotiating line' at all times (Cabinet Office, 2010, B4.14) as they speak on behalf of the UK delegation. Obtaining permission for WG Ministers to attend Council meetings 'is generally not difficult',[21] and WG Ministers regularly attend Council meetings (see Figure 9.2).

Figure 9.2 suggests that the enthusiasm for attendance at Council meetings demonstrated by WG Ministers during the Assembly's first term waned considerably during the second term, and did not increase greatly during the third term. Ministers and officials recognize that attending Council of Ministers meetings offers little scope for influencing policy for several reasons (BBC, 2008a).[22] Firstly, opportunities to promote exclusively Welsh interests are rare, as Ministers must support the UK negotiating position. Secondly, the majority of decisions are reached long before Council meetings take place, namely at

Figure 9.2
Ministerial attendances at EU Council of Ministers meetings

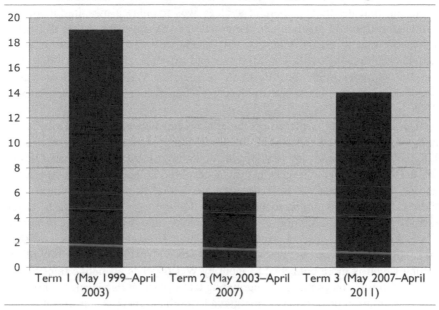

■ Number of Attendances by WG Ministers at EU Council of Ministers meetings.
Source: WG FOI 4347; personal correspondence with WG official.

working group and Committee of the Permanent Representation (COREPER) meetings.[23] Thirdly, substantive negotiating does not take place in the formal sessions of Council meetings. The 'real work' is done behind closed doors, and devolved Ministers seldom have access to these meetings.[24] A former Minister recalled having to return to Wales without taking part in any discussions because the informal meetings took so long.[25]

When Welsh Ministers attend meetings they seldom address Council. Instead, they take turns with Ministers from other devolved administrations to sit in the second row of the UK delegation.[26] Ministers addressed Council meetings five times on behalf of the UK during the first three Assembly terms[27] and they tended to speak at meetings of Councils which have a lower profile, such as the Culture Council at which the Minister for Heritage, Alun Ffred Jones, delivered an address in Welsh in November 2008 (Welsh Assembly Government, 2008; BBC, 2008b).[28] Welsh Ministers appear to value the opportunity to address Council primarily for its symbolic value.[29] According to a former Minister 'in my opinion everything is symbolic . . . when you get to that seat. Trying to influence policy before that stage is far more important'.[30] An official agreed, reasoning that the most important strategy was to 'play a meaningful role in formulating the UK position . . . the critical part is upstream, rather than who sat in the seat'.[31] Benefits of Council attendance include the opportunity to develop relationships with UK Ministers and officials, and the possibility that the UK Minister might be less likely to sacrifice Welsh preferences where negotiations change unexpectedly during a Council meeting (see also Tatham, 2008, pp. 499–502).[32]

Far greater value is placed on the relationship between the WG's officials and UKRep. Representatives of devolved administrations are accredited to UKRep's mission and are issued with diplomatic passports (Cabinet Office, 2010, B4.27).[33] This arrangement 'gives devolved colleagues . . . a degree of access, and a degree of trust between the Member State government and themselves which is unprecedented' except for the case of the Finnish Åland Islands.[34] Their accreditation to UKRep enables devolved officials to attend Council working groups,[35] a privilege which most Brussels-based policy officers take advantage of on an almost weekly basis.[36] Working groups provide a setting which is more congenial to input by WG officials as, unlike ministerial-level meetings, comprehensive negotiating takes place at this level.[37] While the UK's negotiation position is again agreed beforehand there is significant scope for devolved officials to emphasize their territorial preferences within the delegation. Attendance enables WG officials to give simultaneous feedback to the lead negotiator regarding the effect that different policy wordings may have on Wales. Broader benefits include intelligence gathering. By gaining a sense of how Member States are positioning themselves, officials are able to identify potential lobbying partners at the sub-state level.[38]

The importance of maintaining a harmonious relationship with UKRep for the WG's broader strategy of engaging with EU affairs should not be under-estimated. According to a Brussels based WG official, 'one of our main roles is to keep that relationship on a good footing'.[39] The privileges bestowed on the WG by UKRep are not anchored in legislation, and great care is taken to ensure that no reason is given for these privileges to be rescinded. As one devolved official explained, 'we don't own the power. The power is given to us by Whitehall, so we have it but it's not ours. It can be taken away . . . So we need to play by the rules'.[40] The most important of these rules is to maintain the UK position at all times. As two officials said, 'if we were to go around Brussels undermining the UK line publicly then we'd have a slap on the wrist',[41] and while 'UKRep don't really care what we say unless it's a real shocker . . . we as officials certainly feel compelled to play the game'.[42] WG officials must therefore strike a balance between emphasizing the Welsh position and maintaining the UK's line.[43]

EXPLORING ALTERNATIVE CHANNELS OF INTEREST REPRESENTATION

While the WG's strategy in engaging with EU policy processes is centered on cooperating with the UK Government in the formulation and promotion of UK-EU policy, it pursues additional strategies simultaneously. The limitations alluded to above give the WG an incentive to 'use all the levers at [its] disposal'.[44] It targets all institutions which play a significant role in EU policy-making processes, such as the European Commission and the European Parliament, and works with SSEs from across Europe, as well as with regional networks.

The European Commission
The European Commission does not 'have any particular formal level of relations with regions except the relationship [it has] through the Committee of the Regions',[45] a consultative EU institution which the WG views with disdain due to its limited powers.[46] However, Welsh officials are in regular contact 'with many parts of the Commission',[47] mostly through informal, off-the-record telephone calls.[48] While Commission officials are under no obligation to accommodate requests made by the WG, evidence suggests that the Commission responds well to informed input. The WG's office in Brussels secures meetings between Welsh Ministers and senior Commission personnel, and Commissioners are regularly invited to visit Wales.[49] Such visits provide WG officials and Ministers with extensive access to the Commissioner and members of their *cabinets* for an extended period. For instance, the Commissioner for Agriculture, Mariann Fischer Boel, visited Wales in July 2007 (European Commission, 2010)[50] as did the Commissioner for the Environment, Janez Potočnik, in September 2010 (Europa, 2010). Other targets include senior Commission officials from Wales such as Lowri Evans, the head of the Directorate-General for Maritime Affairs and Fisheries.[51] The informality of the WG's relationship with the Commission means that such meetings are not guaranteed. Consequently, establishing and maintaining 'strategically placed contacts', where possible within the Commissioners' *cabinets*, plays a central part in the WG's strategy of targeting the Commission.[52] Furthermore, the WG encourages its

officials to be seconded to the Commission (WG, 2009, p. 8), and 36 WG officials had taken advantage of this opportunity prior to June 2010.[53]

Interaction with the Commission plays a central part in the WG's wider EU interest-promotion strategy. This is partly because the need to maintain the UK position does not apply when the Commission is drafting a proposal, as UK-EU policy is formulated at a later stage.[54] One official explained that:

> What we would tell our guys is "if you can find the Commission person who is sitting with a blank piece of paper about to write a bit of legislation, then get him then." Once he's written that draft . . . then the only influence you really have is going through the UK, and that means a good relationship between our departments and the Whitehall department, and if you don't get that crack then you can forget it really.[55]

Working with MEPs

The European Parliament (EP) plays a leading role in EU policy-making processes, making it an obvious target for the WG. Officials are in regular contact with Welsh MEPs, who are free to promote any agenda they wish, including interests that conflict with the UK Government's preferences. WG officials provide guidance on Welsh issues, usually provided on a non-attributable basis.[56] Officials maintain that they deal with Welsh MEPs from different political parties in the same way, but note that the degree to which they interact with Welsh MEPs varies according to the 'relevance' of the MEP. For instance, parliamentarians who are members of the Agriculture and Rural Development Committee and the Regional Development Committee receive greater 'support'.[57]

As Wales has only four MEPs, the WG also targets MEPs from outside Wales. Officials have met EP rapporteurs on issues relating to the Common Agricultural Policy (CAP) and on the Structural Funds from other Member States. The visit of Deputy Minister for Agriculture, Food, Fisheries and European Programmes, Alun Davies, to Strasbourg for meetings with leading MEPs in December 2011 (WG, 2011) represented a new development.

The importance placed on interaction with MEPs varies according to the policy context. Parliamentary proceedings increase in relevance where the co-decision procedure is used, and there is greater need for independent actors to voice Welsh interests where the UK and the WG's interests diverge.[58] The level of engagement with the EP has increased appreciably since the Lisbon Treaty came into force in 2009, granting the institution co-decision powers on the CAP and Structural Funds.[59]

Working with other SSEs and networks

The WG is a member of several regional networks, including the Conference of European Regions with Legislative Power (REGLEG), the Conference of Peripheral Maritime Regions (CPMR), and the Network to Promote Linguistic Diversity (NPLD).[60] Its officials believe that while some are 'a waste of time' others 'can be incredibly useful'.[61] Regional networks are seen as a good source of information,[62] and as outlets through which the WG may be able to 'convey messages that we perhaps can't convey' when its interests diverge with those of the UK Government.[63] With approximately 300 SSEs represented in Brussels, the WG appreciates that the lobbying efforts of SSEs sharing common interests will be more effective if they present their case with a single voice (NAfW, 2006, p. 10).[64] Regional networks provide a platform from which SSEs can draw attention to its agendas, as well as access to senior policy-makers.[65] The First Minister, Carwyn Jones, and the then Deputy First Minister, Ieuan Wyn Jones, met Commission President Barroso to discuss Cohesion Policy as part of a CPMR delegation in July 2010 (WG, 2010), and an official admitted that 'it would be very difficult' to secure such a meeting under any other circumstances.[66]

The WG also works closely with individual SSEs, encouraging them to lobby their national governments on issues of common interest.[67] The WG has established formal relationships with foreign actors (Cabinet Office, 2010, B4.27), signing Memoranda of Understanding with prominent SSEs including Baden-Württemberg and Catalonia, and with the Latvian state (WG, 2009, pp. 8–9; Royles, 2010, p. 151). Whether practical benefits derive from such agreements is questionable, and Brussels-based officials appear to place greater importance on developing personal contacts with counterparts from other SSEs. The importance of working with other SSEs has increased as officials gained greater experience and understanding of operating in the EU policy making context,[68] and this form of activity currently plays a significant role in the WG's broader engagement with EU policy-making processes.

CONCLUSION

This study has identified that there are two main dimensions to the WG's EU interest representation strategy: firstly, cooperation with the UK Government and secondly, activity that is conducted largely independently of the UK Government where the WG explores alternative channels through the work of its representatives in Brussels. Working with the UK Government in the formulation and promotion of UK-EU policy forms the centrepiece of the strategy. The WG makes a conscious effort to refrain from acting in ways which might jeopardize its relationship with London, displaying caution both in its engagement with the UK Government, and in its interest-promotion activity in Brussels. The WG's willingness to cooperate with the state-level government is reflected in the strategies of many, if not most, other SSEs who attempt to influence EU policy (Tatham, 2010, p. 80). That the WG's strategy is charac-terized by creative mobilization in Brussels is demonstrated in three ways: by the way it works with actors with which it does not have a formal relationship, such as the Commission; by the multiplicity of channels that it explores; and by its ability to balance the need to promote interests which conflict with those of the UK Government while maintaining the UK's negotiating position in public.

By signing and abiding by the Memorandum of Understanding and the accompanying Concordat, it is clear that the WG prefers to rely on the UK Government for its access to EU policy-making processes, rather than to act independently of central government. This suggests that the WG prefers a loosely institutionalized relationship with a large EU Member State to a situation whereby it is free to operate independently but has access to fewer formal channels.

The evidence presented in this study reflects Tatham's finding that SSEs who are included in domestic EU policy-making processes are more likely to work closely with the state-level government (2010). His claim that party political incongruence leads to less cooperation (Tatham, 2010) is not supported in the case of Wales. This is explained by factors that are specific to the case of the WG, including Labour's perception that it has stood to gain more from publicizing conflicts with the UK Government over issues unrelated to EU policy in the period since 2010. This demonstrates that while incongruence increases the potential for intergovernmental tension, this tension will not necessarily manifest itself in the context of EU policy. Sub-state Ministers require a clear political incentive to publicize conflict with the state-level government and such an incentive is less likely to materialize if the saliency of EU policy is low.

Given the difficulties that SSEs face in influencing EU policy debates, especially when acting without the support of their Member State, it is not surprising that the WG has continued to work closely with the UK Government despite changes in the level of political congruence. However, it remains open to possibility that the strategy will change, especially in terms of the way in which intergovernmental relations are carried out at the political level. Regard-less of the degree of political congruence, the WG may choose to openly criticize the UK Government in the context of EU policy where senior figures perceive a significant political advantage from doing so.

NOTES

[1] Sub-state Entities (SSEs) are defined by Tatham as 'the level of government and/or administration immendiately below the state' (2010, p. 12).
[2] Personal correspondence with WG official.
[3] Interview, 30 June 2010.
[4] Interview, 29 June 2010.
[5] Interview, 29 June 2010.
[6] Interview, 29 June 2010.
[7] Interview, 30 June 2010.
[8] Interview, 29 June 2010.
[9] Interviews, 29 June 2010; 30 June 2010; 1 July 2010.
[10] Interview, 29 June 2010.
[11] Interviews, 11 June 2010; 29 June 2010.
[12] Interviews, 29 June 2010; 29 June 2012.
[13] Interview, 11 June 2010.
[14] Interview, 11 June 2010.
[15] Interview, 30 June 2010.
[16] Interviews, 29 June 2010; 1 July 2010.
[17] Interview, 30 June 2010.
[18] Interview, 16 July 2010.
[19] The UK Government eventually agreed to present the views of devolved administrations alongside its own (Interview, 16 July 2010).
[20] Interview, 21 June 2012.
[21] Interview, 30 June 2010.
[22] Interviews, 29 June 2010; 16 July 2010.
[23] Interview, 1 July 2010.
[24] Interview, 30 June 2010.
[25] Interview, 16 July 2010.
[26] Interview, 30 June 2010.
[27] Personal correspondence with WG official.
[28] Interviews, 16 July 2010; 29 June 2010.
[29] Interviews, 29 June 2010; 1 July 2010.
[30] Interview, 16 July 2010.
[31] Interview, 29 June 2010.
[32] Interview, 1 July 2010.
[33] Interviews, 23 June 2010; 30 June 2010; 1 July 2010.
[34] Interview, 30 June 2010.
[35] Interview, 29 June 2010.
[36] Interview, 1 July 2010.
[37] Interview, 1 July 2010.
[38] Interview, 1 July 2010.

[39] Interview, 29 June 2010.
[40] Interview, 1 July 2010.
[41] Interview, 29 June 2010.
[42] Interview, 1 July 2010.
[43] Interview, 29 June 2010.
[44] Interview, 29 June 2010.
[45] Interview, 23 June 2010.
[46] Interview, 29 June 2010.
[47] Interview, 29 April 2010.
[48] Interview, 29 June 2010.
[49] Interview, 29 June 2010.
[50] Interview, 29 June 2010.
[51] Interview, 29 June 2010.
[52] Interview, 29 June 2010.
[53] Welsh Government FOI 4347.
[54] Interview, 29 June 2010.
[55] Interview, 1 July 2010.
[56] Interview, 29 June 2010.
[57] Interview, 21 June 2012.
[58] Interview, 29 June 2010.
[59] Interview, 21 June 2012.
[60] Personal correspondence with WG official.
[61] Interviews, 29 April 2010; 29 June 2010.
[62] Interviews, 29 April 2010; 21 June 2010.
[63] Interviews, 29 June 2010; 1 July 2010.
[64] Interview, 29 June 2010.
[65] Interview, 29 June 2010.
[66] Interview, 29 June 2010.
[67] Interview, 29 June 2010.
[68] Interview, 29 April 2010.

REFERENCES

BBC (2008a). 'Plaid Minister urges independence', 29 March 2008, *http://news.bbc.co.uk/1/hi/wales/7320485.stm* (accessed 23 August 2010).

BBC (2008b). '"Historic" use of Welsh in EU', 20 November 2008, *http://news.bbc.co.uk/1/hi/wales/7739425.stm* (accessed 12 August 2010).

Blatter, J., Kreutzer, M., Rentl, M. and Thiele, J. (2008). 'The Foreign Relations of European regions: competences and strategies', *West European Politics*, 31, 3, 464–90.

Boland, P. (2005). 'An assessment of the Objective 1 Programme in Wales, 1999–2003', *Contemporary Wales*, 17, 66–78.

Bulmer, S., Burch, M., Carter, C. A., Hogwood, P. and Scott, A. (2002). *British Devolution and European Policy-making: Transforming Britain into Multi-level Governance*, Basingstoke: Palgrave.

Carter, C. A. (2002). 'The formulation of UK-EU policy post-devolution: a transformative model of governance?', *Manchester Papers in Policy*, No. 3, Manchester: European Policy Research Unit.

Cole, A., Palmer, R. (2011). 'Europeanising devolution: Wales and the European Union', *British Politics*, 6, 3, 379–96.

Criekemans, D. (2010). 'Regional sub-state diplomacy from a comparative perspective: Quebec, Scotland, Bavaria, Catalonia, Wallonia and Flanders', *The Hague Journal of Diplomacy*, 5, 1, 37–64.

Cabinet Office (2010). *Devolution: Memorandum of Understanding and Supplementary Agreements*, London: The Stationery Office Limited.

European Commission (2010). 'Commissioner Fischer Boel paid a visit to the Royal Welsh Show', European Commission Representation in United Kingdom, *http://ec.europa.eu/ unitedkingdom/about_us/office_in_wales/gallery/boel0707_en.htm* (accessed 31 August 2012).

Euractiv.com (2012) 'Welsh leader: "Our interests in Europe are distinctive from England's"', 31 January 2012, *http://www.euractiv.com/uk-europe/welsh-leader-interests-europe-di-interview-510377* (accessed 24 August 2012).

Europa (2010). *Janez Potocnik European Commissioner for Environment Wales Biodiversity Partnership Annual Conference Keynote Speech*, Bangor University, 16 September 2010, *http://europa.eu/rapid/pressReleasesAction.do?reference=SPEECH/ 10/455&format=HTML&aged=1&language=EN&guiLanguage=en* (accessed 26 July 2011).

Haf, E. (2003). 'Team Wales abroad', *Agenda*, Spring 2003, 66–7.

Hooghe, L. and Marks, G. (1996). '"Europe with the regions": channels of regional representation in the European Union', *Publius: The Journal of Federalism*, 26, 1, 73–91.

House of Commons (2010). Scottish Affairs Select Committee 'Scotland and the UK: cooperation and communication between governments' HC (2009–10) 256 (London: The Stationery Office Limited), *http://www.publications.parliament.uk/pa/cm200910/ cmselect/cmscotaf/256/256.pdf* (accessed 7 February 2012).

Jones B. (2003). 'Wales and the European Union: refining a relationship', in J. M. Magone (ed.), *Regional Institutions and Governance in the European Union*, Westport: Praeger.

Jones, C. (2012). 'The future of the union: Wales', Public lecture delivered at the London School of Economics and Political Science, 8 November 2012, *http://www2. lse.ac.uk/publicEvents/pdf/2012_MT/20121108-CarwynJones-Transcript.pdf* (accessed 26 January 2013).

Keating, M. (2005). *The Government of Scotland: Public Policy Making after Devolution,* Edinburgh: Edinburgh University Press.

Lewis, B. (1998). 'Representing Wales in Europe: the origins and evolution of the Wales European Centre', *Contemporary Wales*, 11, 186–99.

Loughlin, J. (1997). 'Wales in Europe: Welsh regional actors and European integration', *Papers in Planning Research*, No. 157, Cardiff: Department of City and Regional Planning, Cardiff University.

Mamadouh, V. (2001). 'The regions in Brussels: subnational actors in the supranational arena', *Tijschrift voor Economische en Sociale Geografie*, 92, 4, 478–87.

Marks, G., Nielson, F., Ray, L. and Salk, J. (1996). 'Competencies, cracks and conflicts: regional mobilization in the European Union', in G. Marks, F. Scharpf, P. Schmitter and W. Streeck (eds.), *Governance in the European Union*, London: Sage.

Marks, G., Haesly, R. and Mbaye, H.A.D. (2002). 'What do subnational offices think they are doing in Brussels?', *Regional and Federal Studies*, 12, 3, 1–23.

McEwen, N., Swenden, W. and Bolleyer, N. (2012) 'Intergovernmental relations in the UK: continuity in a time of change?', *The British Journal of Politics and International Relations*, 14, 2, 323–43.

Moore, C. (2006). 'Conflicts in representing the regions in Brussels: the case of Wales', *Regional Studies*, 40, 7, 793–9.

Moore, C. (2007). 'The impact of devolution on EU-level representation: British regional offices in Brussels', *Regional and Federal Studies*, 17, 3, 275–91.

Moore, C. (2008). 'Beyond conditionality? Regions from the New EU Member States and their activities in Brussels', *Comparative European Politics*, 6, 212–34.

Moravcsik, A. (1993). 'Preferences and power in the European Community. A liberal intergovernmentalist approach', *Journal of Common Market Studies*, 31, 4, 473–524.

Moravcsik, A. (1998). *The Choice for Europe. Social Purpose and State Power from Messina to Maastricht*, Ithaca, NJ: Cornell University Press.

Morgan, K. (2003). 'How Objective 1 arrived in Wales: the political origins of a coup', *Contemporary Wales*, 15, 20–9.

National Assembly for Wales (2006). 'Assembly Committees: scrutinising and engaging with the European Union's decision-making process', Paper number: 06/007/AD, Cardiff: National Assembly for Wales Members' Research Service, *http://www.assemblywales.org/anna-daniel-scrutiny-eu-policy.pdf* (accessed 20 January 2013).

Palmer, R. (2008). *Devolution, Asymmetry and Europe: Multi-Level Governance in the United Kingdom*, Brussels: P. I. E. Peter Lang.

Putnam, R. D. (1998). 'Diplomacy and domestic politics: the logic of two-level games', *International Organization*, 42, 427–60.

Rawlings, R. (2003). *Delineating Wales*, Cardiff: University of Wales Press.

Royles, E. (2010). 'Small, smart, successful: a nation influencing the twenty-first-century world? The emerging Welsh paradiplomacy', *Contemporary Wales*, 23, 142–70.

Shipton, M. (2009). 'Rhodri Morgan discusses devolution in last interview with the Western Mail', *Western Mail*, 29 December.

Shipton, M. (2011). 'Welsh First Minister Carwyn Jones seeking to forge stronger links in Europe', *Western Mail,* 16 December.

Shipton, M. (2012). 'Carwyn Jones: UK on brink of huge constitutional change', *Western Mail*, 29 March.

Tatham, M. (2008). 'Going solo: direct regional representation in the EU', *Regional and Federal Studies*, 18, 5, 493–515.

Tatham, M. (2010). '*With, without or against you?* The interest representation of states and their sub-state entities in the European Union', unpublished PhD thesis, Florence: European University Institute.

Waltz, K. N. (1979). *Theory of International Politics*, London: Addison-Wesley.

Welsh Assembly Government (2008). Welsh Assembly Government Press Release, *Landmark Use of Welsh in the European Union* (19 November 2008). *http://new.wales. gov.uk/newsroom/welshlanguage/2008/3989122/?lang=en* (accessed 12 August 2010).

Welsh Assembly Government (2009). *Wales and the European Union – A Strategy for the Welsh Assembly Government.*

Welsh Assembly Government (2010). Welsh Assembly Government Press Release, *Welsh Ministers in Brussels to Press Case for Continued EU Funding* (7 July 2010). *http://wales.gov.uk/newsroom/firstminister/2010/100707funding/?lang=en* (accessed 14 August 2010).

Welsh Government (2011). WG Press Release, *Deputy Minister to Raise Welsh Issues in Europe* (13 December 2011). *http://cymru.gov.uk/newsroom/businessandeconomy/ 2011/111212adinbrussels/;jsessionid=vsT9Q2zPgq27pP1HMWGd1zPyyb02VknjC8FJ dHvFTZ0JV7vhxRsv!1219044931?lang=en* (accessed 29 August 2012).

Welsh Government (2012). *Wales and the European Union: The Welsh Government's EU Strategy.*

Williams, P. (2003). 'European structural funds: are they working in Wales?', *Contemporary Wales*, 15, 61–8.

Wyn Jones, R. and Royles, E. (2012). 'Wales in the world: intergovernmental relations and sub-state diplomacy', *British Journal of Politics and International Relations*, 14, 2, 250–69.

10. 'GREY MEN IN GREY SUITS': GENDER AND POLITICAL REPRESENTATION IN LOCAL GOVERNMENT

Nickie Charles and Stephanie Jones

ABSTRACT

Women's representation in local government is significantly lower than it is in the National Assembly for Wales. This article draws on findings from original interview data with councillors and Assembly Members (2003–7) to explore their views on gender equality and the use of positive measures to increase women's political representation. Our findings show that, while gender equality is supported and an increase in the descriptive representation of women is seen as desirable, there is considerable opposition to positive action measures within local government. These findings are situated in the context of the debate over positive measures subsequent upon their adoption by two of the four main political parties in Wales for the first Assembly elections.

INTRODUCTION

In July 2012 the Electoral Reform Society Wales sent out its first electronic newsletter; at the top of the list of features was 'Women still locked out of town halls'. This linked to a report on the 2012 local elections which showed that the rate of increase in women's representation in local government had declined and, although women are now 26.3 per cent of all councillors, 'At this slow rate of progress women will not have an equal voice in Welsh local authorities until 2075' (ERSW, 2012, p. 1). While the proportion of women councillors is far lower than the proportion of women Assembly Members (AMs), there is also a downward trend in women's representation at devolved level (Fox, 2011). The high point of women's representation was in the second Assembly (2003–7) when women were 50 per cent of AMs rising to 52 per cent due to a by-election in Blaenau Gwent. Since 2011, however, the proportion of women AMs has dropped to 42 per cent, almost the level it was after the first Assembly elections in 1999. The unusually high level of women's representation in the Assembly was achieved through the use of positive action measures by Welsh Labour and Plaid Cymru but no such measures have been introduced in local government elections. The Electoral Reform Society Wales report concludes that it is 'vital that parties do more to ensure a greater degree of gender balance at a grassroots level' and suggests that one of the barriers to this being realized is 'the entrenchment of male party elites' (ERSW, 2012, p. 5).

In this article we explore some of the issues raised by attempts to increase women's political representation and how such attempts have been received by AMs and local councillors. In order to do this we draw on the findings of a research project which investigated the gendering of political cultures and processes at different levels of the polity.[1] Before presenting our findings we discuss the arguments for increased political representation of women and the various ways that this can be realized. We then outline differences between political parties in their approaches to this question and the strategies they have adopted in Wales. Although the literature focuses mainly on national and devolved government, our attention will be on local government where there is considerable resistance to positive action.

POLITICAL REPRESENTATION AND GENDER

There is widespread recognition that the proportion of women political representatives should be increased (Evans, 2008; Squires, 2007) and, to this end, political parties and governments around the world have introduced quotas which specify a minimum number or proportion of women (Dahlerup and Friedenvall, 2005; Franceschet et al., 2012; Krook and Squires, 2006). The theoretical basis for this view rests on a range of principles which are taken up in different ways by those advocating for an increase in women's representation (Phillips, 1998; Phillips, 1995; Childs and Cowley, 2010; Krook and O'Brien, 2010). The main grounds on which these arguments are based are equal opportunity and social justice; it is unjust for men to monopolize political representation which should be equally available to women and men. There is also an argument that the composition of a politically representative body should mirror the distribution of different groups in the population; this is known as descriptive representation and is based on the idea that it is only representatives who share the characteristics of those who elect them (class, gender, ethnicity, disability, age, etc.) who can effectively represent the interests of that particular group. It is also argued that increasing women's representation would revitalize democracy and contribute to the legitimacy of the political system which is currently suffering from a 'democratic deficit' (Davies and Williams, 2009). Furthermore, having more women candidates symbolizes a modern political party, making it more attractive to the electorate and enabling women politicians to act as role models, thereby ensuring that talented young women aspire to become political representatives rather than being lost to politics.

ACHIEVING DESCRIPTIVE REPRESENTATION

It is on the basis of one or more of these arguments that the main political parties in Wales agree that there should be more women (and minority ethnic) political representatives. However they disagree on how this should be achieved. There are four main options: do nothing and wait for time to take its course; adopt equality rhetoric (which is making a discursive commitment to equality but doing little about it); promote equality (which involves introducing measures such as training for women and other disadvantaged groups so that the 'playing field' can be levelled and they have a more equal chance of selection); and a more radical form of positive action which includes quotas, either legislated for by government or adopted voluntarily by political parties (Squires, 2005; Campbell and Lovenduski, 2005). This last option includes the measures taken by Welsh Labour and Plaid Cymru in the first Assembly elections in 1999 which resulted in 40 per cent of AMs being women (Charles, 2010).

It has been argued that these different ways of increasing women's political representation relate to different understandings of equality with a key distinction being made between equality of opportunity and equality of outcome (Dahlerup and Friedenvall, 2005). Equality of opportunity is based on a liberal under-standing of equality which relates to notions of the liberal subject and equal treatment; it is assumed that individuals start on a 'level playing field' and any ensuing inequalities arise on the basis of merit and are entirely legitimate (Marshall, 1950). Equality of outcome is more radical, insisting not on equality of treatment, but recognising that different treatment of different groups, particularly those that are disadvantaged by current social arrangements, may result in more equal outcomes (Young, 1990). Different treatment, however, is problematic, because [it stands] in opposition to deeply held beliefs in the liberal democratic principles of individual rights and meritocracy. Promotion of one group over other groups [and] positive discrimination [violate] the principle of equal opportunity. (Welsh and Halcli, 2003, p. 350)

In Wales there is an institutional and ideological commitment to equality of opportunity which is central to the National Assembly for Wales (NAfW), but there appears to be some difference between the political parties in their views on gender equality. These differences are translated into different policies on women's representation. The Liberal Democrats and Conservatives hold an individualistic understanding of gender equality and, in accordance with this, adopt equality rhetoric and measures that will promote equality (such as training or mentoring) (Evans, 2008; Campbell et al., 2007). They oppose other forms of positive action because they are seen as discriminatory and under-mining notions of equality of opportunity (Campbell and Lovenduski, 2005; Campbell et al., 2007; Evans, 2008). The Labour Party and Plaid Cymru, in contrast, have adopted positive measures in recognition of the fact that women as a group are disadvantaged by existing selection practices and procedures. There are, however, ongoing disagreements within these parties about positive measures: Plaid Cymru abandoned the use of zipped lists after the third Assembly elections and Welsh Labour adopted the policy of twinning for the first Assembly elections only.[2]

Disagreement over positive measures and difficulties in implementing them highlight the sometimes problematic relationship between local party branches, where candidates are selected, and central party organizations which are charged with implementing policy decisions. In the main UK parties there is a jealous guarding of the local party's autonomy over candidate selection and, in response to attempts from the centre to increase the number of women selected as candidates, local branches often argue that a local (usually male) candidate should be chosen over and above a woman (Childs and Cowley, 2011; Evans, 2008). This raises questions about attitudes towards women and gender equality at local level and their relation to the gender culture of local politics (Lovenduski, 1996; Perrigo, 1996). Research shows that political represen-tatives at local level have more 'traditional' views on gender than at national level and there is evidence that women chief executives in local government face 'institutionalised sexism' (Fox and Broussine, 2001; Broussine and Fox, 2010; Evans, 2008). Although there is little research focussing solely on Welsh local government, studies of local government in England and Wales find a mixture of attitudes towards gender equality (Welsh and Halcli, 2003) and opposition to positive measures which varies, to some extent, by party (Rallings et al., 2010).

One of the factors associated with the male-domination of local politics is the importance of networks to candidate selection. Existing party members are crucial in encouraging people to stand for election with two in three candidates entering local politics having been asked to stand 'often by fellow party members' (Rallings et al., 2010, p. 377). Such practices are set to reproduce the existing composition of local government which is overwhelmingly male, white and middle class (in England and Wales) (Rallings et al., 2010) and in Wales male, white and rather more working class than in England (WLGA, 2004). Given all this, the Electoral Reform report cited earlier (ERSW, 2012) is correct in its prognosis of slow progress towards gender parity in local government; indeed a recent assessment of the situation across the UK comments that 'recent progress . . . has hardly exceeded gastropodic' (Game, 2009, p. 155) and that responsibility for redressing this imbalance should be placed 'not primarily on members of the under-represented group themselves, but on those who control the recruitment process' (Game, 2009, p. 168).

THE STUDY

In Wales there has been a particular history to attempt to increase women's political representation which, after the second Assembly elections in 2003, resulted in the first legislative assembly in the world to achieve gender parity (Stirbu, 2011; Watt, 2003). This provided an unprecedented opportunity to compare the gendering of political processes and cultures at different levels of the polity where the proportion of women representatives varied significantly. At the time of our research women constituted 52 per cent of AMs, 21.8 per cent of local councillors and only three of the twenty-two council leaders were women. The average figure for the proportion of women councillors masks considerable variation. Prior to the 2008 local elections, 37 per cent of councillors in Cardiff were women, 31 per cent in Swansea and 30 per cent in the Vale of Glamorgan. This compared with Blaenau Gwent where the figure was 9.5 per cent, Anglesey where it was 5 per cent and Merthyr Tydfil where it was 3 per cent. In many councils women were in a very small minority and there was no critical mass of women. A critical mass is usually taken to be around 30 per cent and indicates that women are freer to behave in ways that do not conform to masculinist organizational cultures (Dahlerup, 2006). Given these differences in women's descriptive representation, one of the aims of our research was to investigate how the gender cultures of different political institutions varied and how they related to the views of political representatives on gender equality and positive action.

.Our research began during the second Assembly (2003–7), focusing on the National Assembly for Wales; civil society organizations at the all-Wales and local levels; and local government in three case study areas. Our case study areas differed both in terms of the political composition of local government and in the proportion of women councillors.[3] One was an urban local authority with a Liberal Democrat-led coalition in control of the council where women comprised just under a third of councillors. One was a primarily rural local authority where the council was controlled by an Independent-led coalition, here women comprised under a fifth of councillors. The third was a post-industrial[4] local authority which had for decades been controlled by Labour but at the time of our study was run by an all-party coalition; here fewer than 10 per cent of councillors were women. The councils were characterized by different political cultures which tended to be understood in party political terms by our interviewees rather than in terms of gender. The urban council was seen as 'gladiatorial' and very unpleasant while the other two were perceived as being more consensual: the post-industrial one because, as one councillor put it, it was a dictatorship and everything was decided by the dominant group, and the more rural one because it was a coalition, which involved a relatively large group of Independent councillors. These differences aside, all three shared a similar gender culture which, in contrast to the political and organizational culture of the National Assembly, was highly masculinized and meant that women councillors felt that in order to be accepted and taken seriously by their male colleagues they had to adopt 'masculine' modes of behaviour.

Between 2005 and 2008 we interviewed AMs, councillors and representatives of a range of civil society organizations; we carried out thirty-one interviews with AMs during the second term (2003–7) (see Table 10.1); twenty-one interviews with councillors (see Table 10.2) and six with council officials (three men and three women); twenty-four with representatives of local and six with representatives of all-Wales voluntary organizations, trade unions and an equalities body (of these three were men). In addition we undertook policy analysis and observations at party conferences, the National Assembly and local government. In this paper we draw on interviews with councillors and AMs.

Before discussing our research findings we set our research in the context of attempts to increase women's representation in Wales and the considerable resistance which they generated.

Table 10.1
Gender and party composition of National Assembly at time of interviewing (2006–7)

Political party	Women		Men		Total	
	AMs	Interviewees	AMs	Interviewees	AMs	Interviewees
Conservative	2	0	9	3	11	3
Labour	19	8	10	6	29	14
Liberal Democrat	3	2	3	1	6	3
Plaid Cymru	6	4	6	5	12	9
Independent	1	1	1	1	2	2
Total	31	15	29	16	60	31

Note: We approached women and men AMs from across the political spectrum but were unable to secure interviews with Conservative women AMs.

Table 10.2
Gender and party composition of local government interviewees

Political party	Local authority						
	Rural		Post-industrial		Urban		All
	Women	Men	Women	Men	Women	Men	Total
Conservative	0	0	0	0	0	0	0
Labour	2	1	1	2	1	1	8
Liberal Democrat	1	0	0	0	1	1	3
Plaid Cymru	1	0	0	0	1	0	2
Independent	0	1	0	2	1	1	5
Other	0	1	0	2	0	0	3
Total	4	3	1	6	4	3	21

INCREASING WOMEN'S POLITICAL REPRESENTATION IN WALES

It was at the Labour Party conference of 1989 that it was accepted 'in principle' that 'quotas were the only way to ensure the equal representation of women and men at all levels of the party' (Krook, 2011, pp. 29, 55) and, in 1993, the party adopted a policy of All Women Shortlists (AWS). This was criticized by other parties and by the tabloids as 'privileging special treatment over equal treatment' and possibly being incompatible with the 1975 Sex Discrimination Act (Krook, 2011, pp. 32, 55). It was, however, effective. As the EHRC Wales points out,

There have only ever been thirteen female MPs from Wales since the 'Act of Union' between England and Wales in 1536. Seven of these were selected by all-women shortlists. (2012)

The introduction of AWS 'provoked a furious backlash from reactionary elements within the party' (Davies and Williams, 2009, p. 21) in Wales and elsewhere; they were successfully challenged on grounds of discrimination in employment by two male Labour party members from Leeds and were subsequently withdrawn. In the 1997 general election, because a number of candidates had been selected from AWS prior to this challenge, the proportion of women elected to Westminster doubled from 9 per cent to 18 per cent (Krook and Squires, 2006, p. 49).

In the run up to the elections to the newly-formed NAfW and Scottish Parliament two years later, all the parties except the Tories discussed the adoption of positive action. The Tories were opposed to positive action counterposing it to selection on merit which was their preferred option. The Welsh Liberal Democrats debated various methods, eventually opting for a gender balanced shortlist of candidates for constituency elections; this also happened in Scotland. The Welsh Labour Party and Plaid Cymru adopted different forms of positive action; the former went for twinning and the latter for putting women in first and third place on their regional lists. These measures were highly contentious; one of the reasons Plaid did not adopt twinning was because the Council feared a conservative backlash within the party (Russell et al., 2002) and 'The leaders of Welsh Labour, in contrast to their British and Scottish counterparts, initially expressed strong hostility toward any form of positive action in candidate selection' (Krook, 2011, pp. 38, 55). The adoption of twinning was approved by a narrow margin at the Welsh Labour Party conference in 1998 with nineteen of the forty constituency parties and several important trade unions opposing the measures; there were also threats of legal action and non-cooperation at local level (Krook, 2011). In the event, there was a campaign mounted against twinning, which had its greatest support in 'the south Wales valleys and the Swansea areas' (Edwards and Chapman, 2002, p. 369), and four constituencies, including Blaenau Gwent, had their pairings imposed upon them by Welsh Labour Party headquarters in Cardiff (Edwards and Chapman, 2002, p. 368). Women who were involved in selection processes in this part of Wales and who were from 'local government or academic' rather than trade union backgrounds, experienced hostility, harassment and what can only be seen as sabotage from some members of their constituency parties (Edwards and Chapman, 2002). Accounts of similar experiences emerged in our interviews with AMs.

Edwards and Chapman note that Welsh Labour's selection process for the first Assembly elections involved the completion of 'a detailed application form in which personal sensitivity to issues like equality of opportunity were sought' (Edwards and Chapman, 2002, p. 370). This resulted in the rejection of some 'notable local party personalities' and emphasized the seriousness of the party in ensuring candidates were committed to equal opportunities and avoiding 'traditional ways of selecting the local "favoured son" candidate through old-style patronage rather than merit' (Edwards and Chapman, 2002, p. 370). They argue that the Labour Party in London was able to challenge the 'male-dominated and trade-union dominated selection process' which, prior to 1998/9, had persisted in this area despite the reforms democratizing candidate selection procedures. The second stage of selection involved testing a candidate's ability to speak publicly and, despite training being available for this, was 'biased in favour of articulate people who fitted the New Labour mould' (Edwards and Chapman, 2002, p. 370).

The complexity of the issues involved are clear and relate not only to a culture where traditional views about gender were deeply rooted but also to resentment of central control over the selection process which involved the promotion not only of women but of middle-class candidates in traditionally very working-class areas, a deep hostility to the project of New Labour, and a concern to protect the autonomy of the local constituency party over the selection of local candidates. These issues are all linked and re-emerged in the subsequent conflict over the imposition of AWS in Blaenau Gwent prior to the 2005 general election.

The positive measures taken by Welsh Labour and by Plaid resulted in twenty-four (40 per cent) women being elected as AMs in the first NAfW elections rising to thirty (50 per cent) in the second elections. Since then Plaid has followed Labour in abandoning positive action measures, though Labour is still using AWS for candidate selection in general elections, and, as we have seen, the proportion of women AMs has decreased. At the same time, however, women have been elected as leaders of the Welsh Liberal Democrats (Kirsty Williams in 2008) and Plaid Cymru (Leanne Wood in 2012).

The conflict over AWS arose prior to the 2005 Westminster elections. Labour had decided to apply AWS in at least half of the seats where a Labour MP was retiring and, if their retirement was not announced before the end of 2002, they reserved the right to impose an AWS. In Blaenau Gwent the retirement of the incumbent was announced prior to December 2002 which led to an assumption that AWS would not be imposed (Cutts, Childs and Fieldhouse, 2008). However, Labour's policy was to impose AWS in regions where there was less than 25 per cent female representation amongst MPs; these regions were the North of England and Wales – and five Welsh constituencies (Blaenau Gwent, Llanelli, Newport East, Preseli Pembrokeshire and Swansea East) had an AWS imposed. All were won by Labour women except Preseli and Blaenau, and in Blaenau, not only did the Labour candidate fail to win one of the safest Labour seats in Wales, but she was defeated by an ex-Labour AM, Peter Law, who left the Labour Party in protest at the imposition of AWS and stood as an independent. His death less than a year later resulted in a double by-election. The NAfW election was won by his wife, Trish Law, and the Westminster election was won by a man, Dai Davies; both of whom stood as independents. Only a few days after the election Peter Hain MP, the Welsh Secretary, apologised to 'the people of Blaenau Gwent' for having imposed an All Women Shortlist. 'We sought to present a choice of women only and we over-rode local party wishes and the wishes of the people of Blaneau Gwent' (Childs and Cowley, 2011, p. 17). This message suggests that the commitment of the Labour Party to increasing women's representation may falter when such a commitment is not electorally expedient (Davies and Williams, 2009). Trish Law's election, however, meant that the proportion of women AMs rose to 52 per cent and the idea that the Blaenau electorate were opposed to women candidates could be refuted. Indeed there is no discernible negative effect of women candidates or AWS (Childs and Cowley, 2011) and women candidates may even be preferred by the electorate.

Two of the arguments used against the imposition of an AWS in Blaenau were that the proposed candidate was not local and that she was being imposed by the Blairite centre. However, as Davies and Williams observe, the constituency party could have chosen to support a local, woman candidate (2009, p. 200). It has been noted that arguments about the importance of selecting a local candidate are often advanced in the face of pressure from the centre to select a woman candidate and often result in the selection of a man (Childs and Cowley, 2011; Evans, 2008). This is not only the case in the Labour Party but is also true of the Liberal Democrats and Conservatives and is ostensibly about defending the autonomy of the local party. It has unfortunate consequences for gender equality and women's political representation and 'the issue of women's descriptive representation in the UK – especially the use of measures such as All Women Shortlists (AWS) – has been cast as a zero-sum game against men, especially against "local" men' (Childs and Cowley, 2011, p. 2).

The conflict over AWS in Blaenau was very damaging to the idea of positive action in Wales and more generally; this emerged in our interviews with AMs and with councillors. In what follows we describe the gender culture of local government in our three case study areas before exploring local councillors' understandings of gender equality and feminism and their attitudes towards women's political representation. Such views are significant in light of the fact that local government has to implement policies which have an impact on gender inequalities and may affect the ways in which equality legislation is interpreted and implemented (see for example Charles and Jones, 2010).

A MASCULINIZED CULTURE

Many AMs had been councillors before standing for election to the Assembly (see Table 10.3) or had partners/friends who were councillors so they were able to talk about the gendered culture of local government.

Table 10.3
Number of AMs who had been local councillors

	Women	Men	Total
Conservative	0	2	2
Labour	6	2	8
Liberal Democrat	1	1	2
Plaid Cymru	3	1	4
Independent	0	0	0
Total	10	6	16

One of the women Plaid AMs said:

> you have to remember that I was a member of a Valleys council and it had been controlled by the Labour Party since 1925, it was largely made up of older men who felt that the place for a woman was in the home, and also that they had a right to run everything locally. (Female Plaid AM)

In Wales local government is dominated by older men: 73 per cent of councillors are men and 41 per cent are retired (WLGA, 2008). There are also very few minority ethnic councillors (0.8 per cent during our research period) although, in this respect local government is no different from the Assembly where it is only since the 2007 elections that there have been any minority ethnic AMs.

In contrast to the NAfW where working hours have been designed to be family friendly (Jones et al., 2009; Chaney et al., 2007), the working environment in councils is not family friendly and it is difficult to combine the work of a councillor either with full-time employment or with caring responsibilities. As one of the women Plaid councillors put it:

> For example now, every meeting starts at ten in the morning or at two in the afternoon, so for someone who works full time it's impossible for them to be a councillor . . . nor do I see a crèche or anything being offered . . . I'm afraid that they talk about changes but they aren't ready to change. [*Int: Yes, so you don't see that it is significant?*] It's grey men in grey suits at present, and like that I can see the future. (Female Plaid councillor)

The lack of family-friendly practices reflects the masculinized culture of local government and goes along with the view that politics is a man's world which requires allegedly masculine characteristics of toughness and resilience. This, together with the fact that women are in a minority, means that in order for women to be accepted and taken seriously by male councillors they have to behave like men.

> Women in politics have to be very, very tough and very resilient and very pushy so maybe we have certain features that (laugh) to our personality that, that maybe you would associate with, with a male . . . in politics, you can't be a retiring reclining sort of accepting type of person, you have to have that tough streak and, and be determined and, you know, sometimes I think 'Am I really this kind of person?' (Female Liberal Democrat councillor)

This was the case even in the council where the proportion of women was approaching a critical mass.

Unlike AMs, who thought that there were gendered ways of doing politics, most councillors thought that there was no gender difference in political style and that the gender of a political representative was irrelevant to how they were able to do the job. This is perhaps not surprising if women are in a minority and feel that they have to adopt masculine modes of behaviour in order to survive but it co-existed with a view that women bring different qualities to local politics; they are not so inclined to indulge in political posturing, they are more empathetic and approachable, and they get things done rather than having endless meetings. Moreover, many of the councillors would have liked to see more women councillors and accepted that a wide range of life experiences amongst political representatives is important to ensure that the interests of diverse groups within the population are represented. One of the male council-lors said:

> Well I think it would improve it, to be honest with you, because a woman's aspects in life would, it would bring different aspects to the debate or to the council, you know, I think it's refreshing, to be honest with you, to have women representing different parts of the ward. (Male Independent Councillor)

And a woman spoke about the balance that a greater number of women would bring to the council.

> The Chamber last Wednesday was full . . . I was counting how many were there . . . three women. And it does make a difference to how you, you know, play your part there . . . And I think we would be more effective if we had women there, a more balanced approach to the arguments. (Female Labour Councillor)

One of the male councillors, although he did not think that women and men had different ways of doing politics, thought that there may be an equality issue in having such small numbers of women as councillors.

> It doesn't bode well for equality issues when you have got a council [with a large majority of men], but then that is what people vote for so. You know I am not sure how many candidates stood who were female, I can't remember now it is nearly four years ago, but that is what you get isn't it, you know. (Male Independent Councillor)

These views suggest that the argument about the need to increase the proportion of women political representatives has to some extent been accepted, and that the grounds for this acceptance are based on notions of equality and social justice. There is also a suggestion that women may have different interests from men or at the very least bring a different perspective to bear on political issues. There is, however, a marked hostility to the introduction of measures to achieve such an increase (see also Game, 2009, p. 172) and a lack of gender awareness; this contrasts with the views on these issues which we found amongst AMs.

GENDER AWARENESS

Many AMs were aware that policies and political practices were gendered even those not explicitly about 'women's issues' (Smooth, 2011). They displayed quite a high level of gender awareness (although this varied with party) and an understanding of equalities issues generally, and saw equality as an important principle governing the work of the Assembly.[5] These high levels of gender awareness and commitment to gender equality are to be expected given the selection process gone through by Labour AMs prior to the first NAfW elections and the fact that twenty-three of the thirty-one AMs we interviewed were members of Welsh Labour or Plaid Cymru (Table 10.1) (cf. Campbell et al., 2007). Moreover ten of the women we interviewed and six of the men identified themselves as feminist in response to a question which asked them directly whether they would define themselves in this way.

At local level gender awareness was much less evident. There was little understanding of how policy issues may be gendered although support was expressed for equality of opportunity, often in terms of a denial of gender difference.

> You are a councillor and that's it. My sort of view is that if I have got a leak in the house and I need a plumber I don't care whether the plumber is male, female, black, white, whatever, it is irrelevant, I just want the leak fixed, that's it. (Male Independent Councillor)

Almost all the women councillors understood the culture of local politics to be 'macho' and male dominated but only two (one Labour and one Plaid Cymru) defined themselves as feminist. None of the men defined themselves as feminist and only one talked about the male dominance of political parties at local level. Moreover feminism was seen as a means of promoting women over men rather than as having anything to do with gender equality (see also Welsh and Halcli, 2003). One of the men said:

> if you are a feminist with a belief that women should have an opportunity for opportunity's sake rather than for ability's sake then I would have an issue with that. (Male Independent)

ATTITUDES TOWARDS POSITIVE MEASURES AND SELECTION ON MERIT

Notwithstanding expressions of support for increasing women's representation, it was difficult to see how any increase was to be achieved. Even those who were critical of the male dominance of local politics were not in favour of positive action (with the exception of the two women who defined themselves as feminist) although some were supportive of measures which would promote gender equality. Furthermore some of the councillors saw the whole idea of positive action as a luxury, given the difficulties of finding people who are willing to stand in local elections and who have the necessary skills to do so. One of the Labour women councillors told us:

> I mean we had some people in, some commission, looking at if they could increase numbers of women and they asked me if there is any way it could be done, and I dared to say yes it would be quite easy in our authority because all the wards are multi-members, so you just have to say half the seats are for women, half are for men, huge boos and jeers [*Int: Really*] But it would be really simple to do and without affecting anybody, you could do it when vacancies arose you don't have to chuck people out of their seats to do it. [*Int: But that didn't go down well. Was that across the parties or was that within the Labour Group?*] It was across the board. (Female Labour Councillor)

The arguments used to justify opposition to positive measures were couched in terms of merit and were articulated by women as well as men. Measures such as twinning and all-women shortlists were seen as 'positive discrimination', as running counter to selection on the basis of merit, and as resulting in women who were less good than their male counterparts being selected and elected simply because they were women. This position was supported by claims that gender makes no difference to the effectiveness of a councillor, that there is nothing stopping women standing for selection and election, and that the current selection procedures are meritocratic and ensure that the best person wins.

The view that gender makes no difference to doing politics legitimates the argument that there is no need to take any special measures to ensure an increase in women's representation and, in effect, preserves 'jobs for the boys' (Rallings et al., 2010). One of the male councillors thought there was little that could be done about the under-representation of women – it was 'just how it is'.

> To me it doesn't matter whether there is a man or a woman, we are going out and we are looking at people who are working in the community and it just happens to be the vast majority of people who are doing that are men . . . it just so happens there aren't many women out there who come forward. Whether that's good or whether that's bad is neither here nor there it's just how it is. (Male Independent Councillor)

Several of the men were of the opinion that there was nothing holding women back.

> I don't think any woman would be held back if she went to her ward party or the Labour party or stood on her own . . . Myself, personally, I am not for positive discrimination, if it's all men or all women you can't do anything at all about it but it would be nice to see another, for argument's sake, a third of the council, it would be nice to see a woman's point of view representing the community, why not, they are equal to us . . . But not positive, they got to fight on their own back but they shouldn't be debarred at these places but if you want to do it in life, you will do it, nobody will stop you. (Male Independent Councillor)

Positive action was not only seen as going against selection on merit but could also have negative consequences for women. It was a common view that 'the best person for the job' should be s/elected and that positive discrimination resulted in inferior candidates: 'it is immaterial male or female to myself so long as the best person for the position [is selected]' and positive action results in 'a female in one post because you had to do it, party rules, and what have happened, not up to the standard like' (Male Labour Councillor). Women were not comfortable with this.

> No I don't like it at all. A person should be there because they are the best person for that particular role, and whether you are a man or a woman it shouldn't be – we shouldn't be favoured just because of our sex, I think that's wrong. (Female Labour Councillor)

However, as one of the Labour women commented:

> The party brought in gender balance and men didn't like that, right, you have got to go for the best but women will always be overlooked even if they are the best. (Female Labour Councillor)

Positive measures are seen as giving an unfair advantage to individuals which not only goes against the idea of equal opportunities and equal treatment but can also undermine women's legitimacy as political representatives. This stigmatizing effect has been noted amongst women MPs elected on AWS, at least initially (Childs and Krook, 2012), and testifies to the tension between notions of equal opportunity, which is associated with merit and equal treatment, and treatment based on difference which is seen as privileging certain individuals over others rather than seeking to eliminate group disadvantage and exclusion. Indeed AWS were seen as discriminating against men and creating a backlash. One male councillor who thought the number of women in local government should be increased, when asked how that might be achieved said:

> Well that's the million dollar question isn't it? You could put up all female candidates but I don't think that's the correct way to do it because you end up with a backlash saying that's discrimination against men . . . You know look what happened over in Blaenau Gwent with Peter Law, that is initially what that was about, it was about the fact they were imposing a women only list. (Male Independent)

And two of the male councillors we interviewed had left the Labour party over this issue.

GENDERED NETWORKS

Although almost none of the councillors supported positive action there was some support for equality promotion involving 'women's capacity building' (Dahlerup and Friedenvall, 2005, p. 3) such as training or mentoring. One of the women had become a councillor through mentoring which is a common route into local politics.

> I don't think I would have made the leap from community councillor to city councillor without Sandra saying 'Oh please, come and support me', you know, 'we need more women to move things forward' . . . I don't believe in putting all women forward, I believe in the best person for the job, but I knew I would be able to do it, you know, if I was elected. (Female Liberal Democrat Councillor)

One of the things at issue here is that an increase in women's representation necessarily involves a reduction in the number of men who are able to become councillors and a challenge to the male stranglehold on politics in general and local government in particular. One of the women councillors told us that at local level,

> local councillors feel that their seats would be under threat if they had to make way for women, so they don't want to know. And you get these sort of arguments that people should be appointed on their merits . . . you know it doesn't just happen that the majority of our councillors, the best person just happened to be men, I don't think so. (Female Labour Councillor)

Another woman also spoke about the way men informally select other men to replace them when they decide to retire thereby reproducing the gender inequalities characterizing local government (cf. Rallings et al., 2010).

[we] are now beginning to select or look for people to start coaching or who want to become councillors. And . . . it came up are we going to be encouraging any women, and I think the answer was that, no not necessarily, she puts herself forward . . . But what I saw was a lot of the men who have already earmarked someone who's interested, they are all men that have been earmarked. (Female Labour Councillor)

This underlines the importance of informal, male networks in ensuring that men continue to predominate within local government and gives the lie to the idea that political representatives are selected solely on merit. It also demonstrates resistance on the part of men to recruiting women at local level. Patronage is important and, as we have seen, mentoring is one of the ways in which women are encouraged to stand for election at local level. However, as long as men are in a majority in local parties, it is likely to be men who are mentored rather than women. It was only women in the Labour Party who mentioned recruitment through male networks; men did not talk about this at all, simply claiming that there were no barriers to women standing for election.

CLASS AND LOCAL AUTONOMY

There were two other dimensions of opposition to positive measures which related to class and central party control. These were particularly, though not exclusively, articulated by male Labour councillors. One of them observed that twinning and AWS were simply a means for middle-class women to further their political careers at the expense of working-class men and that what was being forgotten in all the discussion of inequalities was 'postcode discrimination'. And there is indeed a class difference between AMs and councillors which is reflected in their different routes into politics, their different occupations and their differing levels of educational attainment. There is also a resentment of control of what are seen as local selection processes by the centre which is manifest, for the Labour party, in an identification with 'old' rather than 'new' Labour but was also evident in other parties in the form of an assertion of local autonomy over the selection process. Attempts by the centre to encourage women candidates were resisted purely because at local level it was felt to be an imposition of views from elsewhere. In Blaenau Gwent all these things had come together: the candidate who was selected from the AWS was not only a woman and from Cardiff, she was also upwardly mobile with a professional occupation based in England. As one of the Labour councillors said:

the national people are remote from the grass roots, they're remote from the trade unions, they're remote from everyone else because what you've got is a different calibre of Labour politician . . . the Blairs of this world and all those very highly qualified people, and you sometimes wonder whether they have just forgotten where the grass roots is. (Male Labour Councillor)

These observations underline the class differences between the Labour Party leadership and its rank and file and the continuing importance of class politics, particularly in the post-industrial local authority where, as one of the councillors said:

[My] father's generation saw work as with a pick and a shovel, you know, people are being told now that it doesn't necessarily involve physical, manual labour, industrial work . . . it has been difficult for people to absorb, a change from a heavy industrial base to service industries, tourism, this sort of thing. For a generation that has grown up thinking that work involves coal, steel, metal, sweat, it is a bit of something to get used to. (Male Independent Councillor)

These changes also involve a gender shift from male-dominated heavy industry to female-dominated service industries.

CONCLUSIONS

Our evidence suggests that at local level there are both gender differences and differences between parties in views on women's political representation and that these differences relate not only to understandings of gender equality and feminism but also to the masculinist culture of local politics. Although almost all our interviewees were opposed to positive action measures, most of the women recognized the gendered nature of local government and the difficulties this placed in the way of women being selected as candidates and, even though they wanted to be s/elected on merit, there was some recognition that current selection processes were stacked against them. Many of the men, while agreeing that it would be good to have more women as councillors, did not see the male domination of local politics as a problem and were vehemently opposed to any measures which appeared to favour women. At the same time they expressed support for gender equality and equality of opportunity and favoured a gender neutral approach to questions of candidate selection. Women were more likely to recognize that positive steps needed to be taken if women's representation was to increase but it was only the two women who identified themselves as feminist who supported positive action. Men's views were more 'traditional' than women's and took a particular form amongst men associated with the Labour Party, some of whom had lost out as a result of positive action measures. These were also the men who were at the 'sharp end' of the shift from an industrial to a post-industrial economy.

Part of the resistance to positive measures, at least for those in the Labour Party, related to the fact the measures to increase the number of women representatives symbolized processes of modernization and the project of New Labour. Moreover, positive measures were seen by some as benefitting middle-class women over working-class men, and those who were not local over those who were. These are issues which need to be taken into account when consider-ing measures to increase women's political representation. Descriptive representation is not achieved simply by having more women representatives if they are all from the same class and ethnicity although this is an important first step. As Edwards and Chapman (2000) point out, there needs to be diversity amongst women political representatives. Ironically, in 2003 the retiring Labour Party candidate in Blaenau Gwent alluded to this issue when he said that AWS were not about positive discrimination but about imposing the will of the centre: 'why aren't we discriminating in favour of people who are disabled, who come from ethnic minorities (or) who come from working class com-munities' (BBC News, 2003). Such arguments, while having a kernel of truth, are often advanced to render the whole project of positive measures to improve women's representation unwieldy and unworkable and they serve to divert attention from the fact that local government is still dominated by men of a generation and class for whom politics is a man's world and women, if they want to be accepted, have to play by the men's rules.

These findings support the comments of the Electoral Reform Society Wales's report with which we began. Political parties need to do more at local level to ensure a gender balance amongst councillors and part of this, as one of our Labour interviewees said, involves engaging the membership at local level with the issues of women's political representation and the way current s/election methods work against equal opportunities. At the same time, however, parties need to recognize that a diversity of representatives is necessary to achieve descriptive representation, that class, as well as gender and other bases of inequality, needs to be taken into account when considering political repre-sentation, and that positive measures are essential if descriptive representation at local level is to be achieved.

NOTES

[1]   The research was funded by the ESRC (grant number RES 000231185). The research team consisted of Nickie Charles (PI), University of Warwick; Charlotte Aull Davies and Stephanie Jones (Co-Investigators), Swansea University.

[2]   For the first Assembly elections the Labour Party twinned constituencies with each other and each pair had to select one male and one female candidate. Plaid Cymru placed a female candidate first and third on its regional lists, hence the term zipping.

[3]   In order to protect the anonymity of our interviewees we only provide a rough indication of the gender composition of our case study councils. We also give the label 'Independent' to any councillor who is not a member of one of the four main political parties in Wales.

[4]   Post-industrial refers to an area which is not a large conurbation and was previously dominated by coal and/or steel production which has now, to all intents and purposes, ceased.

[5]   Clause 120 of the 1998 Government of Wales Act (Clause 77 in the 2006 Government of Wales Act) obliged the Welsh Assembly Government to consider equality of opportunity throughout all its business. Several of the women who campaigned for this duty to be enshrined in the new institution were AMs and in the second Assembly some were ministers (Mackay, 2004).

REFERENCES

BBC News (2003). 'Labour could reopen women row', 27 June 2003, *http://news.bbc.co.uk/1/hi/wales/3024586.stm* (accessed 20 August 2012).

Bochel, C. and Bochel, H. M. (2006). 'Modernisation or backward step? Women councillors and new decision-making structures in local government', in *Local Government Studies,* 30, 1, 36–50.

Broussine, M. and Fox, R. (2010). 'Rethinking leadership in local government: the place of "feminine" styles in the modernised council', *Local Government Studies*, 28, 4, 91–106.

Campbell, R., Childs, S. and Lovenduski, J. (2010). 'Do women need women representatives?', *British Journal of Political Science*, 40, 1, 171–94.

Campbell, R. and Lovenduski, J. (2005). 'Winning women's votes? The incremental track to equality', *Parliamentary Affairs*, 58, 4, 837–853.

Campbell, R., Childs, S. and Lovenduski, J. (2007). '"It is not about political correctness; it's about being politically effective"; the feminization of the Conservative Party under David Cameron', Paper presented at the PSA Annual Conference, University of Bath, March 22–3.

Chaney, P., Mackay, F. and McAllister, L. (2007). *Women, Politics and Constitutional Change: The First Years of the National Assembly for Wales*, Cardiff: University of Wales Press.

Charles, N. (2010). 'Setting the scene: devolution, gender politics and social justice', in N. Charles and C. A. Davies (eds), *Gender and Social Justice in Wales*, Cardiff: University of Wales Press.

Charles, N. and Jones, S. (2010). 'Developing a domestic abuse strategy', in N. Charles and C. A. Davies (eds), *Gender and Social Justice in Wales*, Cardiff: University of Wales Press.

Childs, S. and Cowley, P. (2011). 'The politics of local presence: is there a case for descriptive representation?', *Political Studies*, 59, 1, 1–19.

Childs, S. and Krook, M. L. (2012). 'Labels and mandates in the United Kingdom', in S. Franceschet, M. L. Krook and J. M. Piscopo (eds), *The Impact of Gender Quotas*, Oxford: Oxford University Press.

Cutts, D., Childs, S. and Fieldhouse, E. (2008). '"This is what happens when you don't listen." All women shortlists at the 2005 general election', *Party Politics*, 14, 5, 575–95.

Davies, N. and Williams, D. (2009). *Clear Red Water: Welsh Devolution and Socialist Politics*, London: Francis Boutle Publishers.

Dahlerup, D. (2006). 'The story of the theory of critical mass', *Politics and Gender*, 2, 4, 511–22.

Dahlerup, D. and Friedenval, L. (2005). 'Quotas as a "fast track" to equal representation for women', *International Feminist Journal of Politics*, 7, 1, 26–48.

Edwards, J. and Chapman, C. (2000). 'Women's political representation in Wales: waving or drowning?', *Contemporary Politics*, 6, 4, 367–81.

EHRC Wales (2012). *Who Runs Wales? 2012*, Cardiff: EHRC Wales.

Electoral Reform Society Wales (2012). *Spotlight on Wales. Women and Local Government*, Cardiff: ERSW, *http://www.electoral-reform.org.uk/images/dynamicImages/file/Wales/Women%20and%20local%20government%20in%20Wales2012.pdf* (acessed 3 February 2013).

Evans, E. (2008). 'Supply or demand? Women candidates and the Liberal Democrats', *The British Journal of Politics and International Relations*, 10, 4, 590–606.

Franceschet, S., Krook, M. L. and Piscopo, J. M. (eds) (2012). *The Impact of Gender Quotas*, Oxford: Oxford University Press.

Fox, R. (2011). '"Boom and bust in women's representation": lessons to be learnt from a decade of devolution', *Parliamentary Affairs*, 64, 1, 193–203.

Fox, P. and Broussine, M. (2001). *Room At The Top? A Study of Women Chief Executives in Local Government in England and Wales*, Bristol: Bristol Business School.

Game, C. (2009). 'Twenty-nine percent women councillors after a mere 100 years', *Public Policy and Administration*, 24, 2, 153–74.

Jones, S., Charles, N. and Davies, C. A. (2009). 'Transforming masculinist political cultures? Doing politics in new political institutions', *Sociological Research Online*, 14, 2/3), *http://www.socresonline.org.uk/14/2/1.html* (accessed 3 February 2013).

Krook, M. L. (2011). *Quotas for Women in Politics: Gender and Candidate Selection Reform Worldwide*, Oxford Scholarship Online.

Krook, M. L. and O'Brien, J. (2010). 'The politics of group representation: quotas for women and minorities worldwide', *Comparative Politics*, 42, 3, 253–72.

Krook, M. L. and Squires, J. (2006). 'Gender quotas in British politics: multiple approaches and methods in feminist research', *British Politics*, 1, 44–66.

Lovenduski, J. (2005). *Feminizing Politics*, Cambridge: Polity Press.

Lovenduski, J. (1996). 'Sex, gender and British politics', in J. Lovenduski and P. Norris (eds), *Women in Politics*, Oxford: Oxford University Press.

Mackay, F. (2004). 'Gender and political representation in the UK: the state of the discipline', *British Journal of Politics and International Relations*, 6, 1, 99–120.

Marshall, T. H. (1950). *Citizenship and Social Class*, Cambridge: Cambridge University Press.

Perrigo, S. (1996). 'Women and change in the Labour Party 1979–1995', in J. Lovenduski and P. Norris (eds), *Women in Politics*, Oxford: Oxford University Press.

Phillips, A. (1991). *Engendering Democracy*, Cambridge: Polity Press.

Phillips, A. (1995). *The Politics of Presence*, Oxford: Clarendon Press.

Phillips, A. (1998). 'Democracy and representation: or, why should it matter who our representatives are?', in A. Phillips (ed.) *Feminism and Politics*, Oxford: Oxford University Press.

Puwar, N. (2004). 'Thinking about making a difference', *British Journal of Politics and International Relations*, 6, 1, 65–80.

Rallings, C., Thrasher, M., Borisyuk, G. and Shears, M. (2010). 'Parties, recruitment and modernisation: evidence from local election candidates', *Local Government Studies*, 36, 3, 361–79.

Russell, M., Mackay, F. and McAllister, L. (2002). 'Women's representation in the Scottish Parliament and National Assembly for Wales: party dynamics for achieving critical mass', *Journal of Legislative Studies*, 8, 2, 49–76.

Smooth, W. (2011). 'Standing for women? Which women? The substantive representation of women's interests and the research imperative of intersectionality', *Politics and Gender*, 7, 3, 436–41.

Squires, J. (2005). 'The implementation of gender quotas in Britain', paper for the International IDEA Project on Electoral Quotas for Women *http://www.quotaproject.org/CS/CS_Britain_Squires.pdf* (accessed 16 December 2012).

Squires, J. (2007). *The New Politics of Gender Equality,* Basingstoke: Palgrave Macmillan.

Stirbu, D. S. (2011). 'Female representation beyond Westminster', *Political Insight*, 2, 3, 32–3.

Watt, N. (2003). 'Equality: women win half Welsh seats', *The Guardian Newspaper*, 3 May 2003.

Welsh, E. and Halcli, A. (2003). 'Accounts of feminism among women local councillors in England', *Women's Studies International Forum*, 26, 4, 345–56.

Welsh Local Government Association (2004). *WLGA Report*, Cardiff: Welsh Local Government Association.

Welsh Local Government Association (2008). *Member Profile 2008* (unpublished data).

Young, I. M. (1990). *Justice and the Politics of Difference*, Princeton, New Jersey: Princeton University Press.

11. 'WE ALWAYS INVITE RESIDENTS TO COME ALONG . . .' DISCOURSES OF CITIZENSHIP AMONG LOCAL GOVERNMENT STAKEHOLDERS

Sally Baker, Brian J. Brown and Howard H. Davis

ABSTRACT

This paper explores the ways in which managers of organizations delivering services to the public in Wales talk about and conceptualize the publics using these services. Topics covered in interviews with these stakeholders include: local democracy; responsibility; behavioural shifts; citizen participation; local specificities; responses to devolution. The themes are analysed in the context of neoliberal welfare reform and the impending financial crisis. The authors review the implicit assumptions in the data. They compare the results of the analysis with wider debates about the erosion of state accountability in relation to rights of citizens and explore the degree to which the views of the stake-holders equate with John Clarke's (2005) 'New Labour's Citizens: activated, empowered, responsibilized, abandoned?' The discussion engages with the question of whether policies in Wales since devolution have promoted a more positive approach to citizenship and participation than in Clarke's dystopian description.

INTRODUCTION

How do managers in organizations which provide services to the public in Wales talk about the publics in receipt of these services? In this paper we explore conceptions of citizenship under a devolved administration that had rejected New Labour ideology and was facing the conundrum of maintaining public services whilst coming to terms with budgetary control imposed from Westminster. Drakeford (2012) provides an excellent account of the political and economic climate in Wales at this time, when many aspects of neoliberal welfare reform were rejected in favour of the 'new set of citizenship rights' based upon the provision of universal, unconditional public services, free at the point of use.

In the mid-1990s, Labour policy rebranded as New Labour explicitly assigned a public participatory role to the recipients of public services – 'service user involvement' or 'citizen participation'. The case for citizen participation was typically framed in terms of positive outcomes such as better services, more appropriately geared to the public's needs. The agenda of public service reform combined the previous Conservative government's vision of public service provision as new managerialism with these themes of citizen participation. Hall (2003) argued that New Labour had two strands, one neoliberal and one social democratic. The latter was constantly being transformed into the former and the citizen-consumer was an example of this – conceptions of citizenship were subordinated and transformed through the imagery of 'user choice'.

Critics have variously questioned this version of the case for participation. Eckert (2011, p. 310) maintains that: 'What we are witnessing is the diminishment of state accountability, particularly in terms of the social rights of citizens'. Yet at the same time there has been a proliferation of ways in which persons are created as legal and civil subjects by the minute administrative practices and classifications of everyday life such as granting tenancies in social housing, administering justice, visiting the doctor, being a member of a voluntary or civic organization and so on (Das, 2011). Good citizenship translates into trying to be a healthy citizen, a responsible tenant or householder and a proficient participant in a variety of therapeutic and wellbeing-enhancing activities, the areas in which the capillary state has been particularly active in infiltrating (Clarke, 2010). The arts of government and the way that governments attempt to produce citizens best suited to fulfilling the government's policies (Rose, 1999; Rose and Osborne, 2000; Rose and Novas, 2005) can be seen as a process of étatization – or growing state dominance – over a variety of spheres including minds and bodies (Mitchell, 2000). The claims that the state can make on the citizen have become 'flexibilized' (Ong, 1998), whilst at the same time the possibilities of citizens making equivalent claims on their states – the social democratic strand – have become less clear cut and, as Das (2004) says, more 'illegible'. In sum, notions of citizenship in terms of collectively held rights have been supplemented by a greater focus on the responsibilities of citizenship exercised through new forms of subjection in workplaces, in public and in private life (Brown and Baker, 2012).

In their sustained critique of New Labour's response to neoliberalism, Clarke and Newman (Clarke 2004, 2005; Clarke et al., 2007; Newman and Clarke, 2009; Vidler and Clarke, 2005) have described the dissolution of the 'public realm' and how policies stressed partnership with communities of place and identity, making an issue out of the politics of representation, and the 'representativeness' of public services. The construction of 'citizen-consumers' was a mechanism for governing the social, and the citizen-consumer displaced the citizen in New Labour's public service reforms (Clarke et al., 2007; Vidler and Clarke, 2005). But representational accuracy does not necessarily rest on the faithful reproduction of the social profile of the wider population within the involved group. Martin (2008) has also argued that the qualities required of involved members of the public are not limited to 'representativeness' or 'expertise', but rather encompass various attributes seen as important in governing the interface between state and society.

An integral part of citizen-consumer participation is a particular type of valorization of the 'ordinary' person, based on the notion that ordinary people are not at heart political (Clarke, 2010). Ordinary people can be used as partners/participants in new assemblages of power and it is their assumed apolitical character, and their capacity to bring values, knowledge and other resources, that are valued as a strategy for governing the social (Clarke, 2010). Martin (2008) noted how ordinary people were used in governmental strategies to depoliticize issues – although they often repoliticized them.

Under New Labour, citizens were the objects of pedagogy, subjected to training for employment, developed to become active citizens and subjected to new governmental strategies on diet, exercise, smoking, parenting, recycling, volunteering and wellbeing. They were brought into closer encounters with government actors through co-production, participation and governance initiatives (Newman, 2010). Newman notes that this has continued under the present Conservative-Liberal Coalition Government, and as Brown and Baker (2012) note, its legacy can be seen in notions such as David Cameron's 'Big Society'.

The stakeholder research described below was designed to continue critical reflection on such themes by exploring the everyday assumptions, talk and practices used by managers of public services. Do they constitute a new rhetoric of citizenship? We focus on the degree to which the views of the stake-holders equate with John Clarke's (2005) 'New Labour's Citizens: activated, empowered, responsibilized, abandoned?'

DATA AND METHODOLOGY

The research in this paper was conducted during the period of UK welfare reform under New Labour (1997–2010) and the subsequent period of transition during the first year of the Westminster Conservative-Liberal Coalition administration. The data are specific to the recent Welsh situation, which can be treated as a test case for alternative policies by a government whose policy-making 'conceptualizes the relation between state and the individual as rooted in shared citizenship' (Drakeford, 2012).

To explore and compare notions of publics and citizen participation across a variety of sectors of delivery, we present the findings of an analysis of semi-structured interviews conducted as part of the 'Localities' programme of the Wales Institute of Social and Economic Research, Data and Methods (WISERD). The sample consisted of managers at the highest level in seven unitary authorities and senior managers in other bodies with responsibility for service delivery. The research partners collaborated to produce 122 individual inter-views from three regions in Wales, north, central and south. The regions are significantly different in population size, and density, economic structure and local government organization so we have selected data from a single region in order to minimize these contrasts and achieve greater depth in the analysis. The aim was to provide insights into stakeholders' perspectives on their localities, local knowledge, policy spaces and the impact of devolution at local and sub-national levels (see Jones et al., 2012). We use a sub-group of twenty-three interviews with senior managers in North Wales (excluding the Isle of Anglesey local authority) working in the following sectors: social care; economic development/regeneration; crime prevention (youth justice, community safety partnerships); education; careers services; housing. Multi-disciplinary working meant that many of the interviewees worked closely with their counterparts in other sectors; the same policies, strategy documents and aspirations were mentioned. Much of this region is disadvantaged socio-economically. It includes a large rural area with sparsely populated uplands, some predominantly Welsh-speaking areas, as well as a more heavily populated coastal region which is a popular retirement destination for migrants from England, and an industrial urban area near the English border. In parts of the region services are delivered bilingually. The interviews were conducted in the last year of the UK New Labour administration, when managers were aware of the forthcoming restrictions on public spending but before they had actually been imposed. Because of devolution, many of the interviewees and the organizations that they repre-sented had responsibilities to, and were influenced by, the Welsh Assembly

Government (WAG, now the Welsh Government) as well as Westminster. A major recent change in the region has been the reorganization of the NHS by the Welsh Government, which resulted in one very big organization replacing a number of smaller ones.

Citizen engagement was one of the core themes of the interview. The largely open question design was informed by academic debates on deliberative democracy, 'upstream' public engagement, and how local knowledge shapes practices of citizenship and community participation. Interviewees were given full opportunity to comment on policies within Wales such as the 'citizen-centred' service delivery advocated in the Beecham Report (2006). We have concentrated our attention on the part of the interview which deals most directly with power, resources, citizenship engagement, consultation and participation. The questions included: 'who makes decisions that affect your patch?' and 'to what extent can people affect decisions about their locality?' Each interview was transcribed in full and each transcript was read independently by all three authors of this paper. A thematic analysis was conducted, with categories developed in a grounded way, that is by identifying what the interviewees see as relevant to the topic and significant in relation to their organizational role. Quotations are identified by the institutional role of the speaker but in order to maintain anonymity, further details such as title and location are not included.

FINDINGS

The views expressed were noticeably homogenous although those which concerned education, housing and economic regeneration showed some local specificity. The first general observation is the notable absence of references to local politics and democracy. The exception is the small number of interviewees who praised some local councillors (in personal terms, irrespective of political allegiance) for their dedication to the local population and area:

> (crime prevention manager): *'the top people are very bothered about the real people at the bottom that they're serving . . . they genuinely seem concerned, . . . to . . . really care . . . councillors, the elected members, they definitely care . . . I know that they still have their politics games.'*

But despite the subject matter of participation there was strikingly little discussion of the public being involved in local democracy or even patterns of voting, and no comment on whether this was an issue of concern. Politics itself is here sidelined into the notion of 'politics games', and what these might mean for the public and their voting behaviour was unexplored.

A second general observation is that the first person pronouns 'we' or 'our' were commonly used by the interviewees to refer to themselves as service providers, along with 'they' or 'them' to refer to the people in receipt of services. Typical phrases are: *'building their confidence so they can do it'*, *'helping people . . . develop themselves into a voice'* and *'these people need more support'*. It suggests that this is not an inclusive discourse of citizenship and that it is usually the service managers rather than the participating citizens who *'set the agenda'* or decide what should be prioritized. There is vocabulary that is specific to certain domains: for example, social care professionals routinely refer to 'service users', other sectors do not. Interviewees referred to 'community' frequently, but never to civil society or the public sphere. There is a single reference to *'our culture as Welsh people'* (which can of course be interpreted as a more inclusive way of speaking or not, depending upon how 'Welsh' is defined). When discussing active citizenship or people 'participating', the notion of 'participation' was used very broadly, usually with reference to aspects of everyday life – going to work or college, spending time on leisure activities, or taking exercise, where these activities involved facilities for which the interviewees were responsible. Their function was to *'service these people'* as one interviewee put it. Rather than espousing Marshall's (1950) classic notion of citizenship in terms of rights, the drift here is towards an altogether more managerial and paternalistic process. Its workings can be seen in the interviewees' talk about the need for behaviour change, their relationship with service users, power and participation, and the barriers to positive change. We will review evidence on each of these themes.

Changing attitudes and behaviour
Change, and the need for it, is a pervasive theme. Interviews were permeated by the assumption that the perceptions and cultures of people using services, the wider population and even the managers themselves needed to change. Culture change was invariably discussed within the context of convincing people to become 'independent' (especially through employment, if possible in the private sector) and not make demands upon public services or claim benefits: (social care manager): *'there's a culture in some families where it's the norm not to work and to survive on state intervention and . . . that's got to change'*. Thus, in common with governmental and popular press discourse, the citizen is a burden on the state rather than, for example an asset to the nation,

and the solution was cast in interior, psychosocial terms – changing cultures or perceptions.

Changing perceptions was deemed important in rather more specific circumstances: for example, in terms of encouraging people to accept tenancies in an area of 'hard to let' housing:

> (community regeneration manager): *'outside this area [there is] some feeling of not wanting to come and live here, it's full of drugs, it's full of this, full of that and it clearly isn't and we're trying to get that message across continually . . . it's very difficult to do that if people are mindset in not wanting their children to go to certain schools but we know that the schools here are performing far better than any school within the county borough.'*

Despite the faith that this manager had in the solution proffered by changing perceptions of this estate, there followed an admission that perhaps the problem identified by potential tenants was indeed more than a matter of perception:

> *'. . . the main crux of this estate is going to be housing . . . if the housing goes over to a registered social landlord I think there's every opportunity that [this estate] will be one of the best communities . . . we are going to struggle if we don't get the finances to change the environment . . . you can change mindsets in communities but you can't change the environment without the money.'*

This interviewee explained that if the housing stock was transferred from the council to a registered social landlord, a substantial investment could be made into the stock in the community regeneration area. However, the tenants of the borough as a whole had previously voted not to transfer the stock and it had now been decided to hold another vote. One group of enterprising tenants had acquired a housing grant and had used it to employ a consultant to advise them as to how to ensure that the housing stock was transferred. The interviewee was clearly anxious about the situation and feared another 'no' vote in the forthcoming ballot. McKee and Cooper (2008) noted that promised investment was often used as an inducement to persuade tenants to vote for housing stock transfer, and it was clear from the interviewee quoted above that investment in this housing estate was badly needed. There was a clash between two groups of 'ordinary' people with different ideas as to the best way of managing the housing estate and the situation had been repoliticized by the tenants.

Changing perceptions was also important for economic regeneration. One response referred to the attempt to persuade organizations to establish themselves or invest in the area:

'we're doing a lot of work recently [for the town] on branding and place marketing and understanding perception . . . until now we probably felt that we haven't got a product to market.'

And changing perceptions was believed to be a solution to the permanent out-migration of younger residents, particularly those deemed more able or aspirational:

(economic regeneration manager): *'young people get [the perception] in school . . . that not too much happens around here . . . once they get that into their mind then it's very difficult to remove that . . . it's good that young people are able to move away. The perception problem around here is that they leave without any thought of coming back ever . . . a lot of valuable work could be done on the perception.'*

In this way, it is as if aspiration itself is being cast as the problem, tempting people away rather than remaining local and running the risk of failure.

It even appears that changing perceptions is a more important topic in crime prevention than detecting/reducing crime itself; talk focussed not so much on patterns of crime as on people's perceptions of crime, particularly whether people 'felt safer'.

The boundary between 'behavioural shifts' and 'changing perceptions' is blurred. Notions of changing perceptions seem to be deployed in the face of intractable problems – a notorious area where people refuse to live, a region that is having difficulty attracting investment or business, or a long history of outward migration of qualified young people. These are problems that Wales has faced for generations and despite numerous 'initiatives', the problems stubbornly remain and it is as if the solution is now to convince people that these are problems only in the eye of the beholder: (economic regeneration manager): *'it isn't what actually is that's the key, but it's the way people see what they think is . . . a lot of policies are done on the basis that people are rational beings and they're not'.* The sense of the citizen as somehow irrational and in need of guidance has permeated the broader policy sphere too (Institute for Government, 2010). Interestingly, elsewhere in the interviews the managers themselves acknowledged that although mindsets can be changed, environments – and perhaps other problems too – need money to change.

User involvement

Comments from social care managers illuminated some of the contradictions and limitations at the heart of the 'service user' notion of participation. This has been embraced by social care perhaps more wholeheartedly than any other sector.

Our interviewees undoubtedly were committed to this notion and believed it to be central to their practice:

> (social care manager): '*I really would like to be able to be have a sustainable participation officer . . . there's a role for somebody like that [a children's rights officer] . . . within the department as well as . . . having people like the Children's Commissioner and us commissioning advocacy services outside as we do . . . trying to maintain children and young people's involvement is a bit like trying to paint the Forth Bridge . . . My head of safeguarding is also I think very committed to children's and young people's participation . . . she's working very hard with her safeguarding unit staff which are the independent reviewing officers and children's protection co-ordinator to really get them to buy in to how important children's participation is . . . we always put on some training events around children's participation every year . . . as a council . . . there are developments around advocacy . . .*'

The description of advocacy which followed shows that this organization has an uncritically positive view of institutionally designed user participation. However, another comment from the same interviewee reveals an underlying weakness:

> '*if the social worker has got children on the child protection register, actually having the time to engage directly with children and get to a point where they can really find out the child's views and help the child's views and help the child to express those views and play a part in any plans that are made for that child is fairly limited.*'

This points to a generic problem with user participation, namely that the social workers are unable to engage with the clients. The reason given in this particular example is time pressure on social workers, yet the data suggests further obstacles too:

> '*we have new generations of social workers coming into the department all of the time . . . by its nature social work training has got to cover such a range of things it's very hit or miss as to how much experience or confidence workers have got about directly engaging with children and young people . . . if you've got an established participation officer, first of all they'd be putting the message across all the time you must directly involve the child and young person and secondly they'd be able to provide support and skills to social workers to help them to be good at engaging with children directly . . . if I have one wish it would be about being able to sort of really strengthen that . . .*'

Thus many social workers may not have learnt how to engage clients and may not use their knowledge and experience creatively to do so. There is also the 'professional instinct' at work, in that the response to 'user involvement' not working as hoped is to import further expertise. Participation officers will also provide a defence for the service in the face of complaint, demonstrating that user involvement is alive and well in the service (Baker, Brown and Gwilym, 2008).

Power and participation

Participation is also a theme in other sectors such as housing and community regeneration. References to 'partnership', the value of 'local knowledge' and the 'user perspective' hint at a more developed, representative, view of power: (housing manager): *'we firmly believe for us to improve services and for tenants to have real influence they should be involved in the management of the organization'.*

This locally rooted housing association has been particularly successful in citizen participation and has a high proportion of tenants on its management board as well as in other decision making forums within the organization. On the other hand, a manager of a community regeneration organization revealed tensions regarding tenants' participation:

> *'we're looking into the board structure with the Welsh Assembly at the moment and the WCVA [Welsh Council for Voluntary Action] as to whether or not we can get more residents on it without sort of offending the voluntary and statutory bodies . . . because it is a community programme . . . [we could give local residents] some added training to go onto the board and build confidence and so forth.'*

This suggests that as McDermont et al. (2009) maintained, the simple 'experience' of an ordinary person is not sufficient for tenant representatives; 'training' was required as well as confidence building before the tenant representatives could participate at board level. Furthermore, in this case citizen participation had to be squeezed in between the interests of other agencies. Comments from this interviewee are consistent with Cruikshank (1999) and Rose (1999) who argue that informing, tutoring, empowering and developing are part of modern governance and new governmentalities of the self. More was revealed regarding the model of citizen participation in this organization:

> *'. . . any resident in [the estate] [can be on the panel] . . . I set the agenda and I give feedback every month and invite people to come along . . . whoever we think is necessary to come along.'*

The tenants then neither 'set the agenda' nor decide who is invited. However:

> (community regeneration manager): '... *we rely a lot on the local people here to tell us what issues and what problems they may have, what knowledge they have of the estate because obviously they can go back many, many years . . . most of our information comes from the local people . . . they're the experts. If you go to the people here, that's where we believe the answers will come from.'*

So the 'people' provide the voice of everyday experience, they are characterized as 'real', spokespersons for *'real peoples' way of doing things'*. They fulfil a pedagogic role in which they teach the agency and supply everyday knowledge to the organization, in the expectation that this knowledge will allow the organization to better respond to the tenants' needs (Martin, 2008). This is a good example of 'vernacular ventriloquism' (Clarke, 2010), in which the voice of the people may be heard, but there is a tenuous and tortuous relationship to power.

The interviewees' view of, and orientation towards, the residents suggests new configurations of professional power which privilege professional conceptions of the purpose of 'empowerment' (Newman, 2010). Thus there seems to be a division between the 'residents-citizens' and the 'professionals-citizens' in this organization:

> '... *we held a child poverty conference which was extremely well attended, they had 120 delegates, we had some keynote speakers from the Assembly . . . it went down extremely well . . . there was residents . . . clearly we always invite residents to come along . . . but yes mainly it was statutory/voluntary groups that came.'*

The view taken here seemed to be that residents' involvement was certainly welcome, that the information provided by them in some contexts was valuable, but 'experts' – or even merely non-residents (the 'professionals' from this organization didn't live on the estate) – were prioritized. The professionals faced dilemmas when the residents were consistently persistent on one matter:

> '*if you were to carry out a survey now . . . a lot of people would say "more things for children to do" . . . but we've done so much for children . . . we're never ever going to get what people want . . . if you had a playground in every corner that would be fine but you can't do that . . . it is difficult at times.'*

This demonstrates the paradox within citizen participation when the citizens request things that the professionals cannot do – or, as suggested by the quote above, do not want to do. As Clarke (2010) noted, ordinary people are not wholly reliable – or predictable – agents. These dilemmas were demonstrated in the data again and again, particularly in community regeneration: *'there's a difference between wanting something and needing something and we have that issue with almost every project'*, and

> *'when somebody's justified the needs so much by you know just handing in a petition after questionnaires, after community appraisals, you do have to check it against real hard data. Now is there truly a need? So we do have the research unit who will provide us with the data. We have a policy manager who will give us an indication of how policy will impact on our work and then we've got the ears on the ground which is this network of officers . . .'*

The extent of such highly managed participation in community regeneration allegedly rooted in the 'expertise' of 'ordinary' people was clear:

> *'we've undertaken a regeneration strategy until 2014 . . . [area plans] are designed by all of the projects and programmes coming down from the Welsh Assembly Government, environment agencies, Countryside Council for Wales, health board, the council, things they know they've programmed in the business plans for the next three or five years. So then you have all the community groups that we know we're working with and what they've got planned for the next three or five years . . . what it also does . . . is identify what should be done . . .'*

Community regeneration not only involves dissuading citizens from pursuing their desired projects, there is also another problem: *'there are always issues that statutory bodies will bring in which are not accepted by communities . . . we take these issues on board'*. Yet despite such obvious micromanagement of citizen participation, an interviewee from the housing sector still felt that there was: *'much more consultation on those issues than would have been if you remain in a local authority . . . now community participation is seen as the way forward . . .'*.

Ultimately though local authorities are seen as very powerful:

> (education): *'Wherever you work in a local authority . . . you have to work very carefully with your political leaders as it were in terms of the elected members of the council because at the end of the day decisions rest with them . . . members here are very involved and very informed I think . . . and very influential in . . . terms of the policy direction that the authority takes.'*

Crime prevention partnerships are also expected to embrace citizen participation, but the data reveals obvious problems here as well as a greater scepticism as to whether it is effective or even wanted:

> '*it is only those concerned few who want to be involved really and the others . . . until something happens that they're not happy with . . . you're not going to hear from them . . . they're not going to engage with you . . . people don't come [to public engagement events] because they genuinely believe that unless they've got something they want to voice . . . basically it's just "oh get on with it", it's what they want you to do isn't it. Just want you to get on with it. So you always have those few people, the same ones really.*'

This represents further confirmation of the contradictions and limitations in the language and practice of participation.

Barriers to change

The interviews provide consistent evidence across a number of sectors to show how discourses of participation are routinely employed to make sense of public service provision in a time of considerable pressure on resources. It is not surprising that the interviews are pervaded by a sense of large-scale, intractable problems. Despite the enormous ambitions of the services and the considerable expectations placed upon them, most interviewees expressed their powerlessness in the face of wider society and forces such as globalization and recognized that there were serious limitations on their ability to effect change. An economic regeneration manager speaks for many when he says: '*what societies are like these days, we have no influence over that*'. He continues,

> '*many authorities who have tried to invent strategies to change the world in their own little patch and failed dismally, because you can't change GDP, you can't change unemployment, you can't change economic activity rates in the global sense . . .*'

and admits that forecasting the demand for skills in even five years' time is to venture into the unknown. Participation needs to be seen in this context of uncertainty. The realization that some social problems and disadvantage stubbornly remain through successive generations in the face of both carrot and stick approaches underlies the thinking which reconceptualizes communities that were previously thought of as wholly problematic in more positive ways according to their 'social capital' or 'resilience':

'There are strong pockets of social capital . . . especially in areas . . . considered to be deprived . . . communities that have nearly had to manage on their own in a way because there haven't been any public services in the areas and very few facilities and resources. The people have pulled together . . . we are trying to better understand . . . what makes people more resilient and enables them to cope with changes in the world surrounding them . . . how we are supporting people to be more resilient in order to prevent them from going into a crisis . . . then asking for more intensive services and more specialised services that are costly to us as a provider within the public sector and also costly to themselves on a personal level . . .'

The communities referred to above were housing estates with a reputation for being particularly resistant to regeneration. There is an admission of service inadequacy and defeat, yet the very survival of the residents is then repackaged as a tribute to their social capital and resilience. The residents' social capital and resilience may well bear fruit, but here it is used to justify further lack of services.

Interviewees using discourses of 'giving people a voice', 'empowering' or other ways of 'enabling' people did not show an awareness that this represents a 'top down' selective approach which is at odds with the universal conception of citizen rights in a democracy. Rather, it is one in which a powerful person decides how much power to share, for example by building 'their' capacity and confidence: (community regeneration manager): *'I hope that it will change in the sense of people having more ambition . . . giving them more confidence running things for themselves because that's what this . . . is all about'.* There is an obvious quality of 'them' and 'us' here, with the interviewees feeling that they have to make good the deficit in their fellow citizens. The publics the interviewees refer to are mostly publics with restricted financial resources and it is often this that is the main factor bringing them into contact with the services. There are certainly people who are disadvantaged or who have encountered problems that do not stem directly from limited income, but it was sometimes assumed that simply being in need of a certain service suggested personal deficit: (community regeneration manager): *'if you're homeless you have some sort of problematic background possibly or financial issues . . . and I think these people need more support . . . '.* Yet a housing manager from a neighbouring authority mentioned that there was a waiting list of 3,000 for a housing stock of six, suggesting that homelessness will not merely be experienced by people with 'problematic backgrounds'.

The context of relatively small local authorities in the study meant that there was much local specificity in the data. Detailed local knowledge not only assisted in the successful delivery of services but also made interviewees less likely to construct the public as inherently problematic, or to use institutional discourses homogenizing publics. Interviewees were aware that delivering services or conceptualizing 'publics' and their needs in Wales is difficult, as one described it, because of, *'the misfits of your physical, political, transportation, economic, language, culture levels . . .'.*

Housing and education managers had a slightly different orientation to the public than interviewees in the other sectors. Education managers expected to provide a service that would see young people fulfilled and happy, not just simply achieving academically or, in the future, economically. As one put it, *'success is where our youngsters perform to the best of their potential . . . being able to access a quality educational provision'.* Their responses contained far less neoliberal ideology than some other interviewees. The term 'citizen' is rarely used in other sectors but is found here, for example in the phrase *'providing a service to the citizens'.* Nearly all pupils in Wales learn in what the Welsh Government describes as 'community comprehensive schooling' and education managers are delivering their services in this context. We may speculate that this informs their view that barriers are external and linked to resource limitations rather than divisions within the public.

In other sectors the discourse is less equal and more closely reflects who holds power and their view of the people they serve. There seems to be an expectation on the part of many of the interviewees that people in receipt of their services should live a middle-class life in miniature on very restricted incomes, sharing the values and lifestyles of interviewees and policymakers. There was little awareness that the publics served by the interviewees might have stimulating interests or abilities of which those operating in top-down hierarchies knew nothing. One of the most interesting themes to emerge was the sense of an alternative to economic and even social regeneration: regeneration of people. This phrase was used by a Communities First manager who explained: *'My remit is broad . . . concentrating on people rather than physical regeneration. It's the regeneration of people and how people can play a part in regeneration, regenerating their own communities . . .'.* This view of people as impoverished potential agents whose agency can be activated by the policies of experts corresponds with Martin's (2011) explanation that those 'in charge' are often responsible for feeding the outputs of participation into the management and delivery of public services. Their views of what is (or is not) a legitimate contribution will have crucial consequences for what is (or is not) drawn upon in informing service provision (Hodge, 2005; Mort et al., 1996; Williams, 2004). It echoes the theme of 'enrolling people' (Clarke, 2010); people have to be discovered and enrolled into the practices and relationships of governmental strategies.

CONCLUSION

The experience reported here supports Touraine's (1995, p. 267) observation, informed by his critique of modernity, that 'today . . . we define ourselves by our needs, our interests, our values or by the communities and traditions we belong to. We no longer define ourselves as citizens . . .'. Against the background of the diminishing importance of class and collective identifications the citizen-consumer has come to prominence. But an underlying complexity reveals the citizen-service user to be a far from active player. Despite being 'consulted', 'involved', 'engaged with' and 'empowered', users of some services are still frequently in such powerless and vulnerable situations that they exert little force as citizens or consumers.

Clarke (2010) and Martin (2008) noted that citizen participation involves a valorization of 'ordinary people', yet our data revealed that the views of ordinary people are over-ridden when deemed necessary; they need to be enrolled and given 'training' and 'confidence building' before participating in decision making bodies, thus assuming a deficit on their part; and representatives from other organizations are sensitive if too many ordinary people are invited onto committees and boards. Our data also demonstrates just how highly managed 'participation' is (Newman, 2010).

Neoliberal assumptions are less prevalent in social policy in Wales than in England, and a different relationship can be expected between the state and the individual. The socio-political roots and affiliation of the managers interviewed for this study, the local councillors and the politicians in the Welsh Government are generally distant from New Labour neoliberalism. The data revealed that a local specificity provided one context in which homogenizing institutionalized discourses were not used. Yet the sometimes intractable problems that the public services are charged with managing or even eradicating, combined with a lack of resources, the consequences of long-term economic decline and a Government of a very different hue in Westminster exercising influence despite devolution, leads to people managing those services often behaving in ways and employing techniques which are very similar to those mobilized under neoliberalism.

The data illustrate the paradox discussed by Clarke (2005, 2010), that of 'empowered' 'valorized' citizens, yet also abandoned by the state in many ways. A rather diminished and depleted view of the community was held by many managers. The citizens using services were seen as perpetually vulnerable, perhaps unable to care for their own children or to maintain their own health and wellbeing, even uneducable. Yet the same citizens were expected to be dutiful, active citizens, participating in pedagogic relationships with the services, sitting on boards and committees as 'equals'. A diminished view of the community by service managers does not yield a level playing field for citizen empowerment and involvement, or active citizenship. The citizen is de-capitalized before entering the field of play. Although some of the publics discussed by the interviewees will be publics to whom it may be very difficult to deliver a service or offer improvements to their lives, stances of independence and initiative are also problematized in the data (especially where this might involve moving away from services), as are people who do not avail themselves of these services. Despite the many references to citizen participation or user involvement in the data, most of the interviewees expected to run the services and make decisions without the users presenting a serious challenge. It was often assumed that the users would not be interested or that if they were to become involved, that would be another task for the services themselves to facilitate, involving for example the 'training' of users. Neo-liberalism may never have been fully alive and well in Wales but the way that the public service managers talk suggests that they rarely challenge neo-liberalism's status as *lingua franca* for communication about participation.

ACKNOWLEDGEMENTS

This publication is based on research supported by the Wales Institute of Social and Economic Research, Data and Methods (WISERD). WISERD is a collaborative venture between the universities of Aberystwyth, Bangor, Cardiff, Glamorgan and Swansea. The research that this publication relates to was funded by the ESRC (grant number: RES-576-25-0021) and the Higher Education Funding Council for Wales.

REFERENCES

Baker, S., Brown, B. J. and Gwilym, H. (2008). 'The rise of the service user', *Soundings*, 40, 18–28.
Beecham Report (2006). *Beyond Boundaries: Citizen Centred Local Services for Wales*, Cardiff: Welsh Assembly Government.

Brown, B. J. and Baker, S. (2012). *Responsible Citizens: Individuals, Health and Policy Under Neoliberalism*, London: Anthem Press.

Clarke, J. (2004). 'Dissolving the public realm? The logics and limits of neoliberalism', *Journal of Social Policy*, 33, 1, 27–48.

Clarke, J. (2005). 'New Labour's citizens: activated, empowered, responsibilized, abandoned?', *Critical Social Policy* 25, 4, 447–63.

Clarke, J. (2010). 'Enrolling ordinary people: governmental strategies and the avoidance of politics?', *Citizenship Studies*, 14, 6, 637–50.

Clarke, J., Newman, J., Smith, N., Vidler, E. and Westmarland, L. (2007). *Creating Citizen-Consumers: Changing Publics and Changing Public Services*, London: Sage.

Cruikshank, B. (1999). *The Will to Empower. Democratic Citizens and Other Subjects*, Ithaca, NY: Cornell University Press.

Das, V. (2004). 'The signature of the state: the paradox of illegibility', in V. Das and D. Poole (eds), *Anthropology in the Margins of the State*, Oxford: James Currey.

Das, V. (2011). 'State, citizenship and the urban poor', *Citizenship Studies*, 15, 3–4, 319–33.

Drakeford, M. (2012). 'Wales in the age of austerity', *Critical Social Policy*, 32, 454–66.

Eckert, J. (2011). 'Introduction: subjects of citizenship', *Citizenship Studies*, 15, 3–4.

Hall, S. (2003). 'New Labour's double-shuffle', *Soundings*, 24, 10–24.

Hodge, S. (2005). 'Participation, discourse and power: a case study in service user involvement', *Critical Social Policy*, 25, 2, 164–79.

Institute for Government (2010). *MINDSPACE: Influencing Behaviour Through Public Policy*, London: Institute for Government.

Jones, L., Mann, R. and Heley, J. (2012). 'Doing space relationally: exploring the meaningful geographies of local government in Wales' *Geoforum*, *http://dx.doi.org/ 10.1016/j.geoforum.2012.11.003* (accessed 21 January 2013).

Marshall, T. H. (1950). *Citizenship and Social Class: And Other Essays*. Cambridge: Cambridge University Press.

Martin, G. P. (2008). '"Ordinary people only": knowledge, representativeness, and the publics of public participation in healthcare', *Sociology of Health & Illness*, 30, 1, 35–54.

Martin, G. P. (2012). 'Public deliberation in action: emotion, inclusion and exclusion in participatory decision making', *Critical Social Policy*, 32, 163–83.

McDermont, M., Cowan, D. and Prendergast, P. (2009). 'Structuring governance: a case study of the new organizational provision of public service delivery', *Critical Social Policy*, 29, 677–702.

McKee, K. and Cooper, V. (2008). 'The paradox of tenant empowerment: regulatory and liberatory possibilities', *Housing, Theory and Society*, 25, 2, 132–46.

Mitchell, T. (2000). *Questions of Modernity*. Minneapolis: University of Minnesota Press.

Mort, M., Harrison, S. and Wistow, G. (1996). 'The user card: picking through the organizational undergrowth in health and social care', *Contemporary Political Studies*, 2, 1133–40.

Newman, J. (2010). 'Towards a pedagogical state? Summoning the "empowered" citizen', *Citizenship Studies*, 14, 6, 711–23.

Newman, J. and Clarke, J. (2009). *Publics, Politics and Power: Remaking the Public in Public Services*, London: Sage.

Ong, A. (1998). 'Flexible citizenship among Chinese cosmopolitans', in P. Cheah and B. Robbins (eds), *Cosmopolitics: Thinking and Feeling Beyond the Nation*, Minneapolis: University of Minnesota Press.

Rhodes, P. and Nocon, A. (1998). 'User involvement and the NHS reforms', *Health Expectations*, 1, 2, 73–81.

Rose, N. (1999). *Powers of Freedom*, Cambridge: Cambridge University Press.

Rose, N. and Novas, C. (2005). 'Biological citizenship', in A. Ong and S. Collier (eds), *Global Assemblages: Technology, Politics and Ethics as Anthropological Problems*, Oxford: Blackwell.

Rose, N. and Osborne, T. (2000). 'Governing cities, governing citizens in democracy', in E. Isin (ed.) *Citizenship and the Global City*, London: Routledge.

Touraine. A. (1995). 'Democracy: from a politics of citizenship to a politics of recognition', in L. Maheu (ed.), *Social Movements and Social Classes*, London: Sage.

Vidler, E. and Clarke, J. (2005). 'Creating citizen-consumers: New Labour and the remaking of public services', *Public Policy and Administration*, 20, 2, 19–37.

Williams, M. (2004). 'Discursive democracy and New Labour: five ways in which decision-makers manage citizen agendas in public participation initiatives', *Sociological Research Online*, 9, 3, *http://www.socresonline.org.uk/9/3/williams.html* (accessed 31 January 2013).

12. HOW SIMILAR OR DIFFERENT ARE THE STRUCTURES OF DEVOLVED GOVERNANCE IN SCOTLAND, WALES AND NORTHERN IRELAND?

Derek Birrell

ABSTRACT

Since the introduction of devolution in 1999 it has become the conventional view that devolution can be described as asymmetrical, implying significant differences between Scotland, Wales and Northern Ireland in terms of the structures and practices of governance. This view was encouraged by a number of factors including the exclusion of England from the devolution arrangements, the predominance of single-country studies and different political histories and party systems. A significant amount of change in devolved governance has been introduced, particularly since 2007, relating to institutions, structures and practices. This paper examines major changes in the core areas of devolved powers, executive government, parliament and assemblies, civil service structures, delegated and local government, financial systems and intergovernmental relations. It identifies and assesses the extent of similarities that have emerged, as well as continuing differences. A number of reasons for a trajectory towards increasing similarities are examined; including the Westminster model, UK Government dominance, policy transfer and an emerging model of devolved governance. The analysis is used to assess the extent of similarities and differences. Finally, some comment is made on the implications of possible future constitutional developments.

INTRODUCTION

In comparisons of the devolved systems of government between Scotland, Wales and Northern Ireland the generalized view has often been expressed that they are asymmetrical. Such an assertion received widespread support in the early years of devolution (Brown, 1998; Curtice, 2001; Leyland, 2002). Expressed simply the assertion was that the devolution process has been asymmetrical in that the nature and degree of devolution has been different in different parts of the United Kingdom (Oliver, 2003). Differences in the sets of devolved powers and forms of government tended to be the main elements identified as asymmetrical (Jeffery and Wincott, 2006, p. 5), with occasional references to the electoral systems, intergovernmental relations and the civil service. As devolution developed this continued to be a dominant view (Hazell and Rawlings, 2005; Jeffrey and Wincott, 2006; Mellett, 2009; and Tierney, 2009). Trench (2007, p. 55) described the devolution arrangements as a whole as profoundly asymmetrical. This view has also largely been endorsed by a range of work in the ESRC Programme on Devolution and Constitutional Change, completed in 2005. A number of general factors set a context for the use of the term 'asymmetric'. Firstly, the view was often based on the absence of devolution for England or the English regions and the consequent substantial lop-sidedness in UK Government arrangements. A second factor was the original more limited devolution of powers to Wales. Thirdly, there was a perception that Northern Ireland was very different from Scotland and Wales with its background of political conflict and violence, its own political history and distinct party politics. Overall these perspectives distracted from comparisons between the three devolved governments, particularly in the working of the totality of their institutions of governance. Ten years on from the beginning of devolution a number of statutory inquiries expressed similar views. The House of Commons report *Devolution: A Decade On* made the precise assertion 'there is an asymmetrical model of devolution' (House of Commons, 2009, para. 10) while the Calman Commission noted that asymmetrical devolution differs in nature and extent in each of the nations and territories to which it has applied (Commission on Scottish Devolution, 2009). A number of factors have encouraged the prominence and durability of the asymmetrical view. There has been a focus in the literature and commentaries on a single-country approach, described and analysed separately and each case addressed with specificity. There has also been a focus on identifying divergence and convergence in the policy outcomes of governmental processes in each country in areas such as criminal justice, education and health (Birrell,

2009) rather than in the institutions and processes of governance. There is at times a possible tendency to exaggerate small differences 'a narcissism of small differences' (Mitchell, 2010a, p. 99) while passing over many similarities. There has, however, been some interest in the need and value of comparing the whole package of devolved arrangements. The overview of the ESRC programme 'Devolution and Constitutional Change' noted a tendency to think of devolution as a set of separate reforms, each tailored to the needs of a particular part of the UK, which was viewed as at best a complacent theory (Devolution and Constitutional Change, 2006). There is also some evidence of recent interest in a transfer of knowledge and practice between the devolved administrations, for example, the Silk Commission in reviewing the powers of the National Assembly for Wales has taken evidence in Scotland and Northern Ireland. The Northern Ireland Assembly, in reviewing the number of MLAs and departments, has looked in detail at Scotland and Wales (Northern Ireland Assembly, 2012).

Since 2007 devolved government has undergone substantial changes in Scotland, Wales and Northern Ireland; in their powers, in the operation of the institutions of governance and in intergovernmental structures. This article summarizes some of the major changes that occurred in this period, compares the changes between Scotland, Wales and Northern Ireland, and identifies similarities in institutions, structures and practices, along with continuing differences. The major areas examined are: devolved powers; forms of executive governance, the operation of Parliament/Assemblies, the civil service structures; delegated and local government and intergovernmental arrangements. This analysis facilitates an examination of the nature of similarities and differences and an assessment of their significance in the working of devolution.

CONVERGENCE IN DEVOLVED POWERS

A growing convergence can be identified in the areas of devolved powers. Since 2007 there has been a major increase in legislative powers of the National Assembly for Wales, one significant increase in devolved powers in Northern Ireland and an incremental increase in Scotland. This has resulted in all three countries now having a more similar system of legislative devolution. The original devolution settlement had not conferred primary law-making powers on the National Assembly for Wales and the transferred functions were specified in the Government of Wales Act 1998. This contrasted with the primary law-making powers of the Scottish Parliament and Northern Ireland Assembly and the listing of non-devolved matters so that all other matters were transferred, a principle which followed the old Stormont model.

A UK White Paper in 2005 had accepted the need for the National Assembly for Wales to secure legislative competencies and the Government of Wales Act (2006) made provision for powers to make primary legislation, although through a complex scheme involving collaboration with Westminster. This Act also made provision for a referendum on the devolution of full law making powers (All Wales Convention, 2009). Following the 'yes' vote, since May 2011 full legislative competence on transferred matters has been devolved, thus removing a major asymmetric feature of devolution. The devolution of policing and justice powers in Northern Ireland brought Northern Ireland into line with Scotland, but not Wales. The overall outcome has been devolution in Wales with still more limited powers but not excessively so. The strongest support for an increase in powers has been in Scotland and some enhancements were contained in the Scotland Act 2012, to operate from 2016, including speed limits, air weapons and drink driving limits, new financial powers, a role in appointments relating to the BBC Trust and the Crown Estate and powers relating to the administration of elections. Northern Ireland remains with the greatest range of devolved powers including social security, employment and equality as well as the recently devolved justice powers.

THE DEVELOPMENT OF FORMS OF GOVERNMENT

The Westminster model of parliamentary government has been described as central to the development of devolution (Mitchell, 2010b). Two key aspects are an executive drawn from the legislature and accountable to it and the broad role of the legislature (Trench, 2010). The operating form of executive government in each country is now similar and based on the Westminster model. This consists of: a form of cabinet government; an office of First Minister, normally a deputy First Minister; senior and junior ministers; Executive sub-committees; a secretariat; ministerial advisers and ministerial codes. The Government of Wales Act (2006) brought Welsh devolution into line with Scotland and Northern Ireland with the establishment of an Executive, separate from the Assembly. In Northern Ireland the power-sharing arrangements of the Northern Ireland Act 1998 and the St Andrews Agreement of 2006 meant a statutory dual position of First and Deputy First Minister drawn from the two largest parties and the sharing of ministerial powers between the main parties, which can be cited as a major continuing asymmetrical feature of the arrangements for executive government. However, coalition government has become common in devolution in Scotland and Wales, although along with periods of minority government and majority government. The consociational arrangements for Northern Ireland also meant the formal absence of the principle of collective responsibility governing Executive decisions. This is unlike Scotland and Wales although the operating arrangements in Northern Ireland are intended to promote consensual decision-making. The principle of ministerial responsibility operates in similar mode in each country, but in practice with a stronger degree of individual ministerial discretion in the Stormont Executive. The precise configuration of ministers' portfolios differs between each administration but a core symmetry can be identified covering the main role, tasks and functions of ministers.

OPERATION OF PARLIAMENT/ASSEMBLIES

The operation of the Scottish Parliament, the National Assembly of Wales and the Northern Ireland Assembly have evolved in largely similar directions. They have adopted similar practices to deal with legislative matters in three different respects: copying Westminster practice, having similar innovations in their operation and in adapting to a relationship with Westminster to suit devolution. All three bodies now deal with a similar range of primary and secondary legislation largely copying Westminster practice. The legislative output in each is dominated by government sponsored public bills but there are provisions for private and hybrid bills. All three bodies have similar mechanisms for legis-lative initiatives by individual members, that is, non-ministerial members, mirroring private members' bills at Westminster. A multi-level process for processing and approving legislation has also mainly symmetrical features in mirroring Westminster practice throughout various stages, involving pre-legis-lative consultation and evidence gathering, committee scrutiny, amendment and further amendment processes and final approval stages. All three legislatures introduced similar innovations, for example, a facility for committees to initiate legislation and have also moved to dual purpose committees to cover both legislation and inquiries. The legislatures in Scotland, Northern Ireland and Wales have also begun to respond to devolution in a further significant convergent way through the development of legislative consent motions, as a procedure to allow Westminster legislation covering devolved matters to apply in Scotland, Wales and Northern Ireland. This process was developed most extensively in Scotland, but has also been adopted in Northern Ireland and Wales.

There is also an extensive degree of similarity in the structure, composition, functions, procedures and coverage of scrutiny committees. Some of the differences which had existed have disappeared with Wales merging subject and legislative committees. The range of statutory and procedural committees is again similar with a key role and status given to public accounts/audit committees and committees for procedure, business and conduct. The Northern Ireland Assembly has lacked some specialist committee coverage in not having a specialist equality committee, or an EU/external affairs committee, although in 2011 the National Assembly for Wales moved to merge some of its specialist committees into wider subject committees, thus becoming more similar to Northern Ireland but different from Scotland. Petitions committees exist in Scotland and Wales to consider public petitions, a process which is not so developed in Northern Ireland. Operational practices are similar in the areas of published departmental responses to committee recommendations, follow-up inquiries and post-legislative scrutiny. Some differences in the operation of committees remain, for example, the use of reporters and substitute members in Scotland and regular meetings with ministers in Wales. Other aspects of parliamentary procedures are largely similar, for example, question time and debates. A further rather hidden similar feature is the range and scope of all-party policy committees.

DEVOLVED CIVIL SERVICE STRUCTURES

With devolution Scotland, Wales and Northern Ireland had to establish a devolved central administration. This was based largely on the existing territorial administration of the UK Government and staffed by civil servants. One asymmetrical feature exists as the separate Northern Ireland Civil Service (NICS) has remained while the devolved civil service in Scotland and Wales is part of the UK Home Civil Service. In practice this has had a limited impact on divergence as traditionally the NICS has adopted the same structure and procedures as the Home Civil Service. The separate Northern Ireland Civil Service Commissioners also tend to follow GB practices. The Head of the Northern Ireland Civil Service along with the Permanent Secretaries of the Scottish and Welsh administrations attend Whitehall meetings of permanent secretaries. Each administration in Scotland, Wales and Northern Ireland has its own civil service code, but they are very similar in content. Each country has dealt with similar issues in relation to the senior civil service, pay, relocation, diversity, use of IT, public sector reform and improving performance. A particular problem has been identified in each administration as a need to develop the policy making capacity and capability of senior civil servants in Edinburgh, Cardiff and Belfast. The devolved administrations in Scotland, Wales and Northern Ireland all operate alongside UK departments in each country administering non-devolved matters, although on a smaller scale in Northern Ireland compared to Scotland and Wales. Although the functions of each devolved administration are similar, the detailed structure and organization does display a degree of divergence. Northern Ireland has kept to a 'mini-Whitehall' structure of separate departments and with a single minister in charge of eleven of the twelve departments. In 2007 Scotland moved to different system of directorates (now thirty-one in total) and with the organization of the civil service administration not necessarily mapping directly with ministers' portfolios. Wales has seven departments but these operate in a corporate manner under the direction of the permanent secretary. Scotland and Northern Ireland both make use of executive agencies within the central administration while Wales does not. As devolution has developed the civil service leadership has become strongly committed to the demands of the devolved governments and systems and removed doubts, especially in Scotland and Wales, about where their loyalty lay.

DELEGATED AND LOCAL GOVERNMENT

The existence of sub-national units of government in Scotland, Wales and Northern Ireland raised the issue of the nature of their relationship to the devolved administrations. Prior to 1999 the three countries all had extensive systems of administration by public bodies/quangos and local government. The quango sector was to produce problems for each of the devolved administrations. All three countries have a substantial number of non-departmental public bodies and other quangos, usually defined in terms of bodies set up by government to carry out public functions at arm's length from government but accountable to government. They normally have the characteristics of a board appointed by the minister, employ their own staff and are allocated their own budget. After devolution many of these bodies came within devolved responsibilities. At the onset of devolution they numbered some 186 in Scotland, 120 in Northern Ireland and 48 in Wales, where they were usually named state sponsored bodies. They constituted a major component of devolved administration and gave rise to a question of the compatibility of the sector with new democratic devolved government. Quangos could be seen as occupying the same ground as devolved administration between UK central government and local government. Their continuing existence developed as a high profile issue with the language of bonfires and culls in Scotland and Wales and led to strategies for a reduction in the number of quangos in Scotland and Wales and a major review in Northern Ireland, as part of a wider review of public administration. The rationales expressed similar ideas about increasing public accountability and, particularly in Scotland and Wales, a principle of absorbing functions into the devolved administration, which would also increase the capacity of devolved government (Birrell, 2008). There was also a convergent policy not to create new quangos unless absolutely necessary. In practice the outcome of the strategies was more limited than expected in reducing the size of the sector in all three countries and there was a common acceptance of the rationale for arms-length bodies in some areas. After 2007 a renewed commitment emerged to reducing the number of quangos with more of an emphasis on the objective of saving money and producing efficiencies. However, in practice, the approach has been slow and cautious in all three countries, using similar mechanisms of mergers, absorption into devolved administrations, occasional abolition or transfer to local government. Despite some divergence in the shape of the sector and government strategies the reality of the institutional endurance of a large quango sector in each country has been noted (Flinders, 2011).

The new devolved institutions of governance also had to interact with much longer established democratically elected bodies in the form of local government. All three devolved governments were to express support for the continuing importance of local government and took the view that devolution would not represent a threat to the role of local government. Extensive systems of local government operated in Scotland and Wales, providing a very large range of services which was a marked divergence with Northern Ireland where since 1972 a local government system with limited functions had been in place. No major structural change has happened in Scotland or Wales and change is still pending in Northern Ireland. Despite fears of a more interventionist approach after devolution the devolved administrations have worked with a partnership approach to relations with local government. This has been seen as even an improvement on pre-devolution relationships (Jeffery, 2006). The devolved administrations have all given an important role to the representative bodies, the Convention of Scottish Local Authorities, the Welsh Local Government Association and the Northern Ireland Association of Local Authorities. A formal concordat with local government has developed in Scotland and

Wales has a statutory Partnership Council, a model which Northern Ireland is likely to follow. Also developed in largely similar ways has been a range of initiatives to improve performance through best value initiatives, outcome and service agreements, audit systems and sharing best practice. A commitment to partnership working with the rest of the public sector has also been a common theme, given particular importance in Wales through the overarching *Making the Connections Strategy*. Wales has developed Local Service Boards and Scotland community planning partnerships to carry forward joined up working and Northern Ireland plans to adopt a form of the Scottish system of community planning for the future. Overall there has been support in the devolved institutions in Scotland, Wales and Northern Ireland for greater cooperation with councils as the way forward rather than any major restructuring or change in functions or moving to a model of more centralized control and command.

INTERGOVERNMENTAL RELATIONS

Comparing the development of institutions and relationships of each devolved government with the UK Government and with each other and also with the EU also demonstrates the development of a strong degree of symmetry. This arises from interaction with the same or similar intergovernmental institutions. All three devolved institutions have a key relationship with their respective Secretaries of State and territorial offices. The general functions of the three UK ministers and the Scotland Office, the Wales Office and the Northern Ireland Office are similar, acting as the lynchpin of the UK Government's relationship with the devolved governments, or 'oiling the wheels of devolution' (Scotland Office, 2010). Politically the Northern Ireland Office has a latent important role. The Scotland Office now has an increased political role. It could be anticipated that with the legislative changes the Wales Office would move to less controversial activities this was not to be the case. The Wales Office contributed to a legal challenge to the first Bill to be passed by the Assembly on the grounds that it effected functions of the Secretary of State and although unsuccessful a further challenge to another Bill seemed possible. Although judicial review becomes a likelihood with devolution, the Wales Office appears to wish to assert a degree of legislative scrutiny. It has proved difficult to set up an inter-governmental forum and for a period a Joint Ministerial Council (JMC), which had no statutory basis, fell into disuse, apart from an EU subcommittee. In 2008 the JMC was re-launched with the support of the new devolved administrations and put on a more positive footing. It has a value in embedding the principle of mutual respect and equity of status between the four governments.

A plenary meeting referred to the JMC as the apex of formal relations between the four governments (Scottish Government, 2010). This equity in status and equity in participation is also to be found in the activities of the devolved governments along with the UK and Irish Governments in the British-Irish Council which also had an uncertain beginning but has become well established with a permanent secretariat and programmes of work. The participating devolved governments have shown a similar degree of commitment and level of participation. The mechanisms and processes through which the devolved administrations relate to the EU through the UK Government also show a great deal of commonality. Devolved ministers attend EU Council meetings as part of UK delegations and can visit commissioners in Brussels. Scotland, Wales and Northern Ireland all have government offices in Brussels under the umbrella of the UK permanent representation and each country can be members of EU sub-national network organizations.

FINANCIAL SYSTEMS

The funding basis of devolution in each country has remained largely unchanged since 1999 based on the application of the Barnett Formula to the major allocation of funding from the UK Treasury. The Barnett Formula governs the majority of the block grant available to the devolved administrations and constitutes the majority of public money that they spend. This has meant similar arrangements for each country as set out in the Treasury statement of funding policy (HM Treasury, 2010). Only limited revenue raising powers were devolved. The main asymmetric feature was a power for Scotland to vary the basic rate of income tax by three pence in the pound but this was never to be used. Devolved financial discretion lies almost wholly in the distribution of the block grant element of the funding allocation and this is a similar feature in all three countries. The Barnett Formula has operated to establish a ceiling on the expenditure of each devolved administration and to keep total expenditure proportionate to each other and to England but does reflect the higher expenditure needs in Scotland, Wales and Northern Ireland (Midwinter, 2007). Amendments to the financial system has been the area most subject to detailed investigation and proposals for change, focussing on devolved financial powers. In Scotland following analysis by the Calman Commission (Commission on Scottish Devolution, 2009) the UK Government introduced in the Scotland Act, 2012, which will mean (from 2016) a reduction in income tax along with a reduction in the block grant, with the Scottish Government free to choose a different rate of income tax as the replacement element. The Scotland Act will also devolve stamp duty land tax and landfill tax and a new capital borrowing power to Scotland and the creation of a new Scottish cash reserve. An inquiry in Wales (Holtham, 2010) suggested a similar measure for Wales, as a way of improving the financial accountability of the Welsh Assembly but the issue was referred for further investigation by a new commission, the Silk Commission (Bowers and Webb, 2012). The Commission has recommended the devolution of smaller taxes, including landfill tax, stamp duty land tax, aggregates levy and air passenger duty; new borrowing powers and also recommended that the Welsh Government should be able to vary income tax rates with the UK tax structure (Commission on Devolution in Wales, 2012). In Northern Ireland proposals for change in financial arrangements have focussed more narrowly on the possible devolution of the power to reduce the rate of corporation tax. If control over corporation tax was devolved to Northern Ireland, Scotland and Wales might expect similar powers. The UK Finance Act 2012 devolved to the Northern Ireland Assembly the power to set air passenger duty rates, but only on direct long haul flights. Current proposals for increasing the fiscal accountability of the devolved administrations may introduce more divergence in the operation of financial powers.

Since 2007 there has been a notable convergence in the scrutiny and over-view of the budget allocation and expenditure process in the Scottish Parliament and the two Assemblies. All three bodies have a finance committee which scrutinizes the annual budget proposals and each government's spending process. The three finance committees take a wider role in also coordinating responses from each subject/department committee on budget proposals. The finance committees also have a role in scrutinizing financial legislation and considering financial information which supports legislative proposals. All three legislatures also have a public accounting committee, a public accounts or audit committee, which have similar functions and methods of operation, largely following West-minster practice.

SIMILARITIES IN GOVERNANCE

There is evidence of a more convergent trajectory since 2007 in terms of powers, institutions and structures and practices. It is possible to examine the main areas of the devolved arrangements and broadly classify them for each country as: similar in most respects to one or both other countries; displaying minor differences, usually reflecting an administrative difference; a different statutory basis or a more marginal and less significant practice; operating with what can be identified as a more major difference in structures and practices.

Table 12.1
Assessment of similarities and differences in core structures

	Scotland	Wales	Northern Ireland
principle of allocation of powers	similar	different	similar
legislative powers	minor differences	major differences	minor differences
cabinet/executive led government	similar	similar	similar
electoral systems reflecting proportionality	similar	similar	minor differences
mostly forms of coalition government	similar	similar	major differences
range of executive and administrative powers	similar	similar	similar
ministerial codes of conduct	similar	similar	similar
role for special advisers	similar	similar	minor differences
unicameral parliament/Assemblies	similar	similar	similar
legislative process	minor differences	minor differences	minor differences
committee system and functions	minor differences	minor differences	minor differences
financial scrutiny	similar	similar	similar
role of secretaries of state and territorial offices	minor differences	minor differences	minor differences
devolved civil service structure	major differences	major differences	major differences
civil service codes and practices	similar	similar	similar
executive agencies	similar	different	similar
concordats with UK departments	similar	similar	similar
extensive quango sector	minor differences	minor differences	major differences
local government	similar	similar	major differences
participation in JMC	similar	similar	similar
participation in British-Irish council	similar	similar	similar
engagement with EU	similar	similar	similar

Source: Adapted from Birrell (2012)

The list has a significance in showing that the three countries share similar components of governance. This assessment does make the judgement that the number of areas of major difference is at present not extensive, although some differences in core institutions may be very significant. The mandatory nature of coalition and power-sharing in Northern Ireland is specific and important politically and constitutionally. Some clear institutional differences may not in practice have important consequences, as in the case of the formally separate Northern Ireland Civil Service. A significant formal difference in powers since 1999, the tax power in Scotland in practice was not significant as a difference as it was never used. Changes may also have at least partially altered the significance of apparent major differences. Devolved legislative powers in Wales have become more similar to those of the legislatures in Scotland and Northern Ireland but a major difference still exists in the constitutional limitations on the scope of Welsh powers because of the listing of transferred powers to Wales in the devolution legislation unlike Scotland and Northern Ireland.

FACTORS INFLUENCING GREATER SIMILARITY

A trend towards greater similarity in the operation of devolution does draw attention to a number of factors influencing this development. The comparison of trends in devolved institutions and processes indicates a role played by four main factors. Firstly, the continuing influence of the Westminster model. Many of the institutions of governance were set up before 1999 in the three devolved countries by the Westminster parliament and many of the three devolved bodies have taken Westminster practice as a reference point for development. The National Assembly for Wales, originally created as a more unique institution, has developed with the increasing assumption of the features of the Westminster model (Trench, 2010, p. 118) and the legislative methods adopted in 2006 for a period can be seen as falling too far out of line with Westminster tradition. New Westminster developments, in such areas as pre-legislative scrutiny, have or are likely to be adopted in all three legislatures. The overall influence of the Westminster model has not prevented some innovations and differences, in Parliamentary/Assembly questions, in petitions committees, in combining legislative committees and subject scrutiny committees and in seating lay-out.

A second factor is the dominant position of the UK Government and the subordinate position of all three devolved governments. Constitutionally, this means that the UK Government can legislate to change the devolved arrangements, and has the final say on proposals for constitutional reform. Devolved institutions are part of the whole UK system and easily relate to Westminster and Whitehall. This has been seen through the adoption of legislative consent motions and developing inter-committee relationships between Parliaments and Assemblies. The UK Government has taken a pragmatic approach with no known preference or agenda for asymmetry or symmetry. Some of the key powers reserved to the UK Government have also had an influence towards convergent forms of governance, particularly through the control of financial allocations, taxation, EU and international matters, equality and social security and employment matters in Great Britain. The influence of the Home Civil Service can at times also be important in imposing similar processes and approaches to governance.

The third factor refers to circumstances where the devolved administrations may engage in policy transfer and copy practices or institutions from each other, that is, not from the example of England. Copying has taken the place in the area of innovative institutions which seem worthy of imitation. Thus the Office of Children's Commissioner was established first in Wales, copied by Northern Ireland and then Scotland. An Office of Older People's Commissioner was introduced in Wales in 2008, and subsequently copied in Northern Ireland. Copying may also operate at the level of improved practice. Wales has been identified as following Scotland in building processes to enhance EU engagement (Carter, 2008, p. 360). If devolved arrangements appear not to be working well or break down then lessons may be learnt from the practices in the other countries (Jeffrey, 2007). Health structures based on a commissioner/provider division were abolished in Scotland, followed by Wales, and may be changed in Northern Ireland. There has also been policy transfer on institutional relationships with local government. Policy copying has been encouraged by intergovernmental activities within Assembly/Parliament committees and the work of the British-Irish Council.

A fourth factor may be suggested as the emergence of a devolved style of government, as devolution has developed. In certain respects change and convergence has been driven by the requirements of devolution. These pressures can be listed as: the growth in powers and activities of devolved government; the significance of ministerial executive powers; Parliament and Assemblies becoming the focus of each country's political decision making; devolved administrations acting as a 'central administration'; a commitment to a participatory ethos with the need for more structures for public participation, consultation and public accessibility; searching for mechanisms for greater efficiency in delivering public services; pursuing methods of more joined-up government and partnership working involving all sectors and ensuring equality of status for each devolved administration in inter-governmental relations.

CONCLUSIONS AND THE FUTURE

It is possible to identify a large measure of similarity in the operation of devolved governance, with an enhancement in similarities in some areas since 2007. These similarities can be found in: the devolution of powers, the status and exercise of executive government, Parliament/Assembly procedures, the legislative process and the operation of scrutiny committees, the functioning of the civil service, the devolved central administration, financial governance, the relationships with quangos and local government and in participation in inter-governmental relations. However, the claim for less asymmetry, particularly since 2007, in institutions, structure and practices has to be balanced and assessed against continuing differences. Among the most important of which are:

- remaining differences in the scope and nature of devolved powers;
- the differential limitations on the scope of Welsh legislative powers;
- tax powers in Scotland;
- the distinctive power-sharing arrangements in Northern Ireland;
- the separate Northern Ireland Civil Service;
- different configuration of devolved central administration.

Trends to date have suggested a justification for amending the general attribution to devolved government of asymmetry. Will future developments in Scotland, Wales and Northern Ireland promote more similarities in the operation of devolution or move towards more differences? A number of scenarios are possible. The question would be made totally irrelevant in the case of Scotland if Scotland was to obtain independence. The second scenario relates to devolution continuing in all three countries and pending changes are implemented in devolved powers and financial arrangements. Following the outcome of current commissions, inquiries and negotiations there will, or is likely to, be some enhancement in non-financial powers. The planned implementation of the Scotland Act 2012 will produce a minor increase in powers and the recommendations of the Silk Commission in Wales may result in some modifications to devolved powers for Wales, possibly related to the boundary between devolved and non-devolved powers and to justice matters. However, it seems unlikely that these developments will lead to major changes in devolved powers. The proposals from current commissions, inquiries and negotiations will be more significant in financial matters. By 2016 there would be arrangements in place for a Scottish income tax, the devolution of minor taxes and borrowing powers. In Wales the Silk Commission has made largely similar recommendations. Northern Ireland has been pressing for the devolution of control over corporation tax rates and, if devolved to Northern Ireland, Scotland and Wales may follow. A limited aspect of Air Passenger Duty has been devolved to Northern Ireland from 2013. Changes in fiscal devolution may lead to some differences in devolved powers but again the powers may end up as being fairly similar. A final scenario is 'devolution max' which is a proposal for the maximum possible devolution of power, leaving the UK Government with only a small range of non-devolved powers. This has been put forward by the SNP and would become an issue after a Scottish vote against independence. However, there has been a call in Wales for a UK constitutional convention, in the context of the Scottish vote on independence, which has invoked the notion of 'asymmetric quasi-federalism' (National Assembly of Wales, 2012). Even devolution max may not necessarily produce major differences the development could be applied to all three countries and Northern Ireland at present is a bit further along the road to devolution max. The most likely future developments would suggest that attention needs to be paid to both similarities and differences, in comparing devolved structures in Scotland, Wales and Northern Ireland.

REFERENCES

All Wales Convention (2009). *All Wales Convention Report, http://wales.gov.uk/docs/ awc/publications/091118thereporten.pdf* (accessed 31 January 2013).
Birrell, D. (2008). 'Devolution and quangos in the United Kingdom: the implementation of principles and policies for rationalisation and democratisation', *Policy Studies*, 29, 1, 35–49.
Birrell, D. (2009).*The Impact of Devolution on Social Policy*, Bristol: Policy Press.
Birrell, D. (2012). *Comparing Devolved Governance*, Basingstoke: Palgrave Macmillan.
Bowers, P. and Webb, D. (2012). *Devolution in Wales: The Silk Commission – Commons Library Standard Note*, London: House of Commons.
Brown, A. (1998). 'Asymmetrical devolution: the Scottish case', *Political Quarterly*, 69, 3, 215–23.
Carter, C. (2008). 'Identifying causality in public institutional change: the adaptation of the National Assembly for Wales to the European Union', *Public Administration*, 86, 2, 345–61.

Commission on Devolution in Wales (2012). *Empowerment and Responsibility: Financial Powers to Strengthen Wales*, *www.commissionondevolutioninwales.independent.gov.uk/ 2012/11/19/tax-and-borrowing-powers-for-wales* (accessed 10 January 2013).

Commission on Scottish Devolution (2009). *Serving Scotland Better: Scotland and the United Kingdom in the 21st Century, Calman Report*, *www.commissiononscottish devolution.org.uk* (accessed 8 April 2012).

Curtice, J. (2001). 'Hopes dashed and fears assuaged', in Trench, A. (ed.) *The State of the Nations 2001*, Thorverton: Imprint Academic.

Devolution and Constitutional Change (2006). *Devolution in the United Kingdom: The Impact on Politics, Economy and Society: An Overview*, London: Economic and Social Research Council.

Flinders, M. (2011). 'Devolution, delegation and the Westminster model: a comparative analysis of developments with the UK, 1998–2009', *Commonwealth and Comparative Politics*, 49, 1, 1–28.

HM Treasury (2010). *Funding the Scottish Parliament, National Assembly for Wales and Northern Ireland Assembly: Statement of Funding Policy*, *http://cdn.hm-treasury.gov.uk/ sr2010_fundingpolicy.pdf* (accessed 31 January 2013).

Hazell, R. and Rawlings, R. (eds.) (2005). *Devolution, Law Making and the Constitution*, Exeter: Imprint Academic.

Holtham, G. (2010). *Final Report, Fairness and Accountability: A New Funding Settlement for Wales*, Cardiff: Independent Commission on Funding and Finance for Wales.

House of Commons (2009). *Devolution: A Decade On*, Justice Committee – Fifth Report, HC529-1, London: The Stationery Office Limited.

Jeffery, C. (2006). 'Devolution and local government', *Publius: The Journal of Federalism*, 36, 1, 57–73.

Jeffery, C. (2007). 'The unfinished business of devolution', *Public Policy and Administration*, 22, 1, 92–108.

Jeffery, C. and Wincott, D. (2006). 'Devolution in the United Kingdom: Statehood and citizenship in transition', *Publius: the Journal of Federalism*, 36, 1, 3–18.

Leyland, P. (2002). 'Devolution, the British constitution and the distribution of power', *Northern Ireland Legal Quarterly*, 53, 4, 408–35.

Mellett, R. (2009). 'A principles-based approach to the Barnett Formula', *The Political Quarterly*, 80, 1, 76–83.

Midwinter, A. (2007). 'The financial framework', in Carmichael, P., Knox, C. and Osborne, R. (eds.) *Devolution and Constitutional Change in Northern Ireland*, Manchester: Manchester University Press.

Mitchell, J. (2010a). 'The narcissism of small differences: Scotland and Westminster', *Parliamentary Affairs*, 63, 1, 98–116.

Mitchell, J. (2010b). 'The Westminster model and the state of unions', *Parliamentary Affairs*, 63, 1, 85–8.

National Assembly for Wales (2012). *Towards a UK Constitutional Convention?*, *www.assemblywales.org/12-023.pdf* (accessed 24 August 2012).

Northern Ireland Assembly (2012). *Reduction in the Number of Northern Ireland Departments*, Assembly and Executive Review Committee, *http://www.niassembly.gov.uk/*

Assembly-Business/Committees/Assembly and Executive-Review/Reports/Review-of-the-Number-of-Members-of-the-Northern-Ireland-Legislative-Assembly-and-of-the-Reduction-in-the-Number-of-Northern-Ireland-Departments/ (accessed 31 January 2013).

Oliver, D. (2003). *Constitutional Reform in the UK*, Oxford: Oxford University Press.

Scotland Office (2010). *Role of Scotland Office Ministers, www.scotlandoffice.gov.uk/scotlandoffice/22.html* (accessed 28 January 2013).

Scottish Government (2010). *Joint Ministerial Committee, http://www.scotland.gov.uk/News/Releases/2010/06/09081633* (accessed 31 January 2013)

Tierney, S. (2009). 'Federalism in a unitary state: a paradox too far?', *Regional and Federal Studies*, 19, 2, 237–55.

Trench, A. (2007). 'The framework of devolution: the formal structure of devolved power', in A. Trench (ed.) *Devolution and Power in the United Kingdom*, Manchester: Manchester University Press.

Trench, A. (2010). 'Wales and the Westminster model', *Parliamentary Affairs*, 63, 1, 117–33.

13. RESEARCH NOTE: OH BROTHER, WHERE ART THOU? THE POSITION OF THE SCOTTISH AND WELSH LIBERAL DEMOCRATS WITHIN THE FEDERAL LIBERAL DEMOCRATS

Adam B. Evans

ABSTRACT

This paper contributes to the growing literature on intra-party politics within state-wide political parties in multi-level systems of governance. Specifically it focuses on the respective positions of the Scottish and Welsh Liberal Democrats within the party federally up to the autumn of 2012. Whilst there has been a longstanding perception that the Scottish Liberal Democrats are a far more influential part of the federal party than their Welsh counterparts, as the early days of the Conservative-Liberal Democrat coalition at Westminster appeared to confirm, this article argues that, in reality, the intra-party dynamics of the Liberal Democrats require a fundamental reinterpretation. By drawing attention to the federal leadership's perceptions of the Welsh party's electoral perform-ance in 2011, the influence of key individuals in the Welsh Liberal Democrats and organizational adaptation by the party in Wales, it is argued that the Welsh party's influence, whilst still bounded, has been enhanced. Furthermore, whilst Scottish interests have certainly been more successful internally than their Welsh counterparts, by reassessing the source of such power, we can see that it is overwhelmingly rooted in Scottish Liberal Democrat Members of Parliament, rather than figures in Edinburgh. The latter is a source of influence that high-lights the unbalanced nature of power within the federal party, with the Scottish and Welsh Liberal Democrats arguably victims of structural deficiencies at the heart of the Liberal Democrats' 'federal' organization.

INTRODUCTION

The Scottish Liberal Democrats have long been considered to be a far more influential part of the federal party than their Welsh counterparts, providing a significant proportion of both the party's MPs and its leaders (Deacon 2007, p. 156; Lynch, 1998, p. 27). The party in Wales, on the other hand, has been described as the 'forgotten part' of the federal Liberal Democrats, and perceived as a far more marginal and insignificant presence (Deacon 2007, pp. 156–8). Indeed, as this paper will show, the early stages of the (2010–) UK Coalition Government appeared to only confirm these perceptions. Not only did the Scottish Liberal Democrats secure two of the Liberal Democrats' five cabinet positions, but the Welsh Liberal Democrats failed to secure their main objective of Barnett reform[1] or even gain a junior ministerial position (Cornock, 2011).

However, whilst acknowledging that the early stages of coalition life appeared to just confirm these longstanding certainties, this article will argue for a reinterpretation of the respective positions of the Scottish and Welsh Liberal Democrats within the party federally. First, whilst acknowledging the historically weak position of the Welsh Liberal Democrats, this paper will outline how perceptions of the Welsh party's electoral performance, individuals' contributions and organizational adaptation have resulted in the Welsh party's influence, whilst still bounded, nevertheless increasing.

Furthermore, whilst Scottish interests have certainly been more successful internally than their Welsh counterparts, by reassessing the source of such power, we can see that it is overwhelmingly rooted in Scottish Liberal Democrat Members of Parliament, rather than figures in Edinburgh. Importantly, this highlights the hierarchical nature of power within the Liberal Democrats federally. Notwithstanding its federal nature it is afflicted by a structural weakness and imbalance of power that sees the party in Wales and Scotland sidelined by an English dominated centre (Holmes, 2007, p. 535).

This article offers a deeper understanding of the intra-party dynamics within the Liberal Democrats, presenting a comparative focus on the Scottish and Welsh branches of the party that has thus far had very limited academic attention. This paper's contention that the Liberal Democrats' intra-party structures have seen English dominance at the expense of the Scottish and Welsh Liberal Democrats appears to confirm rational choice accounts of intra-party relations (most notably associated with Riker, 1964), which expect party structures to largely mimic the organization of state power and focus on what Deschouwer labels the 'core' level of political activity and competition, to protect and promote their own interests and exploit the full potential of the state (see Riker 1964; Deschouwer, 2003, p. 221; Fabre, 2008, pp. 310–11). This is a significant argument given the formal divergence between the United Kingdom's state organization and the federal organization of the Liberal Democrats.

Furthermore, by balancing this focus with an appreciation of the (often neglected) role played by intra-party resource relationships and capacity (in this case the historic organizational reliance on resource-poor branch parties on the party centrally), this article therefore not only offers a fresh source of academic analysis on an often neglected UK political party, but a more multi-dimensional and, therefore, richer contribution to the broader intra-party literature.

METHODOLOGY

This paper is a product of a research project on the Scottish and Welsh Liberal Democrats entitled, *The Squeezed Middle? The Liberal Democrats in Scotland and Wales: A Post-Coalition Reassessment*[2] that has drawn extensively from both quantitative (membership figures, electoral surveys and opinion poll data) and qualitative (party documents, newspaper and journal articles and elite interviews) sources. The latter were the most significant for the purposes of this paper. Elite interviews with senior party figures in the party at both Welsh and federal levels were conducted in 2012.

HISTORICAL CONTEXT

The respective relationships between the Scottish and Welsh Liberal Democrats with the party federally have historically been defined by asymmetry. A disparity of power that has been particularly rooted, according to Deacon (2007), in the growth of the Liberal Democrats and the predecessor SDP-Liberal Alliance from the 1980s at UK level elections. Quite simply, the increased success of the Liberal Democrats in England and Scotland has resulted in a decline in influence internally for the Welsh Liberal Democrats, with Welsh Liberal Democrat MPs representing a decreasing proportion of the Liberal Democrat Parliamentary Party (Deacon, 2007, p. 156).

The Scottish party, on the other hand, has long been a source of senior party recruitment, for example providing UK party leaders Jo Grimond and David Steel in the 1960s and 1970s. Such influence has maintained itself even with the expansion of the federal party's number of MPs, with Scottish Liberal

Democrats still a sizeable proportion of this parliamentary team and still a source of senior UK figures (Lynch, 1998, pp. 16, 27). The imbalanced nature of the Scottish and Welsh Liberal Democrats' influence can be seen even more starkly from the fact that, while the Scottish Party has provided two leaders of the federal party in the past decade, the most senior Welsh figure in this period was Lembit Opik (Deacon, 2008, pp. 1–3). With such obvious asymmetry it is hardly surprising that Deacon (2007, p. 156), has described the Welsh Liberal Democrats not only as the poor relation of the Scottish Liberal Democrats, but as the 'forgotten' part of the federal Liberal Democrat Party.

BLOSSOMING OR WILTING? THE SCOTTISH AND WELSH LIBERAL DEMOCRATS AFTER THE ROSE GARDEN

This imbalance in influence between the Scottish and Welsh Liberal Democrats, within the federal party, appeared to have been exacerbated by the events of the first months of the UK Coalition Government in 2010. For example, the coalition's *Programme for Government* (HM Government, 2010a), delivered a commitment to further Scottish devolution based on the Calman Commission recommendations (HM Government, 2010b, p. 28), with the Scottish Liberal Democrats also securing two of the Liberal Democrats' five cabinet seats, one of which, Danny Alexander MP, is also a member of the 'quad' (consisting also of the Prime Minister, Deputy Prime Minister and Chancellor) that operates as a *de facto* inner cabinet running the coalition (Cornock, 2011; Laws, 2010, p. 14). Such ministerial influence makes it difficult to disagree with one senior Welsh Liberal Democrat's suggestion that Scottish Liberal Democrats are 'hardwired' into the heart of the Coalition Government.[3]

For the Welsh Liberal Democrats, on the other hand, the story could not be more different. Much like the Scottish Liberal Democrats, the Coalition agreement and the allocation of ministerial representation appeared to embody the Welsh party's influence within the Liberal Democrats federally. Whilst the Scottish Liberal Democrats are rooted into the heart of Government, the Welsh Liberal Democrats did not even secure a junior minister, let alone a cabinet position (Cornock, 2011). Furthermore, *Our Programme For Government* (HM Government, 2010a) delivered little evidence of the Welsh party wielding serious influence within the federal organization, with their main objective of Barnett reform embarrassingly failing to materialize, after the Welsh Liberal Democrats had, allegedly, confidently briefed this policy gain to Welsh journalists (Powys, 2010a, Powys, 2010b).

This controversial omission says much about the relative influence of the Scottish and Welsh Liberal Democrats, with Danny Alexander MP alleged to have used his considerable influence to veto the inclusion of Barnett reform in the government's programme.[4] Such tactics are perfectly understandably politically, given that any reform to Barnett would, potentially, result in the Scots being the biggest losers (House of Commons, 2009, p. 60), something that would have serious consequences electorally for the Scottish party. However, this decision still caused astonishment and consternation within the Welsh Liberal Democrats, appearing to symbolize, in the views of one former Welsh Executive Committee member, the marginal position of the Welsh Liberal Democrats at the outset of the Coalition Government.[5]

According to one interviewee, the early months of the coalition saw the Welsh party being ignored by a federal leadership that would fail to adequately consult and/or listen to the Welsh Liberal Democrats on issues as significant as the potential closure of Newport Passport Office or rail electrification in Wales.[6] Indeed it is even alleged that the Welsh party leadership was not given a 'sign off' on the coalition agreement or the 2010 Queen's Speech announcement that the UK Government intended to establish a 'Calman style' commission on future Welsh devolution (Powys, 2010b). It can hardly be surprising that one senior Welsh Liberal Democrat argues that these developments bred a deep 'sense of bitterness' within the Welsh Liberal Democrats, with some members suggesting, according to this source, that the Welsh Liberal Democrats disaffiliate and establish a revised relationship with the federal party along the lines of the Northern Irish Alliance Party.[7]

COALITION 2.0?

The early months of life in coalition, therefore, appeared to confirm the longstanding perceptions of a disparity of influence within the federal Liberal Democrats, with the Welsh party "being ignored and forgotten" as opposed to the Scottish Liberal Democrats' position of influence at the heart of the UK party and coalition Government (Cornock, 2011).[8] However, whilst these are narratives that are certainly rhetorically appealing and have some grounding, they do not paint a full picture of the Scottish and Welsh Liberal Democrats' position within the party federally. Not only do they fail to take into account that there have been some subtle changes to the influence of the Welsh Liberal Democrats since May 2011, but they also fail to appropriately explain the nature of the Scottish party's 'muscle' within the Liberal Democrats.

In terms of the Welsh Liberal Democrats' position within the federal party, there have been a number of subtle changes since 2011. First, a key turning point identified by a number of senior federal and Welsh Liberal Democrat figures, was the 2011 Scottish Parliament and Welsh Assembly elections.[9] Whilst the Welsh party's performance left much to be desired (the Welsh Liberal Democrats lost deposits in seventeen constituencies, coming behind the BNP in four), the scale of the disaster suffered by the Scottish Liberal Democrats, who lost eleven MSPs as opposed to the net loss of just one Welsh Lib Dem AM, appears to have created a perception that the Welsh Liberal Democrats had actually performed relatively well.[10] Indeed, according to one party figure, Nick Clegg MP rang Welsh Liberal Democrat leader Kirsty Williams AM after the results to thank her personally for providing some relatively good news on an otherwise 'terrible' night for the party across the UK.[11]

In addition to this allegedly enhanced reputation, according to one senior Welsh Liberal Democrat a number of important individuals have played a key role in improving the relationship between the Welsh and the Federal Liberal Democrats. Of particular significance, according to this interviewee, has been the role played by figures on key federal organs such as Alison Goldsworthy as Deputy Chair of the Federal Executive, in lobbying for the Welsh party, and Ian Walton on the Federal Conference Committee, in seeking to give greater speaking time to Kirsty Williams and Welsh representatives.[12] Furthermore, Jo Foster's appointment as Deputy Chief of Staff has, this figure also claims, provided the Welsh party with a more friendly voice within the party in London.[13]

However, arguably the most important individual contribution appears to have come from Kirsty Williams. Her forthright style has been jokingly referred to as a 'Kirsty Williams welcome' by Nick Clegg and Vince Cable MP, but it has also been identified as an important part of getting Wales listened to through persevering and putting pressure on the leadership (Williams, 2011). Williams' influence, according to numerous Federal and Welsh Liberal Democrat figures, has not just been bolstered by the 2011 Welsh Assembly results, but also the manner with which the party in Wales fought that election.[14]

Whilst Tavish Scott MSP was, at times, publicly critical of the Coalition Government and Nick Clegg in an attempt to differentiate the Scottish Liberal Democrats from the federal party (Thomson, 2011; Black, 2011), Williams on the other hand has generally avoided this sort of rhetoric, accepting, according to senior Federal and Welsh Liberal Democrats, that the coalition is a fact of life that cannot be avoided.[15] This approach has been compared favourably by these figures to Tavish Scott's strategy, arguing that Williams' more constructive approach helped boost Williams' standing within the federal party and thus increase her and the Welsh party's influence.[16]

Organizational adaptation has also been cited as an important factor in the changing balance of power within the Liberal Democrats since 2011.[17] According to one former Welsh Executive Committee member, the intense frustration that existed within the Welsh Liberal Democrats at their marginalization in the first few months of the UK Coalition Government sparked a number of structural changes designed to boost the Welsh party's links with the centre and its ability to influence federal level decisions.[18] These changes saw weekly phone calls between the Welsh and UK leadership introduced; a development considered particularly effective by one interviewee, due to Williams' enhanced political capital, an important internal change that was further complemented by closer cooperation between special advisors for Liberal Democrat ministers in Whitehall and Assembly staffers.[19]

These dynamics have been so significant, according to this insider, that they have described them as the 'driving force' behind the Welsh Liberal Democrats getting greater influence and being listened to more often.[20] The culmination of which can be seen as the appointment of Baroness Randerson to a junior ministerial position in the Wales Office, the first Welsh Liberal Democrat to be appointed to a ministerial position in the UK Coalition Government.

However, despite these claims that the Welsh Liberal Democrats have secured greater influence, we should be wary of overstating matters. For example, whilst there appears to be a consensus amongst the party insiders interviewed that Wales' influence in the federal party, through the above mentioned developments, has been enhanced,[21] the decision not to give Kirsty Williams a slot at the 2012 Federal Liberal Democrat Autumn conference (whereas the Scottish Liberal Democrats will have speeches from both Michael Moore MP and Willie Rennie MSP) indicates that the Welsh Liberal Democrats' influence is still very limited (Cornock, 2012).

The latter is a point that is ironically reinforced by Baroness Randerson's appointment in the autumn 2012 government reshuffle. Whilst her appointment as a junior Wales Office minister and as the first Welsh Liberal Democrat Coalition Government minister might provide the Welsh Liberal Democrats with greater influence, this appointment pales into insignificance when compared to the, existing and growing, ministerial clout that the Scottish Liberal Democrats have, with the 2012 reshuffle resulting in their two Cabinet Ministers being joined by an additional junior minister, Jo Swinson MP.

The aforementioned role of Kirsty Williams brings us onto the exact nature of the Scottish party's power within the federal Liberal Democrat party. Whilst senior party sources have stressed that Willie Rennie and Kirsty Williams have equal contact with Nick Clegg, they have also suggested that there is an important difference in the authority wielded by these leaders.[22] For example, whilst Williams' position as the most senior figure within the Welsh party appears quite clear cut, these sources have argued that Rennie's authority is less so, surrounded as he is not just by two British cabinet ministers, a newly 'minted' junior minister (in addition to Lord Wallace's ministerial role as Advocate General), but also three former leaders of the Federal party (Lord Steel, Menzies Campbell MP and Charles Kennedy MP). What was earlier mentioned as a sign of strength for the Scottish Liberal Democrats, therefore, appears to be a source of personal weakness for Rennie, with his authority as leader arguably weaker than Williams' due to the seniority of so many Scottish Liberal Democrat figures at the federal level.[23] In fact, when one assesses where Scotland's influence within the federal party derives from, it appears to flow more directly from the party's MPs (for example the prominence of figures such as Danny Alexander, Charles Kennedy and Menzies Campbell in recent years), than from figures in Edinburgh, with even the Scottish Liberal Democrat leader, Willie Rennie, allegedly often kept 'out of the loop' (Torrance, 2012).

STRUCTURAL INEQUALITY: THE LIBERAL DEMOCRATS' ORGANIZATION AND THE INTERNAL IMBALANCE OF POWER

The fact that Scotland's influence within the Liberal Democrats federally appears to stem more from figures at Westminster than from Edinburgh leads us to a fundamental problem at the heart of the Liberal Democrats. Namely, the way power and influence is concentrated within the federal party, something that, as we will now discuss, has become a growing theme in analysis of the internal machinations of the Liberal Democrats. For example, recent analysis undertaken by the Social Liberal Forum has claimed that Liberal Democrat policy making has become increasingly centralized at the elite level of the party, with ministers able to bypass the party's official and well-established policy structures, due to the 'backdoor' negotiations and need for quick decisions that defines life in a coalition government (Hall-Matthews and Buch, 2012, pp. 8–10).

Whilst this criticism is admittedly the product of a faction that sits on the centre-left of the Liberal Democrats, it does find support from recent academic work by Evans and Sanderson-Nash (2011). For Evans and Sanderson-Nash, the increasingly hierarchic nature of the federal Liberal Democrat organization appears to be the product of, what they describe as, 'professionalization' (Evans and Sanderson-Nash, 2011, p. 459). This process, which seems to have largely occurred under Clegg's leadership, has resulted in a more leadership focused political party, as exemplified by a number of important developments (Evans and Sanderson-Nash, 2011, pp. 463–8). Firstly, the establishment of a 'Chief Officers Group', consisting of the Party Leader, the chairs of the Federal Finance and Administration, Federal Conference, Campaigns and Communications Committees, a representative from the Parliamentary Office of the Liberal Democrats (POLD), representatives of the English, Scottish and Welsh parties, the Federal President, Treasurer and Chief Executive, is empowered by the Federal Executive Committee to manage and direct the party (Liberal Democrats 2012, p. 3; Evans and Sanderson-Nash, 2011, p. 464). Second, and just as significantly, is the trend, highlighted by Evans and Sanderson-Nash (2011, p. 469), which has seen the constitutionally sovereign Federal Conference become increasingly a rubber stamp for policy drafted by working groups and the party's policy spokespeople in Parliament.

However, as important as these recent developments have been, there are a number of structural reasons to doubt the effectiveness of the Liberal Democrats' federal organization, with some significant weaknesses that undermine both the party's federal commitments and the Scottish and Welsh Liberal Democrats' positions internally. For example, despite the Liberal Democrats' constitution endowing the Scottish and Welsh Liberal Democrats with a substantial degree of autonomy, in practice there has been a significant degree of policy convergence. This can be partly explained by common values and shared political beliefs amongst Liberal Democrats across the UK (Holmes, 2007, p. 537). However, policy similarity is also unsurprising when placed in the context of resource-poor statewide parties relying heavily on the centre for policy development and finances (Holmes, 2007, p. 536; Bratberg, 2009, p. 74). Indeed, for both Bratberg and Holmes, resource dependency has been one of the most important factors behind Scottish, Welsh and Federal Liberal Democrat policy homogenization (Bratberg, 2009, p. 74; Holmes, 2007, pp. 537–8). Whereas much of the intra-party literature focuses on the importance of external political structures, e.g. state institutions, in shaping intra-party relations (Deschouwer, 2003; Thorlakson, 2009; and Fabre, 2008 all prioritize the role played by formal constitutional structures and electoral considerations in intra-party relations), resource relationships can provide an important variable that enables a richer explanation for the dynamics of intra-party relations.

Aside from the party's federal commitments being bounded by organizational weakness, a further structural weakness within the Liberal Democrats' federal organization and one that has arguably been at the heart of the Scottish and Welsh Liberal Democrats' marginalization is the convergence between the formally distinct English state party and the UK federal party. This convergence occurred with the transfer of the English party's functions to the centre (i.e. policy-making in 1993) leaving the two interchangeable in reality (Holmes, 2007, p. 535). With such interchangeability comes, unsurprisingly, an English dominance over the party's federal processes at the expense of Scotland and Wales according to Holmes (2007, p. 535). It is an argument that finds backing from the evidence of one member of the Federal Executive (FEC) who claimed that FEC meetings often see Scottish and Welsh members 'jumping up and down together saying that it isn't just about England'.[24] Viewed in this light the apparent organizational marginalization of the Scottish and Welsh Liberal Democrats, since the Coalition Government was formed, appears to be almost an inevitable consequence of structural weaknesses that have seen a party that, whilst ostensibly federal, become increasingly leadership-focused and more broadly Anglo-centric (Holmes 2007, p. 535; Evans and Sanderson-Nash, 2011, p. 459).

CONCLUSION

The relative influence of the Scottish and Welsh Liberal Democrats within the party federally has long been regarded as a source of disparity, with the party in Wales considered to have been in the shadow of its more successful Scottish counterpart. As a result the Welsh Liberal Democrats have even been described as the 'forgotten part' of the federal party. Certainly, the early months of the present UK Coalition Government appeared to have exacerbated this asymmetry of influence. Not only did the Scottish Liberal Democrats provide two of the Liberal Democrats' five cabinet positions, one of these led the coalition negotiations and is a member of the 'quad' that governs the coalition. For the Welsh Liberal Democrats, not only was their main objective of Barnett reform foiled (allegedly by the Scottish party), but they failed to secure even one junior ministerial position.

However, despite the early days of life in the coalition appearing to confirm longstanding perceptions of the Scottish Liberal Democrats exerting influence, whilst the party in Wales looks on jealously from the margins, such a narrative fails to provide the full picture of the balance of power within the Liberal Democrats. Indeed, whilst the Welsh Liberal Democrats have had a historically marginal status with the federal party, the Welsh party's influence, whilst still limited, has been enhanced since 2011. Furthermore, whilst Scottish interests have certainly been more successful internally than their Welsh counterparts, a reassessment of this influence shows that the Scottish Liberal Democrats' power flows overwhelmingly from Scottish Liberal Democrat Members of Parliament, not the Scottish party leadership in Edinburgh. This is, therefore, a far more complex story of intra-party relations than is often captured by the limited literature on the Liberal Democrats, with the Scottish and Welsh Liberal Democrats arguably victims of structural deficiencies at the heart of the Liberal Democrats' federal organization.

Beyond this contribution to Liberal Democrat studies, this analysis can also offer some useful contributions to understandings of intra-party dynamics more broadly. The internal dominance enjoyed by the English Liberal Democrats, the roots of the Scottish Liberal Democrats' influence and the Welsh Liberal Democrats' longstanding existence on the margins all appear to confirm Riker's (1964) claim that intra-party relations mirror the state's structures of power, or what Deschouwer usefully describes as the 'core level' of political competition for a political party (Hopkin and Bradbury, 2006, pp. 135–6). Reflecting, in this case, Westminster's continued dominance of British political activity, providing the 'core' focus of the Liberal Democrats' UK organization (a consequence of the party's federal constitution) (Hopkin and Bradbury, 2006, p. 138) and England's predominant position within Westminster politics (Hassan, 2009).

However, the importance of other factors such as intra-party resource relationships, most notably the historical dependency by the Scottish and Welsh Liberal Democrats on the party federally, leads us to a much more dynamic and mutli-dimensional account of intra-party relations than can be wholly explained by the rational choice institutionalist theories of Riker and Deschouwer outlined above. This confirms Hopkin and Bradbury's (2006, p. 150) argument that rational choice institutionalism can provide only a partial account of intra-party dynamics in the UK, thereby underlining the importance of a multi-dimensional and theoretically flexible approach instead.

This paper makes an initial contribution to the study of intra-party relationships in the Liberal Democrats following the 2010 Coalition Government with the Conservatives in Westminster. Certainly there are many more avenues that can and should be explored, in particular the way in which other dimensions beyond resources shape these relations, for example personal networks where there appear to be stark contrasts between the number of well-connected and influential Scottish Liberal Democrat MPs and the relative obscurity of their Welsh counterparts (Deacon, 2008, pp. 1–3). Furthermore, in terms of party organizations that diverge from formal state structures, it would be intriguing to compare the Liberal Democrats with the PSOE in Spain (Fabre, 2008 only offers a limited analysis in the course of a wider comparative article on Spain and the UK), which is another ostensibly federal party in a state operating under a comparable system of multi-level governance.

NOTES

1   Reform of the Barnett Formula, the mechanism that determines the Treasury block grant for Wales. This was foiled allegedly by the Scottish party.
2   MSc Econ Welsh Government and Politics Dissertation, a modified version of which was presented at the 2013 PSA Conference in Cardiff.
3   Author's interview with Federal Party official, 2 April 2012.
4   Author's interview with former Welsh Executive Member, 29 May 2012.
5   Author's interview with former Welsh Executive Member, 29 May 2012.
6   Author's interview with former Welsh Executive Member, 29 May 2012.
7   Author's interview with former Welsh Executive Member, 29 May 2012.
8   Author's interview with former Welsh Executive Member, 29 May 2012.
9   Author's interviews with Federal Executive Committee Member on 2 April 2012; with a Federal Party Employee on 2 May 2012; and with a former Welsh Executive Member on 29 May 2012.
10 Ibid.
11 Author's interview with a former Welsh Executive Member 29 May 2012.
12 Ibid.
13 Ibid.
14 Author's interviews 2 April 2012; 2 May 2012.
15 Author's interviews with a Federal Executive Member, 2 April 2012; and with a Federal Party employee, 2 May 2012.
16 Ibid.
17 Author's interviews with a Federal Executive Member, 2 May 2012; with a former Welsh Executive Member, 29 May 2012.
18 Author's interview with a former Welsh Executive Member, 29 May 2012.
19 Author's interviews with a Federal Executive Member, 2 April 2012; with a former Welsh Executive Member, 29 May 2012.
20 Author's interview with a former Welsh Executive Member, 29 May 2012.
21 Author's interviews with a Federal Executive Member, 2 April 2012; with a Federal Party employee, 2 May 2012; with a former Welsh Executive Member, 29 May 2012.
22 Author's interviews with a Federal Executive Member, 2 April 2012; with a Federal Party employee, 2 May 2012.
23 Author's interview with a Federal Executive Member, 2 April 2012.
24 Author's interview with a Federal Executive Member, 2 April 2012.

REFERENCES

BBC (2012). 'Wales Office: Lib Dem Baroness Randerson made minister', *BBC News*, 5 September 2012, *http://www.bbc.co.uk/news/uk-wales-politics-19496003* (accessed 5 September 2012).

Black, A. (2011). 'Scottish election: Talking nearly over for politicians', *BBC News*, 4 May 2011, *http://www.bbc.co.uk/news/uk-scotland-scotland-politics-13271161* (accessed 6 February 2012).

Black, P. (2012). 'An extra minister', *Peter Black*, 5 September 2012, *http://peterblack. blogspot.co.uk/2012/09/an-extra-minister.html* (accessed 7 September 2012).

Bratberg, Ø. (2009). 'Institutional resilience meets critical junctures: (re)allocation of power in British parties post-devolution', *Publius*, 40, 1, 59–81.

Cornock, D. (2011). 'Nick Clegg interview: deputy PM rails against pessimism', *David Cornock's BBC Blog*, 21 September 2011, *http://www.bbc.co.uk/news/uk-wales-politics-14998531* (accessed 6 February 2012).

Cornock, D. (2012). 'Welsh Lib Dem leader denied party conference platform', *David Cornock's BBC Blog*, 30 August 2012, *http://www.bbc.co.uk/news/uk-wales-politics-19426467* (accessed 30 August 2012).

Deacon, R. (1998). 'The hidden federal party: the policy process of the Welsh Liberal Democrats', *Regional Studies*, 32, 5, 475–9.

Deacon, R. (2007). 'The Welsh Liberal Democrats: from government to opposition and then back again?', *The Political Quarterly*, 78, 1, 156–64.

Deacon, R. (2008). 'Grinding to a halt? The development of the Welsh Liberal Democrats in the twenty-first century?', PSA Paper. Available online at: *http://www.psa.ac.uk/journals/pdf/5/2008/Deacon.pdf* (accessed 3 April 2012).

Deschouwer, K. (2003). 'Political parties in multi-layered systems', *European Urban and Regional Studies*, 10, 3, 213–26.

Detterbeck, K. (2012). *Multi-level Party Politics in Western Europe*, Basingstoke: Palgrave Macmillan.

Evans, E. and Sanderson-Nash, E. (2011). 'From sandals to suits: professionalization, coalition and the Liberal Democrats', *British Journal of Politics and International Relations*, 13, 4, 459–73.

Fabre, E. (2008). 'Party organization in a multi-level system: party organizational change in Spain and the UK', *Regional and Federal Studies*, 18, 4, 309–29.

HM Government (2010a). *The Coalition: Our Programme for Government*, Whitehall: HM Government, *http://www.direct.gov.uk/prod_consum_dg/groups/dg_digitalassets/@dg/@en/documents/digitalasset/dg_187876.pdf* (accessed 12 December 2012).

HM Government (2010b). *Calman Commission Report*, Whitehall: HM Government.

The Guardian (2011a). 'Election results 2011: Scottish parliament results in full', *The Guardian*, 6 May 2011, *http://www.guardian.co.uk/politics/2011/may/05/scotland-election-results-2011* (accessed 1 June 2012).

The Guardian (2011b). 'Election results 2011: Welsh assembly results in full, *The Guardian*, 6 May 2011, *http://www.guardian.co.uk/politics/2011/may/05/welsh-assembly-elections-2011* (accessed 19 April 2012).

Hall-Matthews, D. and Buch, P. (2012). *Liberal Democrat Party Policy-making in Coalition: A Review by the Social Liberal Forum*, London: Social Liberal Forum.

Hassan, G. (2009). 'Reimagining the English question(s): English voices, spaces and institution building', *Public Policy Research*, 16, 2, *http://www.gerryhassan.com/?p=629* (accessed 16 December 2011).

Holmes, A. (2007). 'Devolution, coalitions and the Liberal Democrats: necessary evil or progressive politics', *Parliamentary Affairs*, 60, 4, 527–47.

Hopkin, J. and Bradbury, J. (2006). 'British statewide parties and multi-level politics', *Publius*, 36, 1, 135–52.

House of Commons (2009). *Devolution: A Decade On*, House of Commons Justice Committee, London: The Stationery Office.

Laws, D. (2010). *22 Days in May*, London: Biteback.

Liberal Democrats. (2012). *Reports to Autumn Conference 2012 Brighton*, *http://www.libdems.org.uk/siteFiles/resources/docs/conference/2012-Autumn/Reports%20to%20Autumn%20 Conference%202012.pdf* (accessed 19 November 2012).

Lynch, P. (1998). 'Third party politics in a four party system: the Liberal Democrats in Scotland', *Scottish Affairs*, 22, Winter, 16–32.

Powys, B. (2011). 'Lessons history lessons geography', *Betsan Powys's BBC Blog*, 21 September 2011, *http://www.bbc.co.uk/news/uk-wales-politics-15007341* (accessed 6 February 2012).

Powys, B. (2010b). 'Before, after, ever, after', *Betsan's Blog*, 27 May 2010, *http://www.bbc.co.uk/blogs/thereporters/betsanpowys/2010/05/before_after_ever_after.html* (accessed 6 February 2012).

Powys, B. (2010a). 'Great Expectations', *Betsan's Blog*, 20 May 2010, *http://www.bbc.co.uk/blogs/thereporters/betsanpowys/2010/05/great_expectations.html* (accessed 6 February 2012).

Riker, W. (1964). *Federalism: Origins, Operation, Significance*, Boston: Little Brown.

Thomson, G. (2011). 'Can the SNP wipe out the Scottish Liberal Democrats?', *Huffington Post UK*, 1 July 2011, *http://www.huffingtonpost.co.uk/george-thomson/can-the-snp-wipe-out-the-_b_894175.html* (accessed 6 February 2012).

Thorlakson, L. (2009). 'Patterns of party integration, influence and autonomy in seven federations', *Party Politics*, 15, 2, 157–77.

Torrance, D. (2012). 'Scottish Liberal Democrats: finding compromise', *Holyrood*, 27 February 2012, *http://www.holyrood.com/articles/2012/02/27/scottish-liberal-democrats-finding-compromise/* (accessed 22 May 2012).

Williams, K. (2011). 'Kirsty Williams speech to Lib Dem Conference', *The Daily Telegraph*, 21 September 2011, *http://www.telegraph.co.uk/news/politics/liberaldemocrats/8778766/Lib-Dem-conference-2011-Kirsty-Williams-speech-in-full.html* (accessed 16 April 2012).

14. THE WELSH ECONOMY: A REPORT ON 2012

Jane Bryan and Neil Roche

INTRODUCTION

Since 2008, successive reviews have studied the economic 'mood' in relation to recession or recovery, and noted that few would have believed at the outset how deep or persistent would be this period of global stagnation, which Wales is powerless to avoid or out-manoeuvre. The UK Coalition Government has determinedly refused to waver from its course of austerity, despite provocation from the Keynesian lobby who promote the spending route out of recession (then also relying on inflation to devalue the debts). This commentary will explore the extent to which the UK Coalition aspirations for the private sector to grow jobs to replace those lost in the public sector have been fulfilled, and examine more generally the economic condition of Wales after five years of gloom.

Using the most recent information possible at the time of writing, we comment on Wales and its relative position in the UK on a number of indicators. Housing market and unemployment data are the most up to date. Output; income and expenditure; labour markets: employment and earnings; and regional competitiveness indicators lag by six months to a year. Therefore the data cannot reflect changes arising from current national or global events, or government policy effects. For an appreciation of these we rely on commentary, often from media sources.

In December 2012 the unemployment figures did deliver some surprises showing that private sector employment had grown and indeed, the unemployment figures were the best since 2008. According to the Office for National Statistics the number of people out of work in the UK fell by 82,000 to 2.51 million in the three months to November 2012, with the number of people in work increasing slightly to 29.6 million. The claimant count (the number of people claiming Jobseeker's Allowance) was also down 3,000 from October 2012 to 1.58 million. Unemployment would appear to have peaked in December 2011 and there has been an improving picture since (BBC, 2012). Of course, politicians often sway between citing absolute and relative numbers to suit their arguments, and it is disingenuous perhaps to say that employment levels are their highest and ignore the relative condition in a country with ever-swelling population.

Given the pessimistic headlines and the pervasive sense that the private sector has money to invest but is playing a waiting game, these 'good news' employment figures are counter-intuitive. One explanation is that the private sector is 'under-employing' its workforce with some private sector firms holding on to their experienced employees in anticipation of an up-turn. They can afford to absorb this reduced productivity by paying relatively less each year, as pay rises fall behind inflation exploiting the ever-present fear of redundancy. This does suggest considerable pent-up capacity and an economy that is poised for recovery with no pressure on domestic costs. In October average annual wages grew by 1.3 per cent, which is less than half the rate of inflation (Flanders, 2012).

The minutes of the Bank of England Monetary Policy Committee (MPC) provide useful background reading, and at least an insight into how the highest level of *transparent* economic power in the UK derives its decisions. Interest rates remain at 0.5 per cent even though the headline inflation rate at 2.6 per cent has been 'fuelled' by steeply rising domestic energy prices, and rising university tuition fees. The November 2012 minutes (MPC, 2012) do note an increasing appetite for risk especially in the US financial markets, with the mortgage-backed securities market receiving encouragement from increased activity in the housing sector. However, the markets are extremely sensitive (and very short-sighted) in their response to Barack Obama's on-going battles with the Congressional Budget Office. In order to avert massive future borrowings of nearly $8tn to cover US public spending from 2013 to 2022, the President has to pass unpopular tax rises and spending cuts. He is between a rock and a hard place and faces a series of damaging compromises throughout 2013. It would help global sentiments to settle if the most important economy in the world had a less crippling and adversarial political system.

While the Bank of England notes stabilization in the global economic outlook, they were wary about how far this had transferred to the real economy. The EU composite Purchasing Manager's Index showed contraction in activity toward the end of 2012 and with industrial orders in Germany weakening. Other business surveys also showed weakening. The situation in Greece was not improving. Since 2008, sterling had depreciated helping UK export trade but making imports more expensive. From mid 2011, sterling has strengthened, then hampering the UK's export position.

The much anticipated Olympic Games were a huge success in terms of show-casing the organizational ability, warmth and eccentricity of the British people. Because Britain won the games on the promise that the infrastructure would provide an enduring inheritance for a deprived part of London, it would be unfair to judge their economic impact so soon, and we must satisfy ourselves with theory and anecdote in terms of the short-run effects. Firms in Cardiff have said that they did well as a result of the Olympic football at the Millennium Stadium but some of these businesses will have operated within a corporate bubble and may not necessarily have show-cased Wales or its culture. Some rural tourism businesses, stating that they had already suffered the effects of several summers of poor weather, noted that British holiday makers were staying at home (in front of the television) or making the most of the home games but were not coming to Wales. The role-modelling by British athletes has created a surge in demand for gymnasia membership, cycling, swimming and rowing etc. which, if the enthusiasm persists, will have longer-term health benefits.

OUTPUT, INCOME AND EXPENDITURE

GVA per head of population for 2011 for the UK regions appear in Table 14.1, while similar information for the sub-regions of Wales is given in Table 14.2.

For yet another year, London remains 71 per cent higher than the UK average. This latest data shows Wales to be 25 percentage points below the UK average at 75 per cent with a 1 percentage point improvement on the previous year. The North West is stuck at 85 per cent below the UK average, while Yorkshire's position deteriorated to 82 per cent below the UK average. The North East's position also worsened from 77 per cent to 76 per cent of the UK average failing then to fully recover its pre-recession condition. The relentless differential between London and the regions presents the most powerful of arguments for some form of regional selective assistance. Across the board, however, slow growth is evident. GVA per head for the UK grew only 1.9 per cent over the period.

Household Disposable Income per head for the UK regions, (gross earnings less deductions at source including tax) relating to 2010 is also given in Table 14.1. London's primacy is evident here as well, though clearly the differential is

Table 14.1
Regional accounts

	GVA per head 2011[a]		Household disposable income per head 2010		Individual expenditure per head[b] 2009-2011	
	£	% of UK	£	% of UK	£	% of UK
London	35,638	171	20,238	129	11,773	113
South East	22,369	107	17,610	112	11,887	114
East	19,355	93	16,392	104	11,242	108
South West	19,093	92	15,653	100	10,842	104
East Midlands	18,083	87	14,267	91	10,036	96
West Midlands	17,486	84	14,021	89	9,235	88
North West	17,754	85	14,176	90	9,838	94
Yorkshire & the Humber	17,037	82	13,594	87	9,350	89
North East	15,842	76	13,329	85	9,038	86
England	21,349	102	15,931	101	10,556	101
Scotland	20,571	99	15,342	98	10,421	100
Northern Ireland	16,531	79	13,554	86	10,234	98
WALES	15,696	75	13,783	88	8,840	85
UNITED KINGDOM	20,873	100	15,709	100	10,452	100

Notes:
[a] Figures for GVA 2011 are provisional. GVA per head at current prices on residence base.
[b] Figures from the ONS Family Spending 2012 edition.

Sources:
http://www.ons.gov.uk/ons/dcp171778_291684.pdf
http://www.ons.gov.uk/ons/publications/re-reference-tables.html?edition=tcm%3A77-250794
http://www.ons.gov.uk/ons/rel/family-spending/family-spending/family-spending-2012-edition/index.html

not as great as with GVA showing that profit and taxes are driving a large part of the difference. East Midlands, Yorkshire and Humberside were previously reported as having lost way on this measure but they have since regained their equilibrium, showing no change over the current period. Regions gaining on the UK average were West Midlands, the South West, London and Scotland, with the South East and Northern Ireland falling back slightly. On the whole household disposable income also showed very muted growth over the recent period (growing by 2.4 per cent).

Table 14.2 gives GVA per head figures for the sub regions of Wales for 2011. Cardiff and the Vale of Glamorgan are most prosperous in Wales recording a GVA per head of £21,366 followed closely by Monmouthshire and Newport (£20,355). Cardiff is the only sub-region of Wales that exceeds the

Table 14.2
Sub-regional accounts

	GVA per head 2011[a]		Household disposable income per head, 2010	
	£	% of UK	£	% of UK
West Wales and the Valleys	13,573	65	13,434	86
Isle of Anglesey	12,624	61	14,236	91
Gwynedd	14,379	69	13,158	84
Conwy and Denbighshire	13,116	63	14,152	90
South West Wales	13,097	63	13,619	87
Swansea	15,933	76	13,899	88
Bridgend and Neath Port Talbot	15,440	74	13,769	88
Central Valleys	12,985	62	12,765	81
Gwent Valleys	11,626	56	12,696	81
East Wales	19,309	93	14,380	92
Flintshire and Wrexham	17,820	85	13,948	89
Powys	13,329	64	14,166	90
Cardiff and the Vale of Glamorgan	21,366	102	14,403	92
Monmouthshire and Newport	20,355	98	14,989	95
Wales	15,696	75	13,783	88

Source: Office for National Statistics/Welsh Assembly Government.
https://statswales.wales.gov.uk/Catalogue/Business-Economy-and-Labour-Market/Regional-
Accounts/Gross-Value-Added-GDP/GVA-by-WelshNUTS3Areas-Year
https://statswales.wales.gov.uk/Catalogue/Business-Economy-and-Labour-Market/Regional-
Accounts/Household-Income/GrossDisposableHouseholdIncome-by-Area-Measure

Notes:
[a] Figures for GVA 2011 (sub-regional areas) are provisional.

UK average on this measure. In north Wales, Flintshire and Wrexham have a GVA per head of £17,820, considerably less than the richer south. However, in Wales the differences between west and east exceed those of the north and south, and the poorest regions in Wales lie in the Gwent Valleys, still failing to catch up despite successive waves of inward investment. Here, the industrial past still appears to cast a shadow suppressing employment growth and entre-preneurship and we are reminded of the legendary Upas Tree of Java which could destroy other growth for a radius of 15 miles (Van Stel and Storey, 2004).

The last report (Bryan and Roche, 2012, pp. 118–19) noted sub-regional risers; Newport rising from 95 per cent below UK average to 96 per cent below over the year, Gwynedd (up 3 percentage points to 70 per cent), Anglesey (up 2 percentage points to 57 per cent), Conwy and Denbighshire (up 2 percentage points to 62 per cent), and Bridgend and Neath Port Talbot (up 2 percentage points to 71 per cent) with the rest falling on this measure. It was observed that the pattern of catch-up mirrored the convergence funding area. Now comparing the latest data with the past, we see that this pattern has persisted and in Wales at least, regional disparities have continued to dwindle, with however much more catch-up still required.

Household disposable income per head for the sub-regions of Wales is also reported in this table. Recalling average household disposable income in the UK is £15,709 which is anyway some 30 per cent lower than the London average, Wales' average household income is 14 per cent lower at £13,783. On this measure the differential between sub-regions is more muted than for GVA, with the highest in Monmouthshire and Newport (at £14,989) some 20 per cent more than the lowest of £12,696 in the Gwent Valleys.

Table 14.3 reports identifiable government expenditure on services. Northern Ireland, Scotland and Wales in that order benefit from considerably higher spending than England. The differential between spending in Wales and England (with per capita head spending in Wales some 16 percentage points higher than that of England) is a persistent feature, reflecting England's greater prosperity.

Education, health and social protection (incapacity benefits, income support, tax credits, etc.), absorb the highest spend per capita for each country. Per capita expenditure on health in Wales is 6 percentage points higher than in England, and 5 percentage points higher than the UK average. Meanwhile, spending on education in Wales is 2 percentage points higher than the UK average compared to Scotland where spending on this is 6 percentage points higher than the UK average. These differences, however, are relatively small, with other, smaller budget items giving rise to much larger deviations between the countries. For example, Wales spends nearly two and a half times as much per head on enterprise and economic development than the UK average. Scotland spends £264 per head on environmental protection and £536 per head on transport compared to £202 and £400 respectively in Wales. Northern Ireland still spends nearly twice as much per head as the rest of the UK on public order and safety. It is interesting to note that costs arising from the riots which took place in English cities during August 2011 have not been reflected in the spending patterns reported here or last year.

The Office for National Statistics and the Welsh Government together produce an index of manufacturing output for Wales and the UK. The recent state of the economy is reflected in Figure 14.1. The base period is now 2009. Since the cliff fall of 2007, UK output has experienced a virtual flat-line. The last three quarters do not give cause for optimism. Wales, as a small economy, shows greater volatility. The fall experienced in 2011 can be linked to computer

Table 14.3

Identifiable general government expenditure on services by function: 2010–2011

	£ per head				Index (UK identifiable expenditure = 100)			
	England	Scotland	Wales	N. Ireland	England	Scotland	Wales	N. Ireland
Domestic general public services	117	215	259	261	86	157	190	191
International services	4	4	4	4	100	99	106	99
Defence	1	2	1	0	100	130	108	200
Public order & safety	504	491	497	875	98	96	97	171
Enterprise & economic development	71	184	220	189	78	203	242	208
Science and technology	44	69	36	48	96	151	78	106
Employment policies	59	59	70	119	96	96	114	195
Agriculture, fisheries & forestry	67	184	167	287	76	209	190	325
Transport	344	536	400	360	95	148	110	99
Environment protection	176	264	202	138	96	144	110	75
Housing & community amenities	196	339	242	541	89	154	110	246
Health	1,900	2,072	2,017	2,106	99	108	105	109
Recreation, culture & religion	123	232	201	222	89	168	145	161
Education & training	1,446	1,541	1,485	1,509	99	106	102	103
Social protection	3,582	3,972	4,216	4,008	98	109	115	110
TOTAL	8,634	10,165	10,017	10,668	97	114	113	120

Source: HM Treasury (2012).

Figure 14.1
Index of Production: UK and Wales 2005 Q1 to 2012 Q2 (2009 = 100)

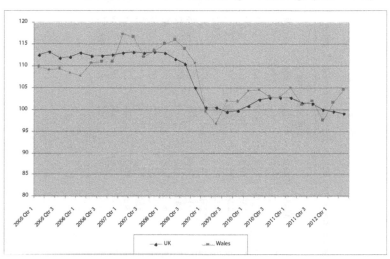

Source: Welsh Government/Office for National Statistics, *http://wales.gov.uk/topics/statistics/ theme/economy/econ-indices/product-construct/?lang=en*

and electronic products and other manufacturing outputs, while the fall in the UK can be attributed to chemicals and pharmaceuticals. The graph tends to suggest that Wales follows rather than leads and a rocky road lies ahead through 2013, as the real economy catches up with the greater optimism evident in the financial markets.

EMPLOYMENT

Table 14.4 shows Annual Population Survey (APS) data for employment by Government Office Regions. These figures are four-quarterly averages, seasonally adjusted, for the periods July 2010 to June 2011, and July 2011 to June 2012. Table 14.4 shows that the employment level in the UK remained relatively stable over the year, rising only slightly year on year by 0.4 per cent, or 119,000 employees, to 28.2 million. In Wales the employment level increased by 1.3 per cent to 1.27 million.

Table 14.4 also shows the employment rate (calculated by dividing the number of people in employment by the total number of people of working age)

Table 14.4

Employment rate: Wales, Great Britain and regions, annual population survey employment, thousands & rate[1]

	Jul 2010–Jun 2011						Jul 2011–Jun 2012					
	Male	Rate (%)*	Female	Rate (%)*	Total	Rate (%)*	Male	Rate (%)*	Female	Rate (%)*	Total	Rate (%)*
London	2040	75.3	1615	60.6	3655	68.0	2055	75.3	1627	60.7	3682	68.1
South East	2132	79.8	1896	69.7	4029	74.7	2160	80.5	1876	68.6	4035	74.5
East	1474	79.9	1238	67.1	2712	73.5	1476	79.6	1276	68.7	2751	74.1
South West	1273	78.1	1136	69.0	2409	73.6	1274	78.1	1140	69.2	2415	73.6
West Midlands	1248	72.8	1065	61.7	2313	67.2	1250	73.0	1073	62.2	2323	67.6
East Midlands	1090	76.0	948	65.8	2038	70.9	1104	76.9	941	65.2	2045	71.1
Yorkshire and the Humber	1246	72.5	1090	63.3	2335	67.9	1243	72.0	1099	63.6	2342	67.8
North West	1620	73.0	1421	63.8	3041	68.4	1611	72.6	1436	64.5	3047	68.5
North East	588	70.0	523	61.6	1111	65.8	585	69.4	522	61.3	1107	65.4
Scotland	1253	75.0	1161	66.9	2415	70.9	1253	75.1	1158	66.9	2412	70.9
Northern Ireland	411	72.0	363	62.5	774	67.2	406	70.7	369	63.2	774	66.9
WALES	653	69.7	601	62.8	1253	66.2	665	71.0	604	63.1	1269	67.0
UNITED KINGDOM	15026	75.3	13057	64.9	28083	70.1	15081	75.4	13121	65.1	28202	70.2

Note 1: * denominator is all persons of working age.
Source: Office for National Statistics (2012a).

for the UK and regions. A regular characteristic of the Welsh economy in recent years has been that, compared to the UK, relatively fewer people in Wales have been in, or searching for work. This has been a concern as low levels of participation are a key factor in GVA per capita differentials. According to the latest figures available at the time of writing this difference in the *employment rate* between Wales and the UK was closing. Whereas the employment rate in the UK averaged 70.2 per cent in July 2011 to June 2012 (increasing by 0.1 of a percentage point from 70.1 per cent in the previous year), in Wales it increased by 0.8 of a percentage point to 67.0 per cent.

Attempts have been made to further close this gap by increasing employment opportunities in Wales. In January 2012, the Welsh Government unveiled a three-year £30m extension to the Skills Growth Fund, aiding training in the workplace and aiming to support the creation of 3,000 new jobs. The programme, which will utilize £17m from the European Social Fund, will run to the end of March 2015. In November 2012 it was confirmed that the Wales Economic Growth Fund would be re-launched by the Welsh Government with £30m being provided for capital funding for investments that will create and retain jobs. Funding of £10m will be allocated in 2013/14 and £20m in 2014/15.

Differences in participation rates between unitary authorities in Wales have however been difficult to address, particularly with regard to male employment rates. Table 14.5 illustrates that the lowest male employment rates in Wales were found in Blaenau Gwent (62.0 per cent), Ceredigion (64.5 per cent), Swansea (65.2 per cent), Rhondda Cynon Taff (65.9 per cent) and Merthyr Tydfil (66.5 per cent). These relatively high figures indicate that contributions to economic output in these areas were still being hindered by factors such as long-term sickness and early retirements. Welsh Government initiatives to bolster sub-regions of the Welsh economy in 2012 included the announcement in May that two further enterprise zones, offering business-friendly planning and lower business rates, were to be set up. The Haven Waterway Enterprise Zone in Pembrokeshire and the Snowdonia Enterprise Zone (centred upon the site of the former Trawsfynydd Power Station) will join the five zones previously announced in 2011.

Table 14.6 shows the employment breakdown by industry sector in Wales and Great Britain for 2010 and 2011. These data are from the Business Register and Employment Survey (BRES). The table shows that there were a total of 26.56 million employee jobs in Great Britain in September 2011, a small decrease (0.1 per cent) from the 26.58 million of the previous September. In Wales there were a total of 1.17 million employee jobs, an increase of 0.4 per

Table 14.5
Male employment rate,[1] Wales unitary authority, July 2011–June 2012

	%		%		%
Anglesey	74.2	Denbighshire	72.3	Powys	77.8
Blaenau Gwent	62.0	Flintshire	81.5	Rhondda Cynon Taff	65.9
Bridgend	74.5	Gwynedd	69.7	Swansea	65.2
Caerphilly	67.2	Merthyr Tydfil	66.5	Torfaen	69.2
Cardiff	69.3	Monmouthshire	79.5	Vale of Glamorgan	72.8
Carmarthenshire	70.6	Neath Port Talbot	67.2	Wrexham	78.4
Ceredigion	64.5	Newport	72.6		
Conwy	72.7	Pembrokeshire	75.4		

[1] Denominator is male persons of working age.

Source: Office for National Statistics (2012a).

Female employment rate,[1] Wales unitary authority, July 2011–June 2012

	%		%		%
Anglesey	69.5	Denbighshire	66.8	Powys	70.2
Blaenau Gwent	55.5	Flintshire	64.9	Rhondda Cynon Taff	58.0
Bridgend	67.0	Gwynedd	65.3	Swansea	59.9
Caerphilly	60.9	Merthyr Tydfil	56.8	Torfaen	62.7
Cardiff	60.4	Monmouthshire	68.5	Vale of Glamorgan	67.2
Carmarthenshire	65.0	Neath Port Talbot	58.3	Wrexham	66.0
Ceredigion	60.0	Newport	63.4		
Conwy	69.2	Pembrokeshire	63.3		

[1] Denominator is female persons of working age.

Source: Office for National Statistics (2012a).

cent. Full-time jobs in Wales increased by 1.3 per cent between 2010 and 2011 while part-time jobs decreased by 1.4 per cent. The number of jobs in the manufacturing sector increased by 5.7 per cent to 135,000 (this represented a gain of 7,000 jobs), reversing the trend in the sector from recent years. Although financial and professional services jobs increased by 2.3 per cent to 164,000 (an increase of 4,000 jobs), Wales still had a far lower proportion of jobs in this sector than the Great Britain average (14 per cent of employment in Wales compared with 21 per cent in Great Britain in 2011). Furthermore, contact centre type roles constitute a large percentage of the jobs in the financial services sector in Wales, and the region is home to very few headquartered firms in this sector (which have the advantage of offering a wider range of employment opportunities).

Wales also features a high level of employment in the non-market, and relatively low productive sectors of public administration, education and health (34 per cent of the total jobs in Wales compared to 28 per cent for Great Britain). Interestingly, despite widespread cuts in public spending, the overall employment level in the non-market sector in Wales remained stable at 403,000 in 2011. Here the decline in the number of jobs in public administration was more than offset by an increase in jobs in health and social work.

The figures just described do not take into account employment gains and losses in 2012. Some of the more notable employment events in Wales are therefore important to outline here. A total of 249 job cuts was announced at the Cardiff headquarters of clothing retailer Peacocks after it was put into administration in January 2012. Difficult trading conditions, combined with a surplus of stores and an unsustainable financial structure, were reported as reasons for the firm's demise. Reduced demand and strong competition were cited by Panasonic Systems Networks Company UK as reasons for reducing its staffing level by 164 at its telephone exchange making facility in Dyffryn, Newport. The company was reportedly planning to centralize production in Vietnam.

Table 14.6
Employee jobs ('000s) in Great Britain and Wales, by industry, 2010 and 2011

	Great Britain			Wales		
	2010	2011	% change	2010	2011	% change
Agriculture and fishing (SIC A,B)	258	257	-0.4	18	17	-5.3
Energy and water (SIC D,E)	280	289	3.2	16	17	4.3
Manufacturing (SIC C)	2,317	2,324	0.3	128	135	5.7
Construction (SIC F)	1,230	1,217	-1.1	58	55	-4.8
Distribution and restaurants (SIC G,I)	6,059	6,074	0.3	271	262	-3.4
Transport and communications (SIC H,J)	2,231	2,256	1.1	63	66	4.8
Financial and Professional services (SIC K,L,M,N)	5,445	5,545	1.8	160	164	2.3
Public admin, education & health (SIC O,P,Q)	7,533	7,399	-1.8	401	403	0.4
Other services (SIC R,S)	1,229	1,201	-2.3	50	51	3.0
Total	26,581	26,562	-0.1	1166	1170	0.4
Full Time	18,019	17,910	-0.6	750	760	1.3
Part Time	8,562	8,652	1.1	416	410	-1.4

Source: Office for National Statistics (2012b).

BAE Systems announced it was to cut 105 jobs at its munitions factory in Glascoed, Monmouthshire. The decision was reportedly made after efficiency improvements resulting from automation at the company, along with reduced demand from the Ministry of Defence. Attenda, a business offering IT hosting solutions, revealed it was creating 150 jobs in Caerphilly over the next three years. The expansion by the company, which has its headquarters in Staines, was supported by a £1.98m financial package from the Welsh Government.

There was mixed news in the automotive sector in Wales. In October it was revealed that the US-owned Meritor brake disc facility in Cwmbran was recruiting 100 people as part of a £36m investment over five years. But in November Italian company, Sogefi, began a ninety-day consultation period over the closure of its Llantrisant car filter factory with the loss of 200 jobs. The company had experienced difficult trading conditions over previous years.

A number of financial service companies with operations in Wales announced job cuts resulting from UK-wide restructuring in early 2012: Lloyds Bank revealed that a total of 200 jobs were to go in Cardiff and Newport; HSBC made 100 job cuts at its Swansea call centre; and at Zurich Insurance 113 jobs were lost in the customer services and claims sections of the company's Cardiff office.

US contact centre company Conduit announced it was to recruit 600 staff at its new base in the Fusion Point office scheme in Cardiff. The investment, which followed the signing of a new contract with British Gas Homecare Service, is to receive training support from the Welsh Government. Also in the contact centre sector: Virgin Media revealed it was taking on 250 workers in Swansea to meet increasing demand for its digital products, and Indian-owned Firstsource created 100 jobs in Cardiff providing customer service functions for satellite broadcaster Sky. However, the AA announced it was reducing its call centre insurance workforce by 400 in Cardiff in order to focus operations in Newcastle.

Remploy, which employs workers with disabilities, announced it was closing five sites in Wales – at Aberdare, Abertillery, Merthyr, Swansea and Wrexham. A total of 189 jobs were lost in Wales as a result of the decision by the UK Government which followed an independent review into the way in which the government spends its disability employment budget. Following a strategic review, the cleaning products company, Jeyes, made it known that it was shutting down its facility in Mold, Flintshire and switching production to Norfolk. A total of 117 jobs were to be lost.

Luxembourg-based aerosol packaging company Ardagh announced it was shutting its factory in Merthyr Tydfil with the loss of 146 jobs. The decision followed a strategic review of its UK manufacturing operations caused by increased competition in challenging economic times.

Tata Steel also announced 500 job losses at its Port Talbot facility due to restructuring of administration posts in a bid to increase competitiveness. Included in the group's rationalizing plans were the closing of sites in Tafarnau-bach (Tredegar) and Cross Keys with the loss of seventy-six and eighty-seven jobs respectively, although relocated work was expected to create thirty-eight jobs in Shotton, North Wales.

Unilever, the consumer products group, announced the closure of two facilities in Wales. Around 100 jobs were to go at Ewloe, Flintshire as the company closed its IT facility there, and a further 250 jobs were cut in Swansea at its personal care products site. The closures came as Unilever sought to concentrate activities at its Port Sunlight, Merseyside base.

Besides the number of jobs available in Wales, the range and quality of the employment opportunities existing in the region are obviously an important concern. Over a number of years there has been an evident lack of opportunities in high level occupations such as research and development (R&D). Table 14.7 shows the breakdown of R&D performed in UK businesses in 2011, by both employment and expenditure, from figures published by the Office for National Statistics in November 2012. There were an estimated 3,000 R&D jobs in

Table 14.7
Breakdown of R&D performed in UK businesses: employment and expenditure, 2011

	Employment FTE[1] 000s	Expenditure £m	Proportion of total expenditure on R&D %
South East	37	4,528	26.0
East of England	31	3,638	20.9
London	11	1,142	6.6
South West	15	1,358	7.8
West Midlands	12	1,237	7.1
East Midlands	12	1,149	6.6
Yorkshire and the Humber	8	543	3.1
North West	13	2,260	13.0
North East	4	259	1.5
Scotland	8	689	4.0
Northern Ireland	4	352	2.0
WALES	3	255	1.5
UNITED KINGDOM	158	17,408	100.0

[1] FTE = Full Time Equivalent employees (i.e. two part-time workers equal one full-time).

Source: Office for National Statistics (2012c).

Wales in 2011, accounting for just 1.9 per cent of the total UK employment in R&D. Expenditure by businesses in Wales on R&D totalled £255 million, or 1.5 per cent of the UK total, even though the region makes up around 5 per cent of the UK population.

There were, however, some notable new R&D investments in Wales during 2012. In April electronics company Panasonic announced plans for a £2m fuel cell research and development centre in Cardiff. The project to adapt and develop fuel cell products for the domestic market will be funded by £450k from the Welsh Government. In December, a £3m research and technology centre (including a clean-room manufacturing resource) was opened by GE Healthcare Life Sciences, also in the capital. The facility will employ over forty scientists and technical support staff. Also, encouragingly, it was revealed that the Welsh Government's Life Sciences strategy will be backed by a £100m investment fund to develop existing start-ups, new businesses and commercialize spin-out companies from research.

UNEMPLOYMENT

Table 14.8 shows a time series of claimant count unemployment rates for the UK and Wales for the decade 2002 to 2011. These data are derived from counts of all persons claiming unemployment-related benefits (i.e. Jobseeker's Allowance), and are adjusted for seasonality (furthermore ONS has revised past data due to the incorporation of updated workforce denominators in the rates). Table

Table 14.8
Annual average unemployment rates (workforce based),
Wales and the United Kingdom, all persons,
claimant count 2002–11

Year	UK	Wales
2002	3.1	3.5
2003	3.0	3.3
2004	2.7	3.0
2005	2.7	2.9
2006	2.9	3.1
2007	2.7	2.8
2008	2.8	3.2
2009	4.7	5.4
2010	4.7	5.2
2011	4.8	5.3

Source: Office for National Statistics (2011d).

14.8 illustrates the impact of the recession on unemployment rates with the UK experiencing a 1.9 percentage point increase from 2.8 per cent in 2008 to 4.7 per cent in 2009, and Wales suffering a 2.2 percentage point increase to 5.4 per cent in 2009. Since then unemployment rates have remained relatively static.

Table 14.9
Unemployment Wales, United Kingdom and regions, claimants, thousands, not seasonally adjusted, November 2010 and November 2011

Area	November 2011			November 2012		
	Male	Female	Total	Male	Female	Total
South East	91.8	47.2	139.0	85.9	47.3	133.2
East	73.5	40.3	113.9	69.6	40.3	109.9
London	142.8	91.9	234.7	132.4	91.3	223.7
South West	59.1	28.8	88.0	56.0	29.1	85.1
West Midlands	110.3	54.2	164.5	102.8	55.8	158.7
East Midlands	69.6	35.1	104.7	66.7	36.6	103.2
Yorkshire and the Humber	107.7	49.3	157.0	105.5	53.4	158.8
North West	133.8	61.7	195.6	129.5	64.5	194.0
North East	60.5	27.4	87.8	62.7	30.7	93.5
Scotland	96.0	42.1	138.0	91.3	42.8	134.1
Northern Ireland	42.1	17.2	59.4	44.9	18.4	63.3
WALES	52.7	23.5	76.2	51.6	25.8	77.4
UNITED KINGDOM	1039.9	518.9	1558.8	999.1	535.9	1535.0

Source: Office for National Statistics (2012d).

Regional changes in the claimant count unemployment numbers for November 2011 and November 2012 can be seen in Table 14.9. This shows a fall in claimants in all of the UK regions except Yorkshire and the Humber (where claimants increased by 1,800 over the year to November 2012), the North East (+5,700 claimants), Northern Ireland (+4,000) and Wales (+1,200). Of these Northern Ireland had the highest proportionate increase in claimant numbers, with a year on year rise of 6.7 per cent (compared to a 1.5 per cent increase in Wales). By gender, unemployment among males in the UK decreased by 40,800 to 999,100 over the year, but with female numbers rising by 17,100 to 535,900. The increase in unemployment in Wales resulted from a rise in female claimants to 25,800. These differences by gender are partly indicative of the fall-out of job opportunities from the public administration sector (following the reigning-in of public spending by the Government in order to reduce national debt levels). The public administration sector has a relatively high proportion of female workers.

The economic profile in Volume 25 of *Contemporary Wales* (Bryan and Roche, 2012) highlighted the lack of employment opportunities, particularly for young people, in the economic climate existing at the time. In November 2011 people aged 24 and under in Wales accounted for over a third (34.9 per cent) of all unemployment claimants in the region. This was a higher proportion than any other UK region. Table 14.10 shows regional claimant count numbers by age category for November 2012. Despite a fall of 3.9 percentage points over the year, Wales remained the region with the highest proportion of young claimants with 31.0 per cent aged 24 or under (or 23,950 people). For the UK as a whole 27.7 per cent of all claimants were represented by those aged 24 and under, a fall of 2.8 percentage points from the same period in the previous year.

Table 14.10
Unemployment by age: Wales, United Kingdom and regions, November 2012

	Aged 24 and under	Aged 25 and over	All claimants	% of all caimants aged 24 and under
South East	34,370	98,250	132,620	25.9
East	30,055	79,780	109,835	27.4
London	49,125	174,110	223,235	22.0
South West	24,480	60,430	84,910	28.8
West Midlands	45,565	112,900	158,465	28.8
East Midlands	30,195	72,945	103,140	29.3
Yorkshire and the Humber	46,825	111,710	158,535	29.5
North West	56,135	137,555	193,690	29.0
North East	28,670	64,490	93,160	30.8
Scotland	36,705	97,105	133,810	27.4
Northern Ireland	17,820	45,105	62,925	28.3
WALES	23,950	53,330	77,280	31.0
UNITED KINGDOM	423,890	1,107,730	1,531,620	27.7

Source: Office for National Statistics (2012d).

Potential job opportunities for young people in the future in Wales were, however, given a boost from some sources in 2012. A new airline maintenance and repair venture was announced in May for St Athan in the Vale of Glamorgan by entrepreneur and musician Bruce Dickinson. Cardiff Aviation was reportedly planning to recruit around 1,000 workers in the first eighteen months of operation with training and skill support being supplied by the Welsh Government. The company has taken a lease on the 132,000 sq. ft. 'Twin Peaks' hangar. Furthermore, derivatives trading company, OSTC, revealed plans for a trading floor to be set up in Swansea with the potential to create around 130 jobs (mainly young graduates). The project was won despite competition from a number of other UK locations and has secured financial support from the Welsh Government. First Minister Carwyn Jones also announced in January 2012 the setting up of a new office in London to encourage business opportunities in Wales. A Welsh Government presence in London had long been argued for by business leaders in order to be in closer proximity to decision makers.

Table 14.11
Unemployment by Unitary Authority and Wales, unadjusted, resident based claimant count with rates, November 2012

	Male		Female		Total	
	number	rate	number	rate	number	rate
Anglesey	1,283	6.3	624	3.0	1,907	4.6
Blaenau Gwent	2,268	10.6	1,215	5.5	3,483	8.0
Bridgend	2,321	5.5	1,138	2.7	3,459	4.1
Caerphilly	3,844	7.1	2,175	3.9	6,019	5.5
Cardiff	7,086	6.1	3,264	2.8	10,350	4.4
Carmarthenshire	2,440	4.5	1,184	2.1	3,624	3.3
Ceredigion	639	2.6	278	1.1	917	1.9
Conwy	1,771	5.5	803	2.5	2,574	4.0
Denbighshire	1,556	5.4	755	2.6	2,311	3.9
Flintshire	1,857	3.9	1,118	2.4	2,975	3.1
Gwynedd	1,613	4.4	736	2.0	2,349	3.2
Merthyr Tydfil	1,497	8.6	817	4.5	2,314	6.5
Monmouthshire	944	3.5	506	1.9	1,450	2.7
Neath Port Talbot	2,023	4.7	1,053	2.4	3,076	3.6
Newport	3,353	7.6	1,719	3.8	5,072	5.7
Pembrokeshire	1,477	4.3	702	2.0	2,179	3.1
Powys	1,243	3.2	635	1.6	1,878	2.4
Rhondda Cynon Taff	4,883	6.6	2,489	3.3	7,372	4.9
Swansea	3,393	4.5	1,619	2.2	5,012	3.3
Torfaen	1,962	7.0	1,003	3.5	2,965	5.2
Vale of Glamorgan	1,837	4.8	822	2.1	2,659	3.4
Wrexham	2,297	5.4	1,135	2.7	3,432	4.0
WALES	51,587	5.5	25,790	2.7	77,377	4.1

Source: Office for National Statistics (2012d).

An underlying concern in the Welsh economy has been the sub-regional disparities in unemployment rates. Table 14.11 illustrates this, showing the claimant count rates for Welsh unitary authorities in November 2012. These rates are calculated by dividing the number of unemployment-related benefit claimants by the local resident population of working age, rather than the local workforce population. Using this denominator prevents distortions from commuting patterns influencing the values.

The highest unemployment rates in Wales were to be found in Blaenau Gwent (up 0.6 of a percentage point over the year to 8.0 per cent) and Merthyr Tydfil (remaining at 6.5 per cent). Notable decreases in unemployment were seen in the Vale of Glamorgan, where the rate fell from 3.9 per cent in November 2011 to 3.4 per cent in November 2012, and Pembrokeshire, where the rate fell to 3.1 per cent (or by 0.4 of a percentage point) from the previous year. In the rural areas of Wales there was a modest increase in the unemployment rate in Gwynedd (up from 3.1 per cent to 3.2 per cent) and a fall in Ceredigion (from 2.1 per cent to 1.9 per cent). In Cardiff the rate remained at 4.4 per cent, whilst Swansea saw a fall from 3.4 per cent to 3.3 per cent. In Wrexham there was an increase from 3.9 per cent to 4.0 per cent and in Newport an increase from 5.3 per cent to 5.7 per cent.

Another feature of the Welsh economy in recent years has been evidence of relatively high levels of economic inactivity. The economically inactive include those who want a job, but have not been seeking work in the previous four weeks, those who want a job and are seeking work, but are not available to start, and those who do not want a job. The economic inactivity rate (working age) is the number of people who are economically inactive aged 16 to 59/64, expressed as a percentage of all working-age people. Table 14.12 highlights Annual Population Survey data for economic inactivity rates for Government Office Regions and Welsh UAs. These figures are four-quarterly averages for the period July 2011 to June 2012. The economic inactivity rate for Wales, at 26.8 per cent, was higher than the rate for the UK as a whole (23.5 per cent), with only Northern Ireland (27.3 per cent) having a higher average rate. Meanwhile, at a sub-regional level in Wales, high proportions of inactivity were found in Ceredigion (34.2 per cent), Neath Port Talbot (30.9 per cent) and Rhondda Cynon Taff (30.6 per cent). Data from the same APS analysis suggest that of all those people classed as economically inactive in Wales, just over a fifth (22.8 per cent) actually wanted to find a job.

There were a few notable announcements in 2012 of infrastructure improvements in Wales having the potential for providing job opportunities. In February 2012 additional funding of up to £170m to improve the condition of the highway network in Wales was made available to local authorities through the UK Government's Public Works Loan Board (PWLB), an agency of the Treasury. The Welsh Government is to coordinate the initiative over the next three years. Also the UK Government Department of Transport confirmed the electrification of the rail network in south Wales with plans to upgrade lines to

Table 14.12
Economic inactivity rates United Kingdom, regions and Wales unitary authorities, combined males and females, July 2011–June 2012

Government office region	Rate	Unitary authority	Rate
South East	20.7	Anglesey	24.3
East	20.4	Blaenau Gwent	30.5
London	25.0	Bridgend	22.7
South West	21.3	Caerphilly	28.4
West Midlands	25.7	Cardiff	28.2
East Midlands	22.5	Carmarthenshire	27.7
Yorkshire and the Humber	24.6	Ceredigion	34.2
North West	24.7	Conwy	23.7
North East	26.2	Denbighshire	25.0
Scotland	22.9	Flintshire	23.3
Northern Ireland	27.3	Gwynedd	28.0
WALES	26.8	Merthyr Tydfil	28.4
UNITED KINGDOM	23.5	Monmouthshire	21.5
		Neath Port Talbot	30.9
		Newport	25.0
		Pembrokeshire	26.0
		Powys	21.7
		Rhondda Cynon Taff	30.6
		Swansea	30.4
		Torfaen	25.1
		Vale of Glamorgan	23.9
		Wrexham	21.8

Source: Office for National Statistics (2012a).

Newport, Cardiff, Swansea and the Valleys. As well as cutting journey times from London to Swansea by twenty minutes, the modifications for electrification will enable newer, longer trains to operate on the lines. The £1bn mainline upgrade to Cardiff is planned to be completed in 2017.

Perhaps giving some more hope for the future in Blaenau Gwent (the area having the highest unemployment rate in Wales during 2012) a proposal for an international motorsports centre at an 830 acre site near to Rassau Industrial Estate was unveiled in August 2012. The £250m private sector regeneration project by The Heads of the Valleys Development Company includes plans for a 3.5 mile racetrack, technology park and support services for the automotive industry.

EARNINGS

Turning the focus to differentials in earnings between Wales and the UK as a whole helps to deepen understanding of issues raised so far in this review. Data from the Annual Survey of Hours and Earnings (ASHE) from previous years has highlighted this discrepancy. Along with low activity rates described in the previous sections, this has been seen to directly contribute to the relatively low levels of GVA per capita generated in Wales. In 2011 average earnings in the Wales, for males and females combined was only 90.8 per cent of the UK average.

Table 14.13 shows an occupational breakdown of earnings for Wales and the UK for April 2012. Full-time employee gross weekly average (median) earnings are given.

Average gross weekly earnings in the UK for all employees (males and females combined) had risen to £505.9, an increase of 1.5 per cent from April 2011. For female workers in the UK average earnings for those in full-time employment increased by 1.9 per cent to £448.6, and for males there was an increase of 1.4 per cent to £545.8. In Wales the average gross weekly earnings for all workers increased to £452.6 (+0.3 per cent from 2011). This was 89.5 per cent of the UK average. Gross weekly average female earnings in Wales increased to £403.9 (+1.4 per cent from 2011) whereas earnings for males remained static at £482.4 (+0.0 per cent).

The widening gap between earnings in Wales compared to the UK was highlighted in the occupational category of managers and senior officials. Here earnings in Wales (males and females combined) were £578.8 in 2012 (falling 0.9 per cent from 2011). This represented just 78.4 per cent of the UK average. In 2011 earnings in this category in Wales had been 81.6 per cent of the UK average.

The ASHE tables for 2012 highlighted that earnings in Wales had decreased from their levels in 2011 in a number of other occupational categories besides managers and senior officials: wages in associate professional and technical occupations in Wales decreased by 1.0 per cent to £513.2 per week in 2012; skilled trade occupations earnings fell by 0.8 per cent to £453.8; and elementary occupations saw a fall of 1.2 per cent to £318.7.

In 2012 UK gross average weekly earnings for males were above the corresponding averages in Wales for every occupational category. The pay differential was largest in the occupational grouping that had the highest average overall pay – that of managers and senior officials. Here, average earnings in Wales were just 75.3 per cent of the UK in 2012, falling from 81.1 per cent

Table 14.13
Average (median) earnings: Wales and UK, £s, all industries and services.
Full-time males and females adult rates, April 2012

| | United Kingdom | | | Wales | | |
	All	Male	Female	All	Male	Female
All	505.9	545.8	448.6	452.6	482.4	403.9
Managers & senior officials	738.4	797.9	625.4	578.8	600.9	529.4
Professional occupations	694.3	739.8	653.3	655.2	696.5	631.8
Associate professional & technical	575.0	617.5	516.5	513.2	560.4	465.2
Administrative & secretarial	393.1	431.0	381.5	369.3	394.0	359.7
Skilled trades occupations	465.7	476.6	346.4	453.8	460.0	342.9
Caring & leisure occupations	332.7	371.5	322.5	326.3	357.4	317.5
Sales & customer service	323.3	338.0	309.1	315.4	323.2	294.6
Process, plant & machine operatives	426.4	441.3	310.9	402.5	421.9	325.9
Elementary occupations	333.0	354.0	279.0	318.7	340.4	264.1

Source: Office for National Statistics (2012e).

in 2011 and 89.9 per cent in 2010. For females in Wales, average weekly pay was higher than the UK average in only one category in 2012, that of process, plant and machine operatives. Here, average earnings in Wales of £325.9 were 4.8 per cent higher than the UK average (£310.9).

The occupational structure prevailing in Wales, with a higher proportion of employment concentrated in lower paid, low-skilled work when compared to the UK average, has been a concern raised in previous editions of *Contemporary Wales*. Table 14.14 uses data from the Annual Population Survey (four quarter average July 2011 to June 2012) to calculate employment shares in each occupation category. The managerial, professional and associate professional categories combined accounted for 43.1 per cent of all employment in the UK, but only 39.1 per cent in Wales. In contrast, Wales had a higher proportion employed in low-skilled elementary occupations, which results in low overall aggregate earnings and, in turn, relatively poor gross value added performance.

Table 14.15 gives full-time gross weekly earnings data by broad industry groups for the UK and Wales. Average weekly pay for service sector employees in Wales (males and females combined), at £441.2, was just 88.0 per cent of the UK average (£501.5). This reflects the low skill quality of many of the employment opportunities in this sector in Wales. Earnings in production industries in Wales in 2012 (£502.4) were only 95.4 per cent of the UK average (£526.5) whereas they had been 98.1 per cent of the UK average in 2011. Manufacturing

Table 14.14
Average gross weekly earnings and employment breakdown
by occupation, Wales and UK

	United Kingdom		Wales	
	Average gross weekly earnings £	% of all employment	Average gross weekly earnings £	% of all employment
Managers & senior officials	738.4	10.1	578.8	9.0
Professional occupations	694.3	19.1	655.2	17.7
Associate professional & technical	575.0	13.9	513.2	12.4
Administrative & secretarial	393.1	11.1	369.3	10.9
Skilled trades occupations	465.7	10.9	453.8	12.5
Caring & leisure occupations	332.7	9.0	326.3	9.9
Sales & customer service	323.3	8.1	315.4	8.6
Process, plant & machine operatives	426.4	6.4	402.5	7.0
Elementary occupations	333.0	10.9	318.7	11.4
All	505.9	100.0	452.6	100.0

Sources:
Earnings – Office for National Statistics (2012e).
Employment – Office for National Statistics (2012a).

industries wages in Wales also showed a relative decline against the UK average falling from 100 per cent of the UK average in 2011 to 96.8 per cent in 2012.

Table 14.16 shows average (median) gross weekly earnings for full-time employees by unitary authority in Wales for April 2012. With the small sample sizes involved it is not advisable to make year-on-year comparisons, but the data can illuminate broad differences in earnings across the region. The highest average weekly earnings were seen in Flintshire (£503.1), Bridgend (£498.0), the Vale of Glamorgan (£496.4) and Neath Port Talbot (also £496.4). The lowest earnings, meanwhile, were found in Blaenau Gwent (£382.1), Gwynedd (£398.9) and Powys (£399.7).

Table 14.15
Average (median) Gross Weekly Pay (£) by Broad Industry Groupings,
Full-Time Employees,[1] United Kingdom and Wales, 2012

	Males			Females			All		
	UK	Wales	% UK	UK	Wales	% UK	UK	Wales	% UK
All industries and services	546.1	482.4	88.3	448.7	403.9	90.0	506.0	452.6	89.4
All index of production industries	555.8	543.6	97.8	402.7	366.4	91.0	526.5	502.4	95.4
All manufacturing	543.6	539.7	99.3	395.2	358.9	90.8	515.9	499.3	96.8
All service industries	544.2	464.4	85.3	453.7	409.8	90.3	501.5	441.2	88.0

[1] Employees on adult rates whose pay for the survey pay-period was not affected by absence.
Source: Office for National Statistics (2012e).

Table 14.16
Average (median) gross weekly earnings £s, Wales and unitary authorities
All, male and female full-time employees on adult rates, 2012, workplace based

	All FT	Male FT	Female FT	All change
Flintshire	503.1	563.7	372.7	-0.5
Bridgend	498.0	512.3	439.4	4.0
The Vale of Glamorgan	496.4	566.6	405.1	-6.8
Neath Port Talbot	496.4	554.6	375.7	-0.7
Cardiff	485.7	513.9	447.7	0.8
Denbighshire	456.7	454.4	468.0	-1.1
Isle of Anglesey	456.5	498.3	342.1	7.4
Conwy	454.0	503.9	397.6	9.2
Caerphilly	452.3	483.4	402.5	4.2
Wrexham	450.9	477.6	376.4	6.8
Newport	450.5	450.5	450.4	-4.0
Monmouthshire	443.1	503.2	387.9	-2.0
Swansea	440.8	450.3	416.8	0.0
Rhondda Cynon Taff	431.5	441.3	418.2	-0.3
Carmarthenshire	418.4	419.2	412.1	1.0
Pembrokeshire	412.2	436.1	350.3	-10.4
Torfaen	408.8	486.6	344.8	-0.9
Merthyr Tydfil	406.3	403.6	405.4	-1.5
Ceredigion	403.4	456.6	364.1	-3.9
Powys	399.7	442.2	344.0	1.0
Gwynedd	398.9	406.9	361.3	-3.5
Blaenau Gwent	382.1	438.0	345.1	-3.9
WALES	452.6	482.4	403.9	0.3

Employees on adult rates whose pay for the survey pay-period was not affected by absence.
Source: Office for National Statistics (2012e).

HOUSING MARKETS

The housing markets have experienced a particularly long period of subdued performance. It remained difficult to get a mortgage through 2010 and 2011 and it was hoped that the coalition's new housing strategy announced in November 2011 comprising a mortgage indemnity scheme would assist first time buyers. This coupled with the 'Get Britain Building Fund' of £400m was hoped to reinvigorate moth-balled building projects.

The Bank of England's Credit Conditions Survey undertaken in the final Quarter of 2012 reported that secured credit to households had increased in the three months to mid-December 2012, and that this was driven in part by the Funding for Lending Scheme (Bank of England, 2012). The availability of unsecured credit to households had also risen slightly in 2012 Q4, and it was anticipated that this trend would continue into 2013 Q1.

The same report also noted that the demand for secured lending for house purchase had increased in 2012 Q4, with lenders also expecting further increases in the first part of 2013. This demand was for both prime lending and buy-to-let lending. The Chief Economist at the Halifax was not able to observe any particular strong direction in either supply or demand behaviours, predicting continued house price stability for 2013.

So what happened in 2012? UK house prices, annual and monthly changes as at October 2012 are shown in Table 14.17, sourced from the Land Registry.

Table 14.17
Land Registry regional data

Land Registry House Price Index October 2012

	Monthly change %	Annual change %	Average price (£)
North West	-0.1	-1.2	109,361
Wales	1.5	1.0	118,215
London	1.0	7.0	364,574
West Midlands	1.1	0.1	130,088
Yorkshire & the Humber	-0.4	-2.1	116,365
South West	0.0	0.9	171,695
North East	-4.2	-5.8	96,061
East Midlands	-0.1	-0.3	122,716
South East	-0.3	1.4	209,137
East	0.8	2.2	175,821
England & Wales	-0.3	1.1	161,605

Source: Land Registry (2012).

Table 14.18
Average house price by Welsh unitary authority, twelve months to October 2012

Local authority	Average house price (£) October 2012	Monthly change (%)	Annual change (%)
Blaenau Gwent	61,749	-3.4	-13.5
Bridgend	114,459	0.7	-1.8
Caerphilly	98,316	-0.4	-1.2
Cardiff	141,930	0.6	-1.1
Carmarthenshire	107,177	3.4	-1.1
Ceredigion	161,013	0.0	0.4
Conwy	131,310	1.6	-4.3
Denbighshire	115,803	-0.1	-1.7
Flintshire	127,451	2.6	0.5
Gwynedd	136,083	-3.4	-3.7
Isle of Anglesey	128,799	-0.6	-5.4
Merthyr Tydfil	72,283	3.2	4.7
Monmouthshire	174,552	2.3	-2.4
Neath Port Talbot	85,062	0.6	2.3
Newport	114,136	1.3	-0.5
Pembrokeshire	135,081	-1.8	-4.7
Powys	149,462	-0.4	0.7
Rhondda Cynon Taff	72,952	0.3	-2.3
Swansea	112,345	-0.2	-2.4
The Vale of Glamorgan	155,321	0.3	0.1
Torfaen	103,406	-2.1	-2.9
Wrexham	109,261	-2.6	-9.6

Twelve months to October 2012.

Source: Land Registry (2012).

The last commentary reported the average price at November 2011 was £160,780 in England and Wales, which by October 2012 had risen marginally to £161,605. The average house price in Wales was £118,215 by October 2012, compared to £118,320 in the year to November 2011.

The last report also showed house prices to have dropped in *all* regions except London, with the North East experiencing the greatest decline; down by 5.4 per cent. In the latest period to October 2012, house prices dropped in only four regions (North West, -1.2 per cent; Yorkshire and Humber, -2.1 per cent; North East, -5.8 per cent and East Midlands, -0.3 per cent). London, always buoyant, experienced a rise of 7 per cent, while house prices in Wales rose by 1 per cent.

Table 14.18 reports average house prices by Welsh Unitary Authority (also sourced from the Land Registry). 2011 delivered some punishing falls over the year, particularly in Merthyr Tydfil (-8.6 per cent), with many experiencing falls of around 5 per cent to 6 per cent. In 2012 the two biggest falls were Blaenau Gwent (-13.5 per cent) and Wrexham (-9.6 per cent). Blaenau Gwent had been a 'gainer' in 2011. In six unitary authorities house prices rose to October 2012, with the strongest growth in Merthyr Tydfil (4.7 per cent). Most of the growth shown was muted. It should be noted that the headline figures are volatile being based often on small sales volumes. The requirement for large deposits is still keeping first time buyers out of a market which continues to be dominated by equity rich home buyers and investors. On a purely anecdotal level, stock values of private sector construction firms were showing buoyancy in the early part of 2013 reflecting land banked at competitive prices, and previously moth-balled building plots were showing signs of fresh activity.

REGIONAL COMPETITIVENESS

Table 14.19 reports on regional competitiveness indicators, with gross disposable household income data repeated from earlier Table 14.1. GVA data given here is workplace rather than household based. Other important competitiveness indicators such as the proportion of the population over 16 years claiming income support and manufacturing investment data are reviewed. Claimant count figures reflect conditions prevailing in 2011 hence there is a significant lag, as with manufacturing investment data.

It would be both gratifying and interesting to be able to observe change over time in terms of Wales' position in relation to the UK average on gross disposable income and gross value added measures. However, over successive years of commentary, no change can be reported, and it becomes clearer each year that devolution does not deliver a magic economic bullet. The claimant count figures do show some improvement on the previous year across the UK regions, while each region maintains its relative position in the rankings. Wales's claimant count was reported as 6.2 per cent of the working population in the previous commentary; while still in the bottom half of the rankings this has improved to 5.7 per cent.

Wales has always enjoyed a strong history with respect to attracting foreign inward investment, reflecting its well-developed infrastructure links, manufacturing competence and competitive cost base for investors. However, foreign inward investment is footloose and it is well-known that in recent years the UK

Table 14.19
Regional competitiveness

Region	Gross disposable household income per head 2010 (UK=100)	Gross value added, workplace basis per head 2010 (UK=100)	Proportion of income support claimants (in population over 16) Aug 2011	Manufacturing investment by foreign and UK owned companies 2008 (£m)		Manufacturing investment by foreign and UK owned companies 2009 (£m)	
				Foreign	*UK*	*Foreign*	*UK*
London	129	171	5.4	176	571	210	436
South East	112	107	3.3	385	607	371	480
East	104	93	3.6	282	561	446	483
South West	100	91	3.9	322	482	328	435
West Midlands	89	83	5.0	508	427	483	555
East Midlands	91	88	4.2	372	638	334	387
Yorkshire & the Humber	90	83	4.6	564	597	488	537
North West	90	85	5.8	817	1024	708	719
North East	85	77	5.9	361	305	205	195
England	101	102	4.6	3787	5213	3573	4226
Scotland	98	99	5.3	350	748	305	583
Northern Ireland	86	76	7.7	117	299	107	272
WALES	88	74	5.7	563	254	366	214

Sources:
Regional Economic Performance Indicators, BIS, May 2012.
GVA figures – Office for National Statistics.

http://www.bis.gov.uk/analysis/statistics/sub-national-statistics/regional-economic-performance-indicators has lost out to Eastern Europe. In 2009 Wales attracted £366m of foreign investment compared to £563m the previous year. That this reflects generally poor investment levels in absolute terms is indicated by comparing other UK regions with the previous year, and indeed total foreign investment for *England* is down slightly from £3787m to £3573m. The North and Midlands were the losers while the winners were London, the South West and particularly the East.

UK investment in manufacturing is also down over the period from £5213m to £4226m and on this measure there is one convincing winner: the West Midlands, up from £427m to £555m, with all other regions experiencing declines in UK investment in manufacturing, and particularly the East Midlands down to £387m from £638m. In summary, the figures, while out of date, show the long-lasting deleterious effects on investment confidence of the 2007 credit crunch.

OVERVIEW

Here we make a number of observations from the preceding commentary. While Wales shows no sign of catching up with the UK average on the GVA measure there is some good news. The employment rate gap between Wales and the UK has closed slightly. Moreover, according to the Business Register and Employment Survey the number of jobs in manufacturing in September 2011 had risen over the year by 5.7 per cent to 135,000, which was a gain of 7,000 jobs.

The failure of successive policy efforts to reduce the R&D activity gap that exists between Wales and the rest of the UK (with for example the Technium business innovation centres in Wales) proves how difficult it is for public sector interventions to pump-prime the private sector. Nevertheless, it is impossible to predict how much poorer this situation might be without such efforts. Hence, investment plans by Panasonic, supported by Welsh Government funds, must be welcomed, as is GE Healthcare Life Sciences' £3m research and technology centre, any spin-outs from which will receive Welsh Government support.

Given the perception of poor wage settlements and even downward pressure on earnings that have been a feature of 2012, the earning levels reported for Wales have held up reasonably well, and there were signs that disparities within Wales had narrowed again through 2011. The time lag on data is a confounding factor for any such commentary, but writing here at the beginning of 2013 there are outward signs that the human spirit is growing weary of prolonged pessimism and the financial markets are becoming more bullish, and no one wants a triple dip.

REFERENCES

BBC (2012). 'Economy tracker: unemployment', *BBC News*, December 2012, *http:// www.bbc.co.uk/news/10604117* (accessed 18 January 2013).

Bank of England (2012). *Credit Conditions Survey 2012 Q4*, *http://www.bankofengland. co.uk/publications/Documents/other/monetary/ccs/creditconditionssurvey130103.pdf* (accessed 8 January 2013).

Flanders, S. (2012). 'UK unemployment: jobs up, pay down', *BBC News*, *http://www. bbc.co.uk/news/business-20697050* (accessed 18 January 2013).

HM Treasury (2012). *Public Expenditure Statistical Analysis 2011*, London: HM Treasury, *http://www.hm-treasury.gov.uk/d/natstats_statistical_bulletin_july2012.pdf* (accessed 14 January 2013).

Land Registry (2012). *House Price Index*, London: Land Registry, *http://www.land registry.gov.uk/_-data/assets/file/0009/28728/october-hpi-report.pdf* (accessed 14 January 2013).

Monetary Policy Committee (2012). *Minutes of the Monetary Policy Committee Meeting, 7 and 8 November 2012*, *http://www.bankofengland.co.uk/publications/minutes/ Documents/mpc/pdf/2012/mpc1211.pdf* (accessed 18 January 2013).

Office for National Statistics (2012a). *Annual Population Survey*, Newport: ONS.

Office for National Statistics (2012b). *Business Register and Employment Survey*, Newport: ONS.

Office for National Statistics (2012c). *UK Business Enterprise Research and Development 2011*, Newport: ONS. *http://www.ons.gov.uk/ons/dcp171778_287868.pdf* (accessed 14 January 2013).

Office for National Statistics (2012d). *Claimant Count*, Newport: ONS.

Office for National Statistics (2012e). *Annual Survey of Hours and Earnings*, Newport: ONS.

Van Stel, A. and Storey, D. (2004). 'The link between firm births and job creation: Is there a Upas Tree effect?', *Regional Studies*, 38, 8, 893–909, *http://dx.doi.org/ 10.1080/0034340042000280929* (accessed 16 January 2013).

15. LEGISLATING FOR WALES 2012

Marie Navarro

INTRODUCTION

2012 will be remembered as the year when the first Welsh Acts were made in Wales in 600 years. But as the National Assembly enacted its first two Acts in 2012, its legislative competence was also tested by a legal challenge in the Supreme Court to the first Bill passed and a threat of a challenge to the second Bill. 2012 was a surprising year in that there was initially a slow build-up of the amount of legislation being introduced in the Assembly which culminated in some legal turmoil at the end of the year with the referral to the Supreme Court.

As well as the challenges to the Welsh laws, the extent of the devolved competences is also being explored by the Silk Commission. Part 2 of its recommendations are expected to suggest ways to refine or even to re-define the Assembly's competence. Finally, the First Minister of Wales is also calling for possible expansions of the Assembly's competence by calling for example for the devolution of the Severn Bridge poll or by launching a debate on whether Wales should have its own legal jurisdiction. Thus the boundaries of devolution will continue to be an important part of Welsh debates in 2013.

Several Bills were introduced in the Assembly in 2012, consequently some general conclusions can begin to be drawn about the quality of drafting of Welsh Bills. There seem to be no more criticisms that the drafting of the laws made in Wales is defective. This marks a stepping stone in the devolution process when it seems that the legal drafting capacity of Wales has stepped up to the mark. The quality of the first Bill passed has been noted by the Supreme Court.

The Supreme Court's decision on the legality of the first Bill has slightly moved the boundaries of devolution and it has provided the first set of principles which will assist in the consideration of the future competence issues in relation to Welsh Bills. The favourable decision to Wales means that the Assembly can make incursions to non-devolved areas as long as such incursions are incidental or consequential provisions. The law of devolution in Wales has never been never dull and particularly not so at the end of 2012.

LAW MAKING IN WALES

In 2012, two Acts were passed and several Bills were introduced in the Assembly both by the Welsh Government and Assembly Members.

Assembly Acts
Out of five Bills introduced in the first year of the Fourth Assembly (May 2011-July 2012), two were passed in 2012.

The first two Acts passed by the National Assembly for Wales are the Local Government Byelaws (Wales) Act 2012 and the National Assembly for Wales (Official Languages) Act 2012.

Following the referral of the Local Government Byelaws (Wales) Bill to the Supreme Court, the National Assembly for Wales (Official Languages) Bill received Royal Assent first on 12 November 2012. The Local Government Byelaws (Wales) Bill received Royal Assent on 29 November 2012.

The Local Government Byelaws (Wales) Act 2012
The purpose of the Local Government Byelaws (Wales) Act 2012 is to simplify the procedures for the making and enforcing of local authority byelaws. This is achieved by enhancing the current process for making such byelaws which currently requires confirmation by Welsh Ministers or the Secretary of State and by introducing an alternative procedure which removes the need for such confirmation for specific byelaws. The Act also provides local authorities with an alternative option for the enforcement of byelaws through the introduction of fixed penalty notices.[1]

It is interesting to note that the Act also 'recasts and consolidates' existing byelaw provisions contained in the Local Government Act 1972. The Explanatory Memorandum explains that 'This is a step towards the development of a Welsh Statute Book and makes the key legislative provisions relating to making, confirming and enforcing byelaws in Wales accessible in a single enactment' (NAfW, 2011a, para 1.1).

The National Assembly for Wales (Official Languages) Act 2012
The purpose of the National Assembly for Wales (Official Languages) Act 2012 is to place clear duties on the National Assembly for Wales and on the

Assembly Commission in relation to the provision of bilingual services duties imposed on them by the Government of Wales Act 2006.

Competence issues

During the passage of both Bills, the Wales Office raised questions as to whether the Bills were within the competence of the Assembly.

Referral to the Supreme Court

The Secretary of State for Wales, David Jones MP, referred both of the Bills to the Attorney General, Dominic Grieve, suggesting that both Bills should be referred to the Supreme Court. Under section 112 of the Government of Wales Act, the Secretary of State cannot refer Bills to the Supreme Court directly and the power only belongs to the Attorney General or the Counsel General. Under the procedure, the Attorney General has four weeks from the passing of the Bill by the Assembly to make the referral. The purpose of the referral to the Supreme Court is to ask the Court whether the Bill, or any provision of the Bill, would be within the Assembly's legislative competence before the Bill can become an Act. It is a form of preventative control to ensure the legality of the Bill before it becomes enforceable law.

In relation to the National Assembly for Wales (Official Languages) Bill, the Secretary of State for Wales argued that the provision contained in the Welsh Bill which stated 'The official languages of the Assembly are English and Welsh,' was outside of the legislative competence of the Assembly because under Schedule 7 to GOWA, the Assembly can only legislate about the Welsh language. The Assembly's Chief Legal Adviser argued that the provision was within the competence of the Assembly because the provision was not a substantial provision. He added that the Bill only contained a subsidiary reference to the English language and that the provision did not affect in any way the status of the English language. In his opinion, the Bill only restated the obligation contained in GOWA to ensure that both languages were treated according to the principle of equality in Assembly proceedings. It was claimed therefore that the provision was within the competence of the Assembly as it was incidental to, or consequential on other provisions contained in the Bill as allowed by GOWA section 118(6). The Attorney General chose not to refer the Bill to the Supreme Court.

The Local Government Byelaws (Wales) Bill was passed by the Assembly on 3 July 2012 and it was referred to the Supreme Court by the Attorney General on 31 July 2012 just as the four week delay was about to expire. The case was heard on 9 and 10 October 2012. The Supreme Court's judgement was given on 21 November 2012.

The appellant in the case was the Attorney General for England and Wales and the respondents were the National Assembly for Wales Commission, the Counsel General for Wales and the Attorney General for Northern Ireland. Two issues were put to the Court: first whether sections 6 and 9 of the Local Government Byelaws (Wales) Bill were within the legislative competence of the National Assembly for Wales and secondly clarification was sought from the Court as to how 'incidental to, or consequential on' should be interpreted. Welsh Bill clauses under GOWA are referred to as sections.

Section 6 of the Bill created a new procedure for making byelaws and therefore replaced the procedure contained in the Local Government Act 1972. The new procedure would apply only in relation to byelaws made under enactments specified in Schedule 1 to the Bill. Section 9 of the Bill allowed the Welsh Ministers to modify the list of enactments contained in Schedule 1.

The procedure in the Local Government Act 1972, which the Welsh Bill would replace, contains a default provision according to which, in the absence of a confirming authority being specified in an enactment allowing byelaws to be made, the Secretary of State was the default confirming authority (section 236(11) of the 1972 Act). The power was devolved concurrently to the Welsh Ministers and the Secretary of State in 1999.[2]

The Secretary of State's power contained in section 236(11) was the source of the competence dispute referred to the Supreme Court. The question was whether the Assembly could remove that power by section 6 of the Welsh Bill which provided that byelaws made under the enactments listed in Schedule 1 do not need to be confirmed (by anyone) and therefore disapplied section 236(11) for those byelaws.

Under the Government of Wales Act 2006, Schedule 7, Part 2, a provision of an Assembly Act cannot remove any pre-commencement function of a Minister of the Crown (i.e. the function of an English Secretary of State contained in an Act made prior to May 2011). However, Part 3 of the same Schedule allows such removal in two specific circumstances: if the Secretary of State consents to the removal or if the removal is incidental to or consequential on other provision in the Bill (Schedule 7, Part 3).

The Secretary of State for Wales, at the time Cheryl Gillan MP, did not give consent to the removal of functions operated by sections 6 and 9 of the Welsh Bill. It transpires from a disclosure of information under the Freedom of Information Act (Welsh Government, 2012a) that she had told the First Minister in a letter dated 1 May 2012 that she was prepared to consent to the removal of function contained in section 6 but only if the Welsh Government amended section 9 of the Bill so that it included a requirement for her consent before the power to amend Schedule 1 was used. Section 9 was not amended in this way.

The arguments before the Court were as follows. According to the Assembly Commission, all the enactments contained in Schedule 1 to the Welsh Bill specified a confirming authority (the Welsh Ministers in all instances) and therefore the default provisions of section 236(11) did not apply. Consequently no pre-commencement function of a Minister of the Crown had been affected and the Bill was within the legislative competence of the Assembly. The Commission added that if the Court were to find that a pre-commencement function was affected, then the removal would be incidental to or consequential on the provisions of the Bill.

In an alternative argument, the Welsh Government's Counsel General agreed with the UK Attorney General that section 6 of the Bill did remove a pre-commencement Ministerial function, namely section 236(11) because Schedule 1 contained three enactments to which section 236(11) would apply. Both also agreed that the function contained in section 236(11) was a concurrent power of the Secretary of State and of the Welsh Ministers. It was also argued that while section 6 of the Welsh Bill did remove a concurrent power of the Secretary of State, section 9 by adding further enactments to the Schedule could potentially remove the concurrent default power of the Secretary of State to confirm bye-laws.

The disagreement between the Counsel General and the Attorney General related to whether the removal of this concurrent power fell within or outside the exception contained in Part 3 of Schedule 7. If the removal was within the exception then it was within the competence of the Assembly, if not, the provisions were outside the legislative competence of the Assembly.

The Court was asked to decide whether the removal of the concurrent power was 'incidental to or consequential on another provision of the Bill' which is the wording of the exception. This question of interpretation of the exception is the reason why the Attorney General for Northern Ireland joined in the case as the same wording appears in the Northern Ireland Act 1998.

In assessing whether both sections 6 and 9 of the Bill were within the exception contained in Schedule 7 Part 3, the Court considered that one of the purposes of the Byelaws Bill (the primary purpose) was streamlining and modernizing the making of byelaws (which the Court pointed out had also happened in relation to England). They added that retaining the concurrent power of the Secretary of State would undermine the primary purpose of the Bill. They also pointed to the fact that the concurrent power of the Secretary of

State was a default power, which had not been used since 1999 and that the byelaws captured by the enactments listed in Schedule 1 would be for the Welsh Ministers rather than the Secretary of State to confirm as they related to 'local, small scale (but important) issues'. Therefore the Court concluded that the removal of the function was incidental or consequential on the provisions of the Bill.

The Court stated in its judgement that

> The answer to the question whether a particular provision in an enactment is 'incidental to, or consequential on' another provision, obviously turns on the facts of the particular case. The answer may to some extent be a question of fact and degree, and it should turn on substance rather than form, although, of course, in any well drafted Bill, the substance will be reflected in the form, at least in relation to that sort of question. (The Supreme Court, 2012, Paragraph 49)

and added that

> although this is a successful outcome for the Assembly and the Counsel General, it cannot be regarded as a setback in practical terms for the Secretary of State. Somewhat curiously, the conclusion I have reached as to the effect of section 9 is one which reflects the terms on which she was prepared to give her consent to Section 6 of the Bill. (The Supreme Court, 2012, Paragraph 67)

This implies that what constitutes a primary provision or an incidental provision in any given Bill can only be decided in each particular case. This points to the possibility of other disputes in the future in particular as the Court's comments seem to encourage the Secretary of State to continue to assess Welsh Bills.

The UK Attorney General further argued that section 9 by allowing further enactments to be added to Schedule 1 and therefore to be exempt from the concurrent power does 'confer' on the Welsh Ministers a power to remove or modify a pre-commencement function of a Minister of the Crown, and therefore is outside of the competence of the Assembly. The Court decided that if the power had been unlimited and of general effect then it would clearly be outside of the competence of the Assembly, but as the power identifies the enactments under which the Welsh Ministers are the confirming authority and if the removal of the power is incidental or consequential as in the case of section 6, then such removal of function is within the competence of the Assembly.

Finally, it is worth reporting that the Court also provided an explanation of the meaning of 'concurrent powers'. Three possible meanings were given by the different parties during the proceedings and the Court agreed with the Counsel General's interpretation of the term. In the opinion of the Court, concurrent powers means that both the Welsh Ministers and the Secretary of State own the power and that it is for them as a matter of administrative arrangement to decide in each case who is best to exercise the power in the particular circumstance. Lord Hope was reported to have praised the drafting of the Bill (Welsh Government, 2012b), saying that the Bill 'was "very well drafted". He described the Welsh draftsmen as "using their own lines, but applying the same standards" as Parliamentary draftsmen.' (George, 2012)

The importance of the case is that the Court did not give the narrowest interpretation to the exception contained in Part 3 of Schedule 7 which would have made the operation of Part 4 very difficult. However, the case also demonstrates that the incursions into the non-devolved subjects must be limited as the Court explained that if incursions were unlimited and of general effect the provisions would clearly be outside of the Assembly's competence.

This leads me to conclude that following this judgement nothing is fully retained in relation to Wales and that there can be lawful, though limited, incursions into non-devolved subjects. The decision slightly moves the boundaries of the devolution settlement. This can cast some new light in relation to the interpretation of the legislative competence of the Assembly but it also shows that the new balance is delicate and that each case will be different.

One can only wonder whether, and if so, how, this judgement will affect other Bills in particular the Human Transplantation (Wales) Bill.

Role of the Secretary of State for Wales

As explained above, under the Government of Wales Act 2006, the Secretary of State cannot refer Bills to the Supreme Court directly. However, he or she can only 'intervene' in very specific cases listed in section 114 of GOWA 2006. Under that section, in particular circumstances, the Secretary of State can make an Order preventing the Assembly Clerk from submitting a Welsh Bill for Royal Assent.

Devolution Guidance Note 9 however clearly explains that:

> The UK Government expects any concerns which could risk triggering an intervention to be resolved in practice during the passage of the Assembly Bill. It is therefore important that Departments respond to Wales Office write-rounds and monitor the progress of Assembly legislation, informing the Wales Office and the Welsh Government if any concerns arise. (Cabinet Office, 2012, Paragraph 77)

Under the Guidance Note, it is the Secretary of State's role to write

> at official level to Departments when a Bill is introduced in the Assembly, and again once the Assembly passes a Bill, to seek views on whether the Secretary of State should exercise her powers of intervention, and to ask on behalf of the Attorney General whether the Bill raises issues of legislative competence. (Cabinet Office, 2012, Paragraph 75)

The Supreme Court seemed to encourage that role. The Attorney General then decides whether or not to refer the Bill to the Supreme Court.

The referral procedure, it should be stressed, is of a preventative nature and the Supreme Court recognized that it was better to use this procedure at an early stage and before the law is enforceable rather than wait for a devolution issue procedure under Schedule 9 to GOWA to be initiated once the law has been commenced.

Reflecting the UK Government guidance, the UK Government stressed that referring the Bill to the Supreme Court did not demonstrate that 'an "anti-devolutionist" approach was being taken, but rather a desire to ensure that laws passed by the assembly are within their powers.' (Mason, 2012) Whilst recognizing that the issue was a technical one, they were also clear that there was a principle at stake.

Former Welsh Secretary Cheryl Gillan explained that, in her opinion,

> The secretary of state for Wales and the attorney general are custodians of the devolution settlement for Wales and have a duty to ensure that the provisions of the Government of Wales Act 2006 are complied with. (BBC, 2012b)

She added that at the time, the UK Government made every attempt to resolve the issue with the Welsh Government during the passage of the Bill. This is required by the Devolution Guidance Note 9 and generally the Wales Office's position echoes the various Devolution Guidance Notes and the Memorandum of Understanding policies.

This is the reason given for the intervention of the Wales Office in relation to the first two Acts passed by the Assembly.

Lessons learnt in the Assembly from the referral

The Assembly Constitutional and Legislative Affairs Committee (CLA Committee)
The referral of the Bill to the Supreme Court, and the consideration to refer the second, came as a surprise to most. The Assembly had not been previously

informed that there had been any questions raised by the Wales Office about the competence of the Assembly in relation to two sections.

To ensure the Assembly's awareness of competence disputes, the CLA Committee has decided to ask each Minister in charge of a Bill at Stage 1 whether they have been made aware whether there are any issues of competence raised by the Wales Office. Accordingly, the Committee has created a new section of their reports on Bills which is dedicated to legislative competence.

As an example, Part 4 of their report on the Public Audit (Wales) Bill records that the Minister has been made aware of one competence issue being raised 'which relates to whether the Assembly has legislative competence to make provision to change the audit arrangements for Chief Constables in Wales.' (NAfW, 2012b). The Minister added, 'We are in on-going discussions with the Wales Office regarding this matter' (NAfW, 2012b, Paragraph 22). Subsequently the Committee recommended 'that the Minister explains, during the Stage 1 debate on the general principles of the Bill, the outcome of her discussions with the Wales Office about whether the Assembly has legislative competence in respect of the audit arrangements for Chief Constables in Wales' (NAfW, 2012b, Paragraph 24).

It can therefore be expected that in the future there will be less surprises about central government's concerns in relation to the issues of competence. Any future question about the Assembly's competence on specific Bill provisions should be raised in the Assembly and be debated before any future Bill is passed by the Assembly.

Assembly Bills
In addition to the two Acts passed by the Assembly and to the three Bills introduced in the year 2011–12, four new Bills have been introduced in the second half of the calendar year (July–December 2012). They include two Government Bills and two Members Bills.

The School Standards and Organization (Wales) Bill was introduced on 23 April 2012. The government Bill includes provision for intervening in schools causing concern, school improvement, school organization, Welsh in education strategic plans, annual parents meetings, school-based counselling, primary school free breakfast initiatives and flexible charging for school meals. It is worth noting that an impressive number of 141 amendments were agreed at Stage 2 (NAfW, 2012c). Most amendments came from the Government and while some were of a technical nature many were substantive. Three non-government amendments were also accepted at Stage 2.

The Food Hygiene Rating (Wales) Bill was introduced on 28 May 2012. The government Bill includes provision for food authorities to operate a food hygiene rating scheme and places a duty on food businesses to display their food hygiene rating at their establishment. Forty-one amendments were agreed at Stage 2, all proposed by the government (NAfW, 2012c).

The Public Audit (Wales) Bill was introduced on 9 July 2012. The government Bill aims to strengthen and improve the accountability and governance arrangements relating to the Auditor General for Wales (AGW) and the Wales Audit Office (WAO) whilst protecting the AGW's independence and objectivity. The general principles of the Bill were agreed on 4 December 2012.

The Local Government (Democracy) (Wales) Bill was introduced on 26 November 2012. The provisions of the Bill are intended to reform the organization and functions of the Local Government Boundary Commission for Wales. The Bill also contains provisions which would amend the Local Government (Wales) Measure 2011 in relation to the responsibilities of the Independent Remuneration Panel for Wales and the structure of local authority audit committees.

The Human Transplantation (Wales) Bill was introduced on 3 December 2012. The Bill aims to increase the number of organs and tissues available for transplant by introducing a soft opt-out system of organ and tissue donation in Wales. I refer the reader to last year's report on the potential legal issues raised by this particular Bill (Navarro, 2012). The fact that the Bill has been introduced means that the Presiding Officer has issued her formal legal statement that the Bill would be within the competence of the Assembly. The Supreme Court judgement on the Byelaws Bill could imply that it would be more likely that the Bill is within competence as some provisions could potentially fall within the incidental and consequential provision category. But the Court has emphasized that what is incidental and consequential is a subjective decision and this might not be the end of the story. It will be fascinating to observe the journey of the Bill.

The Regulated Mobile Home Sites (Wales) Bill was introduced by Peter Black AM. Peter Black AM was successful in a legislative ballot on 29 November 2011 and he was given leave to proceed with the Bill by the Assembly on 1 February 2012. The Business Committee has remitted the Bill to the Communities, Equality and Local Government Committee. The Bill was then introduced on 24 October 2012. The purpose of the Bill is to establish a licensing regime for mobile home sites in Wales and to make further provision in relation to the management of such sites and the agreements under which mobile homes are stationed on them.

The Recovery of Medical Costs for Asbestos Diseases (Wales) Bill. Mick Antoniw AM was successful in a legislative ballot on 21 March 2012 and given leave to proceed with his Bill by the Assembly on 16 May 2012. The Business Committee has remitted the Bill to the Health and Social Care Committee. The Bill was then introduced on 3 December 2012. The purpose of the Bill is to enable the Welsh Ministers to recover from a compensator (being a person by or on behalf of whom a compensation payment is made to or in respect of a victim of asbestos-related disease), certain costs incurred by the NHS in Wales in providing care and treatment to the victim of an asbestos-related disease.

According to the Welsh Government legislative programme for 2012–13, five more Bills are to be expected before July 2013: the **Control of Dogs Bill** (to introduce changes to current dangerous dogs legislation to protect the public by promoting responsible dog ownership); the **Social Services (Wales) Bill** (to provide a coherent legal framework to transform social services in Wales); the **Active Travel Bill** (to introduce a duty to provide walking and cycling paths in areas to help the people of Wales become healthier, more active and more environmentally aware); the **Further and Higher Education Bill** (to take forward proposals for further education by seeking to reform the functions of the Higher Education Funding Council for Wales and the introduction of a more co-ordinated approach between all providers of post-16 education) and the **Education (Wales) Bill** (to set out requirements for the registration of the education workforce; reform of the statutory framework for children and young people with special educational needs, and the registration of children of compulsory school age who are home educated among other provisions).

Subordinate Legislation
In 2012, the CLA Committee considered nearly 200 SIs out of which 158 SIs were subject to the negative resolution procedure and 31 SIs were subject to the affirmative resolution procedure.

The Assembly has also considered the draft Order creating the new body in Wales called 'Natural Resources Wales' which will replace the Environment Agency Wales, the Countryside Council for Wales and the Forestry Commission Wales. At the end of 2012, it was considering an early draft order listing the new body's functions. The procedure for the scrutiny of these orders, which is longer than the normal parliamentary procedures, is set out in the Public Bodies Act 2011 (c.24) at sections 13 and 19. The procedure is being monitored by the Assembly to see if it could be adopted for other subordinate legislation which requires enhanced scrutiny.[3] The two draft Natural Resources Wales Orders have been considered both by the CLA Committee and by the Environment and Sustainability Committee.

The CLA Committee has also considered three Consent Memoranda in relation to the Advisory Committee on Hazardous Substances (Abolition) Order 2012 (NAfW, 2012d), the British Waterways Board (Transfer of Functions) Order 2012 (NAfW, 2012e) and the Local Better Regulation Office (Dissolution, Transfer of Functions, etc.) Order 2012 (NAfW, 2012f).

Finally, the Assembly's Members Research Service produced an excellent document which lists all subordinate legislation made under the Measures passed during the third Assembly (NAfW, 2012g). It is an interesting read which could be the basis for future post-legislative scrutiny to be carried out by the Assembly.

Quality of Welsh legislation

Improvement in the drafting of Bills and of their explanatory material
Despite the fact that the First Minister has claimed that a fall in the number of civil servants in Wales has made it more difficult to draw up legislation in Wales, there has been a noticeable general improvement in the drafting of Welsh Bills in the fourth Assembly. It is interesting to note that, by contrast with the third Assembly, there have been no statements in Assembly Committees' reports that the scrutiny of the legislation was impaired by the poor quality of the explanatory memoranda or by the drafting of Bill which included the use of wide framework provisions. This is a welcome improvement which confirms the First Minister's statement that 'he believed Wales had "come a long way" since pre-devolution, where civil servants in the Wales Office would have been incapable of drafting laws' (Henry, 2012).

The general improvement is also confirmed in the contents of the Constitutional and Legislative Affairs Committee reports on the Bills. The reports generally contain very few adverse comments and the recommendations conform to what is to be expected by a Committee carrying out the scrutiny of Bills. The CLA Committee has therefore recommended a few increases in the procedural controls to apply to specific subordinate legislation and also recommended that few provisions were to be made on the face of the Bill rather than being left to subordinate legislation. The quality of the drafting of the first Assembly Act has also been noted by Lord Hope during the hearing of the Supreme Court case. This is a very positive lesson learnt in 2012.

While the Welsh Government has improved on its drafting of Bills, questions must still be raised about the number of amendments proposed to the School Standards and Organization Bill at Stage 2 showing that there is still room for improvement in the drafting of Bills and in the development of drafting principles. Several amendments related to the use of the expression 'by order' in the phrase 'the Welsh Ministers may by order' to allow greater executive flexibility in the way in which the power is used. Over time, such amendments should no longer be moved as more drafting conventions are established. It remains to be seen if this great number of amendments being proposed and agreed was a one-off. On the other hand, the number of amendments agreed shows that a Bill can truly be improved during its passage in the Assembly and that non-government amendments can be accepted by the Welsh Government.

Better control of subordinate legislation making powers

During the fourth Assembly, all powers to make subordinate legislation in Bills have been subjected to either the affirmative resolution procedure or the negative resolution procedure. It seems that a drafting convention has arisen in Wales whereby the negative resolution procedure has become the default procedure to apply to the making of SIs by the Welsh Ministers. This means that, unlike previous legislation, no subordinate legislation made by the Welsh Ministers under Welsh Acts avoid some control by the Assembly. This is different to the UK where it is estimated that only 50 per cent of the subordinate legislation made by UK Government Ministers is subject to parliamentary control procedures.

Extensive consultation

Another general improvement in the law made post-devolution lies in the extensive use of Bill consultation by the Welsh Ministers on Green Papers, White Papers and draft Bills. Except for the Byelaws Bill, which was the first to be introduced in the Assembly, all Bills which have been introduced up to December 2012 have been the subject of some form of pre-legislative scrutiny either by consultation on Green or White Papers or draft Bills or a combination of the three. Some of the Bills have been consulted upon twice as was the Human Transplantation Bill (White Paper and draft Bill). This is another positive evolution of the law made in Wales.

Counsel General – Access to legislation and consolidation

In June 2012, the Counsel General gave an oral statement updating the Assembly on the progress made by his office since his previous oral statement on 4 October 2011 on access to Welsh legislation and developing a Welsh Statute Book (NAfW, 2012h). He highlighted the progress made to improve the legislation.gov.uk website which is achieved in three separate ways. 'First, two new officials have recently been recruited by the Welsh Government to begin the process of updating Welsh provisions on that website.' Secondly, the National Archives had also begun a process of signposting the territorial application of statutory provisions. 'The intention is that the reader will be assisted in identifying whether a provision applies, for example, to Wales only, to England only, or to England and Wales. This is a significant point in what is a complex system of dual legislatures'. Thirdly, he explained that the legislation.gov.uk team recently came to Cardiff to test new functionality for its site, including an option to navigate the site in Welsh and to access and view both language versions of Welsh legislation side by side.

In relation to the development of an encyclopaedia of Welsh law 'helpful to lawyers and non-lawyers alike', he explained that the Welsh Government had begun 'a process of collaborating with Westlaw, one of the UK's main legal publishers, with a view to developing an online service. The intention is to develop a new website that will be available free of charge to the public.' He added it was early days, but this was a very exciting development. Westlaw UK Insight[4] was launched in December 2012.

The Counsel General also spoke of the intention of creating Welsh Acts which stand alone, separate to UK Acts. He explained that this involved revising, codifying and consolidating the law, where possible drafting laws afresh, instead of amending existing provisions. Such a practice he claimed allows the development of Welsh-language texts, because, 'as things stand, most of the existing text of legislation that can be amended is in English only.' He added that 'where practicable, new legislation in Cardiff should be drafted in a way that simplifies the statute book by consolidating Welsh legislation and separating it from legislation that also applies to England.' He was therefore pleased to report that consolidation had been 'a feature of a number of the Bills that the Government has introduced or is consulting upon and this approach permeates the drafting method applied by office of the legislative counsel of the Welsh Government.' Examples included the School Standards and Organization Bill, the Human Transplantation Bills and the Local Democracy Bill. He added that his office had started 'assessing the feasibility of developing a separate fast-track consolidation programme to run alongside the main legislative programme' but that this project was at early stage. He concluded that 'good progress' had been made but much more needed to be done to promote clarity and improve access to Welsh law. To him, 'accessing the law is an essential part of the democratic process. It is vital to the people of Wales's understanding of the huge impact that work done here in Cardiff on their behalf by you, our legislature, already has and will increasingly have on the things that most matter to them in their daily lives: their health, environment, homes, education, local administration and so on' (NAfW, 2012h).[5] He had promised another update at the end of 2012, but this had not taken place by the end of 2012.

The CLA Committee in its consideration of the School Standards Bill welcomed the consolidation of the law on intervention in schools and local authorities and school organization provided for by the School Standards Bill (NAfW, 2012i). They explained that bringing together a number of provisions currently found in several existing statutes greatly enhanced the clarity of the law relating to education in Wales. The Committee added that they hoped that the Welsh Government would apply the same consolidating principles to other Bills introduced in the future. In the same report, the CLA Committee recommended that the Welsh Government should provide Tables of Derivations for all Bills which contain consolidation provisions in their explanatory memoranda in order to improve the scrutiny of consolidation provisions in Assembly Bills (NAfW, 2012i, Recommendation 8).

A Table of Derivations shows the connections between the provisions of the Bill and the equivalent provisions in existing statutes which are repealed and restated in the Bill.

In relation to the Byelaws Bill, the CLA Committee considered whether the Bill achieved its stated objective of consolidating relevant provisions and whether a greater degree of consolidation could have been achieved. They concluded that they accepted the Minister's explanation that consolidating the old byelaw-making powers on the face of the Bill 'would not have been practical' and were therefore content with the issue being dealt with in Schedules (NAfW, 2012j, Paras. 13 and 15).

Legislative Consent Motions
There has been a significant increase in the number of Legislative Consent Motions (LCMs) by which the Assembly agrees that Westminster legislates for Wales in relation to devolved subjects. The third Assembly (2007–2011) had considered and voted on 16 LCMs, refusing one of them. The fourth Assembly has considered 14 LCMs in 2012 alone.

Legislative Consent Memoranda and Motions are as follows (NAfW, 2013):

2012

UK Bill	Legislative Consent Memoranda Laid before the Assembly
Welfare Reform Bill	3 January 2012
Financial Services Bill	3 February 2012
Local Government Finance Bill	28 May 2012
Enterprise and Regulatory Reform Bill	12 June 2012, 10 July 2012, 5 October 2012
Disabled Persons' Parking Badges Bill	10 July 2012
Public Service Pensions Bill	2 October 2012
Prevention of Social Housing Fraud Bill	30 October 2012
Crime and Courts Bill	6 November 2012
Energy Bill [2012]	4 December 2012
Growth and Infrastructure Bill	13 December 2012, 18 December 2012
Marine Navigation No. 2 Bill	21 December 2012

Some of the UK Bills have given rise to several Legislative Consent Motions such as the Growth and Infrastructure Bill and the Enterprise and Regulatory Reform Bill. This means that in addition to the original Bill, amendments moved in Westminster related to devolved subjects and the Assembly needed to agree their inclusion in the UK Bill. The list above show that even in fields which are generally not devolved, provisions can touch upon the devolved subjects, for example the Crime and Courts Bill.

LAW MAKING IN WESTMINSTER FOR WALES

Several Bills were introduced in the session 2012–13 which contain special provisions for Wales. Most of the relevant Bills (in addition to those listed above in relation to LCMs) proposed to devolve new powers to the Welsh Ministers. Four of those Bills have become Acts in 2012.

UK Bills

The parliamentary session started on 9 May 2012. Since then, many Bills having an impact on Wales or proposing to make provision within the devolved competence or devolving further powers to the Welsh Ministers have been introduced. No Bill has proposed to amend the competences of the Assembly in 2012.

The Finance Bill 2012,[6] a UK Government Bill, re-introduced on 11 May 2012 by Mr David Gauke (HM Treasury) proposes to grant certain duties, to alter other duties, and to amend the law relating to the National Debt and the Public Revenue and to make further provision in connection with finance. It received Royal Assent on 17 July 2012. The Bill proposed to devolve executive powers to the Welsh Ministers in relation to the expenditure on plant and machinery for use in designated assisted areas and in relation to the definition of "pre-eminent property" for items with a purely Welsh interest. Such property includes among others: any picture, print, book, manuscript, work of art, scientific object or other thing that the Welsh Ministers are satisfied is pre-eminent for their national, scientific, historic or artistic interest.

Financial Services Bill 2012,[7] a UK Government Bill, re-introduced on 11 May 2012 by Mr George Osborne (HM Treasury) proposes to amend the Bank of England Act 1998, the Financial Services and Markets Act 2000 and the Banking Act 2009, to make other provision about financial services and markets, to make provision about the exercise of certain statutory functions relating to building societies, friendly societies and other mutual societies, to amend section 785 of the Companies Act 2006, to make provision enabling the Director of Savings to provide services to other public bodies and for connected purposes. The Bill makes provision in relation to matters which are within the competence of the National Assembly for Wales and a Legislative Consent Memorandum was laid before the Assembly by the Welsh Ministers in relation to the functions of the Consumer Financial Education Body on 21 March 2012. The Legislative Consent Motion was considered and agreed by the Assembly on 27 March 2012. The Bill received Royal Assent 19 December 2012.

The Marine Navigation Bill,[8] a Private Members' Bill (starting in the House of Lords), was introduced by Lord Berkeley on 16 May 2012. The Bill proposes to make provision about marine navigation and to devolve to the Welsh Ministers the power to make harbour closure orders. The Bill had its first reading on 15 May 2012 and is awaiting a second reading.

The **Marine Navigation (No. 2) Bill,**[9] a Private Members' Bill was introduced by Sheryll Murray, Baroness Wilcox on 16 May 2012. The Bill proposes to make provision in relation to marine navigation and harbours. It also proposed to devolve to the Welsh Ministers the power to make harbour closure and to make the Welsh Ministers the 'designated harbour authority'. The Bill had its second reading in January 2013 and is awaiting the start of its Committee Stage.

The Local Government Finance Bill 2012,[10] a UK Government Bill, introduced by Eric Pickles and Baroness Hanham (Department for Communities and Local Government), was passed and it received Royal Assent on 31 October 2012. The Bill proposed to make provision about non-domestic rating; to make provision about grants to local authorities; to make provision about council tax; to make provision about the supply of information for purposes relating to rates in Northern Ireland; and for connected purposes. A Legislative Consent Memorandum[11] was laid in the Assembly by the Welsh Minister on 28 May 2012 to seek the Assembly's agreement that the clauses which relate to the Welsh Ministers being given executive powers to require specified authorities in Wales to introduce localized council tax reduction schemes in Wales, and prescribe for the parameters within which such schemes should operate; and to introduce regulations which provide for powers to investigate and prosecute fraud and overpayment errors in relation to council tax could be included in the UK Bill. It received Royal Assent on 31 October 2012.

The House of Lords Reform Bill 2012,[12] a UK Government Bill, was introduced by Nick Clegg (Cabinet Office) on 27 June 2012 but it did not proceed beyond Second Reading. The Bill proposed to make provision about the membership of the House of Lords; the disclaimer of life peerages; to abolish the jurisdiction of the House of Lords in relation to peerage claims. Under the Bill, the House of Lords will be composed of elected members ('ordinary elected members') and appointed members ('ordinary appointed members', 'named' and 'ordinary' Lords Spiritual and 'ministerial members').

The House would have been progressively reformed and there would initially have been 120 ordinary elected members for all districts of the United Kingdom. Wales is a district for this purpose and is initially entitled to return 6 'ordinary elected members'. At a later stage, a fully reformed House of Lords would have consisted of 450 members – 360 elected and 90 appointed – together with up to 12 Lords Spiritual and any ministerial members. The Bill would have also given the Secretary of State powers to make secondary legislation about the conduct of House of Lords elections similar to the powers to make secondary legislation about the conduct of elections to the European Parliament, the Scottish Parliament and the National Assembly for Wales.

The Social Care Portability Bill,[13] a Private Members' Bill, was introduced by Baroness Campbell of Surbiton on 26 June 2012. The Bill proposes to provide for the portability of care packages to promote independent living for disabled persons by local authorities in England and Wales; and for connected purposes. The Bill devolves powers to the Welsh Ministers to make regulations in relation to the performance of the authorities' duties to provide care packages (subject to negative resolution procedure) and to commence the provisions of the Act. The Bill is awaiting a second reading.

The Prevention of Social Housing Fraud Bill,[14] a Private Members' Bill, was introduced by Richard Harrington and Baroness Eaton on 20 June 2012. The Bill proposes to devolve the power to make regulations in relation to the loss of assured tenancy status to Welsh Ministers and to make regulations to provide for the creation of an offence that may be committed by a person by refusing or failing to provide any information or document when required to do so by or under regulations under section 7. The Bill was at its Third Reading in the House of Lords at the end of 2012.

The Public Service Pensions Bill[15] 2012, a UK Government Bill, was introduced by Mr George Osborne (HM Treasury). The Bill proposes to make provision for the creation of public service pension schemes for the payment of pensions and other benefits to persons in public service. The Bill devolves to the Welsh Ministers the power to make regulations setting out schemes in relation to fire and rescue workers in Wales. The Explanatory Notes explain that 'The consent of the National Assembly for Wales will be sought in relation to provisions in this Bill which apply to new pension schemes for public bodies and statutory office holders. The National Assembly for Wales has competence in relation to pension schemes for Assembly Members, Welsh Ministers and members of local authorities.' The Bill was at Report Stage in the House of Lords in January 2013.

The Energy Bill 2012,[16] a UK Government Bill, was introduced by Mr Edward Davey (Department of Energy and Climate Change). The Bill was at Committee Stage in the Commons at the end of 2012. The Bill proposes to make provision for or in connection with reforming the electricity market to encourage low carbon electricity generation or ensuring security of supply; for the establishment and functions of the Office for Nuclear Regulation; about the government pipe-line and storage system and rights exercisable in relation to it; about the designation of a strategy and policy statement; for the making of orders requiring regulated persons to provide redress to consumers of gas or electricity; about offshore transmission of electricity during a commissioning period; for imposing further fees in respect of nuclear decommissioning costs; and for connected purposes.

The Explanatory Notes state that 'all provisions in this Bill apply to Wales (although there are no government pipeline and storage system assets in Wales)'. The Bill requires the Secretary of State to consult the Welsh Ministers before making an Order under Chapter 2 (Contracts for Difference) of Part 1 (Electricity Market Reform) or before issuing a direction under clause 39 (Suspension, etc. of emissions limit in exceptional circumstances), before making regulations under clause 38 (Duty not to exceed annual carbon dioxide emissions limit), before reviewing the strategy and policy statement under Part 4 of the Act under clause 112 (Review) and 113 (Procedural requirements) and before modifying licences under Part 4 of Schedule 3 (Investment contracts). The Bill imposes a duty on the Welsh Ministers to make arrangements for monitoring compliance with, and enforcement of, the emissions limit duty in Wales. The Bill includes a power to make by regulations any provision mentioned in Schedule 5 (monitoring compliance with, and enforcement of, the emissions limit duty) under Chapter 8 (Emissions performance standard) of Part 1 (Electricity Market Reform) of the Bill. The Welsh Ministers would have a power to require the Office for Nuclear Regulation to provide information and advice to them under clause 68 (Provision of information or advice to relevant authorities) and Schedule 9 (Disclosure of information, Part 3 – Protected information: permitted disclosures and restrictions on use) allows the disclosure of information to the Welsh Ministers.

The Growth and Infrastructure Bill,[17] a UK Government Bill, was introduced by Eric Pickles and Baroness Hanham (Department for Communities and Local Government) in October 2012. The Bill was at Committee Stage in the House of Lords in January 2013. The Bill proposes to devolve to the Welsh Ministers powers in relation to the stopping up and diversion of highways, the power to postpone compilation of Welsh rating lists and the power to provide for fees to amend registers of land registered as town or village green.

The Statute Law (Repeals) Bill 2012,[18] a UK Government Bill, was introduced in the House of Lords by Lord McNally and Chris Grayling (Ministry of Justice). The Bill was at Third Reading in the House of Commons in January 2013. The Bill proposes to promote the reform of the statute law by the repeal, in accordance with recommendations of the Law Commission and the Scottish

Law Commission, of certain enactments which are no longer of practical utility. The Bill would repeal certain spent Acts applying to England and Wales and to Wales only such as the Bristol and South Wales Junction Railway Act 1846 (9 & 10 Vict. c.cv), the Prince of Wales's Hospital Plymouth Act 1934 (24 & 25 Geo.5 c.lii) or the Aberdare and Central Wales Junction Railway Act 1866 (29 & 30 Vict. c.ccciv).

The UK Department for Education has also consulted on a future **Children and Families Bill**.[19] A Green Paper was published in March 2012 which explains that the Bill's adoption provisions would apply to England and the Government will discuss with the Welsh Ministers whether it would be extended to Wales.

The list shows that there is still a significant number of UK Bills which relate to Wales and which propose to devolve powers to the Welsh Ministers. The difference is that now UK Bills require LCMs agreed by the Assembly for any such matters.

DEVOLUTION COMMISSIONS AND COMMITTEES

Many commissions and committees have been created in 2012 in London following the progress of Alex Salmond's independence proposals. The referendum he has successfully campaigned for raises many questions about the structure and future of the UK. These questions have important consequences in Wales.

The Silk Commission

The Commission on Devolution in Wales, the 'Silk Commission', follows on from the Commission on Scottish Devolution, the 'Calman Commission'. The Scottish Commission was accountable to both the UK and Scottish Governments and it reported in December 2009.

Following this precedent, in October 2011, Welsh Secretary Cheryl Gillan launched 'The Commission on Devolution in Wales' to be chaired by Paul Silk, former Clerk to the National Assembly for Wales and a Clerk in the House of Commons. The Silk Commission is composed of political members from the different political parties represented in the Welsh Assembly and it is required to review both the present financial and constitutional arrangements in Wales. The commission's work was split in two parts: first the consideration of the financial arrangements and secondly the consideration of the constitutional arrangements of devolution in Wales. The Commission reported its findings on Part I (financial accountability) in November 2012 (Commission on Devolution in Wales, 2012a). Work on Part II commenced at the end of 2012.

The UK Government have declared that they would issue an initial response to the Silk Commission in Spring 2013 but it is interesting to note, that in relation to Part I the Welsh Secretary of State has already hinted in January 2013 that implementation of some of the Silk Commission's Part I recommendations could take place much sooner than most anticipated, as the devolution of small taxes could be operated through an ordinary UK Finance Bill, which could even be the 2013's Finance Bill (ITV Wales, 2013).

The terms of reference in relation to Part II (powers of the National Assembly for Wales) are: 'To review the powers of the National Assembly for Wales in the light of experience and to recommend modifications to the present constitutional arrangements that would enable the United Kingdom Parliament and the National Assembly for Wales to better serve the people of Wales' (Commission on Devolution in Wales, 2012b). The Commission will report its findings on Part II by Spring 2014.

The Commission issued a call for evidence on 29 November 2012. They also produced a guide on the current Welsh devolution settlement (Commission on Devolution in Wales, 2012c). The Commission held its first Part II meeting on 14 December 2012. The findings of the Commission will be a fascinating read in 2014 and both the written and oral evidence received will give plenty of food for thought in 2013.

The Welsh Government have already stated that they would advocate in their evidence moving towards a 'reserved model' of devolution, along the lines of the Scotland and Northern Ireland Acts. They emphasized that this was recommended by the Richard Commission report published in 2004 (Welsh Government, 2012c). Under such a model only what is not devolved to Wales would be legally listed.

The Welsh Government has also flagged up other problems around a perceived lack of legislative competence in certain areas, for example, in relation to the proposals of the UK Government to abolish the Agricultural Wage Board, which the Welsh Government would like to keep.[20] In December 2012, the Welsh Government also asked the UK Minister for Disabled People, Esther McVey, to devolve the funding, assets, land, buildings and contracts of the two remaining Remploy factories in Wales to the Welsh Government in order to create a viable social enterprise (Welsh Government, 2012d).

The Welsh Jurisdiction question
In order to inform their evidence to the Silk Commission, the Welsh Government undertook a consultation exercise and initiated a public debate[21] on the need (or not) to establish a separate jurisdiction in Wales. The consultation

opened on 27 March 2012 and closed on the 19 June 2012. The government received sixty-eight written responses.

To inform that debate, the Assembly CLA Committee decided to launch its own inquiry into the establishment of a separate Welsh jurisdiction. The Committee focussed on the technical aspects of the question and in particular it considered the following matters:

- the meaning of the term 'separate Welsh jurisdiction';
- the potential benefits, barriers and costs of introducing a separate Welsh juris-diction;
- the practical implications of a separate jurisdiction for the legal profession and the public; and
- the operation of other small jurisdictions in the UK, particularly those, such as Northern Ireland, that use a common law system.[22]

At the conclusion of the inquiry, the Chair of the Committee declared that

> The Committee believes that a separate legal jurisdiction system in Wales is con-stitutionally viable, but the issue of whether one should be established or not is ultimately a political decision . . . It became clear during the course of our inquiry however that an emerging Welsh legal identity will, in the short term, require practical changes to the current system . . . Such changes would also have the added benefit of making a move to a separate jurisdiction easier in the future, if such a decision is made. (National Assembly for Wales, 2012l)

In its report published in December 2012, the Committee made the following recommendations 'which seek to ensure that practical steps are taken within current structures to make the administration of justice more responsive to the needs of Wales':

- As a body of Welsh law evolves over time, we recommend that additional legal training is put in place to allow specialisms to develop, reflecting the legal tradi-tions and emerging legal identity of Wales. This should include raising awareness in England of the growing divergence between the laws applicable in England and Wales
- We recommend that the Civil Procedure Rules are amended to ensure that public law cases which deal primarily with Welsh issues should generally be commenced or transferred to the administrative court in Cardiff
- We recommend that a body should be entrusted with reviewing and assisting with the consolidation of Welsh law. Such a body could form part of the existing Law Commission for England and Wales or be a newly established body

- We recommend that a presumption should be established in favour of commencing and hearing in Welsh courts all cases relating to laws made bilingually in the English and Welsh languages. (NAfW, 2012m)

The Welsh Government will respond to this inquiry and they will reveal their position on having a separate Welsh jurisdiction when they publish their evidence to the Silk Commission in Spring 2013.

In the meantime, in November 2012, the Counsel General, Theodore Huckle QC, hinted that the question was complex and he highlighted the practical implications of the project, explaining that for a separate jurisdiction to be meaningful and efficient the criminal justice system and the police might need to be devolved too (Welsh Government, 2012f). He also highlighted the great potential costs of the operation and questioned whether Wales could afford presently such a move. He declared that 'It would be of limited or even dubious worth pursuing a separate legal jurisdiction "in principle" if Welsh Ministers and the Assembly did not also obtain a reasonably full set of powers in relation to justice' (BBC, 2012c). He added that the Welsh Government *will* want the creation of a separate jurisdiction but that the question was around the timescales (BBC, 2012d). Many more practical issues and well as theoretical points around the constitutional arrangements for Wales will be raised and debated following from the evidence which the Silk Commission will receive and publish. Debates are expected throughout 2013 on the need for further devolution or less devolution in Wales (Shipton, 2013).

Commission on the Consequences of Devolution for the House of Commons

The UK Government created a Commission in 2012 to explore options for the reform of the internal processes of Westminster following from devolution. The Commission is referred to, generally, as 'The McKay Commission' or 'The West Lothian Commission'. This Commission was established in January 2012 by the Parliamentary Secretary, Mr Mark Harper.

The Commission was set up to explore what is generally referred to as 'The West Lothian question' (the question of the role at Westminster of Members representing constituencies in parts of the United Kingdom to which a measure of self-government in domestic affairs has been granted) and also the 'English Question' (the wider issue of how England should be governed post devolution) could be taken account in the working practices of Westminster. Bearing these questions in mind the Commission's terms of reference are: 'To consider how the House of Commons might deal with legislation which affects only part of the United Kingdom, following the devolution of certain legislative powers to the Scottish Parliament, the Northern Ireland Assembly and the National Assembly for Wales.' The Commission will 'focus on Parliamentary business and procedure' (The McKay Commission, 2012).

The Commission consists of a panel of six independent, non-partisan experts, chaired by Sir William McKay, including Sir Emyr Jones Parry GCMG. Its work began in February 2012 and it is expected to report in the next parliamentary session. The Commission gathered oral evidence throughout the United Kingdom at the end of 2012 and held an evidence session in Cardiff on 24 July 2012.[23]

House of Commons Inquiry – 'Do we need a constitutional convention for the UK?'

Finally, it is worth noting that the House of Commons' Political and Constitutional Reform Committee launched an inquiry on 19 April entitled 'Do we need a constitutional convention for the UK?'[24] The inquiry aims to look at how a convention might allow a debate on the future of the Union as a whole, rather than piecemeal through a focus on specific issues or nations and the Committee will consider the grounds and basis for establishing a convention: its composition, remit and working methods. The Committee was still taking oral evidence at the end of 2012. This answers the calls of the Welsh First Minister who has repeatedly has claimed[25] that such convention was necessary to prepare the future of the UK (Jones, 2012).

CONCLUSION

As the Assembly grasps its new powers and produces its first Acts, its legislative competence has been questioned in the Supreme Court and it is being considered by the Silk Commission. Scotland is currently a main driver of the future of devolution in Scotland, the UK and Wales and the existence and work of the Silk Commission demonstrates that there is a redefining movement of devolution in the UK and in relation to Wales. It remains to be seen what will be the extent of the changes proposed by central government for Wales and what will be recommended by the Silk Commission. Will Wales see yet another profound change of its competence or will it just be offered a light tweaking of the current system which has just come into effect following the 2011 referendum?

In 2012, the Bills introduced in the Assembly were better drafted than the Proposed Measures were in the third Assembly. Wales is learning and is producing better drafted laws. The scope of the Bills is also increasing as Bills with wider subject matters have started to be introduced at the end of 2012. At the same time, the Welsh devolution boundaries have been tested by the Supreme Court. The judgement was specific and it seems to imply that more referrals will take place as the nature of 'incidental' provisions needs to be examined in each particular case.

Potential changes to the Welsh competence are on their way through the work of the Silk Commission and through the progress of devolution in Scotland and answers will be given in 2014 with possible changes being decided in 2015. Meanwhile, in 2013 the Assembly will start looking at important pieces of legislation. One can only wonder what their journey will be and if they will end up in the Supreme Court again.

NOTES

[1] Explanatory Notes to the Act available at *http://www.legislation.gov.uk/anaw/2012/2/pdfs/anawen_20120002_mi.pdf* (accessed 8 January 2013).

[2] The National Assembly for Wales (Transfer of Functions) Order 1999 (SI. 1999/No. 672).

[3] A full list of the subordinate legislate legislation which is subject to special requirements is available on the Assembly's website at *http://www.assemblywales.org/bus home/bus legislation/bus fourth legislation sub/bus legislation sub specific requirements.htm* (accessed 8 January 2013) This list gives access to both draft Orders relating the Natural Resources Wales.

[4] *http://www.westlaw.co.uk/insight/*

[5] See also Welsh Government, 2012g.

[6] Bill 325 2010–2012 (as introduced), available at *http://services.parliament.uk/bills/2012-13/financeno4.html* (accessed 8 January 2013).

[7] HC Bill 278 2010-2012 (as introduced), available at *http://services.parliament.uk/bills/2012-13/financialservices.html* (accessed 8 January 2013).

[8] HL Bill 14 2012-13, as introduced, available at *http://services.parliament.uk/bills/2012-13/marinenavigation.html* (accessed 8 January 2013).

[9] HC Bill 019 2012-13 (as introduced), available at *http://services.parliament.uk/bills/2012-13/marinenavigationno2.html* (accessed 9 January 2013).

[10] HC Bill 265 2010-12 (as introduced), available at *http://services.parliament.uk/bills/2012-13/localgovernmentfinance.html* (accessed 9 January 2013).

[11] NAW, LCM-LD8918 – Legislative Consent Memorandum – Local Government Finance Bill, available at *http://www.assemblywales.org/bus-home/bus-business-fourth-assembly-laid-docs.htm?act=dis&id=234629&ds=5/2012* (accessed 9 January 2013).

[12] HC Bill 52 2012-13 (as introduced), available at *http://services.parliament.uk/bills/2012-13/houseoflordsreform.html* (accessed 9 January 2013).

[13] HL Bill 32 2012-13 (as introduced), available at *http://services.parliament.uk/bills/2012-13/socialcareportability.html* (accessed 15 January 2013).

[14] HC Bill 16 2012-13 as introduced, *http://services.parliament.uk/bills/2012-13/preventionofsocialhousingfraud.html* (accessed 15 January 2013).

[15] HC Bill 70 2012-13 (as introduced), available at *http://services.parliament.uk/bills/2012-13/publicservicepensions.html* (accessed 15 January 2013).

[16] HC Bill 100 2012-13 (as introduced), available at *http://services.parliament.uk/bills/2012-13/energy.html* (accessed 15 January 2013).

[17] HC Bill 075 2012-13 (as introduced), available at *http://services.parliament.uk/bills/2012-13/growthandinfrastructure.html* (accessed 15 January 2013).

[18] HL Bill 042 2012-13 (as introduced), available at *http://services.parliament.uk/bills/2012-13/statutelawrepeals.html* (accessed 15 January 2013).

[19] Department of Education, Press Notice, 9 May 2012, available at *http://www.education.gov.uk/a00208753/childrens-bill-family-support* (accessed 15 January 2013).

[20] See for example Cornock, 2012.

[21] See Welsh Government (2012e) consultation webpage which includes a list of all responses.

[22] See National Assembly for Wales, 2012k.

[23] See *http://tmc.independent.gov.uk/cardiff-24-july-2012/* (accessed 20 January 2013).

[24] See House of Commons Political and Constitutional Reform Committee, Inquiry webpage, *http://www.parliament.uk/business/committees/committees-a-z/commons-select/political-and-constitutional-reform-committee/inquiries/parliament-2010/constitutional-convention-for-the-uk/* (accessed 20 January 2013).

[25] See also NAfW, 2012n.

REFERENCES

BBC (2012a). 'Welsh language: no equality bill Supreme Court challenge', *BBC News Wales*, 1 November 2012, *http://www.bbc.co.uk/news/uk-wales-politics-20171491* (accessed 8 January 2013).

BBC (2012b), 'Attorney general in court challenge to first Welsh Bill', *BBC News Wales*, 31 July 2012, *http://www.bbc.co.uk/news/uk-wales-politics-19055404* (accessed 8 January 2013).

BBC (2012c). 'Theo Huckle links legal shake-up to powers over police', *BBC News Wales*, 15 November 2012, *http://www.bbc.co.uk/news/uk-wales-politics-20342576* (accessed 20 January 2013).

BBC (2012d). 'Theo Huckle on Welsh legal system and police devolution', *BBC News Wales,* 16 November 2012, *http://www.bbc.co.uk/news/uk-wales-20353777* (accessed 20 January 2013).

Cabinet Office (2012). 'Devolution Guidance Note 9: Parliamentary and Assembly Primary Legislation Affecting Wales', *http://www.cabinetoffice.gov.uk/sites/default/ files/resources/DGN-9-Parliamentary-and-Assembly-Primary-Legislation-Affecting-Wales.pdf* (accessed 3 February 2013).

Commission on Devolution in Wales (2012a). *Empowerment and Responsibility: Financial Powers to Strengthen Wales, November 2012, http://commissionondevolution inwales.independent.gov.uk/files/2013/01/English-WEB-main-report1.pdf* (accessed 15 January 2013).

Commission on Devolution in Wales (2012b). *Commission on Devolution in Wales: Terms of Reference, http://commissionondevolutioninwales.independent.gov.uk/files/ 2011/11/Commission-ToR-Final.pdf* (accessed 3 February 2013).

Commission on Devolution in Wales (2012c). *The Current Devolution Settlement,* November 2012, *http://commissionondevolutioninwales.independent.gov.uk/files/2012/11/ Current-devolution-settlement.pdf* (accessed 20 January 2013).

Cornock, D. (2012). 'Wales v Westminster: round 94 – this time, on farming', *BBC News Wales,* 16 October 2012, *http://www.bbc.co.uk/news/uk-wales-politics-19964382* (accessed 20 January 2013).

George, M. (2012). 'Supreme Court dictates pace of Welsh devolution', *Click on Wales,* 15 October 2012, *http://www.clickonwales.org/2012/10/supreme-court-dictates-direction-of-welsh-devolution-journey/* (accessed 17 December 2012).

Henry, G. (2012). 'Carwyn Jones blames civil service redundancies for legislation "challenge"', *Wales Online,* 15 November 2012, *http://www.walesonline.co.uk/news/ welsh-politics/welsh-politics-news/2012/11/15/carwyn-jones-blames-civil-service-redundancies-for-legislation-challenge-91466-32234300/#ixzz2Jf0sHFHl* (accessed 25 January 2013).

HM Government (2012*). Local Government Byelaws (Wales) Act 2012 2012 aw 2 Explanatory Notes, http://www.legislation.gov.uk/anaw/2012/2/pdfs/anawen_20120002 _mi.pdf* (accessed 8 January 2013).

ITV Wales (2013). 'Wales tax powers sooner than expected?', *ITV Wales,* 23 January 2013, *http://www.itv.com/news/wales/update/2013-01-23/wales-tax-powers-sooner-than-expected/* (accessed 15 January 2013).

Jones, C. (2012). *Constitutional convention for the UK?,* Unlock Democracy Lecture, 12 July 2012, *http://www.clickonwales.org/2012/09/constitutional-convention-for-the-uk/* (accessed 20 January 2013).

Mason, T. (2012). 'Why are UK and Welsh governments at odds over a Bill?', *BBC News Wales,* 30 July 2012, *http://www.bbc.co.uk/news/uk-wales-politics-19057221* (accessed 8 January 2013).

National Assembly for Wales (2011a). *Local Government Byelaws (Wales) Bill, Explanatory Memorandum to Local Government Byelaws (Wales) Bill, http://www.assembly wales.org/bus-home/bus-business-fourth-assembly-laid-docs/pri-ld8734-em-e.pdf?lang option=3&ttl=PRI-LD8734-EM%20-%20Local%20Government%20Byelaws%20% 28Wales%29%20Bill%20-%20EXPLANATORY%20MEMORANDUM* (accessed 8 January 2013).

National Assembly for Wales (2012a). *National Assembly for Wales Official Languages Bill, Briefing note in relation to legislative competence,* Chief Legal Adviser, *http://*

www.senedd.assemblywales.org/documents/s10317/Briefing%20note%20on%20the%
20Bill%20in%20relation%20to%20legislative%20competence%20Chief%20Legal%
20Adviser%20National%20Assem.pdf (accessed 8 January 2013).

National Assembly for Wales (2012b). *Report on the Public Audit (Wales) Bill, November 2012*, National Assembly for Wales Constitutional and Legislative Affairs Committee, *http://www.assemblywales.org/bus-home/bus-business-fourth-assembly-laid-docs/cr-ld9101-e.pdf?langoption=3&ttl=CR-LD9101%20-%20Constitutional%20and%20Legislative%20Affairs%20Committee%20Report%20on%20the%20Public%20Audit%20(Wales)%20Bill* (accessed 3 February 2013).

National Assembly for Wales (2012c). *Local Government Byelaws (Wales) Bill: Summary of changes made at Stage 2 – Bill Summary paper*, Research Service, *http://www.assemblywales.org/bus-home/research/bus-assembly-research-publications/research-constitution.htm?act=dis&id=234751&ds=5/2012* (accessed 3 February 2013).

National Assembly for Wales (2012d). *Constitutional and Legislative Affairs Committee, Report on The Advisory Committee on Hazardous Substances (Abolition) Order 2012*, *http://www.senedd.assemblywales.org/documents/s7276/Advisory%20Committee%20on%20Hazardous%20Substances%20Abolition%20Order%202012%20-%20March%202012.pdf* (accessed 3 February 2013).

National Assembly for Wales (2012e). *Constitutional and Legislative Affairs Committee, Report on the British Waterways Board (Transfer of Functions) Order 2012, http://assemblywales.org/bus-home/bus-business-fourth-assembly-laid-docs.htm?act=dis&id=232415&ds=3/2012* (accessed 3 February 2013).

National Assembly for Wales (2012f). *Report of the Constitutional and Legislative Affairs Committee on the 'The Local Better Regulation Office (Dissolution and Transfer of Functions, Etc.) Order 2012', http://www.assemblywales.org/bus-home/bus-business-fourth-assembly-laid-docs.htm?act=dis&id=229733&ds=1/2012* (accessed 3 February 2013).

National Assembly for Wales (2012g). *Subordinate Legislation made by Welsh Ministers under Assembly Measures*, October 2012, *http://www.assemblywales.org/bus-home/research/bus-assembly-research-publications/research-constitution.htm?act=dis&id=239489&ds=11/2012* (accessed 3 February 2013).

National Assembly for Wales (2012h). *Statement: Access to Welsh Laws and Developing a Welsh Statute Book – An Update*, The Record of Proceedings 26 June 2012, *http://www.assemblywales.org/bus-home/bus-chamber-fourth-assembly-rop.htm?act=dis&id=235738&ds=6%2F2012#hygyr* (accessed 8 January 2013).

National Assembly for Wales (2012i). *Report on the School Standards and Organisation Bill (October 2012)*, National Assembly for Wales Constitutional and Legislative Affairs Committee, *http://www.assemblywales.org/bus-home/bus-business-fourth-assembly-laid-docs/cr-ld9053-e.pdf?langoption=3&ttl=CR-LD9053%20-%20Constitutional%20and%20Legislative%20Affairs%20%20Committee%20-%20The%20School%20Standards%20and%20Organisation%20%28Wales%29%20Bill%20* (accessed 3 February 2013).

National Assembly for Wales (2012j). *Report on the Local Government Byelaws (Wales) Bill* (CR-LD8852) National Assembly for Wales Constitutional and Legislative Affairs Committee, *http://www.assemblywales.org/bus-home/bus-business-fourth-assembly-laid-docs.htm?act=dis&id=231851&ds=3/2012* (accessed 3 February 2013).

National Assembly for Wales (2012k). *Inquiry into the Establishment of a Separate Welsh Jurisdiction,* National Assembly for Wales Constitutional and Legislative Affairs Committee, *http://www.senedd.assemblywales.org/mgIssueHistoryHome.aspx? IId=2594* (accessed 20 January 2013).

National Assembly for Wales (2012l). 'National Assembly Committee recommends important changes to the existing England and Wales jurisdiction', *National Assembly for Wales News,* 13 December 2012, *http://www.assemblywales.org/newhome/new-news-fourth-assembly.htm?act=dis&id=241545&ds=12/2012* (accessed 20 January 2013).

National Assembly for Wales (2012m). *Inquiry into a Separate Welsh Jurisdiction,* December 2012, National Assembly for Wales Constitutional and Legal Affairs Committee, *http://www.assemblywales.org/bus-home/bus-business-fourth-assembly-laid-docs/ cr-ld9135-e.pdf?langoption=3&ttl=CR-LD9135%20-%20Constitutional%20and%20 Legislative%20Affairs%20Committee%20-%20Inquiry%20into%20a%20Separate% 20Welsh%20Jurisdiction* (accessed 20 January 2013).

National Assembly for Wales (2012n). *Towards a Constitutional Convention,* National Assembly for Wales, May 2012, *http://www.assemblywales.org/12-023.pdf* (accessed 28 January 2013).

National Assembly for Wales (2013). *Legislative Consent Motions, http://www.assembly wales.org/bus-home/research/bus-assembly-publications-monitoring-services/bus-lcm_ monitor.htm* (accessed 3 February 2013).

Navarro, M. (2012). 'Legislating for Wales 2011–12', *Contemporary Wales,* 25, 15–39.

Shipton, M. (2012). 'Westminster must not try power grab from National Assembly, warns MP', *Wales Online,* 11 January 2013, *http://www.walesonline.co.uk/news/welsh-politics/welsh-politics-news/2013/01/11/westminster-must-not-try-power-grab-from-national-assembly-warns-mp-91466-32584865/* (accessed 20 January 2013).

The McKay Commission (2012) Written Ministerial Statement – 17 January 2012, *http://tmc.independent.gov.uk/key-documents/written-ministerial-statement-17-january-2012/* (accessed 20 January 2013).

The Supreme Court (2012). *Judgement Local Government Byelaws Wales Bill 2012 – Reference by the Attorney General for England and Wales,* Michaelmas Term [2012] UKSC 53, *http://www.supremecourt.gov.uk/decided-cases/docs/UKSC_2012_0185_ Judgment.pdf* (accessed 8 January 2013).

Welsh Government (2012a). *Lgo 31 Correspondence on the Local Government Byelaws (Wales) Bill,* Disclosure Log 5 September 2012, *http://wales.gov.uk/publications/ accessinfo/disclogs/dr2012/julsep/lclgov1/dllgo31/?lang=en* (accessed 25 January 2013).

Welsh Government (2012b). *Written Statement – Supreme Court Judgment – Local Government Byelaws (Wales) Bill Reference,* 21 November 2012, *http://wales.gov.uk/ about/cabinet/cabinetstatements/2012/byelawsbill/?lang=en* (accessed 17 December 2012).

Welsh Government (2012c). *The Future of the Union: Wales,* Lecture by the First Minister of Wales, the Rt Hon Carwyn Jones AM, at the London School of Economics, 8 November 2012, *http://wales.gov.uk/newsroom/articles/firstminister/121112future union/?lang=en* (accessed 20 January 2013).

Welsh Government (2012d). 'Welsh Government asks for the devolution of Remploy', *Welsh Government News*, 6 December 2012, *http://wales.gov.uk/newsroom/education andskills/2012/121206remploy/?lang=en* (accessed 20 January 2013).

Welsh Government (2012e). *Consultation on a Separate Legal Jurisdiction for Wales*, *http://wales.gov.uk/consultations/finance/seplegaljurisdiction/?lang=en* (accessed 20 January 2013).

Welsh Government (2012f). *Wales, a Jurisdiction?*, The Counsel General to the Society of Legal Scholars, 15 November 2012, *http://wales.gov.uk/about/counselgeneral2/cg statements/cgspeech151112/?lang=en* (accessed 20 January 2013).

Welsh Government (2012g). *Speech – Access to Legislation*, Counsel General to the Association of Welsh District Judges, 26 September 2012, *http://wales.gov.uk/docs/ caecd/publications/130114welshdistrictjudgesspeech260912.pdf* (accessed 8 January 2013).

BOOK REVIEWS

Richard Wyn Jones and Roger Scully (2012). *Wales Says Yes: Devolution and the 2011 Welsh Referendum,* **Cardiff: University of Wales Press.**

This important and timely book offers both the only detailed retrospective on the 2011 constitutional process on Wales and, in the depth of its coverage and range of its scholarship, a landmark contribution to the literature on constitutional change in Britain since 1997.

As the authors concede, the 2011 process can scarcely be described as dramatic. The Welsh electorate did not in general engage enthusiastically with the referendum but, as the authors also point out, this is itself a reflection on the nature of Welsh politics. The notion of the 2011 referendum as a damp squib might cause the reader to ask, is the subject worthy of a book-length treatment? The authors answer this question in the preface to the book. The 2011 referendum is important for a number of other reasons. The substance of the issue at stake, while not headline grabbing, is potentially significant for the powers of the National Assembly; it marks a potentially important step on the Welsh trajectory towards a legislative assembly along the Scottish and Northern Irish models. More importantly, the book offers a broad and rich account of a number of important research questions in both political science and constitutional law, as well as a detailed account of Welsh devolution which reflects upon the authors' extensive scholarship in the area for many years; for these reasons it is most welcome and will richly reward careful study.

Another significant issue which the book brings out well is the use of the referendum itself. When addressed in the context also of the AV referendum in 2011 the Welsh process helps further to embed direct democracy as central to the process of constitutional change in the UK. The House of Lords Constitution Committee addressed this issue at length in 2009 and while generally sceptical of referendums it concluded that where they are to be used they should be reserved only for major constitutional matters. This seems to be a definite trend when we think also of the commitment in the European Union Act 2011 to referendums for future significant treaty changes, and the proposed referendum for Scotland, scheduled for 2014.

In light of this broader context this book offers very important empirical data as well as analytical insight which helps us identify comparative lessons which the Welsh process has to offer. As for the referendum itself, the authors show how the initiation of such a process, in the absence of constitutional regulation setting out clearly when a referendum must be held, can be subject to the vagaries of internal party struggles (as were the 1975 and 1979 referendums of course), or to deal-making between parties (the AV and Welsh referendums in 2011). The authors persuasively demonstrate that there was no need in constitutional terms for the 2011 referendum in Wales, and that it was very much the consequence of political imperatives. They also show the perils of holding a referendum when the public are largely disengaged, both 2011 referendums suffer from this failing.

In broader terms, the book will be an excellent guide to Welsh devolution particularly for students new to the subject. Chapters 1 and 2 offer a thorough and clear history of the devolution movement and process going back to the 1970s, explaining how the aspiration for legislative devolution first emerged, missed opportunities and general apathy, all of which is essential background to the 2011 event. Other historical issues which are mirrored for example in Scotland are the significance of the Thatcher era to the rise in support for devolution, and the ongoing process of devolution since 1997. An interesting discussion is offered as to whether or not the flexibility of the UK constitution which has allowed for a never-ending constitutional process is good or bad. A plea for some level of stability, to let changes bed down is interesting. It seems to be a fruitless plea however, particularly when we look to Scotland which is seemingly embarked on an unending constitutional process, the outcomes of which may well have significance for Wales, perhaps prompting another round of constitutional debate in Cardiff.

The book is also illuminating in discussing the detail of the campaign, the results and in explaining voting patterns. Here the authors offer Wales as a case study, providing broader insights which will be of great value to specialists in political behaviour, elections and voting.

The book ends by highlighting how entrenched devolution now is. The 2011 issue did not spark much popular interest but this is not indicative of a broader disillusionment with devolution as a project. The narrowness of the victory for devolution in the 1997 referendum led many to question the legitimacy of the whole National Assembly project, but polls now suggest that the constitutional issue facing Wales is very much what kind of devolved government Wales should have, rather than whether devolution works for Wales at all; and whether the 2011 process will presage possibly a new area of Welsh jurisdiction, and an organic form of specifically 'Welsh' law.

The book also offers timely lessons for the proposed process in Scotland in 2014. The authors raise issues with regard to how the Political Parties, Elections and Referendums Act regulate campaign groups and campaign finance. They also comment that the main issue from 2011 may well be turnout and that 'if you wish to engage most of the public in a referendum, you need to present them with clear alternatives so that the consequences of a Yes and No vote can be readily understood' (p. 167). This is clearly central to the ongoing debate in Scotland, and indicates that proper deliberation can only take place where there is a level playing field, a well-informed public and a range of options that are both considered to be significant by the people and offered in a clear way. On this issue as on many others this book offers illuminating and insightful comment. Devolution in the UK has been a largely disjointed and disconnected process; this is not a criticism, simply a statement of fact. It has allowed for the three devolved territories to set their own priorities and proceed at their own pace. It is therefore the job of scholars to try to draw comparisons, connections and lessons of broader reach from each of these cases. This book succeeds admirably not only in its review of the 2011 process, but also in explaining Welsh devolution's historical trajectory and in offering insights and lessons which have broader resonance for devolution scholars across the UK.

Stephen Tierney
University of Edinburgh

Gideon Calder, Jeremy Gass and Kirsten Merrill-Glover (eds) (2012). *Changing Directions of the British Welfare State*, Cardiff: University of Wales Press.

This book, published in the year of the Beveridge Report's seventieth birthday, was conceived on the sixtieth birthday of the 'appointed day' of the welfare state. It has three stated aims (pp. 5–6). The first is historical: to consider the record of the British welfare state since the late 1940s – with an emphasis, in *some* chapters, on the Welsh context (my emphasis). The second is critical: to evaluate the aims, principles and ambitions of the welfare state as conceived by government, social commentators and other agencies. The third aim is to consider the priorities of welfare provision as we face the future.

In addition to an Introduction and Conclusion, there are two parts with five chapters each. The first part focuses on Beveridge's 'five giants' of want, disease, ignorance, squalor and idleness. The second part examines 'five challenges' of gender, race, disability, devolution and 'the start and end of life' (itself in two parts, with different authors). It is welcome to see a clear framework, and the five giants are a good starting point. However, the challenges perhaps need a clearer justification. It is unclear why they were selected. Were they neglected by Beveridge (e.g. disability), incorrectly (with hindsight?) conceptualized by Beveridge (e.g. women's status and employment) or arisen since Beveridge's Report (e.g. immigration, changes in family structure)? The final chapter sums up the book very clearly. It is stated that there is a 'striking ambivalence about the achievements of the welfare state found in all the contributions to this book' (p. 213). On the one hand, there is recognition of the 'undoubted improvements in people's quality of life', but the welfare state has not succeeded in eradicating Beveridge's five giants, and has limited impact on inequality (pp. 214–15).

Although all the chapters provide useful material, personal favourites will depend on preferences in terms of style and topic. I enjoyed Mike Sullivan's discussion of equality, Dave Byrne's literary pot shots at merchant bankers (although this felt a little like shooting fish in a barrel) and Mark Drakeford's 'history as biography' discussion of devolution (albeit perhaps through rose-coloured spectacles). Moreover, Drakeford's chapter illustrated one of the disappointing features of the rest of the book, in that the historical and contemporary material on Wales was rather uneven. Although 'many chapters make mention of a special connection between Welsh political traditions and the welfare state' (p. 13), there is little detail on this. There are the usual nods to Bevan (or Aneurin, or Nye, depending on familiarity – but not to Ni, his wife Jennie Lee's term). However, there is little on James Griffiths, the 'architect of Labour's social insurance social security system' (as Drakeford, p. 183, puts it. According to a fellow Labour MP, Griffiths had 'all the Welsh eloquence of Bevan without the egotism'). There was some material on 'devolution' before and after 1999, but little attempt to examine the distinctiveness of the Welsh dimension (see Powell, 2006). In my view, one example of this missed opportunity was in the areas of race and diversity. Margaret Thatcher's speech on being 'swamped by alien cultures' is mentioned (p. 146) but the same phrase has been used by some nationalists concerning recent English immigration. Similarly, areas such as Tiger Bay had many 'Windrush moments' before 1948.

The aims of the book are only partially met, with a rather mixed pattern between the contributors. I would have liked to have seen a stronger editorial hand, guiding towards a more common chapter template. The 'historical' aim was largely achieved. The contributors broadly provide informed and readable, if not ground-breaking, historical accounts. However, the degree of historical depth and detail varied significantly, as did the attention given to the Welsh context.

Achieving the 'critical' aim was more problematic. This was because there was limited discussion of the often unclear and shifting aims, principles and ambitions of the welfare state, and little attention to evaluation principles. Moreover, there was little discussion that these aims may differ significantly between different stakeholders such as 'government, social commentators and other agencies'. For example, it is stated that the second key theme in the book is of inequality (p. 215). However, it can be argued that the 'strategy of equality' of the welfare state is often opaque and ambiguous, and varies over time and between different services and governments. There is a tendency for the authors to conduct trial by hindsight and find the welfare state guilty of a charge that it never accepted. It is admitted that 'most of the criticisms of the welfare state in these contributions look through a contemporary lens, in that they use modern standards to appraise the welfare state's achievements' (p. 215). In short, different degrees of success can be claimed depending on the evaluative template adopted (e.g. the rather different equality aims associated with Beveridge, Bevan, Tawney, Marshall, etc. – see Powell, 1995).

The third aim of considering the future priorities of welfare provision is also problematic. Bevan may have asked 'why gaze into the crystal when you can read it in the book', but there is relatively little in this book: it is admitted that 'the various chapters have relatively little to say about the future directions for the welfare state' (p. 217).

In conclusion, the book fell between two stools to some extent. On the one hand, the £85 hardback nature of the book probably mean that it will be useful for students as a library resource, but will be unlikely to challenge long-established and best-selling introductory social policy students texts in the UK. On the other hand, there is insufficient Welsh material to focus on social policy in Wales. With small changes in direction and a large change in price (paperback version) it could be an invaluable exploration of the British and Welsh welfare state.

REFERENCES

Powell, M. (1995). 'The strategy of equality revisited', *Journal of Social Policy*, 24, 2, 163–185.
Powell, M. (2006). 'What was Wales? Towards a contextual approach to medical history', in P. Michael and C. Webster (eds), *Health and Society in Twentieth-Century Wales*, Cardiff: University of Wales Press.

Martin Powell
Health Services Management Centre, Birmingham University

GUIDELINES FOR CONTRIBUTORS
OF ARTICLES

GENERAL POLICY

Contemporary Wales is an annual review of economic and social developments and trends in Wales. It provides an authoritative analysis drawing upon the most up-to-date research, and represents the only comprehensive source of analysis across the range of economic and social research about Wales. It is a University of Wales Press journal published once a year, and contains articles selected for their quality and significance to contemporary society in Wales. Submissions are refereed and are accepted for publication on the assumption that they have not been previously published and are not currently being sub-mitted to any other journal. The normal maximum length for articles is about 5,000 words. An abstract of up to 200 words is required.

Contemporary Wales welcomes articles submitted for publication in Welsh. English language abstracts of articles in Welsh will be included in the journal. In addition, we will endeavour to secure funding for English translations of the articles following hardcopy publication in the journal. If successful, translations will be available on the *Contemporary Wales* pages of Ingenta at http://ingenta connect.com/content/uwp.

COPYRIGHT

Copyright in the articles in printed and electronic forms will be retained by the University of Wales, but the right to reproduce their own articles by photo-copying is granted to the contributors provided that the copies are not offered for sale. Contributors should obtain the necessary permission to use material already protected by copyright.

OPEN ACCESS REQUIREMENTS

It is incumbent on contributors to *Contemporary Wales* to state clearly if they have an Open Access requirement when submitting an article. In accordance with RCUK policy on Open Access, this applies to articles which acknowledge Research Council funding, that are submitted for publication in journals from 1 April 2013. All papers must include details of the funding that supported the research and, if applicable, a statement on how the underlying research materials – such as data, samples or models – can be accessed. For further information please see the RCUK website http://www.rcuk.ac.uk/documents/documents/RCUKOpenAccessPolicy.pdf

PREPARATION OF TYPESCRIPTS

If possible, please email papers as Word attachments to one of the editors:

Elin Royles: ear@aber.ac.uk
Paul Chaney: chaneyp@cardiff.ac.uk

If email is not possible, please post three copies on single-sided A4 to one of the editors:

Elin Royles
Sefydliad Gwleidyddiaeth Cymru
Adran Gwleidyddiaeth Ryngwladol
Prifysgol Aberystwyth
Aberystwyth
Ceredigion SY23 3FE

Paul Chaney
Cardiff School of Social Sciences
The Glamorgan Building
King Edward VII Avenue
Cardiff CF10 3WT

The editors can provide further guidance as to the form and style in which contributions should be submitted, but the following gives a brief guide for potential contributors. Additional general information is available from the UWP. Articles submitted should be typed (Times New Roman, 12 point) using double spacing with wide margins, unjustified on the right. Pages should be numbered throughout consecutively.

PREPARATION OF TYPESCRIPTS ON DISK

Once a paper has been accepted for publication, an electronic version should
sent to the editors by e-mail. Authors should retain a back-up copy of their
papers electronically and as a printout. Word versions of the paper are preferred,
but other softwares may be acceptable – please contact University of Wales Press
for further information. The editors would be grateful if contributors would
submit accepted articles in house style according to the guidelines provided
here and in line with copies of the journal.

Notes and references
Notes and references should be supplied at the end of the article, also in double
spacing. Notes should be numbered consecutively. References should be in
alphabetical order of author (see below for style).

Tables, maps and diagrams
These will eventually appear within the printed page but should be provided on
separate pages in the typescript and their position indicated by a marginal note
in the text. Tables and figures should be provided in separate Excel or tiff files,
not embedded in Word. Some other kinds of software may be acceptable –
please contact University of Wales Press for further information. All figures,
diagrams, maps, charts, etc. must be saved in *black only*, not full colour, and
should be saved at 1,200 pixels per inch.

Diagrams and maps may be submitted in the best possible condition on
paper if the contributor is unable to supply a disk version. References in the text
to illustrative material should take the form 'Table 1', 'Table 2', etc. for tables
and 'Figure 1', 'Figure 2', etc. for other illustrations including maps. Do not
use references such as 'in the following diagram' since there is no guarantee
that pagination will allow this precise positioning. The tables and figures will
eventually be labelled 'Table 1.1', 'Figure 2.1', etc. according to the number of
the chapter in which they appear.

STYLE OF TEXT

Quotations within running text should be in single quote marks (double for
quotes within quotes). Quotations of more than forty-five words should be
indented without quotation marks and with a line space before and after.

Underline or type in italic any words which are to appear in italic. In English-
language articles, single words or short phrases in any language other than

English should be in italic, but longer quotations in another language should be in roman within single quotation marks.

Dates should be expressed as 1 January 1999; the 1990s; the twentieth century (but 'a twentieth-century record'); 1988–9; 1914–18 (not 1914–8). Numbers up to ninety-nine should be spelt out in full except in a list of statistics or in percentages (e.g. 25 per cent).

Use -ize endings when given as an alternative to -ise, for example, realize, privatize, organize; but note analyse, franchise, advertise.

Capitalization should be kept to a minimum in the text. For titles, initial capitals should only be used when attached to a personal name (thus 'President Clinton', but 'the president of the United States').

Journal style is that 'south' in 'south Wales' should take lower case (also 'north', 'east', 'west' Wales/England, etc.), since this is not a specific political, administrative or geographical region. South America or South Africa would take upper case since the term refers to the name of a continent or political entity respectively. When referring to a specific area for economic assessment, e.g. the South West of England, upper case may be used for clarity.

REFERENCES

References in the text should be given in the Harvard system in the following format:

(Dower, 1977), (Welsh Office, 1986), (White and Higgs, 1997).
(Gripaios et al., 1995a).

The form of references listed under the heading 'References' at the end of the text should be as follows:

Ambrose, P. (1974). *The Quiet Revolution*, London: Chatto and Windus.

Buller, H. and Hoggart, K. (1994b). 'The social integration of British home owners into French rural communities', *Journal of Rural Studies*, 10, 2, 197–210.

Dower, M. (1977). 'Planning aspects of second homes', in Coppock, J. T. (ed.), *Second Homes: Curse or Blessing?*, Oxford: Pergamon Press.

Note the use of lower case for all initial letters except the first in an article or unpublished thesis title, and capitals for initial letters of all significant words in book and journal titles.

Publications by the same author in the same year should be differentiated by means of a, b, c, etc. after the year of publication, both in the text reference and in the list of references.

PROOFS AND COMPLIMENTARY COPIES

Checking of proofs will be done by editors, with contributors expected to reply promptly to queries. Upon publication, contributors will receive one complimentary copy of the issue of the journal in which their article appears.

In addition, as a contributor to a University of Wales Press publication, after 09/10 authors can purchase any UWP titles, including journals (inc. hardcopies of CW), at 25% discount. The contact for this is Charlotte Austin at UWP (c.austin@wales.ac.uk).

Editorial Board of *Contemporary Wales*

Professor Huw Beynon, Cardiff University
Professor Douglas Caulkins, Grinnell College, Iowa
Professor Chris Harvie, Universität Tübingen
Professor Michael Hechter, University of Washington
Dr Nigel O'Leary, Swansea University
Professor Wayne Parsons, Queen Mary College, University of London
Dr Richard Wyn Jones, Cardiff University

Contemporary Wales
Volume 26